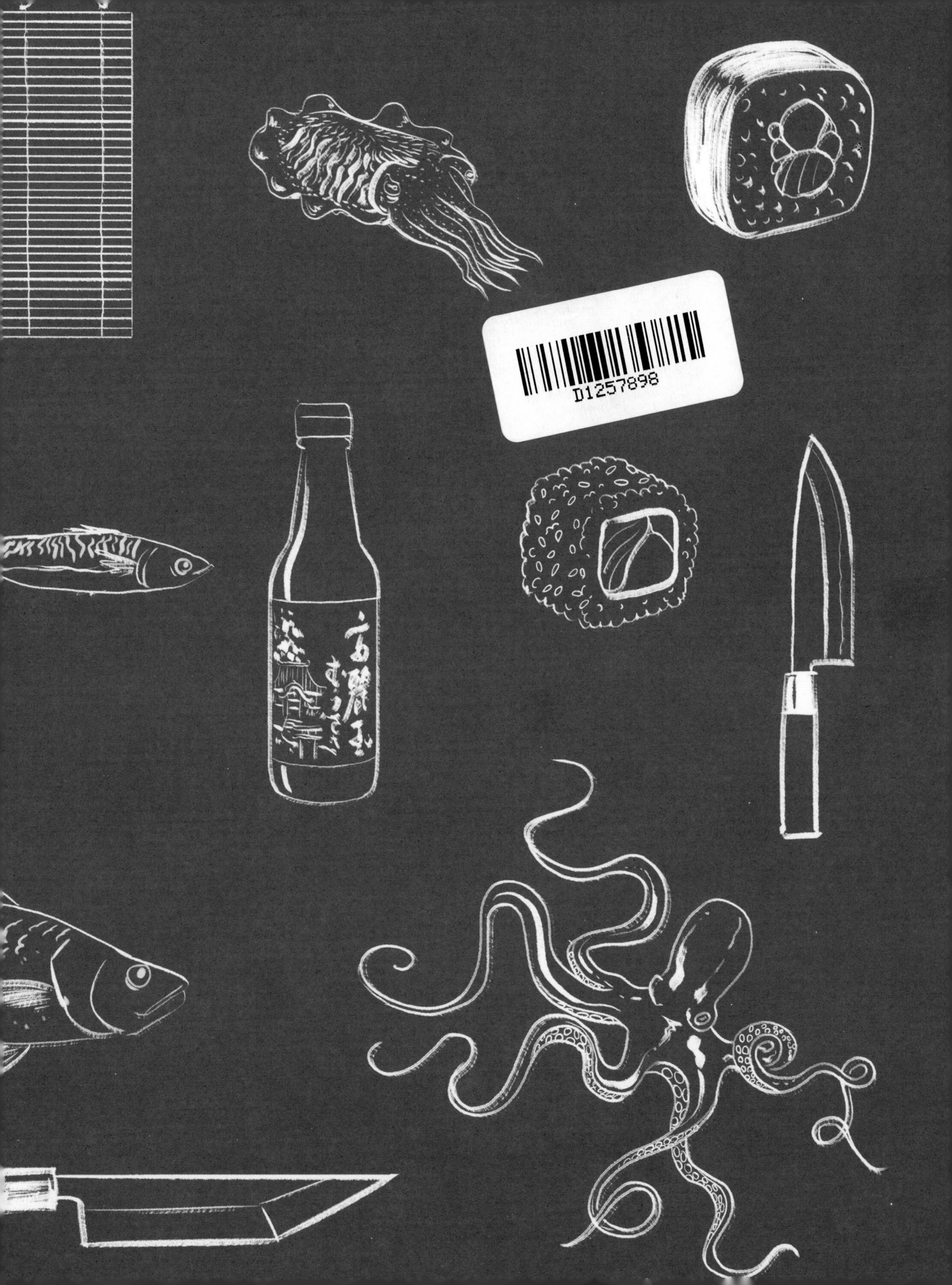

THE ART OF SUSHI

SCRIPT, ART AND COLOR
FRANCKIE ALARCON

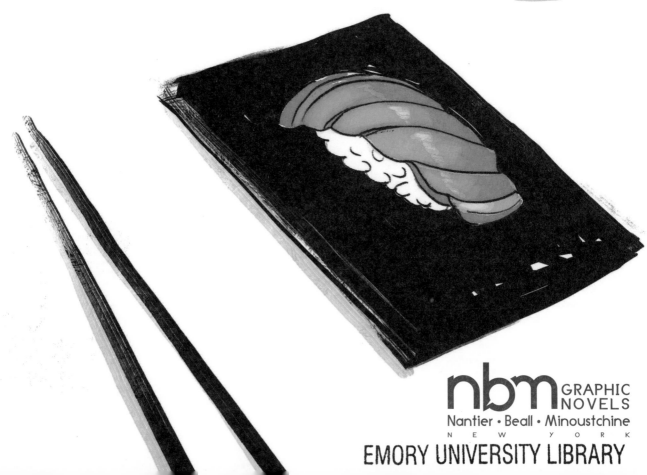

nbm GRAPHIC NOVELS
Nantier • Beall • Minoustchine
NEW YORK

A very, very big thank you to Rica, without whom this book would never have seen the light of day.
To David, with whom it is my great fortune to share a love of sushi and sake.
To Chloé Vollmer-Lo for her magnificent photos that inspired me.
To Marilyne, my first reader and provider of daily moral support throughout the entire process of creating this book, I could not have finished it without her help, commitment, and kindness.

A very big thank you to:
Yannick Alléno for his expertise and his generosity
Chihiro Masui for her precious advice
Hachiro Mizutani for his kindness and his singular knowledge
"Taku" and Nina Nikhou for welcoming us
Daisuke Okada for an unforgettable lesson and sushi dinner
Yasunari Okazaki for an exceptional culinary experience
Koko Okuda, guide to all the twists and turns of Tsukiji

I will never forget, in Japan and in France:
A meal of sushi and song with Hide and Kana, the gargantuan dinner and the nighttime fishing trip with Kenji and his family, the ceramics lesson with Shikamaru Takeshita, discovering rice paddies with Mr. Yamazaki, sake tastings with our friend Hiroyuki Toshikubo, eel fishing and dinner with Yoshiyuki Saita and Mrs. Tanemura, the smells of shoyu at Yohishi Yaguta's and of nori at Maruyama's, the wasabi lesson with Olivier Derenne, our meetings with Mr. Fujita, France Ikejime, Sylvain Huet, Toshiro Kuroda, Tsunahiro Yamamura, Kayoko Shibata…

Franckie
www.franckiealarcon.com

Also available by Alarcon:
The Secrets of Chocolate: A Gourmand's Trip Through a Top Chef's Atelier

See previews, get exclusives
and order from:
NBMPUB.COM
We have hundreds of graphic novels available. Subscribe to our monthly newsletter
Follow us on Facebook & Instagram (nbmgraphicnovels), Twitter (@nbmpub).

NBM Graphic Novels
160 Broadway, Suite 700, East Wing,
New York, NY 10038
Catalog available by request

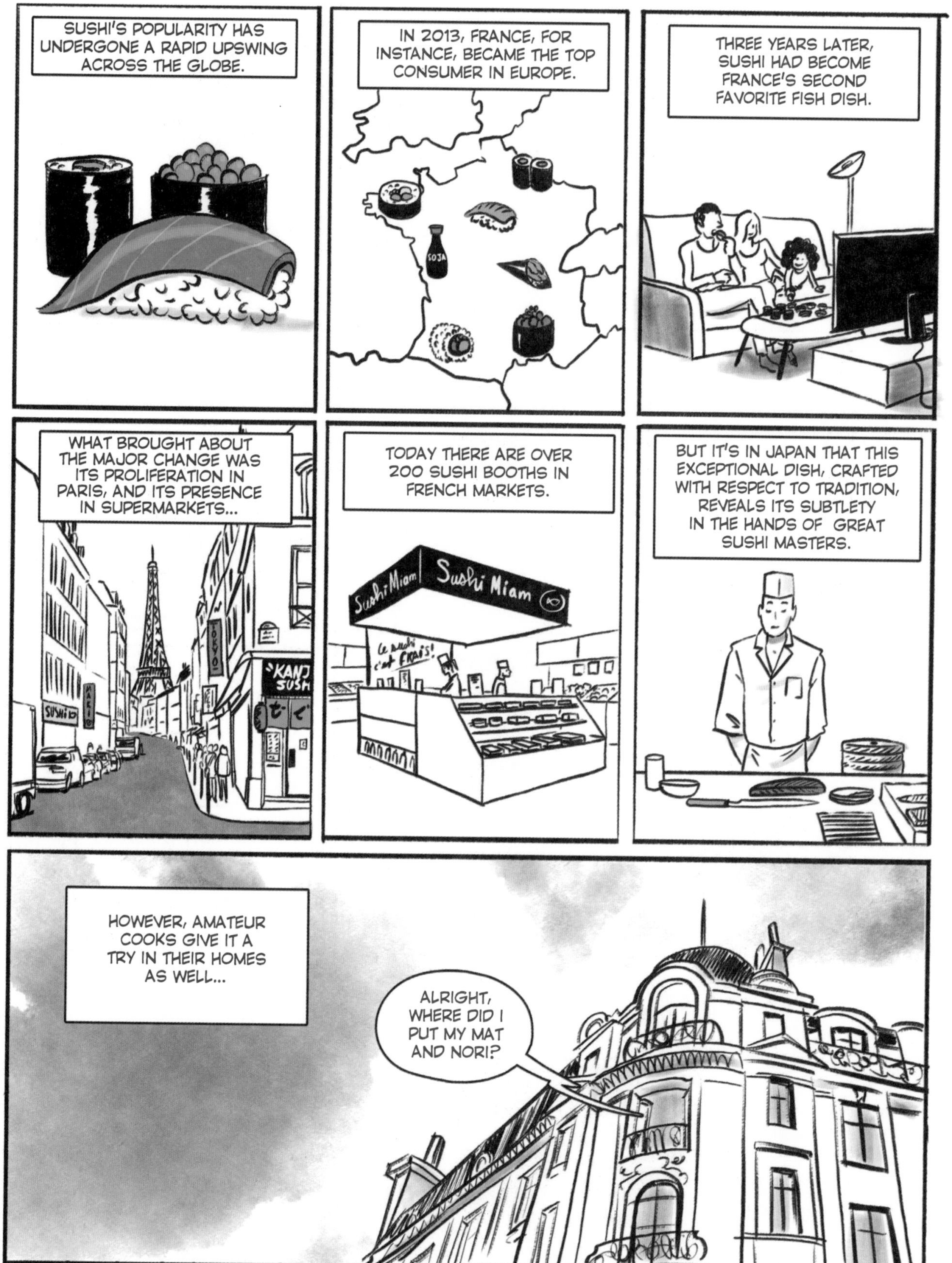
SUSHI'S POPULARITY HAS UNDERGONE A RAPID UPSWING ACROSS THE GLOBE.
IN 2013, FRANCE, FOR INSTANCE, BECAME THE TOP CONSUMER IN EUROPE.
SOJA
THREE YEARS LATER, SUSHI HAD BECOME FRANCE'S SECOND FAVORITE FISH DISH.
WHAT BROUGHT ABOUT THE MAJOR CHANGE WAS ITS PROLIFERATION IN PARIS, AND ITS PRESENCE IN SUPERMARKETS...
TODAY THERE ARE OVER 200 SUSHI BOOTHS IN FRENCH MARKETS.
Sushi Miam
Sushi Miam
BUT IT'S IN JAPAN THAT THIS EXCEPTIONAL DISH, CRAFTED WITH RESPECT TO TRADITION, REVEALS ITS SUBTLETY IN THE HANDS OF GREAT SUSHI MASTERS.
HOWEVER, AMATEUR COOKS GIVE IT A TRY IN THEIR HOMES AS WELL...
ALRIGHT, WHERE DID I PUT MY MAT AND NORI?

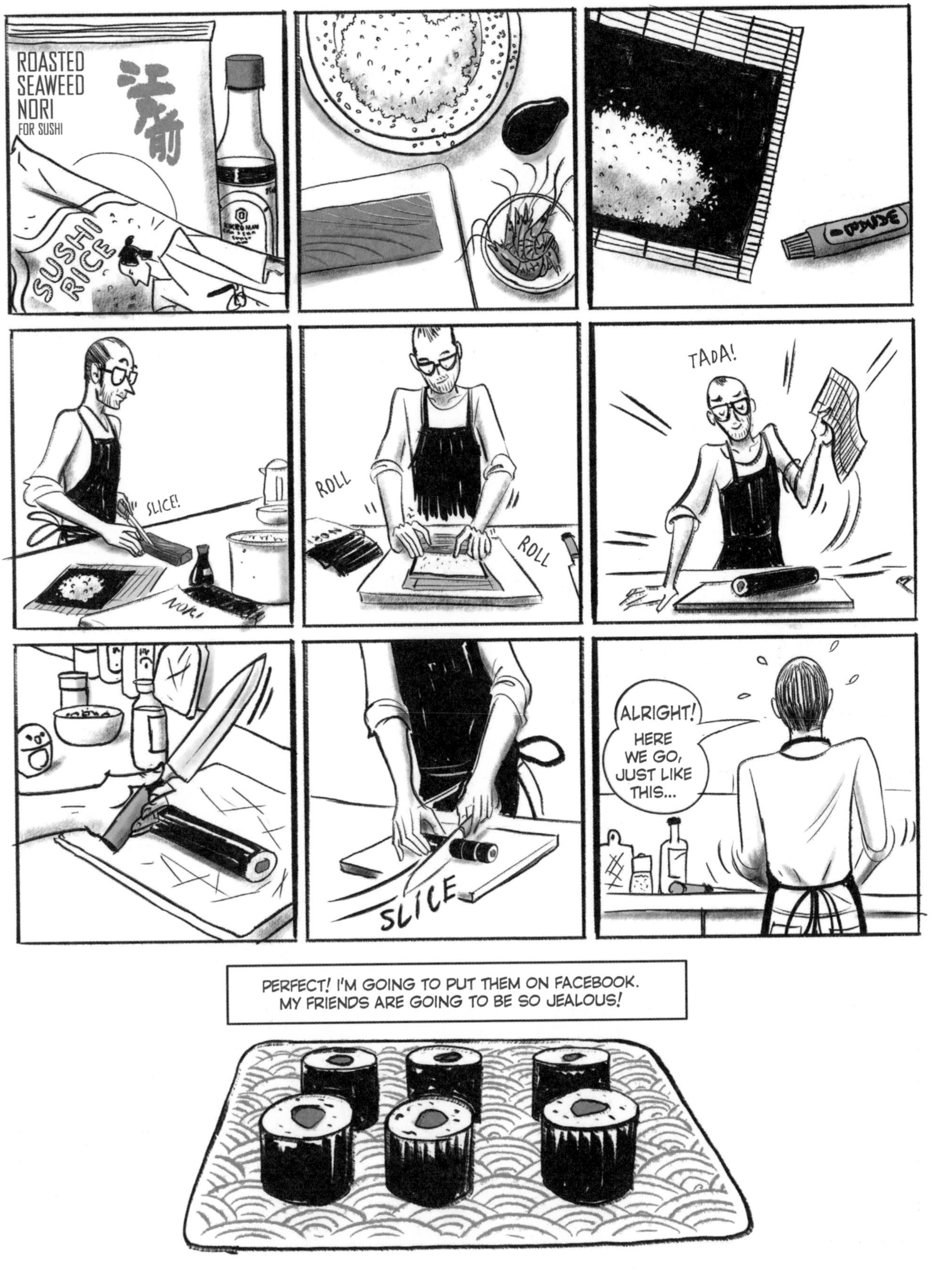
ROASTED SEAWEED NORI FOR SUSHI
SUSHI RICE
SLICE!
NORI
ROLL
ROLL
TADA!
SLICE
ALRIGHT!
HERE WE GO, JUST LIKE THIS...
PERFECT! I'M GOING TO PUT THEM ON FACEBOOK. MY FRIENDS ARE GOING TO BE SO JEALOUS!

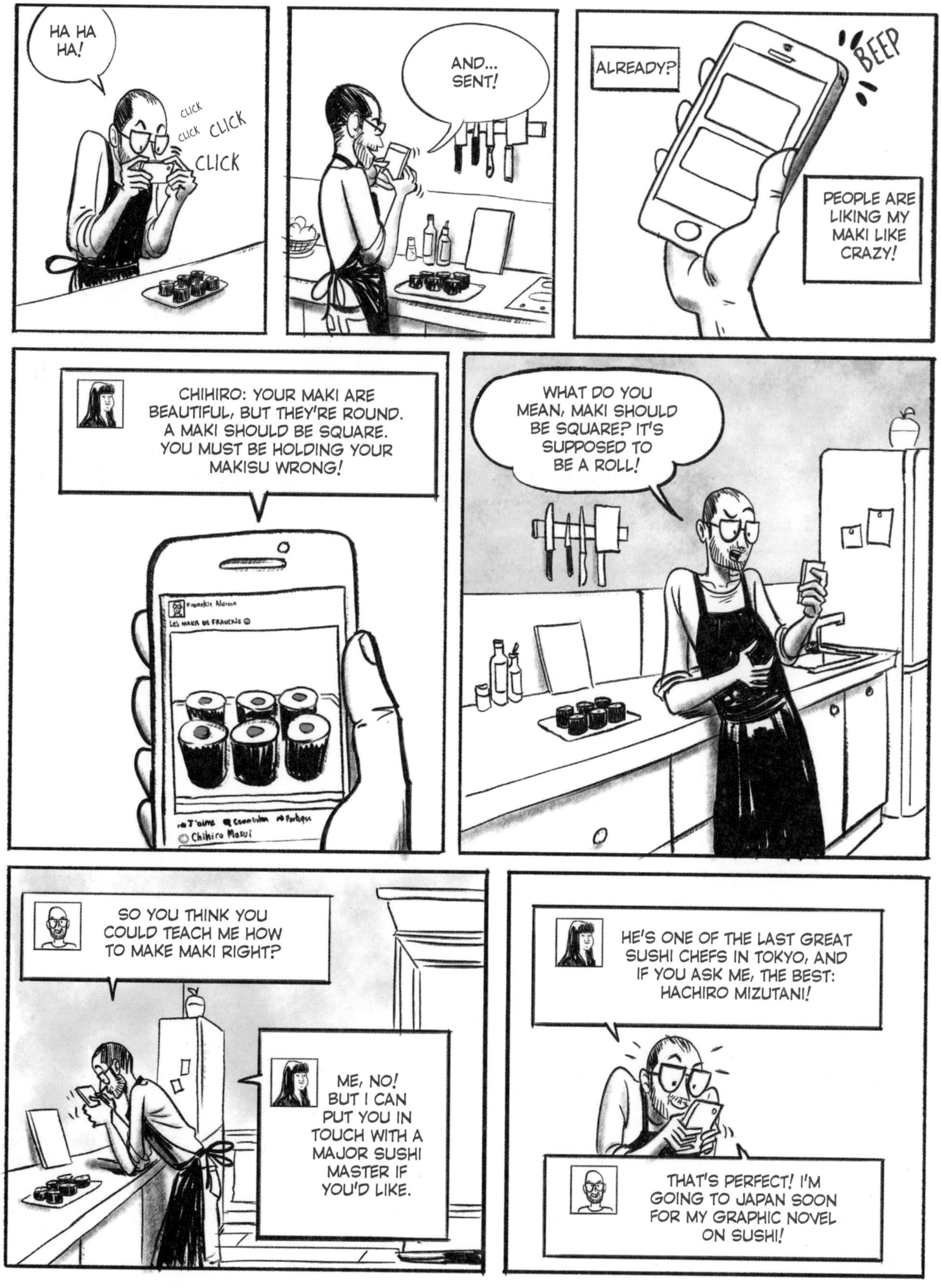
HA HA HA!
CLICK CLICK CLICK CLICK
AND... SENT!
ALREADY?
BEEP
PEOPLE ARE LIKING MY MAKI LIKE CRAZY!
CHIHIRO: YOUR MAKI ARE BEAUTIFUL, BUT THEY'RE ROUND. A MAKI SHOULD BE SQUARE. YOU MUST BE HOLDING YOUR MAKISU WRONG!
Chihiro Masui
WHAT DO YOU MEAN, MAKI SHOULD BE SQUARE? IT'S SUPPOSED TO BE A ROLL!
SO YOU THINK YOU COULD TEACH ME HOW TO MAKE MAKI RIGHT?
ME, NO! BUT I CAN PUT YOU IN TOUCH WITH A MAJOR SUSHI MASTER IF YOU'D LIKE.
HE'S ONE OF THE LAST GREAT SUSHI CHEFS IN TOKYO, AND IF YOU ASK ME, THE BEST: HACHIRO MIZUTANI!
THAT'S PERFECT! I'M GOING TO JAPAN SOON FOR MY GRAPHIC NOVEL ON SUSHI!

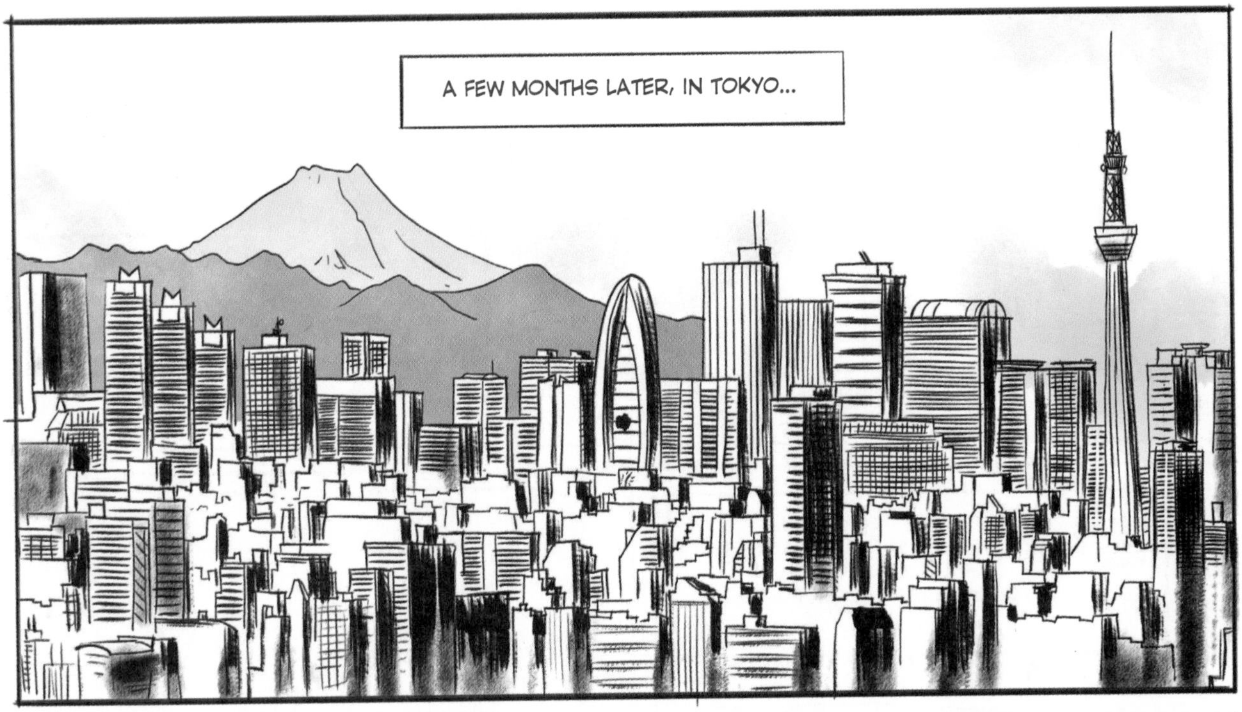
A FEW MONTHS LATER, IN TOKYO...

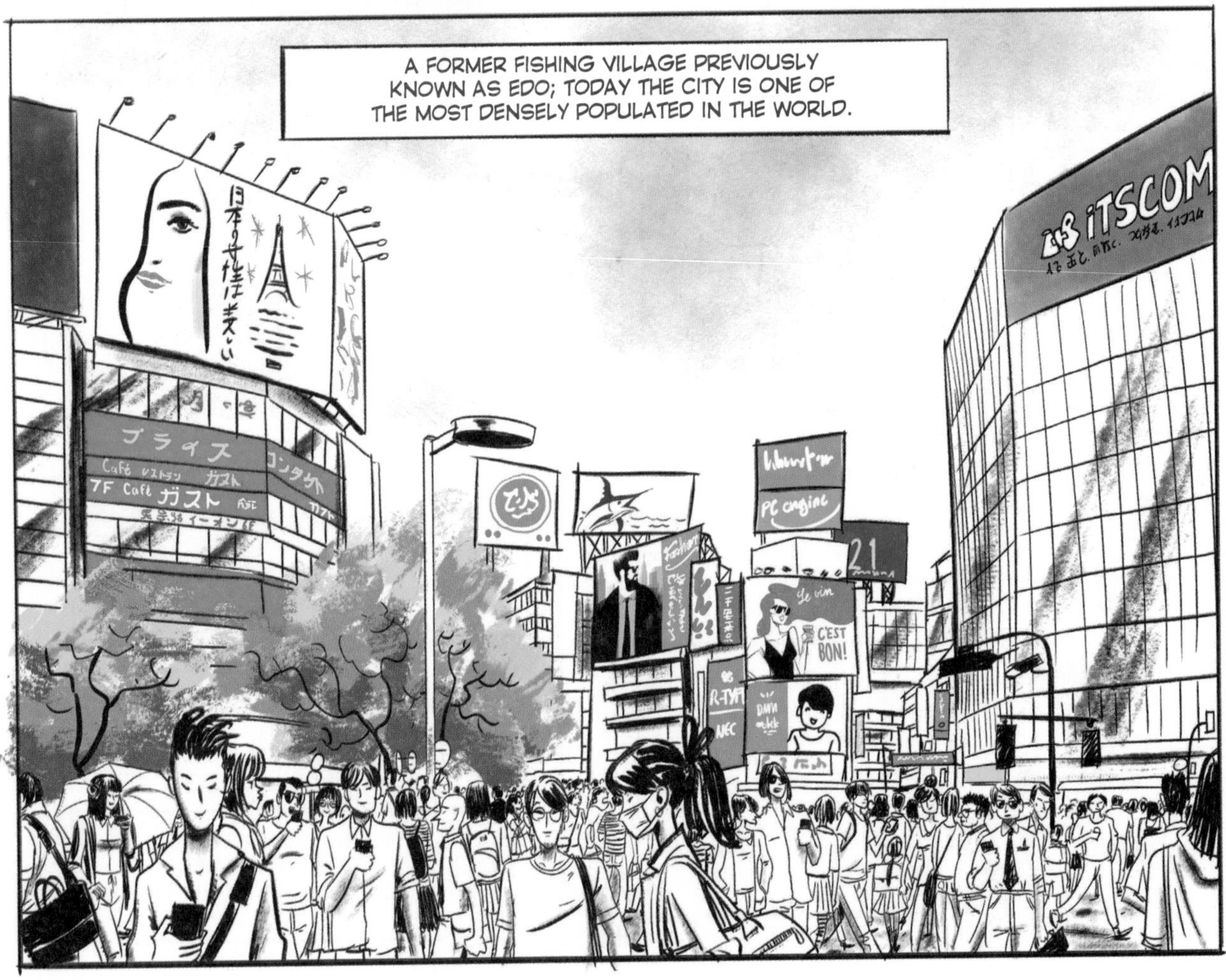
A FORMER FISHING VILLAGE PREVIOUSLY KNOWN AS EDO; TODAY THE CITY IS ONE OF THE MOST DENSELY POPULATED IN THE WORLD.
iTSCOM
プライス
7F Café ガスト
PC engine
21
Le vin
C'EST BON!
NEC

IT WAS HERE, IN THE CAPITAL, THAT MODERN SUSHI WAS BORN!

BUT BEFORE BECOMING THE SYMBOL OF JAPANESE FOOD
TO THE WORLD, IT UNDERWENT YEARS OF EVOLUTION.

IN THE 8TH CENTURY A TECHNIQUE ORIGINATING FROM CHINA WAS INTRODUCED TO JAPAN: FISH COOKED AND CONSERVED IN COOKED RICE FOR SEVERAL MONTHS BEFORE BEING EATEN. THE RICE IS LATER DISCARDED.

IN THE 12TH-CENTURY, THE METHOD EVOLVES. NOW FERMENTATION CAN LAST A MONTH AND THE RICE CAN BE EATEN WITH THE FISH!

THROUGHOUT THE 18TH CENTURY, THE FERMENTATION TIME IS REDUCED TO JUST A FEW DAYS. THE RICE AND THE FISH ARE PRESSED IN A WOODEN TRAY WITH VINEGAR TO GET THE FERMENTED TASTE OF YESTERYEAR.

MODERN SUSHI, ALSO CALLED NIGIRI SUSHI, APPEARED AT THE BEGINNING OF THE 19TH-CENTURY IN TOKYO. STREET FOOD FOR LABORERS, IT IS CRAFTED WITH FRESH FISH, COOKED OR MARINATED, FROM TOKYO BAY, PLACED UPON A LARGE BALL OF VINEGARED RICE.

THE LARGER, ORIGINAL SUSHI IS THEN SPLIT IN TWO TO FORM SMALLER BITES WHICH ARE SOLD IN PAIRS. THE INVENTION OF REFRIGERATION ALSO ALLOWS FOR THE USE OF OTHER RAW FISH WHICH HAD BEEN, UP TO THIS POINT, UNEXPLOITED OR UNSUITABLE FOR SERVING (MAINLY BECAUSE OF BACTERIA).

TODAY SUSHI IS AVAILABLE IN DIFFERENT FORMS.

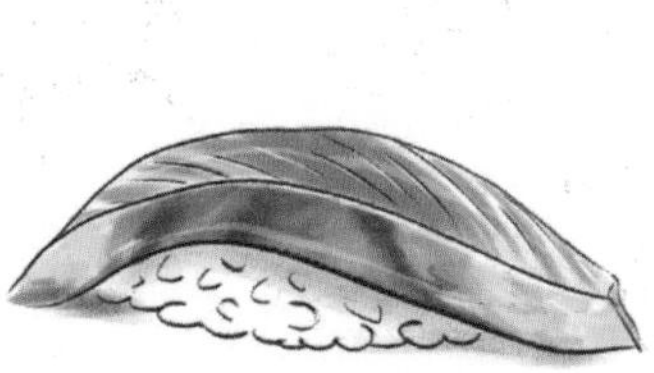

THE BEST KNOWN, NIGIRI SUSHI, IS THE MAIN BENCHMARK FOR EVALUATING A GREAT JAPANESE TABLE.

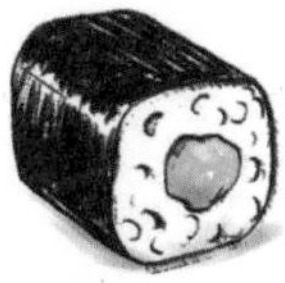

HOSO MAKI MEANS "LITTLE ROLL." IT'S RICE ENVELOPED IN SEAWEED NORI WITH ONLY ONE INGREDIENT INSIDE (EITHER FISH OR A VEGETABLE).

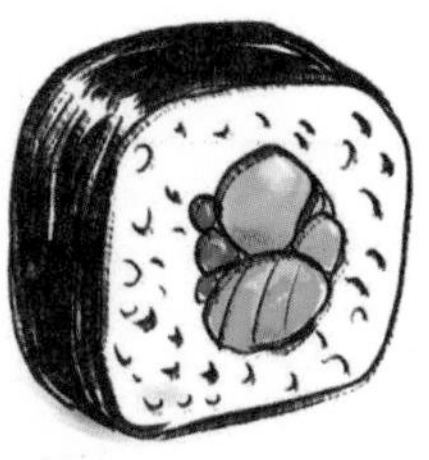

THE FUTO MAKI, ITS BIG BROTHER, CONTAINS MULTIPLE INGREDIENTS.

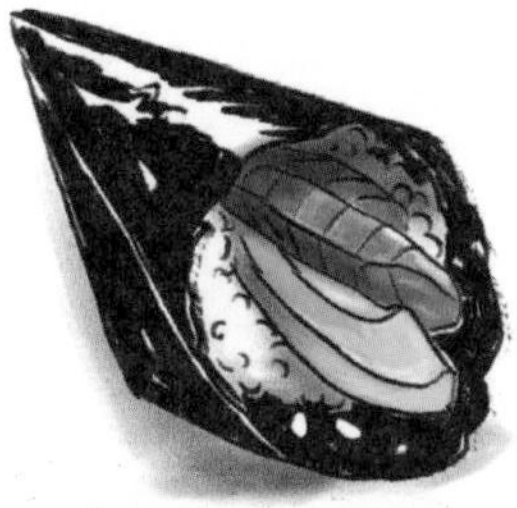

TEMAKI SUSHI IS A CONE MADE OF NORI DRESSED WITH RICE AND OTHER ELEMENTS. IT'S EATEN OFTEN AT HOME WHERE EVERYONE CAN PUT IN IT WHAT THEY WISH.

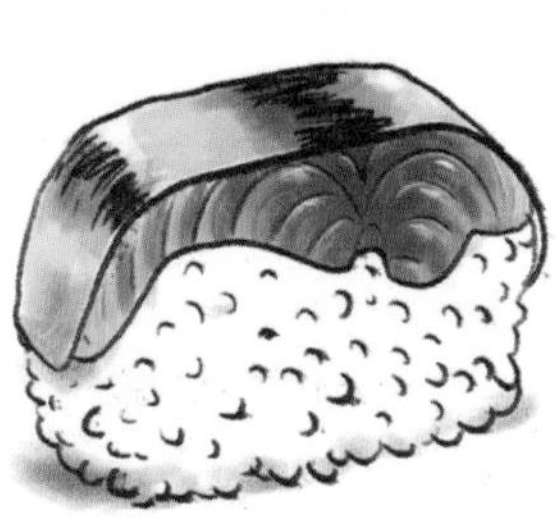

NARE SUSHI IS THE CONTEMPORARY VERSION OF THE ORIGINAL FERMENTED SUSHI. IT MAKES FOR A BITE THAT IS STRONG IN TASTE AND IN SMELL, FOR THOSE WITH SEASONED PALATES.

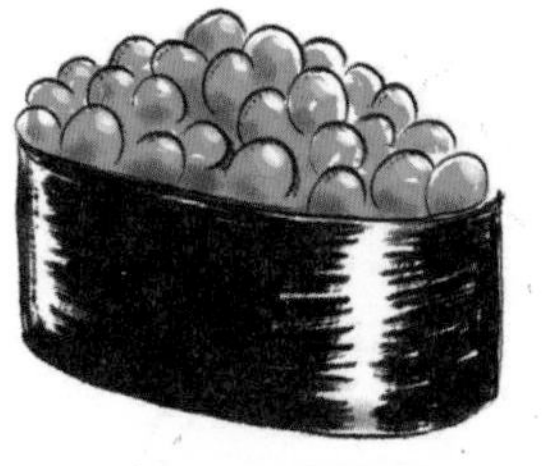

GUNKAN MAKI GETS ITS NAME FROM ITS ARMORED FORM (GUNKAN IN JAPANESE). IT HOLDS TOGETHER RICE AND ANOTHER INGREDIENT TOO DIFFICULT TO CONTAIN IN SUSHI OR MAKI (LIKE FISH EGGS OR SEA URCHIN).

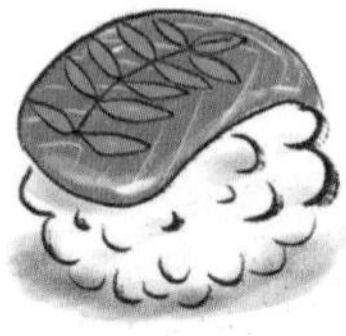

TEMARI SUSHI COMES IN THE FORM OF A LITTLE BALL.

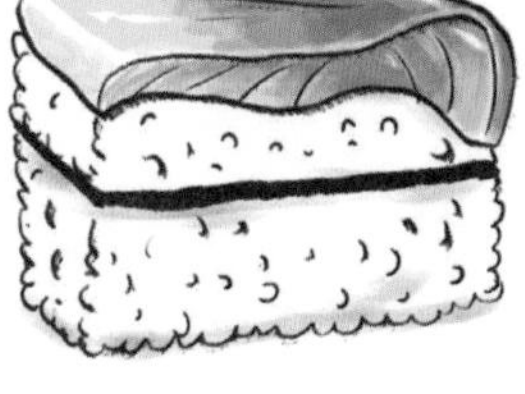

BATTERA SUSHI (OR OSHI SUSHI) IS PRESSED (BUT NOT FERMENTED) IN A WOODEN MOLD. IT CAN BE MADE UP OF DIFFERENT LAYERS OF INGREDIENTS.

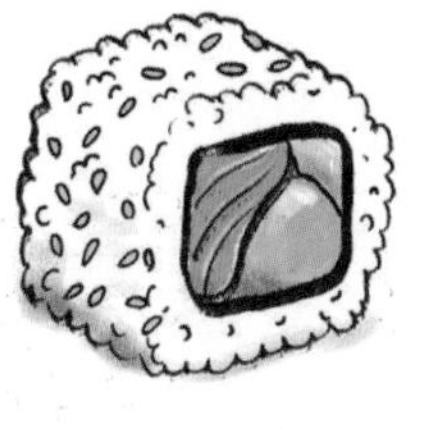

THE CALIFORNIA ROLL IS THE MOST WELL-KNOWN VARIANT OF URAMAKI, OR INVERTED MAKI. THE RICE SURROUNDS THE SEAWEED AND OTHER INGREDIENTS. THE RICE IS SPRINKLED WITH SESAME SEEDS.

Mizutani
Traditional sushi

HACHIRO MIZUTANI, A THREE MICHELIN STAR CHEF, IS ONE OF THE GREATEST SUSHI MASTERS IN JAPAN.
IN HIS CAREER, HE WORKED ALONGSIDE JIRO ONO, THE OTHER GLOBAL
REFERENCE FOR THIS CUISINE'S KNOWLEDGE AND TRADITIONS.

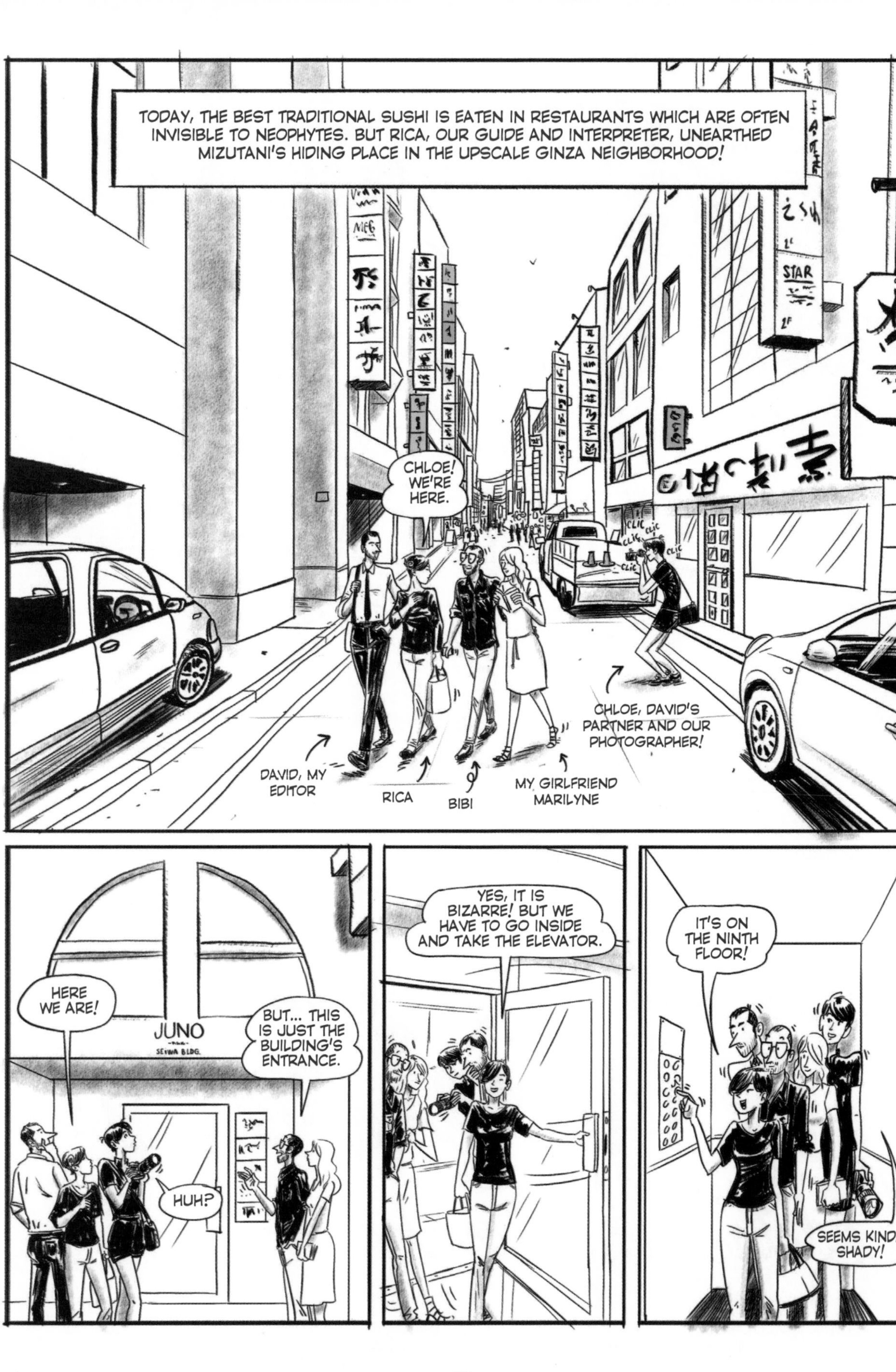
TODAY, THE BEST TRADITIONAL SUSHI IS EATEN IN RESTAURANTS WHICH ARE OFTEN INVISIBLE TO NEOPHYTES. BUT RICA, OUR GUIDE AND INTERPRETER, UNEARTHED MIZUTANI'S HIDING PLACE IN THE UPSCALE GINZA NEIGHBORHOOD!
CHLOE! WE'RE HERE.
CLIC CLIC CLIC CLIC CLIC
STAR
CHLOE, DAVID'S PARTNER AND OUR PHOTOGRAPHER!
DAVID, MY EDITOR
RICA
BIBI
MY GIRLFRIEND MARILYNE
HERE WE ARE!
JUNO
SEIWA BLDG.
BUT... THIS IS JUST THE BUILDING'S ENTRANCE.
HUH?
YES, IT IS BIZARRE! BUT WE HAVE TO GO INSIDE AND TAKE THE ELEVATOR.
IT'S ON THE NINTH FLOOR!
SEEMS KINDA SHADY!

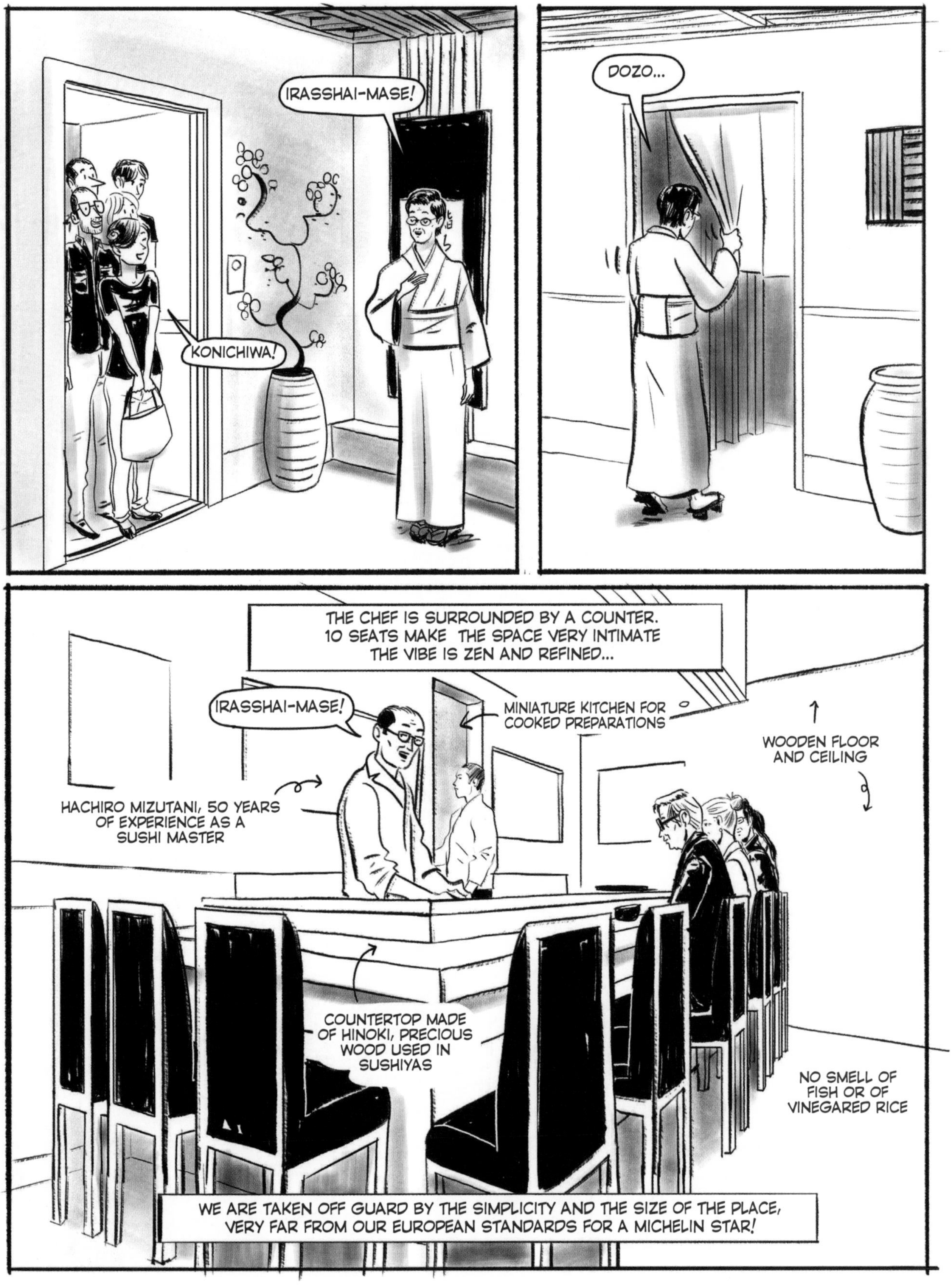
IRASSHAI-MASE!
KONICHIWA!
DOZO...
THE CHEF IS SURROUNDED BY A COUNTER.
10 SEATS MAKE THE SPACE VERY INTIMATE
THE VIBE IS ZEN AND REFINED...
IRASSHAI-MASE!
MINIATURE KITCHEN FOR COOKED PREPARATIONS
WOODEN FLOOR AND CEILING
HACHIRO MIZUTANI, 50 YEARS OF EXPERIENCE AS A SUSHI MASTER
COUNTERTOP MADE OF HINOKI, PRECIOUS WOOD USED IN SUSHIYAS
NO SMELL OF FISH OR OF VINEGARED RICE
WE ARE TAKEN OFF GUARD BY THE SIMPLICITY AND THE SIZE OF THE PLACE,
VERY FAR FROM OUR EUROPEAN STANDARDS FOR A MICHELIN STAR!

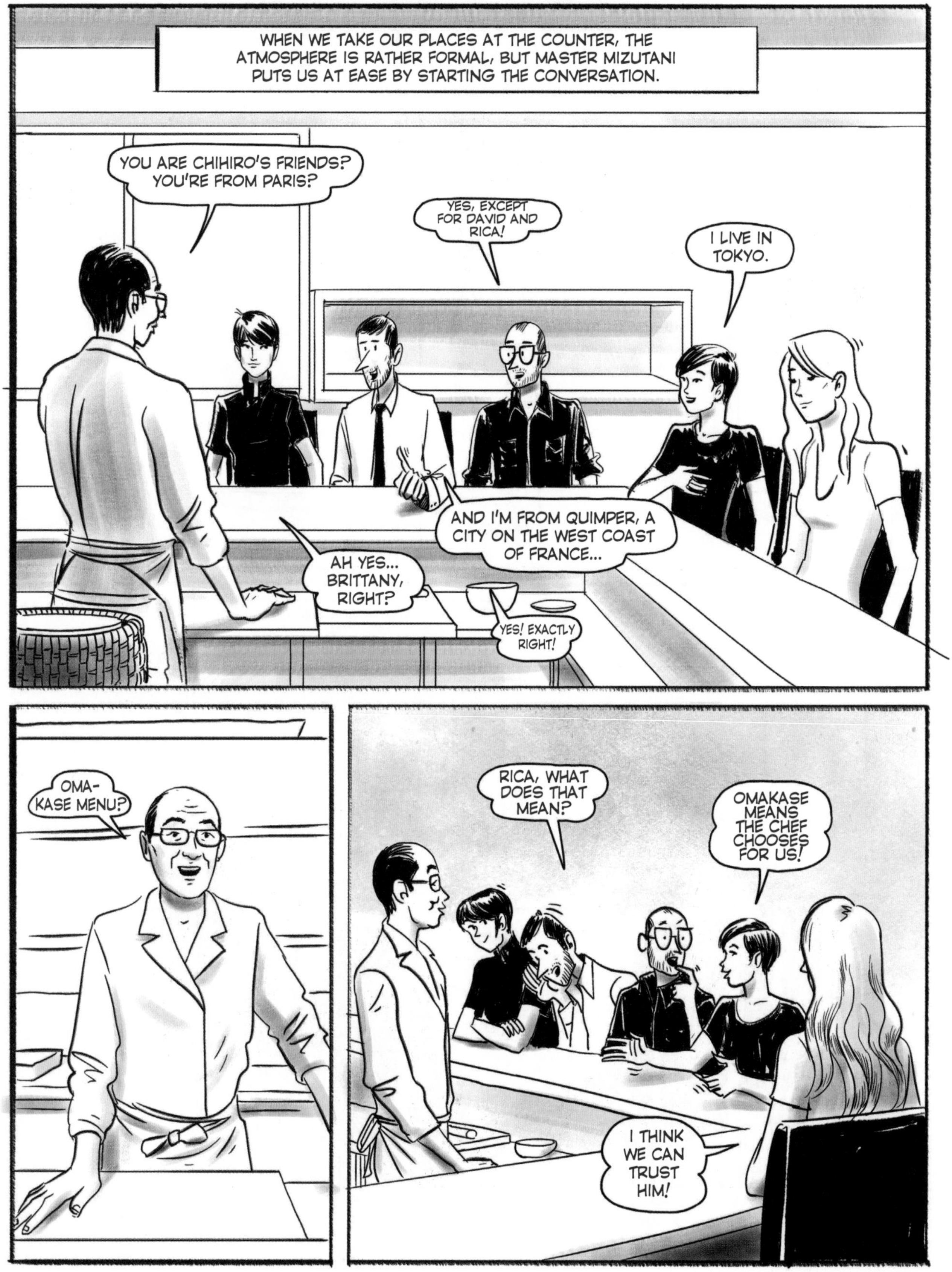
WHEN WE TAKE OUR PLACES AT THE COUNTER, THE ATMOSPHERE IS RATHER FORMAL, BUT MASTER MIZUTANI PUTS US AT EASE BY STARTING THE CONVERSATION.
YOU ARE CHIHIRO'S FRIENDS? YOU'RE FROM PARIS?
YES, EXCEPT FOR DAVID AND RICA!
I LIVE IN TOKYO.
AND I'M FROM QUIMPER, A CITY ON THE WEST COAST OF FRANCE...
AH YES... BRITTANY, RIGHT?
YES! EXACTLY RIGHT!
OMA-KASE MENU?
RICA, WHAT DOES THAT MEAN?
OMAKASE MEANS THE CHEF CHOOSES FOR US!
I THINK WE CAN TRUST HIM!

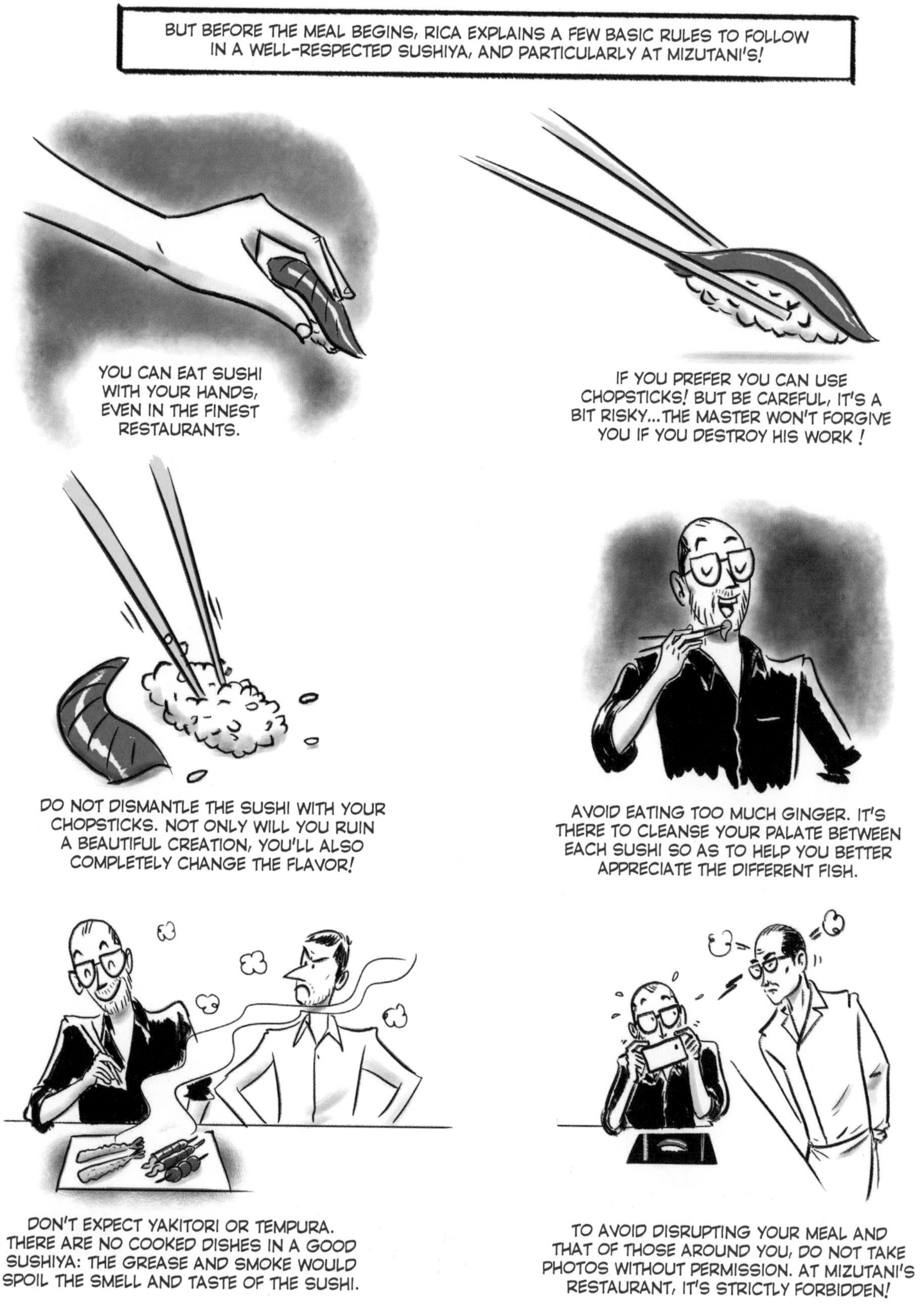

BUT BEFORE THE MEAL BEGINS, RICA EXPLAINS A FEW BASIC RULES TO FOLLOW IN A WELL-RESPECTED SUSHIYA, AND PARTICULARLY AT MIZUTANI'S!
YOU CAN EAT SUSHI WITH YOUR HANDS, EVEN IN THE FINEST RESTAURANTS.
IF YOU PREFER YOU CAN USE CHOPSTICKS! BUT BE CAREFUL, IT'S A BIT RISKY...THE MASTER WON'T FORGIVE YOU IF YOU DESTROY HIS WORK !
DO NOT DISMANTLE THE SUSHI WITH YOUR CHOPSTICKS. NOT ONLY WILL YOU RUIN A BEAUTIFUL CREATION, YOU'LL ALSO COMPLETELY CHANGE THE FLAVOR!
AVOID EATING TOO MUCH GINGER. IT'S THERE TO CLEANSE YOUR PALATE BETWEEN EACH SUSHI SO AS TO HELP YOU BETTER APPRECIATE THE DIFFERENT FISH.
DON'T EXPECT YAKITORI OR TEMPURA. THERE ARE NO COOKED DISHES IN A GOOD SUSHIYA: THE GREASE AND SMOKE WOULD SPOIL THE SMELL AND TASTE OF THE SUSHI.
TO AVOID DISRUPTING YOUR MEAL AND THAT OF THOSE AROUND YOU, DO NOT TAKE PHOTOS WITHOUT PERMISSION. AT MIZUTANI'S RESTAURANT, IT'S STRICTLY FORBIDDEN!

WITH THESE RULES IN MIND, THE MARVELOUS PROCESS OF THE CHEF'S SUSHI CAN BEGIN. THE TASTES AND TEXTURES REACH CRESCENDO.

MIZUTANI BEGINS BY CUTTING HIRAME, A DELICATE WHITE FISH MUCH LIKE A FLOUNDER.

THEN HE FORMS A BALL OF RICE WITH HIS RIGHT HAND...

...TAKES A PINCH OF FRESH WASABI WITH THE TIP OF HIS INDEX FINGER...

... AND SPREADS IT OUT DELICATELY ON THE SLICE OF FISH.

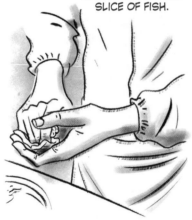

HE SETS THE BALL OF RICE THAT HE HAD KEPT IN THE PALM OF HIS HAND...

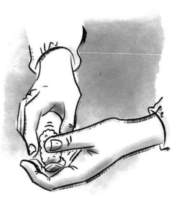

... AND WITH A PRECISE AND ELEGANT GESTURE HE BRINGS ALL THE COMPONENTS TOGETHER!

THE FINISHING TOUCH: THE FISH RECEIVES A BRUSHSTROKE OF A HOUSE SAUCE CALLED NIKIRI MADE FROM SOY, MIRIN* AND SAKE!

*VERY SWEET COOKING SAKE

MIZUTANI SETS A SUSHI BEFORE EACH DINER ON A SMALL BLACK LACQUERED BOARD...

14

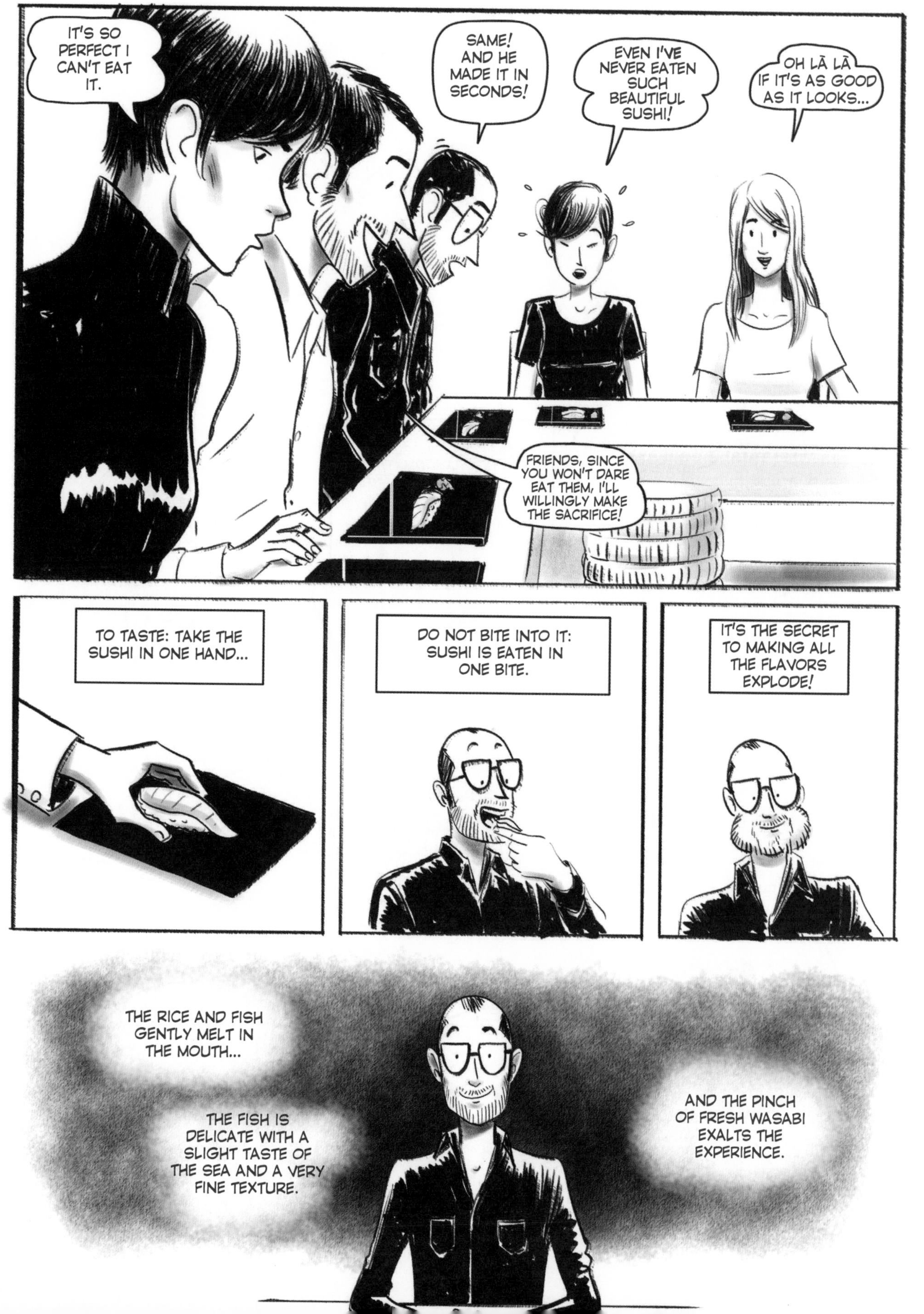
IT'S SO PERFECT I CAN'T EAT IT.
SAME! AND HE MADE IT IN SECONDS!
EVEN I'VE NEVER EATEN SUCH BEAUTIFUL SUSHI!
OH LÃ LÃ IF IT'S AS GOOD AS IT LOOKS...
FRIENDS, SINCE YOU WON'T DARE EAT THEM, I'LL WILLINGLY MAKE THE SACRIFICE!
TO TASTE: TAKE THE SUSHI IN ONE HAND...
DO NOT BITE INTO IT: SUSHI IS EATEN IN ONE BITE.
IT'S THE SECRET TO MAKING ALL THE FLAVORS EXPLODE!
THE RICE AND FISH GENTLY MELT IN THE MOUTH...
THE FISH IS DELICATE WITH A SLIGHT TASTE OF THE SEA AND A VERY FINE TEXTURE.
AND THE PINCH OF FRESH WASABI EXALTS THE EXPERIENCE.

THE EXPLORATION CONTINUES, ITS TEMPO MARKED BY THE PRECISE AND ELEGANT GESTURES OF THE SUSHI MASTER!

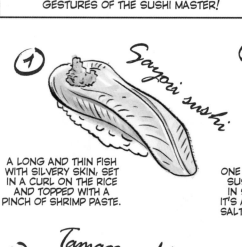

① *Sayori sushi*

A LONG AND THIN FISH WITH SILVERY SKIN, SET IN A CURL ON THE RICE AND TOPPED WITH A PINCH OF SHRIMP PASTE.

② *Kohada sushi*

ONE OF THE MOST BEAUTIFUL SUSHIS! MARINATED FIRST IN SALT THEN IN VINEGAR, IT'S ALL AT ONCE SWEET AND SALTY WITH A SOFT TEXTURE.

③ *Cuttlefish sushi*

HATCH MARKED CUTS MAKE TASTING EASIER. IT'S TENDER AND MELTS IN THE MOUTH. IT'S THE EXACT OPPOSITE OF PLAIN CUTTLEFISH.

⑯ *Tamago-yaki*

A SLIGHTLY SWEET SHRIMP PASTE "OMELET" IDEAL FOR THE END OF THE MEAL.

THE ORDER OF SUSHI IS NOT RANDOM. THE CHEF RANKS THE FISH FROM THE SOFTEST AND SWEETEST TO THE FATTIEST, DENSEST, AND STRONGEST IN FLAVOR.

⑮ *Anago sushi*

THE FAMOUS EEL COOKED IN TERIYAKI* SAUCE. A MELT-IN-YOUR-MOUTH FATTY AND SWEET TREAT.

Ikura gunkan

⑭

FRESH SALMON EGGS LIGHTLY MARINATED BY THE CHEF ALL WRAPPED UP IN CRUNCHY NORI.

A SAUCE MADE OF SAKE, SOY, AND SUGAR.

⑬ *Samel sushi*

ONE OF MY FAVORITES! A FIRM FLESHED FISH TASTING OF THE SEA WITH AN ALMOST METALLIC FLAVOR.

⑫ *Shima-aji sushi*

MULTIPLE TEXTURES. THE SKIN IS SLIGHTLY TOUGH — THE FISH IS DENSE AND FATTY — WHICH MAKES FOR A UNIQUE TASTING SUSHI.

WITH EACH AND EVERY SUSHI, WE ARE IMPRESSED BY MIZUTANI'S RIGOR AND AGILITY...

BUT MOSTLY WE'RE TRANSFIXED BY THE HINTS OF CERTAIN TASTES THAT WE WEREN'T EXPECTING.

④ *Akami*

THEN ARRIVES THE TRILOGY OF TUNA WHICH STARTS WITH THE LEAST FATTY PIECE. IT TASTES LIGHT AND SLIGHTLY METALLIC.

⑤ *Chutoro*

ITS LAYERED CUT IS MAGNIFICENT. IT POSSESSES ALL AT ONCE THE FINENESS OF THE AKAMI AND THE FATTINESS OF THE OTORO.

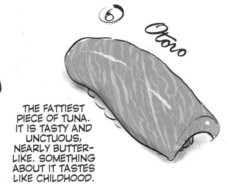

⑥ *Otoro*

THE FATTIEST PIECE OF TUNA. IT IS TASTY AND UNCTUOUS, NEARLY BUTTER-LIKE. SOMETHING ABOUT IT TASTES LIKE CHILDHOOD.

⑦ *Miru-gai sushi*

A TYPE OF CLAM THAT IS VERY RARE EVEN IN JAPAN. IT IS SERVED RAW AND TASTES SWEET.

⑧ *Shako sushi*

THE TENDER FLESH OF THIS TYPE OF SLIPPER LOBSTER TASTES SLIGHTLY NUTTY.

⑪ *Ebi sushi*

A PLUMP SUSHI VISUALLY APPEALING WITH ITS LIVELY ORANGE COLOR. IT'S BEGGING TO BE EATEN!

⑩ *Abalone sushi*

THE ABALONE IS VERY TENDER AFTER BEING COOKED IN SAKE, AN UNPRECEDENTED TASTE FOR US THAT, PREPARED IN THIS WAY, IS NOT THE SLIGHTEST BIT RUBBERY.

⑨ *Uni gunkan maki*

A SMALL "ARMORED" SUSHI (REMEMBER?) SERVED WITH SEA URCHIN. IT'S A GENTLE BOMB OF SALTY SEA FLAVOR!

YOU ALRIGHT?

THINK YOU'LL RECOVER?

HA HA! WHAT ABOUT YOU? YOU HOLDING UP?

CHIHIRO TOLD ME THAT YOU ARE HER FAVORITE SUSHIYA... NOW I KNOW WHY!

SHE SAID THAT?

SHE ALSO TOLD ME A VERY FUNNY STORY ABOUT YOUR LAST TRIP TO PARIS...

PARIS, APRIL 2015. FIRST MEETING WITH CHIHIRO MASUI, JOURNALIST AND COOKBOOK AUTHOR.

IN 2007 MIZUTANI CAME TO PARIS TO PRESENT HIS WORK.

I TOOK HIM TO ONE OF THE BEST MARKETS SO HE COULD CHOOSE HIS FISH...

Carte des vins
Rouge
- Domaine de P.Thun
- le Temps des cerises
- Rupatel
Blanc
- Vin du Rhin
- L'emphibolite

18

IT WAS OUR THIRD TIME AROUND THE ROWS OF FISHMONGERS. HE SEEMED WORRIED...

SO, DO YOU SEE ANYTHING YOU LIKE?

THE PROBLEM IS THAT ALL THESE FISH ARE DEAD...

UHH... YEA... WE'RE IN PARIS!

BUT THEY'RE VERY, VERY DEAD!!!

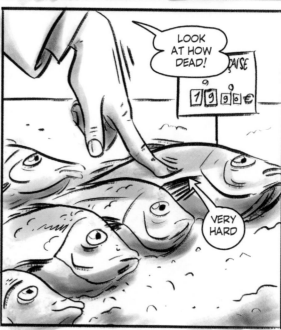

LOOK AT HOW DEAD!

VERY HARD

UNTIL THAT DAY I BELIEVED THAT A GOOD FISH SHOULD BE FIRM.

BUT THERE THEY WERE STIFF LIKE CADAVERS...

AND FOR HIM, A FISH IN THIS STATE IS NO LONGER EDIBLE BECAUSE HE CAN'T CONTROL THE MATURATION!

THIS MATURATION IS PRECISELY WHAT ALLOWS THE FLAVORS OF THE FISH TO DEVELOP.

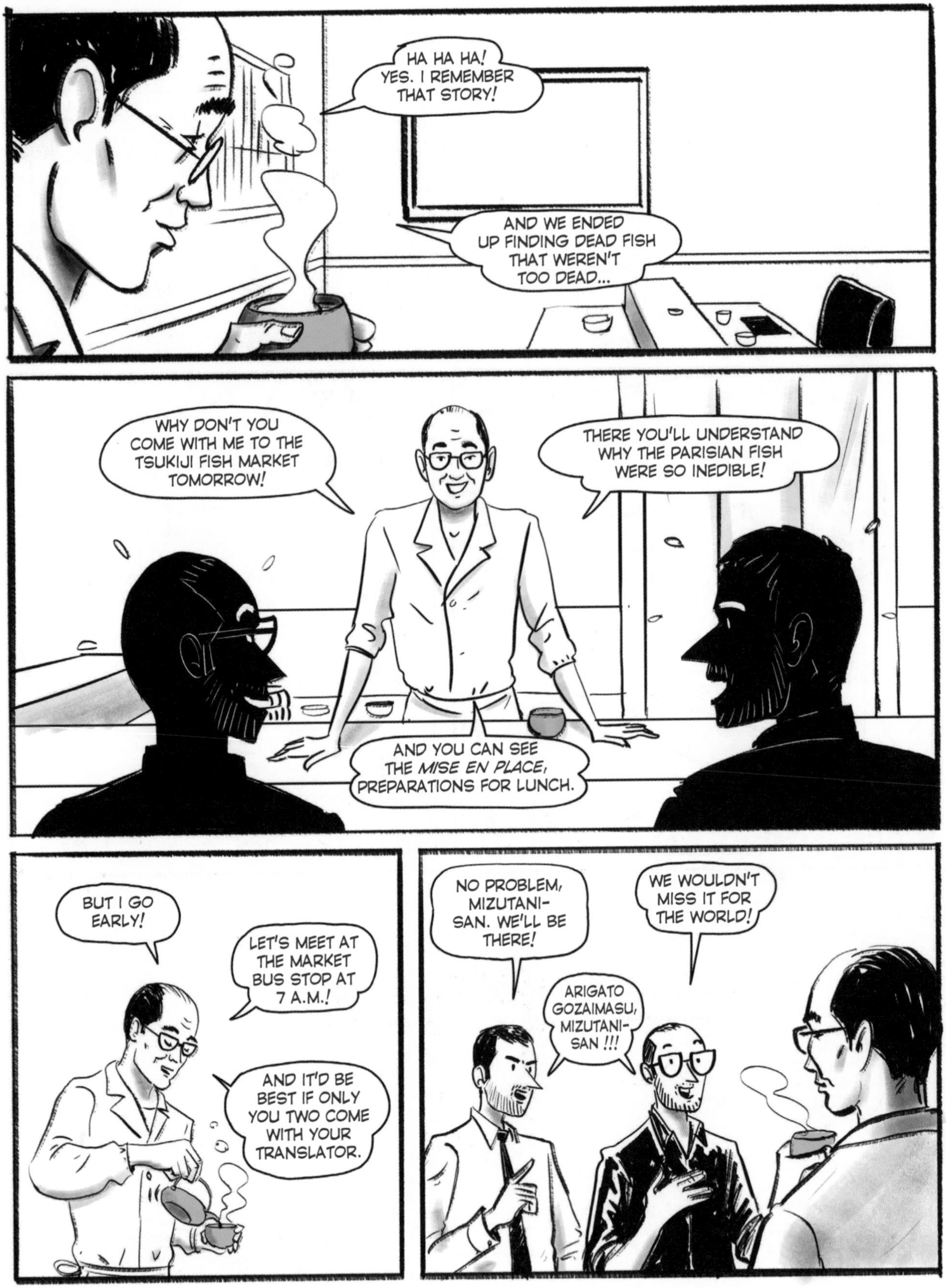

HA HA HA! YES. I REMEMBER THAT STORY!
AND WE ENDED UP FINDING DEAD FISH THAT WEREN'T TOO DEAD...
WHY DON'T YOU COME WITH ME TO THE TSUKIJI FISH MARKET TOMORROW!
THERE YOU'LL UNDERSTAND WHY THE PARISIAN FISH WERE SO INEDIBLE!
AND YOU CAN SEE THE *MISE EN PLACE*, PREPARATIONS FOR LUNCH.
BUT I GO EARLY!
LET'S MEET AT THE MARKET BUS STOP AT 7 A.M.!
AND IT'D BE BEST IF ONLY YOU TWO COME WITH YOUR TRANSLATOR.
NO PROBLEM, MIZUTANI-SAN. WE'LL BE THERE!
WE WOULDN'T MISS IT FOR THE WORLD!
ARIGATO GOZAIMASU, MIZUTANI-SAN !!!

TSUKIJI MARKET*, 7 A.M.! IT'S THE BIGGEST FISH MARKET IN THE WORLD WITH OVER 10,000 EMPLOYEES AND MORE THAN 450 SPECIES FROM ALL OVER THE WORLD.

THIS PLACE IS SWARMING! IT'S NUTS!

WE'RE EARLY SO WE'LL BE SURE NOT TO MISS MIZUTANI!

IN JAPAN IT'S VERY IMPOLITE TO BE LATE, FRANCKIE-SAN!

*OPENED IN 1935, TSUKIJI MOVED ON OCTOBER 11, 2018 (AFTER OUR TRIP) TO TOYOSU, A TOTALLY NEW MARKET FURTHER SOUTH OF TOKYO.

WOAH! TUNA!

WATCH OUT WHEN YOU CROSS. THEY DON'T YIELD FOR PEDESTRIANS!

AND BE CAREFUL NOT TO GET IN THE WAY. THEY CAN KICK US OUT!!!

THEY'RE GOING FULL STEAM AHEAD WITH THEIR LITTLE CARTS!

OH THERE'S THE BUS!

HELLO, MR. MIZUTANI!

HELLO, EVERYONE!

21

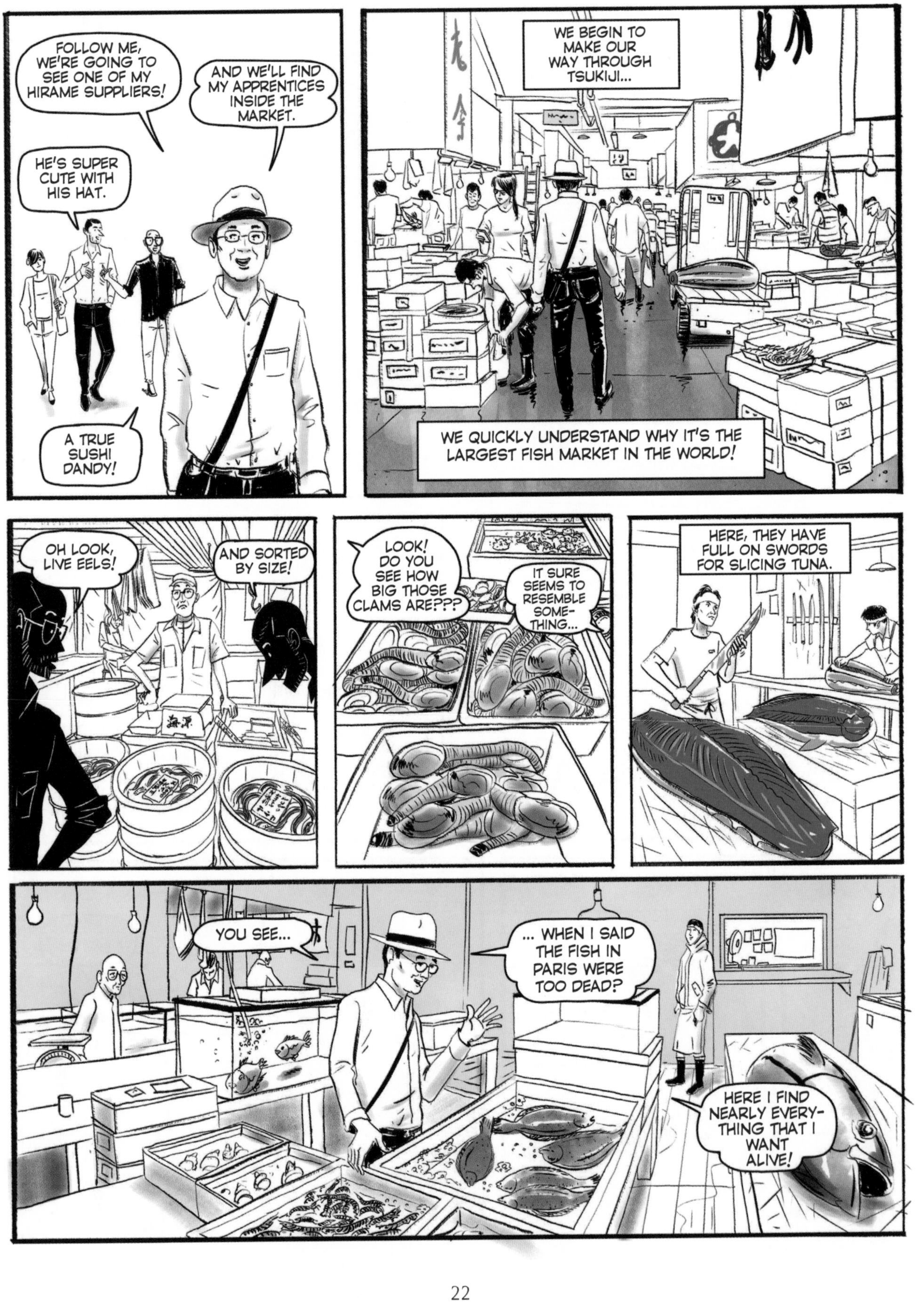
FOLLOW ME, WE'RE GOING TO SEE ONE OF MY HIRAME SUPPLIERS!
AND WE'LL FIND MY APPRENTICES INSIDE THE MARKET.
HE'S SUPER CUTE WITH HIS HAT.
A TRUE SUSHI DANDY!
WE BEGIN TO MAKE OUR WAY THROUGH TSUKIJI...
WE QUICKLY UNDERSTAND WHY IT'S THE LARGEST FISH MARKET IN THE WORLD!
OH LOOK, LIVE EELS!
AND SORTED BY SIZE!
LOOK! DO YOU SEE HOW BIG THOSE CLAMS ARE???
IT SURE SEEMS TO RESEMBLE SOME-THING...
HERE, THEY HAVE FULL ON SWORDS FOR SLICING TUNA.
YOU SEE...
... WHEN I SAID THE FISH IN PARIS WERE TOO DEAD?
HERE I FIND NEARLY EVERY-THING THAT I WANT ALIVE!

COME SEE! THIS HERE IS HIRAME. I SERVED YOU SOME LAST NIGHT.

I'M GOING TO ASK MY SUPPLIER TO PREPARE IT!

MIZUTANI INTRODUCES US, FOLLOWED BY JAPANESE GREETINGS. THE TWO FRIENDS DISCUSS FISH...

MITZUTANI SEEMS TO HAVE VERY SPECIFIC DEMANDS.

ONCE THE FISH ARE CHOSEN, AN EMPLOYEE PLACES A STRUGGLING HIRAME ON THE CUTTING BOARD...

SPLAT! SPLAT! SPLAT!

... AND GIVES IT A CLEAN AND PRECISE CUT JUST BELOW ITS HEAD...

CRAC!

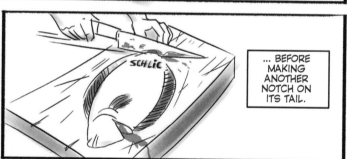

SCHLIC

... BEFORE MAKING ANOTHER NOTCH ON ITS TAIL.

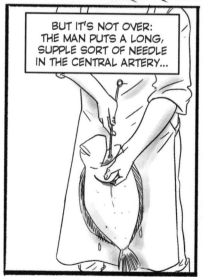

BUT IT'S NOT OVER: THE MAN PUTS A LONG, SUPPLE SORT OF NEEDLE IN THE CENTRAL ARTERY...

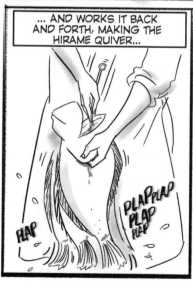

... AND WORKS IT BACK AND FORTH, MAKING THE HIRAME QUIVER...

PLAP

PLAPPLAP PLAP PLAP

FINALLY IT STOPS MOVING.

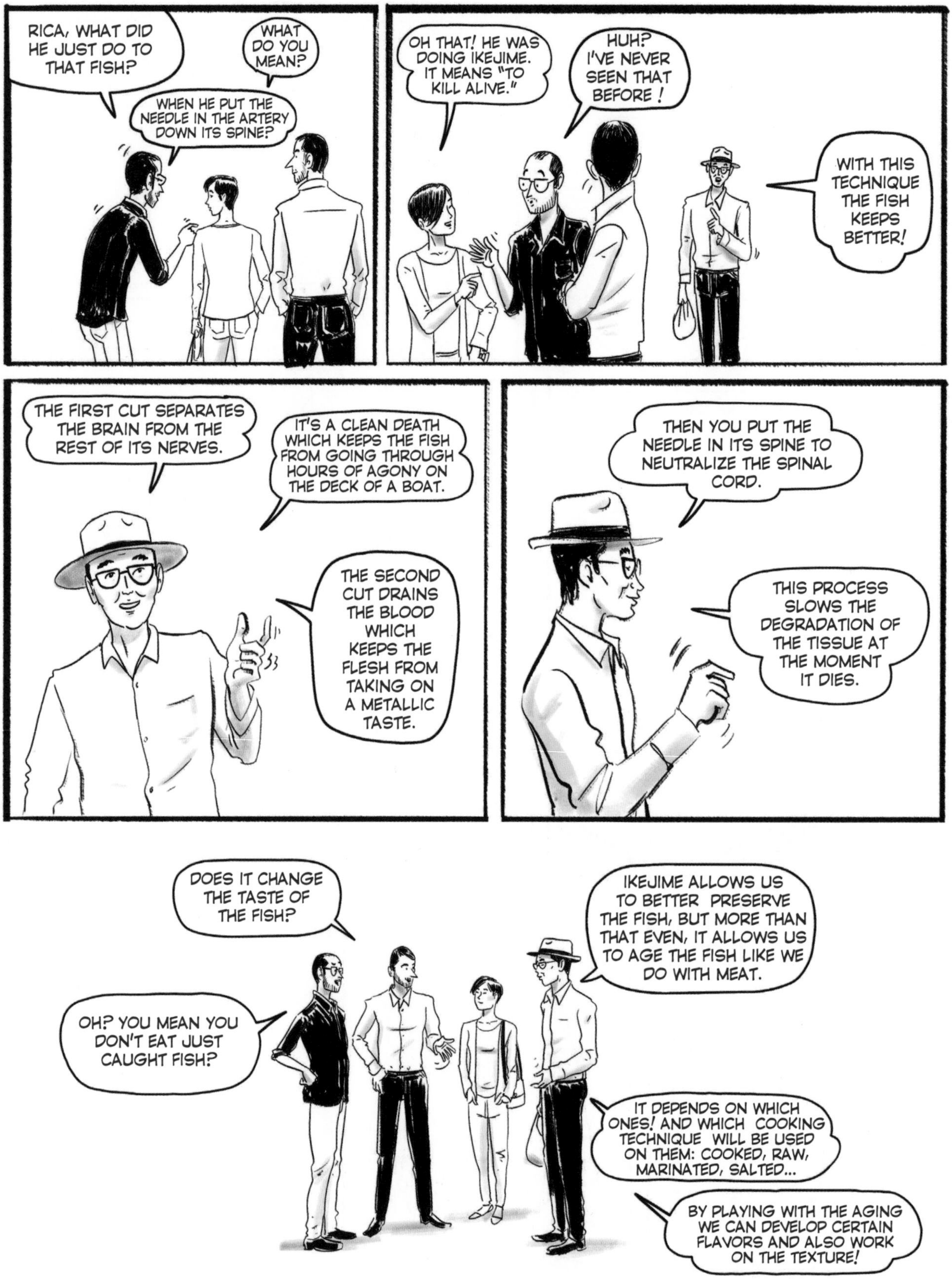
RICA, WHAT DID HE JUST DO TO THAT FISH?
WHAT DO YOU MEAN?
WHEN HE PUT THE NEEDLE IN THE ARTERY DOWN ITS SPINE?
OH THAT! HE WAS DOING IKEJIME. IT MEANS "TO KILL ALIVE."
HUH? I'VE NEVER SEEN THAT BEFORE !
WITH THIS TECHNIQUE THE FISH KEEPS BETTER!
THE FIRST CUT SEPARATES THE BRAIN FROM THE REST OF ITS NERVES.
IT'S A CLEAN DEATH WHICH KEEPS THE FISH FROM GOING THROUGH HOURS OF AGONY ON THE DECK OF A BOAT.
THE SECOND CUT DRAINS THE BLOOD WHICH KEEPS THE FLESH FROM TAKING ON A METALLIC TASTE.
THEN YOU PUT THE NEEDLE IN ITS SPINE TO NEUTRALIZE THE SPINAL CORD.
THIS PROCESS SLOWS THE DEGRADATION OF THE TISSUE AT THE MOMENT IT DIES.
DOES IT CHANGE THE TASTE OF THE FISH?
IKEJIME ALLOWS US TO BETTER PRESERVE THE FISH, BUT MORE THAN THAT EVEN, IT ALLOWS US TO AGE THE FISH LIKE WE DO WITH MEAT.
OH? YOU MEAN YOU DON'T EAT JUST CAUGHT FISH?
IT DEPENDS ON WHICH ONES! AND WHICH COOKING TECHNIQUE WILL BE USED ON THEM: COOKED, RAW, MARINATED, SALTED...
BY PLAYING WITH THE AGING WE CAN DEVELOP CERTAIN FLAVORS AND ALSO WORK ON THE TEXTURE!

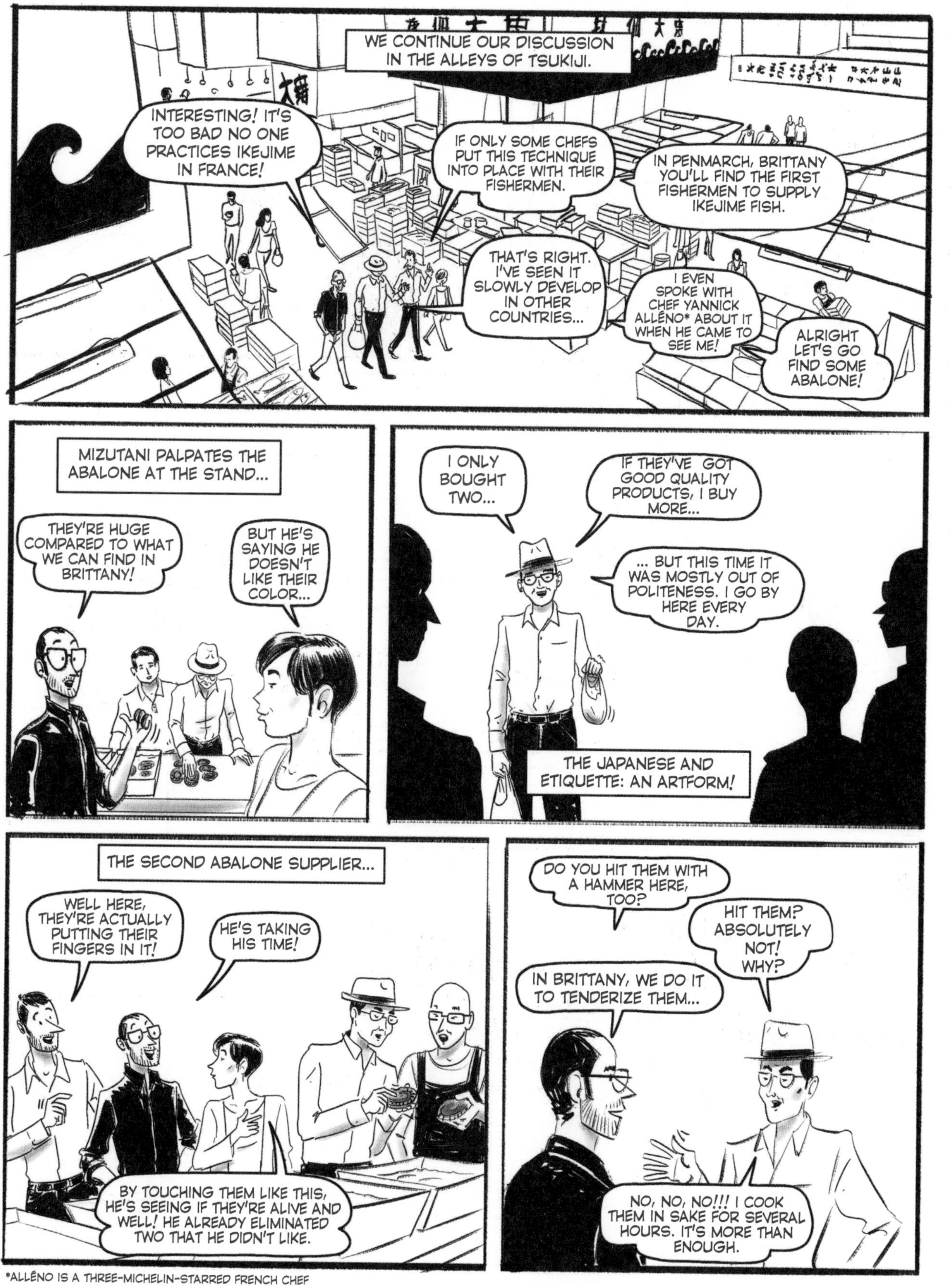
WE CONTINUE OUR DISCUSSION IN THE ALLEYS OF TSUKIJI.
INTERESTING! IT'S TOO BAD NO ONE PRACTICES IKEJIME IN FRANCE!
IF ONLY SOME CHEFS PUT THIS TECHNIQUE INTO PLACE WITH THEIR FISHERMEN.
IN PENMARCH, BRITTANY YOU'LL FIND THE FIRST FISHERMEN TO SUPPLY IKEJIME FISH.
THAT'S RIGHT. I'VE SEEN IT SLOWLY DEVELOP IN OTHER COUNTRIES...
I EVEN SPOKE WITH CHEF YANNICK ALLÉNO* ABOUT IT WHEN HE CAME TO SEE ME!
ALRIGHT LET'S GO FIND SOME ABALONE!
MIZUTANI PALPATES THE ABALONE AT THE STAND...
THEY'RE HUGE COMPARED TO WHAT WE CAN FIND IN BRITTANY!
BUT HE'S SAYING HE DOESN'T LIKE THEIR COLOR...
I ONLY BOUGHT TWO...
IF THEY'VE GOT GOOD QUALITY PRODUCTS, I BUY MORE...
... BUT THIS TIME IT WAS MOSTLY OUT OF POLITENESS. I GO BY HERE EVERY DAY.
THE JAPANESE AND ETIQUETTE: AN ARTFORM!
THE SECOND ABALONE SUPPLIER...
WELL HERE, THEY'RE ACTUALLY PUTTING THEIR FINGERS IN IT!
HE'S TAKING HIS TIME!
BY TOUCHING THEM LIKE THIS, HE'S SEEING IF THEY'RE ALIVE AND WELL! HE ALREADY ELIMINATED TWO THAT HE DIDN'T LIKE.
DO YOU HIT THEM WITH A HAMMER HERE, TOO?
HIT THEM? ABSOLUTELY NOT! WHY?
IN BRITTANY, WE DO IT TO TENDERIZE THEM...
NO, NO, NO!!! I COOK THEM IN SAKE FOR SEVERAL HOURS. IT'S MORE THAN ENOUGH.

*ALLÉNO IS A THREE-MICHELIN-STARRED FRENCH CHEF

OFF TOWARDS OUR LAST STOP OF THE MORNING: TUNA!

I'VE BEEN DOING BUSINESS WITH MR. FUJITA, MY TUNA SUPPLIER, FOR OVER 20 YEARS.

WE ONLY WORK WITH FRESH TUNA FROM OMA, A SMALL FISHING PORT IN NORTHERN JAPAN.

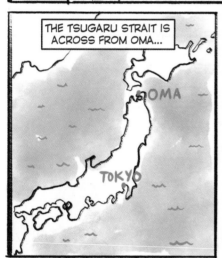

THE TSUGARU STRAIT IS ACROSS FROM OMA...

OMA

TOKYO

THAT'S WHERE SMALLER FISHING BOATS FIGHT TO CATCH THE TUNA MIGRATING NORTH.

SINCE THE FISHING AREA IS NEAR THE PORT, THEY PRACTICE IKEJIME QUICKLY ON WHARF: IT'S WHAT MAKES OMA TUNA SUCH A DISTINCT AND QUALITY PRODUCT.

NO FREEZING, NO FILETING. WE CALL IT THE DIAMOND OF THE SEA!

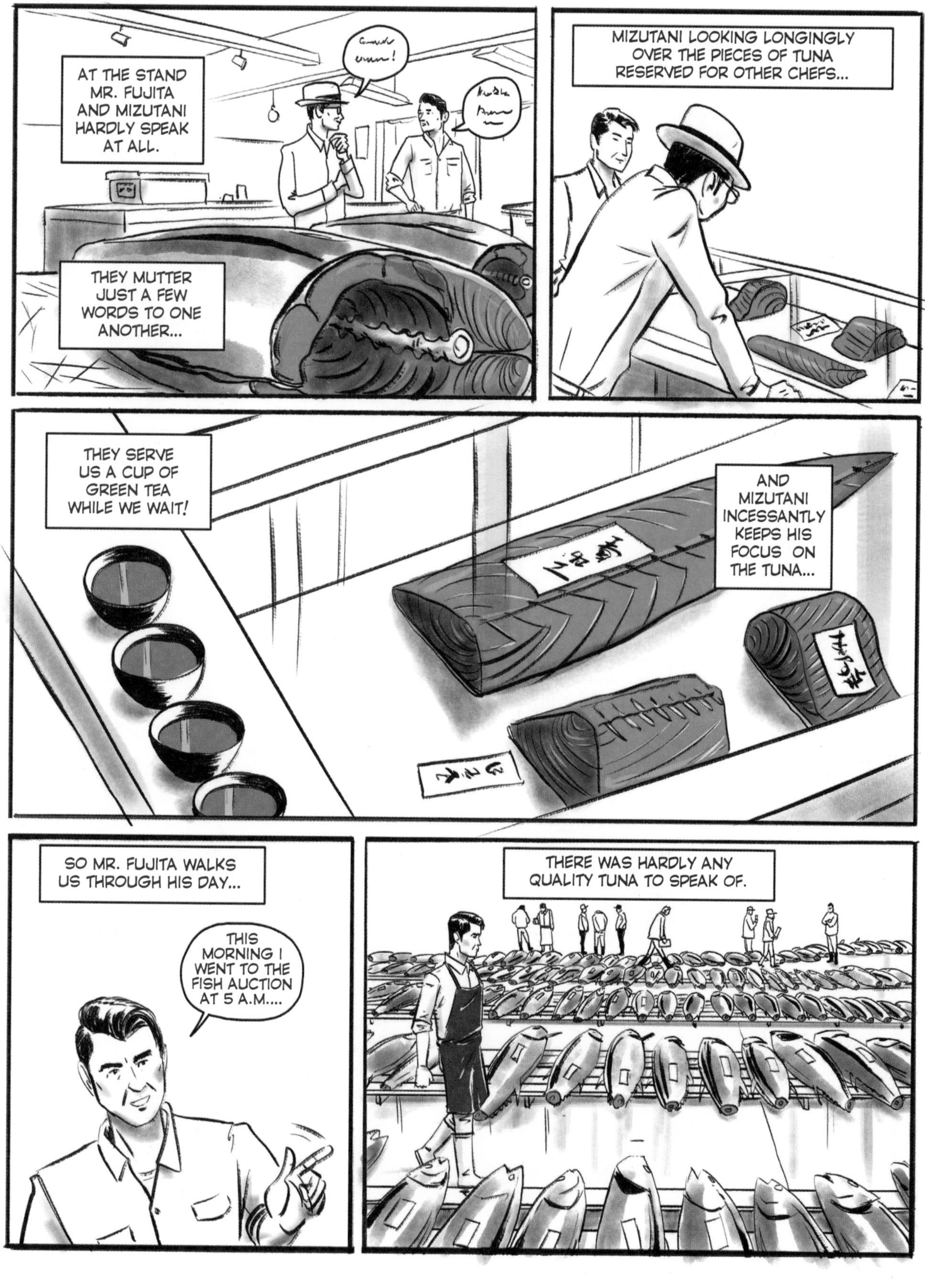
AT THE STAND MR. FUJITA AND MIZUTANI HARDLY SPEAK AT ALL.
THEY MUTTER JUST A FEW WORDS TO ONE ANOTHER...
MIZUTANI LOOKING LONGINGLY OVER THE PIECES OF TUNA RESERVED FOR OTHER CHEFS...
THEY SERVE US A CUP OF GREEN TEA WHILE WE WAIT!
AND MIZUTANI INCESSANTLY KEEPS HIS FOCUS ON THE TUNA...
SO MR. FUJITA WALKS US THROUGH HIS DAY...
THIS MORNING I WENT TO THE FISH AUCTION AT 5 A.M....
THERE WAS HARDLY ANY QUALITY TUNA TO SPEAK OF.

TO SEE IF THE TUNA IS GOOD, YOU CAN TAKE A SMALL BIT OF FLESH FROM THE TAIL OF THE FISH.

HE USES A FLASHLIGHT TO INSPECT THE COLOR OF THE FLESH.

BY SQUEEZING IT BETWEEN YOUR FINGERS, YOU CAN FEEL IF IT IS FATTY, FIRM, ETC.

I HAVE A TUNA HERE FROM THIS MORNING BUT IT'S NOT GOOD ENOUGH FOR YOU...

CAN I SEE IT ANYWAY?

OF COURSE!

BUT I NEED TO PREPARE IT FIRST!

MR. FUJITA BEGINS BY CUTTING OFF THE HEAD WITH A HUGE BLADE...

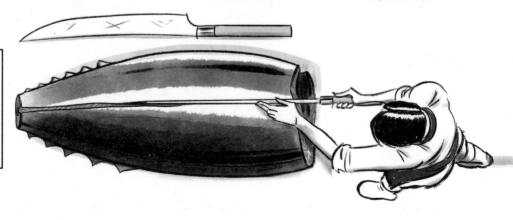

NEXT, HE TAKES A SWORD AND MAKES AN INCISION ALONG THE LENGTH OF THE TUNA.

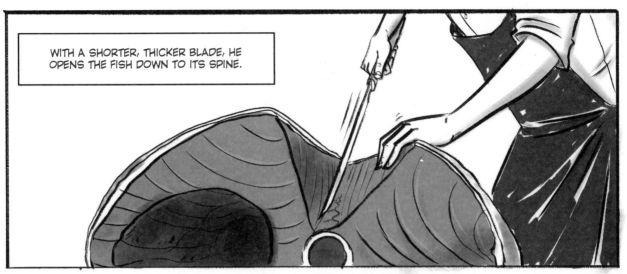

WITH A SHORTER, THICKER BLADE, HE OPENS THE FISH DOWN TO ITS SPINE.

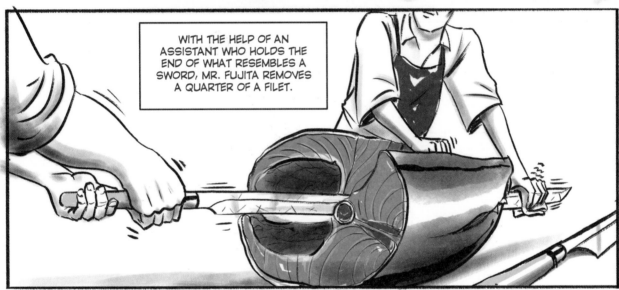

WITH THE HELP OF AN ASSISTANT WHO HOLDS THE END OF WHAT RESEMBLES A SWORD, MR. FUJITA REMOVES A QUARTER OF A FILET.

ONCE REMOVED, THE CUT IS PLACED ON A BOARD SO IT CAN BE MOVED TO ANOTHER WORK SURFACE.

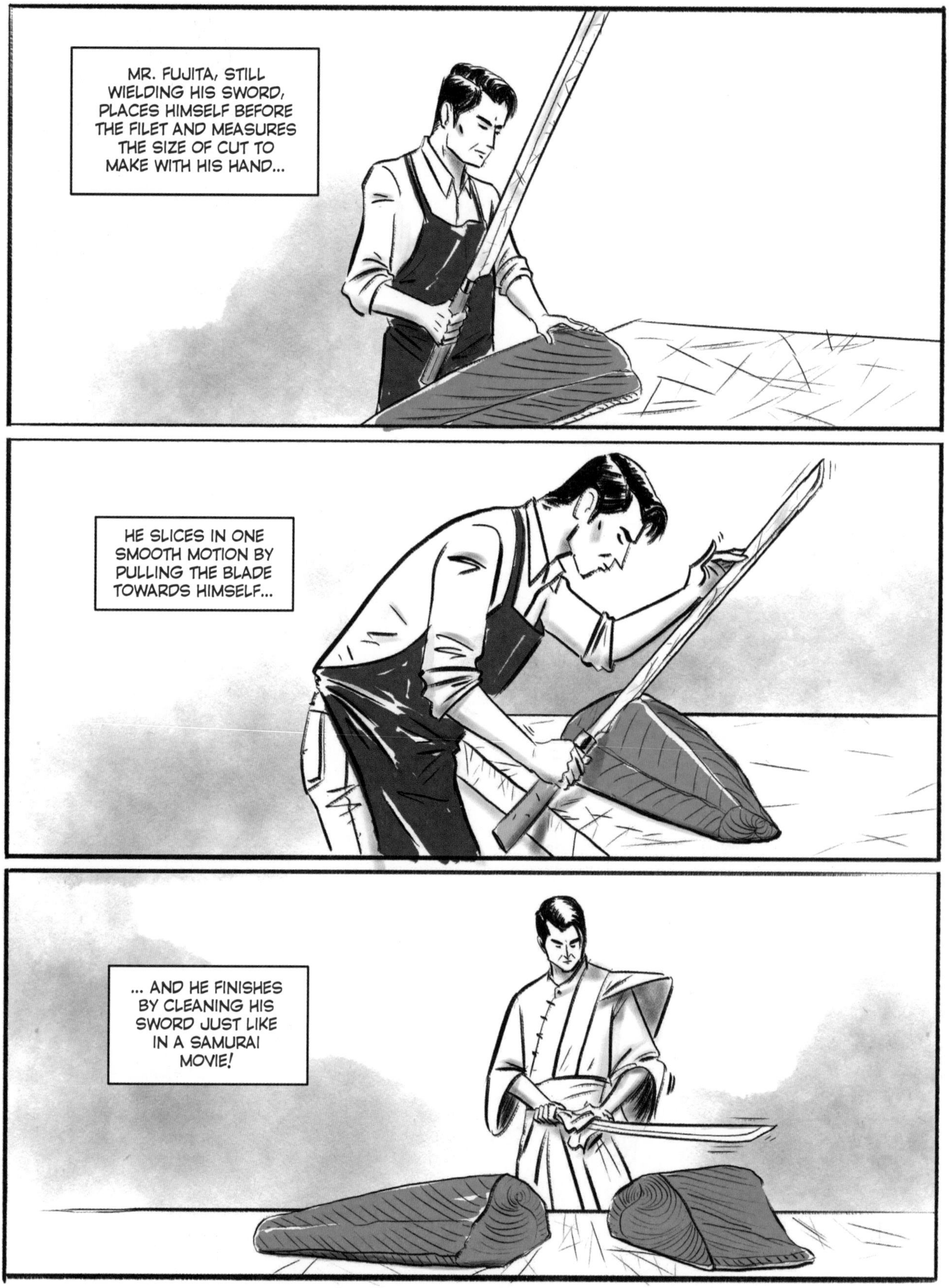
MR. FUJITA, STILL WIELDING HIS SWORD, PLACES HIMSELF BEFORE THE FILET AND MEASURES THE SIZE OF CUT TO MAKE WITH HIS HAND...
HE SLICES IN ONE SMOOTH MOTION BY PULLING THE BLADE TOWARDS HIMSELF...
... AND HE FINISHES BY CLEANING HIS SWORD JUST LIKE IN A SAMURAI MOVIE!

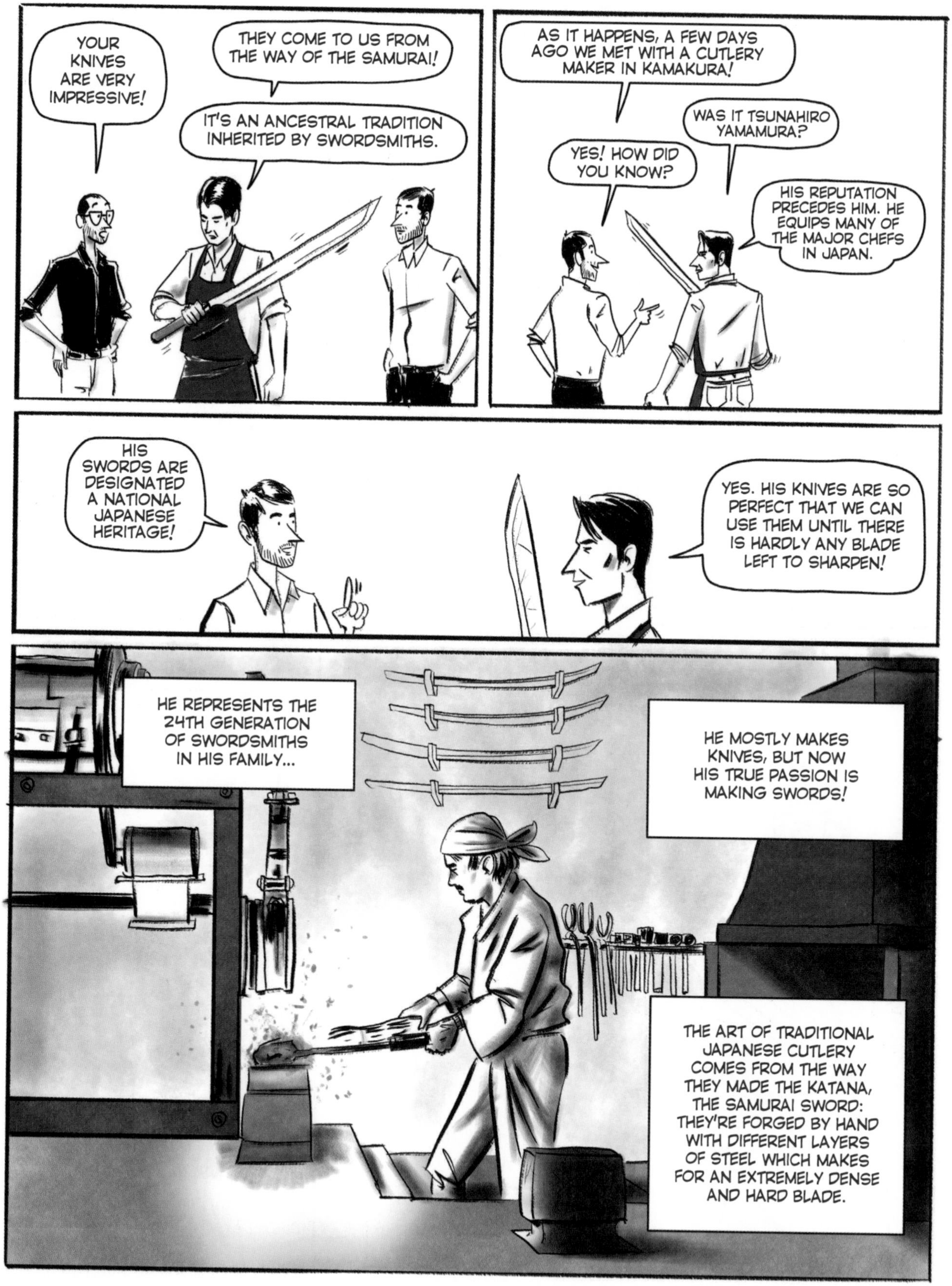
YOUR KNIVES ARE VERY IMPRESSIVE!
THEY COME TO US FROM THE WAY OF THE SAMURAI!
IT'S AN ANCESTRAL TRADITION INHERITED BY SWORDSMITHS.
AS IT HAPPENS, A FEW DAYS AGO WE MET WITH A CUTLERY MAKER IN KAMAKURA!
WAS IT TSUNAHIRO YAMAMURA?
YES! HOW DID YOU KNOW?
HIS REPUTATION PRECEDES HIM. HE EQUIPS MANY OF THE MAJOR CHEFS IN JAPAN.
HIS SWORDS ARE DESIGNATED A NATIONAL JAPANESE HERITAGE!
YES. HIS KNIVES ARE SO PERFECT THAT WE CAN USE THEM UNTIL THERE IS HARDLY ANY BLADE LEFT TO SHARPEN!
HE REPRESENTS THE 24TH GENERATION OF SWORDSMITHS IN HIS FAMILY...
HE MOSTLY MAKES KNIVES, BUT NOW HIS TRUE PASSION IS MAKING SWORDS!
THE ART OF TRADITIONAL JAPANESE CUTLERY COMES FROM THE WAY THEY MADE THE KATANA, THE SAMURAI SWORD: THEY'RE FORGED BY HAND WITH DIFFERENT LAYERS OF STEEL WHICH MAKES FOR AN EXTREMELY DENSE AND HARD BLADE.

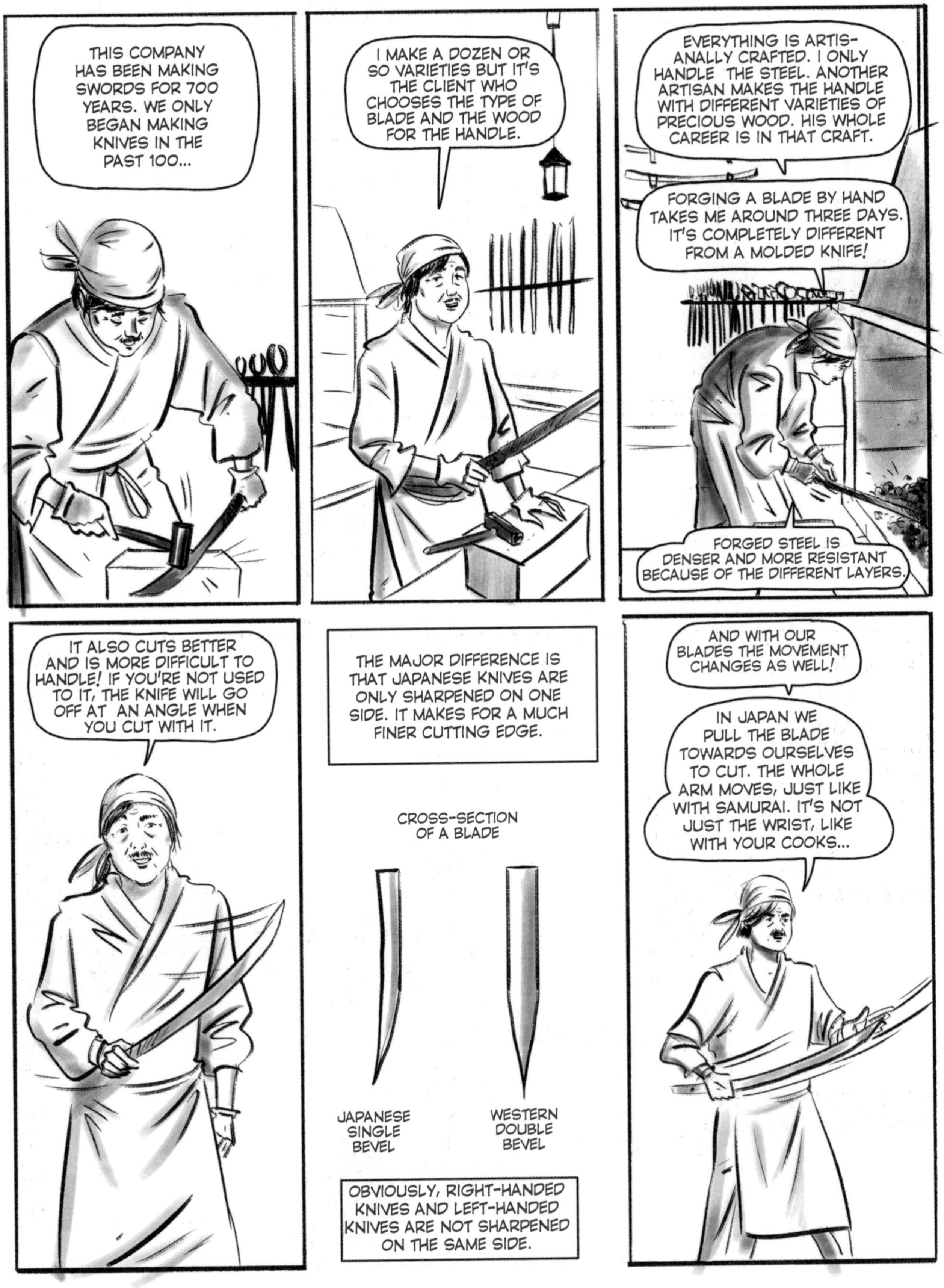
THIS COMPANY HAS BEEN MAKING SWORDS FOR 700 YEARS. WE ONLY BEGAN MAKING KNIVES IN THE PAST 100...
I MAKE A DOZEN OR SO VARIETIES BUT IT'S THE CLIENT WHO CHOOSES THE TYPE OF BLADE AND THE WOOD FOR THE HANDLE.
EVERYTHING IS ARTISANALLY CRAFTED. I ONLY HANDLE THE STEEL. ANOTHER ARTISAN MAKES THE HANDLE WITH DIFFERENT VARIETIES OF PRECIOUS WOOD. HIS WHOLE CAREER IS IN THAT CRAFT.
FORGING A BLADE BY HAND TAKES ME AROUND THREE DAYS. IT'S COMPLETELY DIFFERENT FROM A MOLDED KNIFE!
FORGED STEEL IS DENSER AND MORE RESISTANT BECAUSE OF THE DIFFERENT LAYERS.
IT ALSO CUTS BETTER AND IS MORE DIFFICULT TO HANDLE! IF YOU'RE NOT USED TO IT, THE KNIFE WILL GO OFF AT AN ANGLE WHEN YOU CUT WITH IT.
THE MAJOR DIFFERENCE IS THAT JAPANESE KNIVES ARE ONLY SHARPENED ON ONE SIDE. IT MAKES FOR A MUCH FINER CUTTING EDGE.
CROSS-SECTION OF A BLADE
JAPANESE SINGLE BEVEL
WESTERN DOUBLE BEVEL
OBVIOUSLY, RIGHT-HANDED KNIVES AND LEFT-HANDED KNIVES ARE NOT SHARPENED ON THE SAME SIDE.
AND WITH OUR BLADES THE MOVEMENT CHANGES AS WELL!
IN JAPAN WE PULL THE BLADE TOWARDS OURSELVES TO CUT. THE WHOLE ARM MOVES, JUST LIKE WITH SAMURAI. IT'S NOT JUST THE WRIST, LIKE WITH YOUR COOKS...

AS YOU CAN SEE, JAPANESE KNIVES COME IN ALL DIFFERENT SHAPES, SIZES, AND CUTTING EDGES.

EACH KNIFE IS DESIGNED FOR A SPECIFIC INGREDIENT. IT'S ACTUALLY THE FISH WHO MAKES THE KNIFE!

THE MOST COMMON, OR MOST NOTEWORTHY, BLADES IN SUSHI ARE THESE:

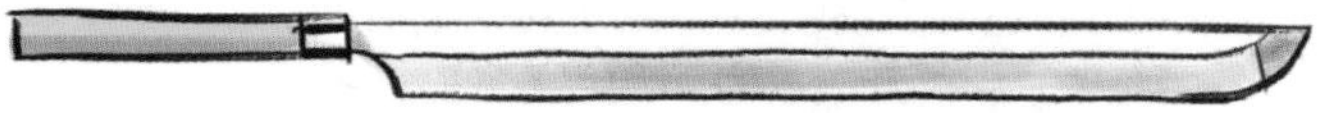

Maguro bocho and Oroshi bocho

THESE ARE THE SWORDS USED TO CUT TUNA. THE BLADE CAN BE UP TO 5 FEET LONG! IT IS FORBIDDEN TO TAKE THEM OUTSIDE OF TSUKIJI. HOWEVER, THEY'VE BEEN FOUND AMONG CERTAIN YAKUZA...

Deba

ONE OF THE MOST COMMON. HEAVY, THICK, AND RESILIENT, IT MEASURES FROM 16 UP TO 22 CENTIMETERS IN LENGTH. THE FORWARD PART OF THE BLADE IS FOR CUTTING FILETS WHILE THE BACK PART IS USED TO CLEANLY CUT THROUGH BONES AND TO REMOVE FISH HEADS.

Yanagi

ITS LONG, THIN BLADE IS FOR CUTTING SASHIMI WITH ONE SMOOTH MOTION. CHEFS USE BLADES THAT CAN REACH UP TO 30 CENTIMETERS LONG!

Fuguhiki

FINER AND MORE FLEXIBLE THAN THE YANAGI, IT ALLOWS FOR MORE PRECISION. AS ITS NAME MIGHT SUGGEST, IT IS USED TO CUT FUGU, A FISH THAT IS FAMOUS FOR BEING DEADLY IF IT IS POORLY PREPARED.

Unagisaki

UNAGI MEANS "EEL." YOU PLANT THE SHARP POINT OF THE KNIFE NEAR THE HEAD OF THE FISH BEFORE FILETING IT BY SLICING IT ALONG ITS SPINE.

Takohiki

IF YOU LIKE SQUID, YOU MIGHT HAVE RECOGNIZED THE WORD TAKO, TO WHICH THIS BLADE IS DEDICATED.

Santoku

ITS NAME MEANS "THREE VIRTUES." IT IS A POLYVALENT BLADE MADE FOR CUTTING VEGETABLES, MEAT OR FISH. IT'S THE JAPANESE VERSION OF THE CHEF'S KNIFE. IT CAN ALSO BE FOUND IN PEOPLE'S HOMES.

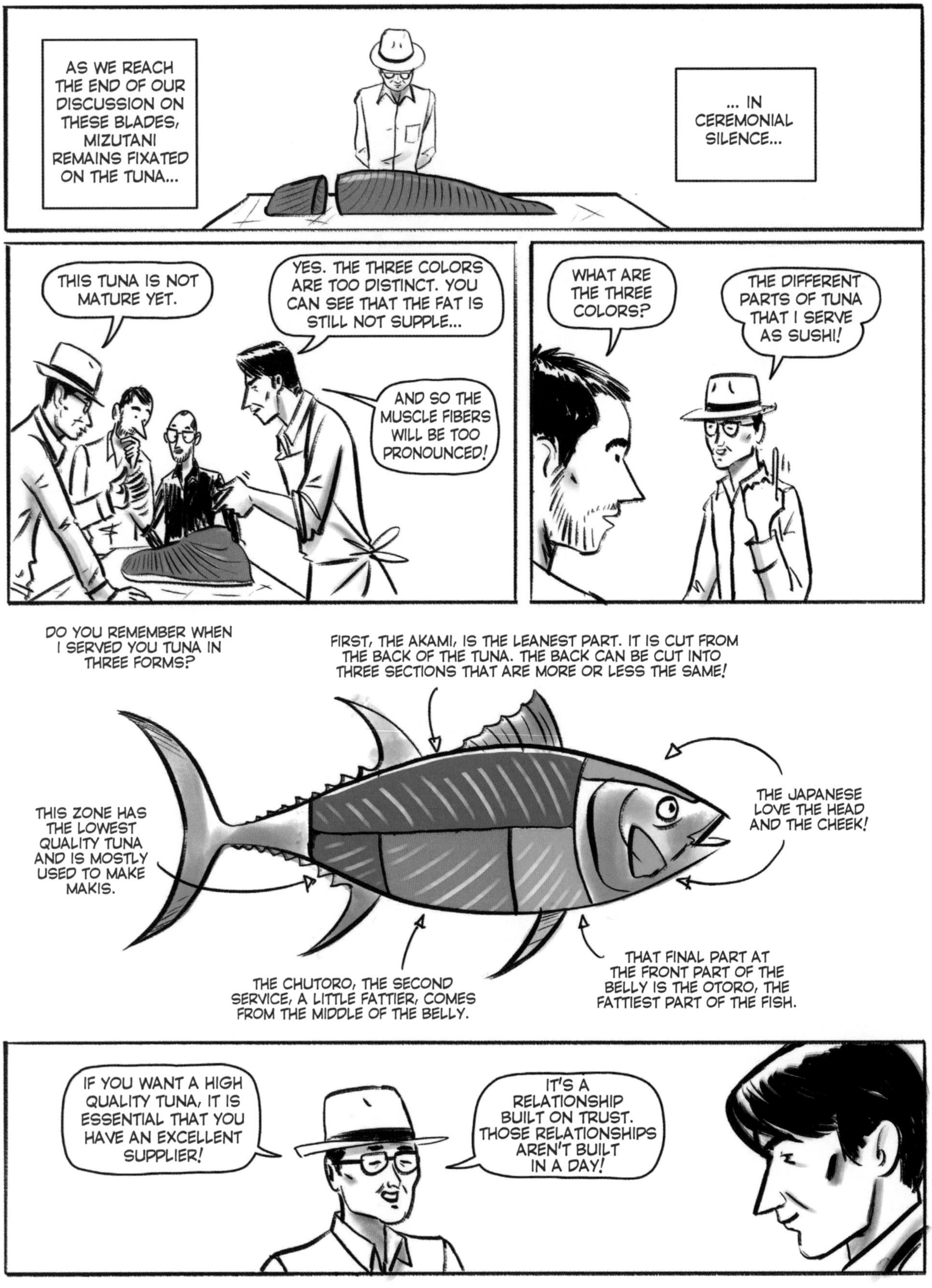
AS WE REACH THE END OF OUR DISCUSSION ON THESE BLADES, MIZUTANI REMAINS FIXATED ON THE TUNA...
... IN CEREMONIAL SILENCE...
THIS TUNA IS NOT MATURE YET.
YES. THE THREE COLORS ARE TOO DISTINCT. YOU CAN SEE THAT THE FAT IS STILL NOT SUPPLE...
AND SO THE MUSCLE FIBERS WILL BE TOO PRONOUNCED!
WHAT ARE THE THREE COLORS?
THE DIFFERENT PARTS OF TUNA THAT I SERVE AS SUSHI!
DO YOU REMEMBER WHEN I SERVED YOU TUNA IN THREE FORMS?
FIRST, THE AKAMI, IS THE LEANEST PART. IT IS CUT FROM THE BACK OF THE TUNA. THE BACK CAN BE CUT INTO THREE SECTIONS THAT ARE MORE OR LESS THE SAME!
THIS ZONE HAS THE LOWEST QUALITY TUNA AND IS MOSTLY USED TO MAKE MAKIS.
THE JAPANESE LOVE THE HEAD AND THE CHEEK!
THE CHUTORO, THE SECOND SERVICE, A LITTLE FATTIER, COMES FROM THE MIDDLE OF THE BELLY.
THAT FINAL PART AT THE FRONT PART OF THE BELLY IS THE OTORO, THE FATTIEST PART OF THE FISH.
IF YOU WANT A HIGH QUALITY TUNA, IT IS ESSENTIAL THAT YOU HAVE AN EXCELLENT SUPPLIER!
IT'S A RELATIONSHIP BUILT ON TRUST. THOSE RELATIONSHIPS AREN'T BUILT IN A DAY!

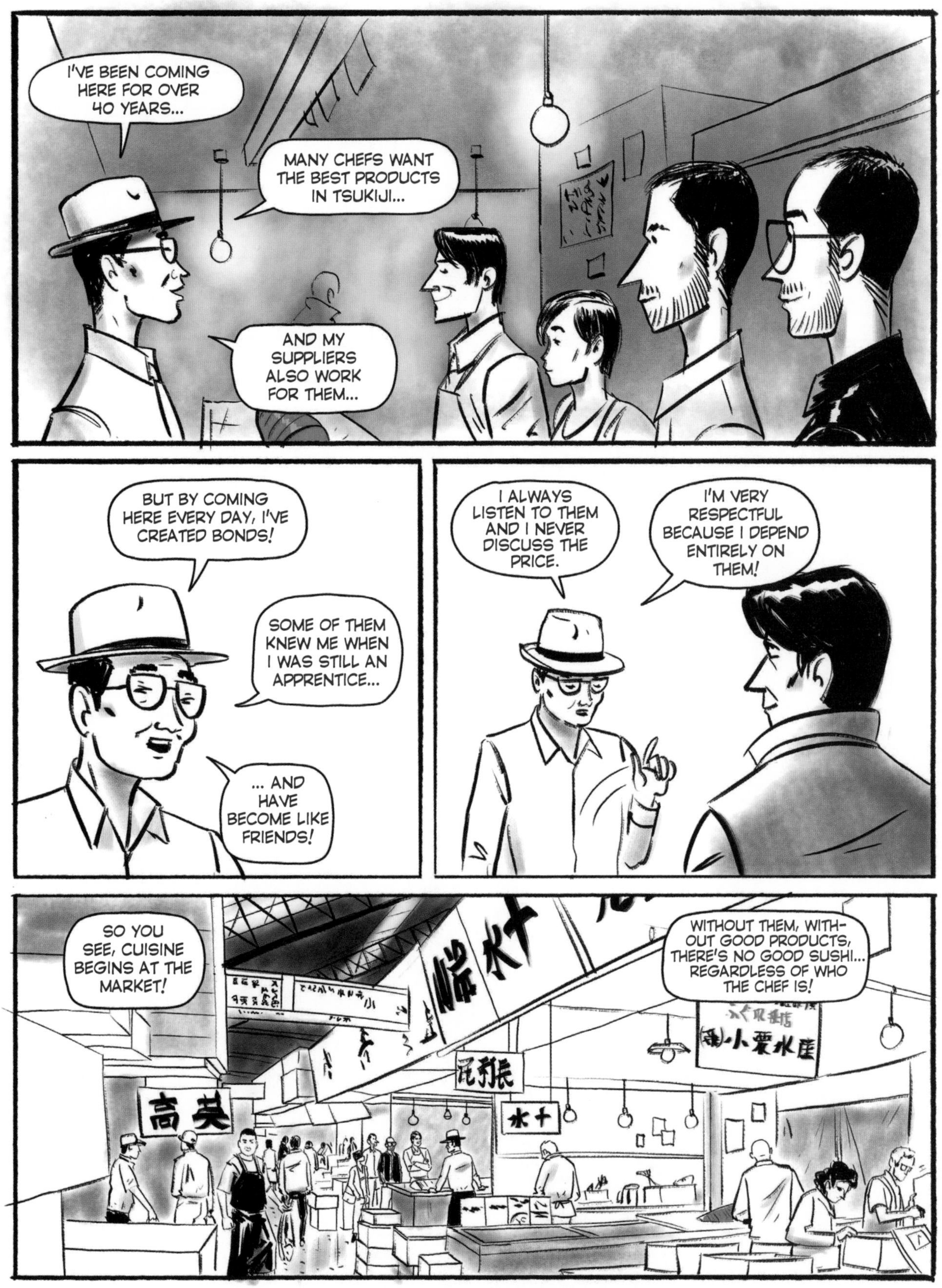
I'VE BEEN COMING HERE FOR OVER 40 YEARS...
MANY CHEFS WANT THE BEST PRODUCTS IN TSUKIJI...
AND MY SUPPLIERS ALSO WORK FOR THEM...
BUT BY COMING HERE EVERY DAY, I'VE CREATED BONDS!
SOME OF THEM KNEW ME WHEN I WAS STILL AN APPRENTICE...
... AND HAVE BECOME LIKE FRIENDS!
I ALWAYS LISTEN TO THEM AND I NEVER DISCUSS THE PRICE.
I'M VERY RESPECTFUL BECAUSE I DEPEND ENTIRELY ON THEM!
SO YOU SEE, CUISINE BEGINS AT THE MARKET!
WITHOUT THEM, WITHOUT GOOD PRODUCTS, THERE'S NO GOOD SUSHI... REGARDLESS OF WHO THE CHEF IS!
高英
水十

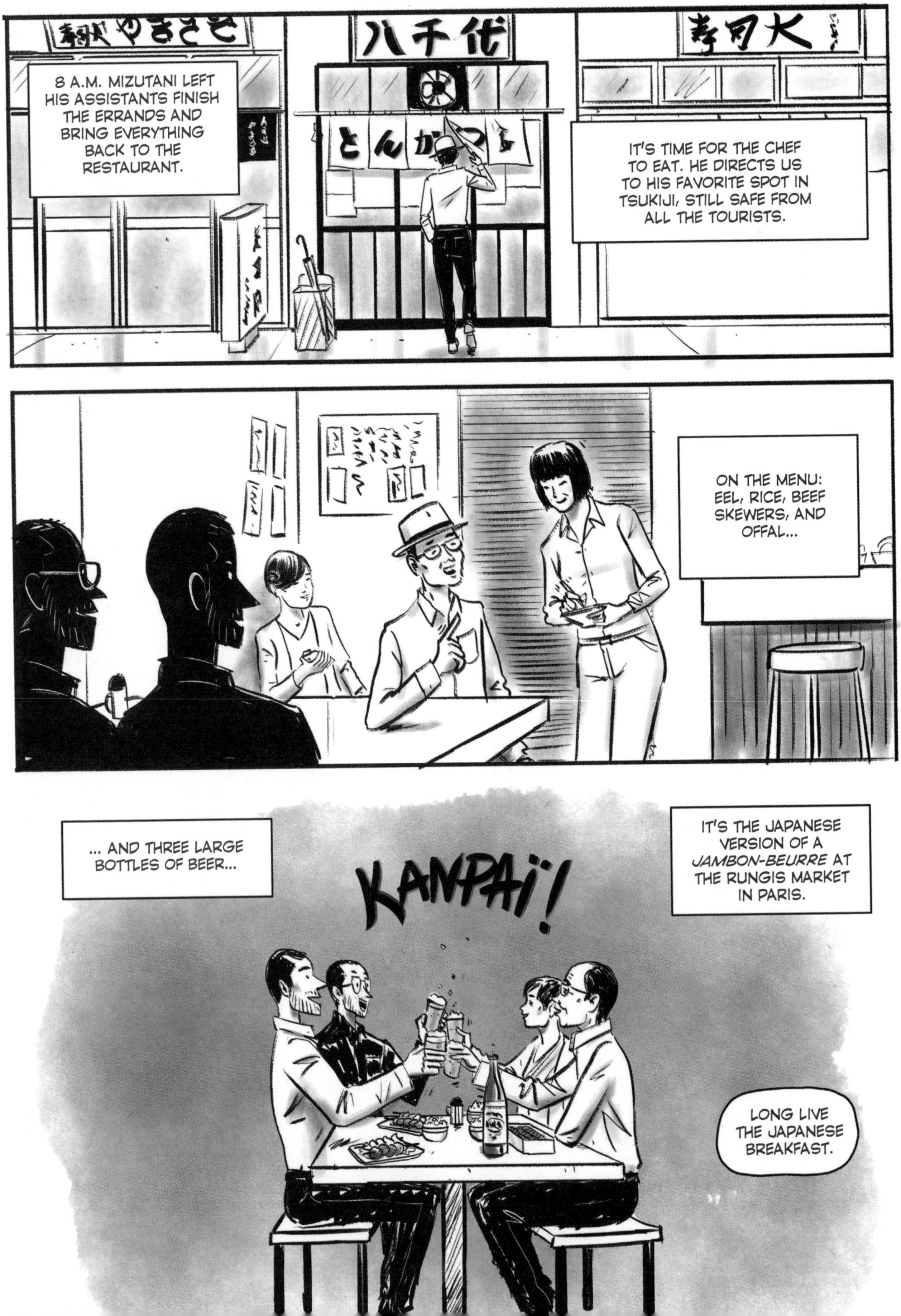

八千代
とんかつ
8 A.M. MIZUTANI LEFT HIS ASSISTANTS FINISH THE ERRANDS AND BRING EVERYTHING BACK TO THE RESTAURANT.
IT'S TIME FOR THE CHEF TO EAT. HE DIRECTS US TO HIS FAVORITE SPOT IN TSUKIJI, STILL SAFE FROM ALL THE TOURISTS.
ON THE MENU: EEL, RICE, BEEF SKEWERS, AND OFFAL...
... AND THREE LARGE BOTTLES OF BEER...
KANPAÏ!
IT'S THE JAPANESE VERSION OF A *JAMBON-BEURRE* AT THE RUNGIS MARKET IN PARIS.
LONG LIVE THE JAPANESE BREAKFAST.

9:30 A.M. WE'RE BACK IN THE RESTAURANT. THE APPRENTICES ARE ALREADY WORKING ON THE *MISE EN PLACE** IN THE TINY KITCHEN, HARDLY BIGGER THAN A BROOM CLOSET.

CLEANS THE FISH.

SEPARATING, CLEANING, AND BRUSHING THE ABALONE!

IN HIS UNIFORM, MIZUTANI BEGINS A SERIES OF PREPARATIONS...

COOKING THE ABALONE IN SAKE...

CUTTING AND COOKING THE EEL IN A BROTH MADE UP OF SHOYU, MIRIN, SUGAR, AND WATER...

AND THE INDISPENSABLE INGREDIENT: SUSHI RICE!

SOMETIMES THE APPRENTICES GET TO REMOVE THE FILETS. BUT...

THE RICE IS ALWAYS ME! I DO EACH STEP: WASHING, COOKING, AND SEASONING.

SUSHI IS 80% RICE SO IT HAS TO BE PERFECT!

RICE COOKER

NEXT, BACK BEHIND HIS COUNTER, HE GETS TO WORK ON THE HIRAME.

DID YOU NOTICE AT TSUKIJI...?

IT DIDN'T SMELL LIKE FISH!

THAT'S BECAUSE WE USUALLY BUY THE PRODUCTS ALIVE. THERE IS ALSO IKEJIME. THEN, EVEN WHEN THEY'RE DEAD, WE DON'T PILE THEM UP IN THE STANDS.

THEY'RE GROUPED BY TYPE AND WE AVOID PUTTING THE SKIN IN DIRECT CONTACT WITH THE ICE. IT BURNS THE FLESH WHICH IS BAD FOR THE TASTE AND THE SMELL.

MORE THAN ANYTHING, IT'S ABOUT CLEANLINESS! EVERYTHING SHOULD BE CLEANED, ALL THE TIME, TO AVOID THE FISH SMELL.

*PREPARATION OF THE INGREDIENTS

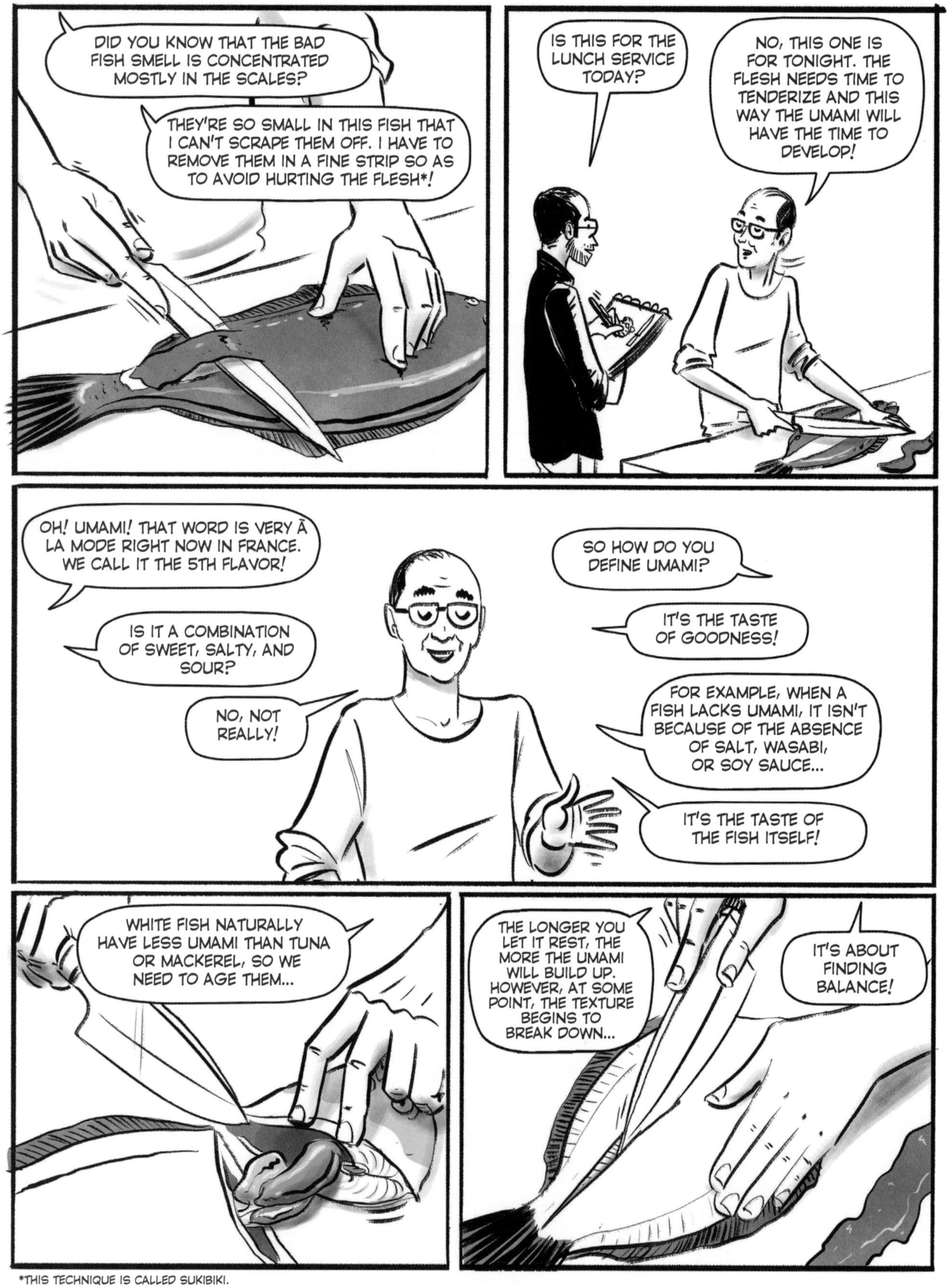
DID YOU KNOW THAT THE BAD FISH SMELL IS CONCENTRATED MOSTLY IN THE SCALES?
THEY'RE SO SMALL IN THIS FISH THAT I CAN'T SCRAPE THEM OFF. I HAVE TO REMOVE THEM IN A FINE STRIP SO AS TO AVOID HURTING THE FLESH*!
IS THIS FOR THE LUNCH SERVICE TODAY?
NO, THIS ONE IS FOR TONIGHT. THE FLESH NEEDS TIME TO TENDERIZE AND THIS WAY THE UMAMI WILL HAVE THE TIME TO DEVELOP!
OH! UMAMI! THAT WORD IS VERY À LA MODE RIGHT NOW IN FRANCE. WE CALL IT THE 5TH FLAVOR!
SO HOW DO YOU DEFINE UMAMI?
IS IT A COMBINATION OF SWEET, SALTY, AND SOUR?
IT'S THE TASTE OF GOODNESS!
NO, NOT REALLY!
FOR EXAMPLE, WHEN A FISH LACKS UMAMI, IT ISN'T BECAUSE OF THE ABSENCE OF SALT, WASABI, OR SOY SAUCE...
IT'S THE TASTE OF THE FISH ITSELF!
WHITE FISH NATURALLY HAVE LESS UMAMI THAN TUNA OR MACKEREL, SO WE NEED TO AGE THEM...
THE LONGER YOU LET IT REST, THE MORE THE UMAMI WILL BUILD UP. HOWEVER, AT SOME POINT, THE TEXTURE BEGINS TO BREAK DOWN...
IT'S ABOUT FINDING BALANCE!

*THIS TECHNIQUE IS CALLED SUKIBIKI.

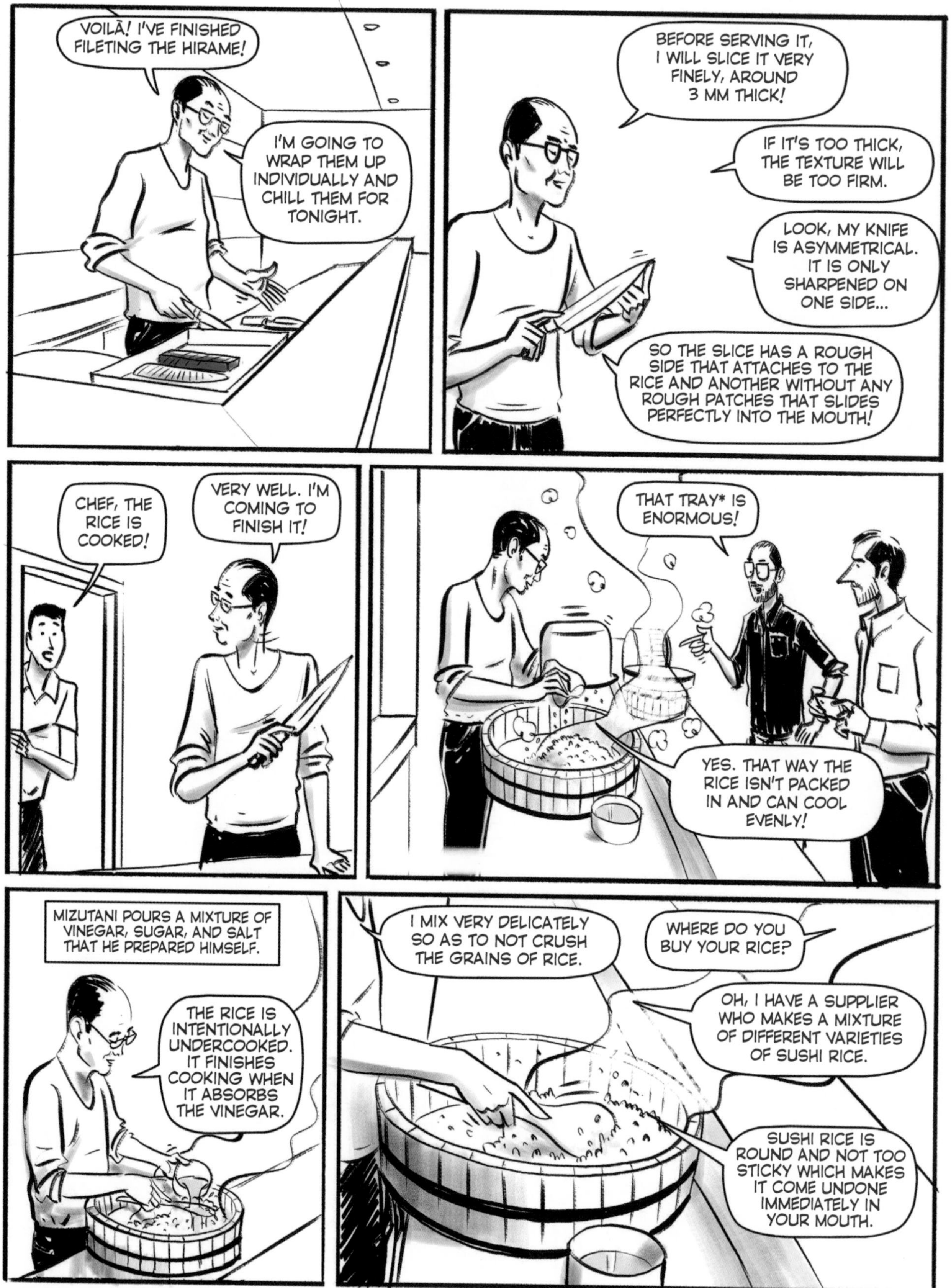
VOILÀ! I'VE FINISHED FILETING THE HIRAME!
I'M GOING TO WRAP THEM UP INDIVIDUALLY AND CHILL THEM FOR TONIGHT.
BEFORE SERVING IT, I WILL SLICE IT VERY FINELY, AROUND 3 MM THICK!
IF IT'S TOO THICK, THE TEXTURE WILL BE TOO FIRM.
LOOK, MY KNIFE IS ASYMMETRICAL. IT IS ONLY SHARPENED ON ONE SIDE...
SO THE SLICE HAS A ROUGH SIDE THAT ATTACHES TO THE RICE AND ANOTHER WITHOUT ANY ROUGH PATCHES THAT SLIDES PERFECTLY INTO THE MOUTH!
CHEF, THE RICE IS COOKED!
VERY WELL. I'M COMING TO FINISH IT!
THAT TRAY* IS ENORMOUS!
YES. THAT WAY THE RICE ISN'T PACKED IN AND CAN COOL EVENLY!
MIZUTANI POURS A MIXTURE OF VINEGAR, SUGAR, AND SALT THAT HE PREPARED HIMSELF.
THE RICE IS INTENTIONALLY UNDERCOOKED. IT FINISHES COOKING WHEN IT ABSORBS THE VINEGAR.
I MIX VERY DELICATELY SO AS TO NOT CRUSH THE GRAINS OF RICE.
WHERE DO YOU BUY YOUR RICE?
OH, I HAVE A SUPPLIER WHO MAKES A MIXTURE OF DIFFERENT VARIETIES OF SUSHI RICE.
SUSHI RICE IS ROUND AND NOT TOO STICKY WHICH MAKES IT COME UNDONE IMMEDIATELY IN YOUR MOUTH.

*THE REAL NAME IS HANGIRI OR HANDAI.

FOR THE VINEGAR MIXTURE, I KEEP THAT SECRET!

SHOOT...

I'M GOING TO LET THE RICE REST JUST OVER AN HOUR!

BUT I HAVE TO USE IT QUICKLY...

TWO HOURS MAX. LONGER THAN THAT AND ITS TASTE CHANGES. IT'S FAR LESS DELICIOUS!

ALRIGHT. LET'S GET TO THE PREPARATIONS FOR THE EBI SHRIMP...

THEY'RE BEAUTIFUL. WE'RE RIGHT AT THE BEGINNING OF THE SEASON!

YOU KNOW WE'RE LUCKY? JAPAN IS A LONG, SKINNY ISLAND WITH AN OCEAN ON EACH SIDE...

IN FRANCE YOU CAN'T HAVE AS MANY DIFFERENT SUSHI AS WE DO.

IF YOU MOVE FROM NORTH TO SOUTH, THE SEASONAL CLIMATES VARY WIDELY. THIS GIVES US A GREAT VARIETY OF FISH!

NEVER-THELESS, SUSHI IS PHENOMENALLY SUCCESSFUL THERE!

SKEWER FOR IMPALING THE SHRIMP

YES IT WAS DURING THE MAD COW OUTBREAK AND SWINE FLU PANDEMIC THAT SUSHI BECAME POPULAR AROUND THE WORLD!

IN FRANCE SUSHI HAS A REPUTATION FOR BEING A VERY HEALTHY FOOD.

WELL, IT'S TRUE THAT THE JAPANESE ARE ALL VERY THIN!!!

AND VISUALLY JAPANESE FOOD IS COLORFUL AND AESTHETICALLY PLEASING!

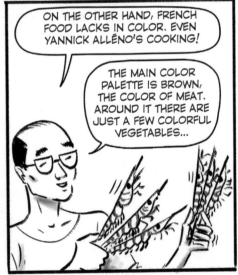

ON THE OTHER HAND, FRENCH FOOD LACKS IN COLOR. EVEN YANNICK ALLÉNO'S COOKING!

THE MAIN COLOR PALETTE IS BROWN, THE COLOR OF MEAT. AROUND IT THERE ARE JUST A FEW COLORFUL VEGETABLES...

THE SKEWER SERVES TO KEEP THE SHRIMP STRAIGHT AFTER IT IS COOKED.

40

WHAT'S MORE, CONTEMPORARY FRENCH CUISINE IS HIGHLY INFLUENCED BY KAISEKI*!

FIRST OFF THE PORTIONS ARE SMALLER...

... THEN THE TASTING MENUS WITH THE MULTITUDE OF SMALL PLATES, THAT REALLY COMES FROM OUR TRADITIONAL CUISINES.

HE PLUNGES THE SHRIMP IN BOILING SALT WATER.

*JAPANESE HAUTE CUISINE.

TEN YEARS AGO YANNICK ALLÉNO CAME TO SEE ME TO LEARN ABOUT FISH. LATER ON HE WAS AWARDED 3 MICHELIN STARS!

HE IS A VERY TECHNICAL, BUT ALSO VERY CREATIVE COOK!

HOW ABOUT YOU. HAVE YOU EVER BEEN INFLUENCED BY FRENCH CUISINE?

I'VE NEVER BEEN INFLUENCED BY ANY FOREIGN CUISINES...

NEVER!

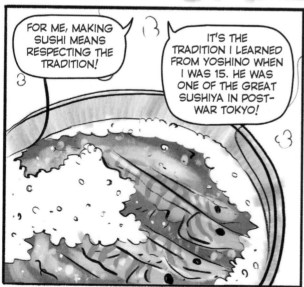

FOR ME, MAKING SUSHI MEANS RESPECTING THE TRADITION!

IT'S THE TRADITION I LEARNED FROM YOSHINO WHEN I WAS 15. HE WAS ONE OF THE GREAT SUSHIYA IN POST-WAR TOKYO!

I WAS AN APPRENTICE. AFTER THE LAST CLIENTS LEFT, I SLEPT IN THE RESTAURANT!

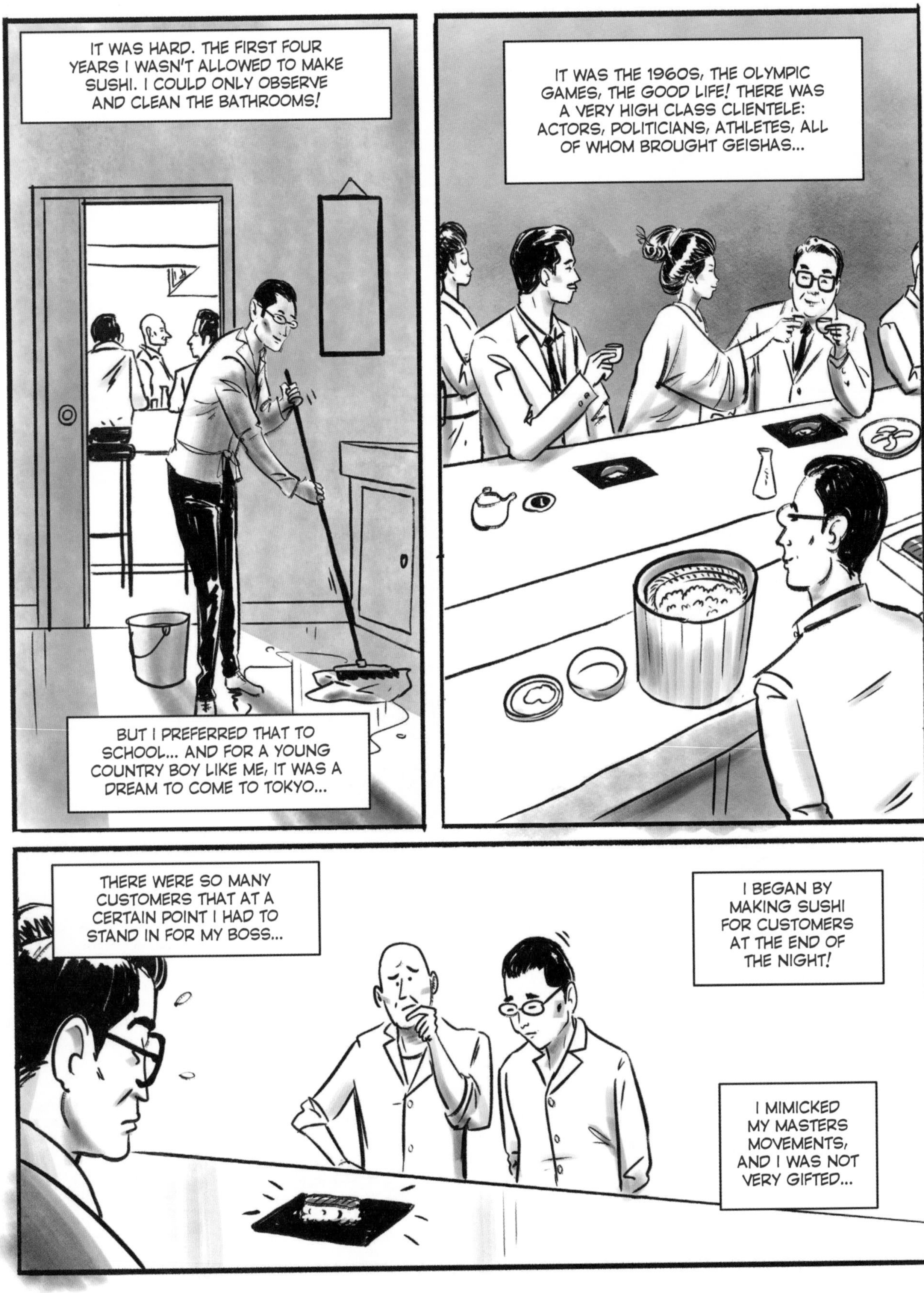
IT WAS HARD. THE FIRST FOUR YEARS I WASN'T ALLOWED TO MAKE SUSHI. I COULD ONLY OBSERVE AND CLEAN THE BATHROOMS!
BUT I PREFERRED THAT TO SCHOOL... AND FOR A YOUNG COUNTRY BOY LIKE ME, IT WAS A DREAM TO COME TO TOKYO...
IT WAS THE 1960S, THE OLYMPIC GAMES, THE GOOD LIFE! THERE WAS A VERY HIGH CLASS CLIENTELE: ACTORS, POLITICIANS, ATHLETES, ALL OF WHOM BROUGHT GEISHAS...
THERE WERE SO MANY CUSTOMERS THAT AT A CERTAIN POINT I HAD TO STAND IN FOR MY BOSS...
I BEGAN BY MAKING SUSHI FOR CUSTOMERS AT THE END OF THE NIGHT!
I MIMICKED MY MASTERS MOVEMENTS, AND I WAS NOT VERY GIFTED...

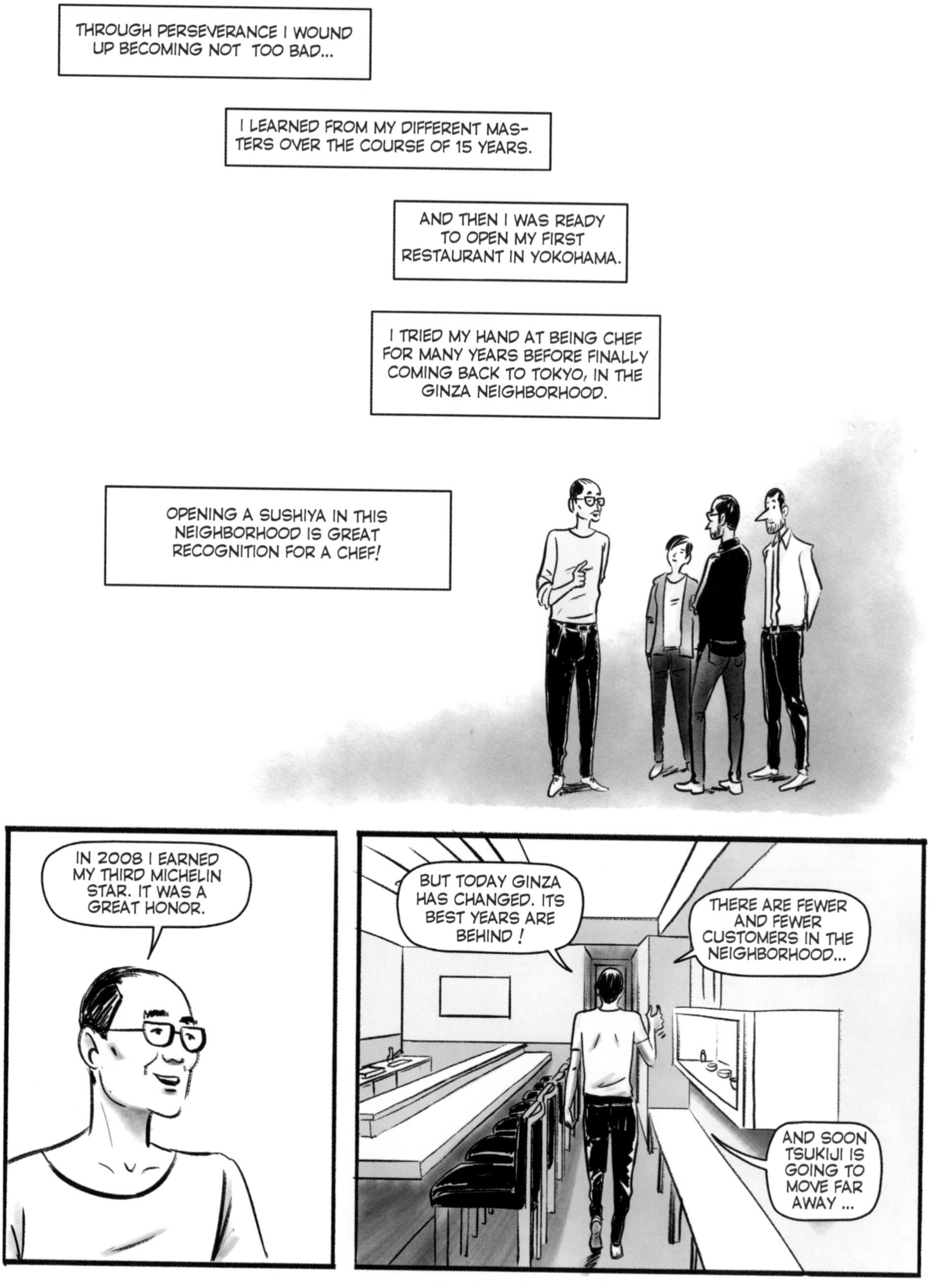
THROUGH PERSEVERANCE I WOUND UP BECOMING NOT TOO BAD...
I LEARNED FROM MY DIFFERENT MASTERS OVER THE COURSE OF 15 YEARS.
AND THEN I WAS READY TO OPEN MY FIRST RESTAURANT IN YOKOHAMA.
I TRIED MY HAND AT BEING CHEF FOR MANY YEARS BEFORE FINALLY COMING BACK TO TOKYO, IN THE GINZA NEIGHBORHOOD.
OPENING A SUSHIYA IN THIS NEIGHBORHOOD IS GREAT RECOGNITION FOR A CHEF!
IN 2008 I EARNED MY THIRD MICHELIN STAR. IT WAS A GREAT HONOR.
BUT TODAY GINZA HAS CHANGED. ITS BEST YEARS ARE BEHIND !
THERE ARE FEWER AND FEWER CUSTOMERS IN THE NEIGHBORHOOD...
AND SOON TSUKIJI IS GOING TO MOVE FAR AWAY ...

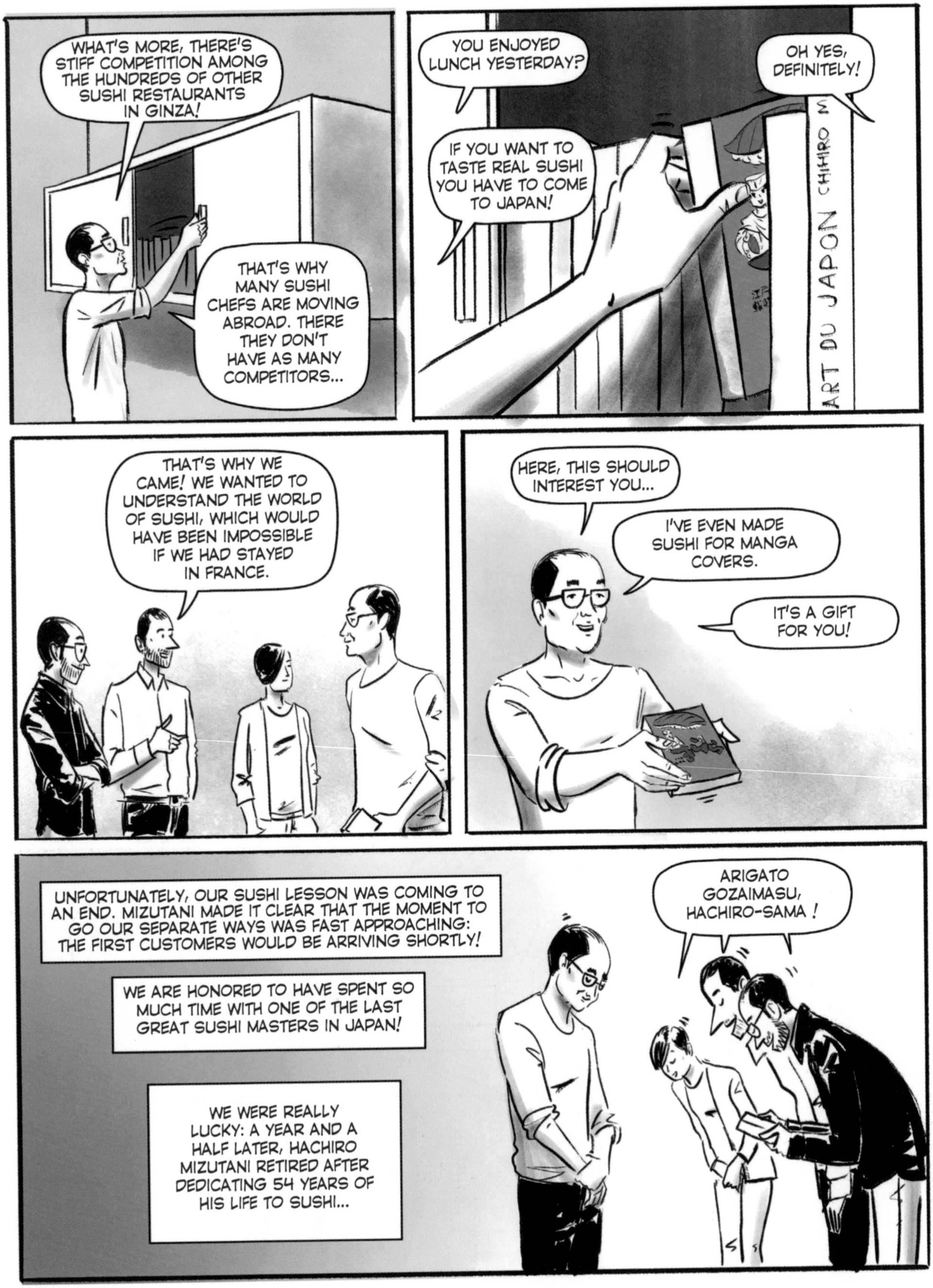
WHAT'S MORE, THERE'S STIFF COMPETITION AMONG THE HUNDREDS OF OTHER SUSHI RESTAURANTS IN GINZA!
THAT'S WHY MANY SUSHI CHEFS ARE MOVING ABROAD. THERE THEY DON'T HAVE AS MANY COMPETITORS...
YOU ENJOYED LUNCH YESTERDAY?
OH YES, DEFINITELY!
IF YOU WANT TO TASTE REAL SUSHI YOU HAVE TO COME TO JAPAN!
ART DU JAPON CHIHIRO M
THAT'S WHY WE CAME! WE WANTED TO UNDERSTAND THE WORLD OF SUSHI, WHICH WOULD HAVE BEEN IMPOSSIBLE IF WE HAD STAYED IN FRANCE.
HERE, THIS SHOULD INTEREST YOU...
I'VE EVEN MADE SUSHI FOR MANGA COVERS.
IT'S A GIFT FOR YOU!
UNFORTUNATELY, OUR SUSHI LESSON WAS COMING TO AN END. MIZUTANI MADE IT CLEAR THAT THE MOMENT TO GO OUR SEPARATE WAYS WAS FAST APPROACHING: THE FIRST CUSTOMERS WOULD BE ARRIVING SHORTLY!
WE ARE HONORED TO HAVE SPENT SO MUCH TIME WITH ONE OF THE LAST GREAT SUSHI MASTERS IN JAPAN!
WE WERE REALLY LUCKY: A YEAR AND A HALF LATER, HACHIRO MIZUTANI RETIRED AFTER DEDICATING 54 YEARS OF HIS LIFE TO SUSHI...
ARIGATO GOZAIMASU, HACHIRO-SAMA !

Okada
Modern sushi

OKADA, A YOUNG CHEF WORKING TO MAKE SUSHI MORE ACCESSIBLE, GETS HIS PRODUCTS
DIRECTLY FROM THE FISHERMEN THEMSELVES, USES FISH WE NORMALLY WOULDN'T EAT AS
SUSHI. HE DOESN'T HAVE A COUNTER IN HIS RESTAURANT, WHICH IS ALSO A SMALL SHOP.
IN SHORT, HIS SUSHI JOURNEY IS OFF THE BEATEN PATH.

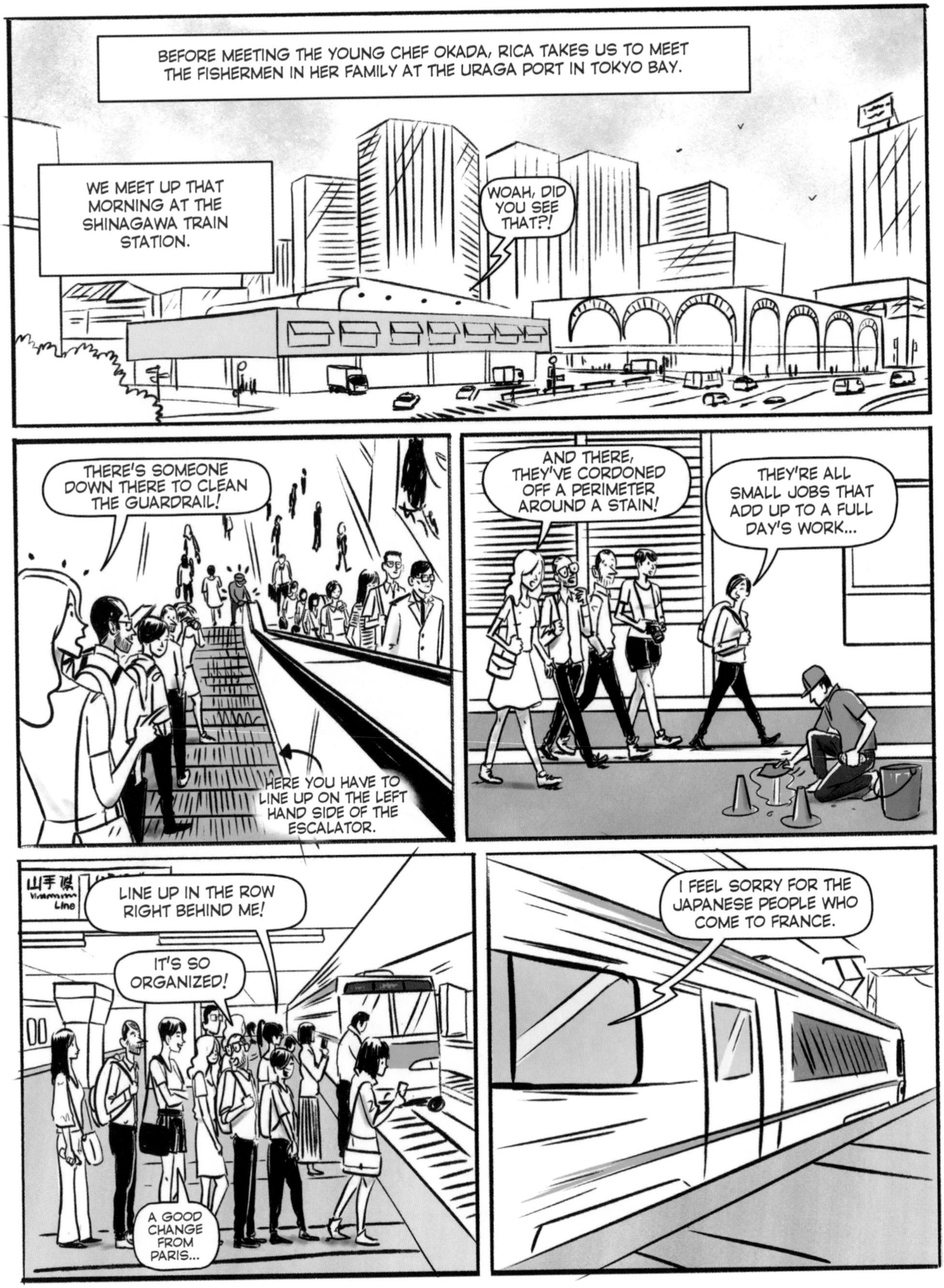

BEFORE MEETING THE YOUNG CHEF OKADA, RICA TAKES US TO MEET THE FISHERMEN IN HER FAMILY AT THE URAGA PORT IN TOKYO BAY.
WE MEET UP THAT MORNING AT THE SHINAGAWA TRAIN STATION.
WOAH, DID YOU SEE THAT?!
THERE'S SOMEONE DOWN THERE TO CLEAN THE GUARDRAIL!
HERE YOU HAVE TO LINE UP ON THE LEFT HAND SIDE OF THE ESCALATOR.
AND THERE, THEY'VE CORDONED OFF A PERIMETER AROUND A STAIN!
THEY'RE ALL SMALL JOBS THAT ADD UP TO A FULL DAY'S WORK...
山手線
Line
LINE UP IN THE ROW RIGHT BEHIND ME!
IT'S SO ORGANIZED!
A GOOD CHANGE FROM PARIS...
I FEEL SORRY FOR THE JAPANESE PEOPLE WHO COME TO FRANCE.

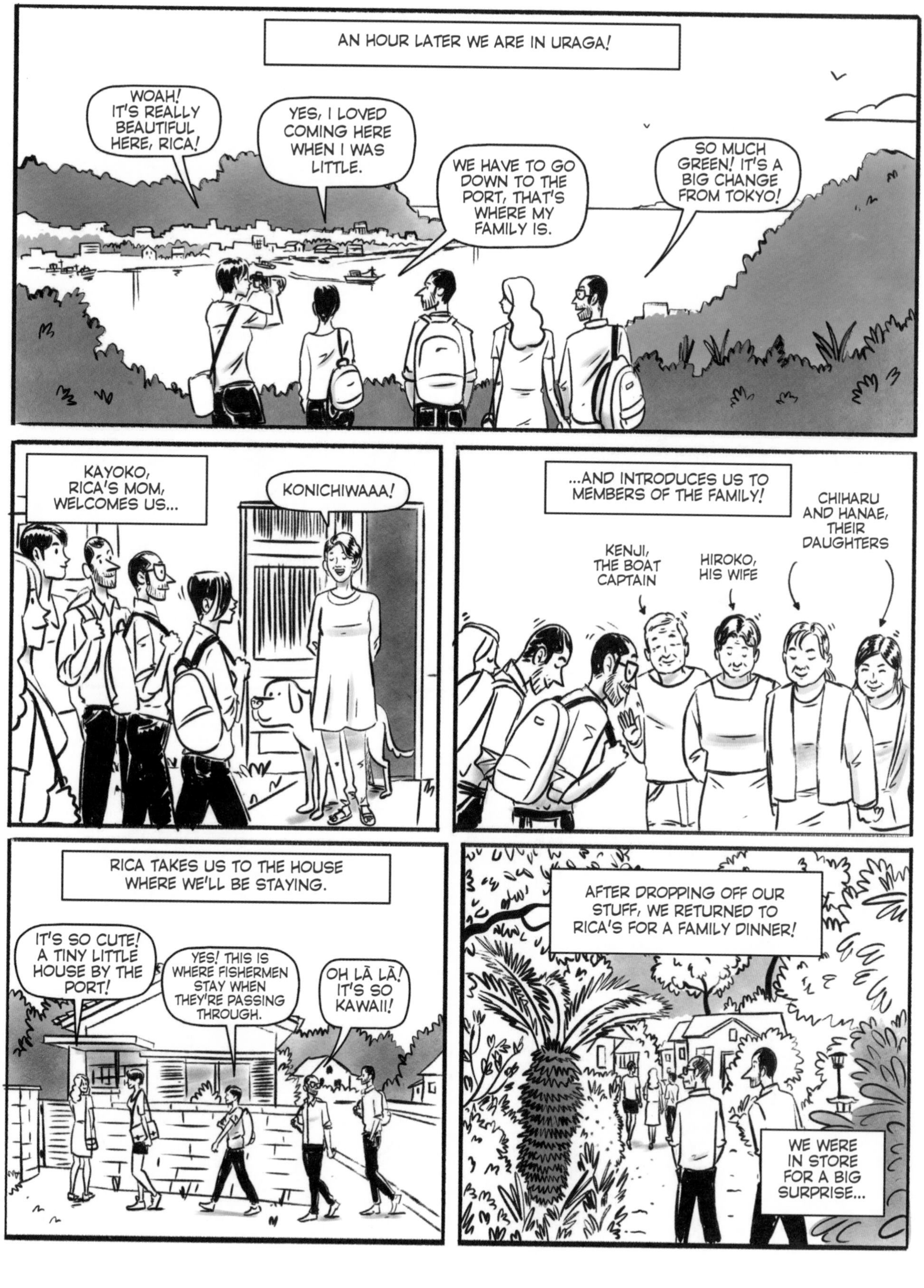
AN HOUR LATER WE ARE IN URAGA!
WOAH! IT'S REALLY BEAUTIFUL HERE, RICA!
YES, I LOVED COMING HERE WHEN I WAS LITTLE.
WE HAVE TO GO DOWN TO THE PORT, THAT'S WHERE MY FAMILY IS.
SO MUCH GREEN! IT'S A BIG CHANGE FROM TOKYO!
KAYOKO, RICA'S MOM, WELCOMES US...
KONICHIWAAA!
...AND INTRODUCES US TO MEMBERS OF THE FAMILY!
KENJI, THE BOAT CAPTAIN
HIROKO, HIS WIFE
CHIHARU AND HANAE, THEIR DAUGHTERS
RICA TAKES US TO THE HOUSE WHERE WE'LL BE STAYING.
IT'S SO CUTE! A TINY LITTLE HOUSE BY THE PORT!
YES! THIS IS WHERE FISHERMEN STAY WHEN THEY'RE PASSING THROUGH.
OH LÃ LÃ! IT'S SO KAWAII!
AFTER DROPPING OFF OUR STUFF, WE RETURNED TO RICA'S FOR A FAMILY DINNER!
WE WERE IN STORE FOR A BIG SURPRISE...

A GARGANTUAN FEAST!

OCTOPUS SASHIMI!

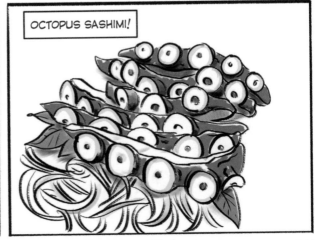

GRILLED SHELLFISH...

PRESSED ANCHOVY SUSHI...

FINGER-LINGS...

CRAB...

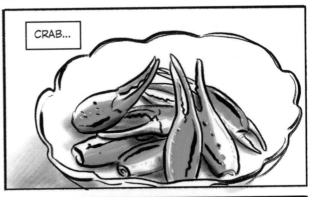

TATAKI SASHIMI OF SKIPJACK TUNA...

VEGETABLE TEMPURA...

...ALL WASHED DOWN WITH BEER AND SAKE!

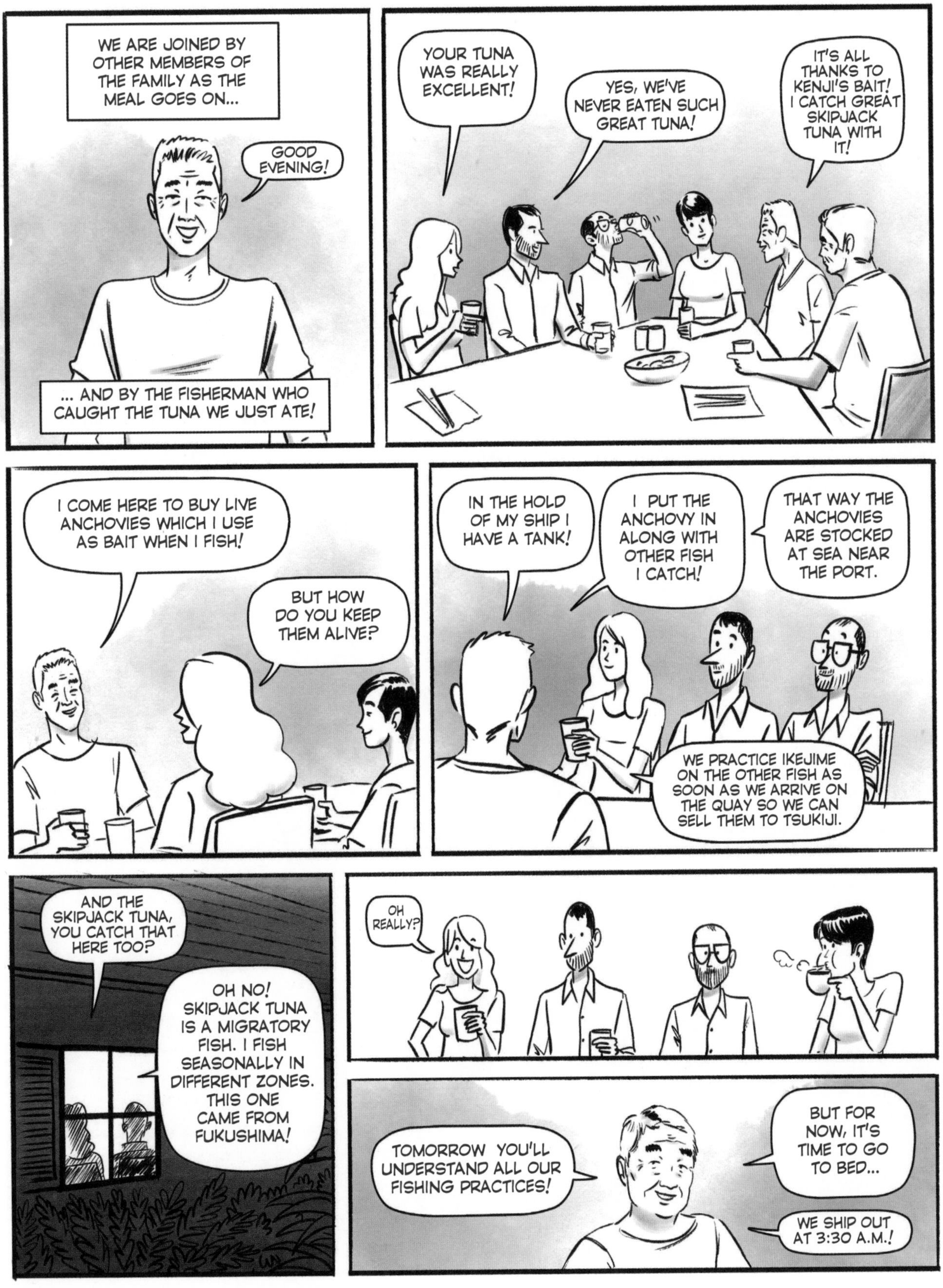
WE ARE JOINED BY OTHER MEMBERS OF THE FAMILY AS THE MEAL GOES ON...
GOOD EVENING!
... AND BY THE FISHERMAN WHO CAUGHT THE TUNA WE JUST ATE!
YOUR TUNA WAS REALLY EXCELLENT!
YES, WE'VE NEVER EATEN SUCH GREAT TUNA!
IT'S ALL THANKS TO KENJI'S BAIT! I CATCH GREAT SKIPJACK TUNA WITH IT!
I COME HERE TO BUY LIVE ANCHOVIES WHICH I USE AS BAIT WHEN I FISH!
BUT HOW DO YOU KEEP THEM ALIVE?
IN THE HOLD OF MY SHIP I HAVE A TANK!
I PUT THE ANCHOVY IN ALONG WITH OTHER FISH I CATCH!
THAT WAY THE ANCHOVIES ARE STOCKED AT SEA NEAR THE PORT.
WE PRACTICE IKEJIME ON THE OTHER FISH AS SOON AS WE ARRIVE ON THE QUAY SO WE CAN SELL THEM TO TSUKIJI.
AND THE SKIPJACK TUNA, YOU CATCH THAT HERE TOO?
OH NO! SKIPJACK TUNA IS A MIGRATORY FISH. I FISH SEASONALLY IN DIFFERENT ZONES. THIS ONE CAME FROM FUKUSHIMA!
OH REALLY?
TOMORROW YOU'LL UNDERSTAND ALL OUR FISHING PRACTICES!
BUT FOR NOW, IT'S TIME TO GO TO BED...
WE SHIP OUT AT 3:30 A.M.!

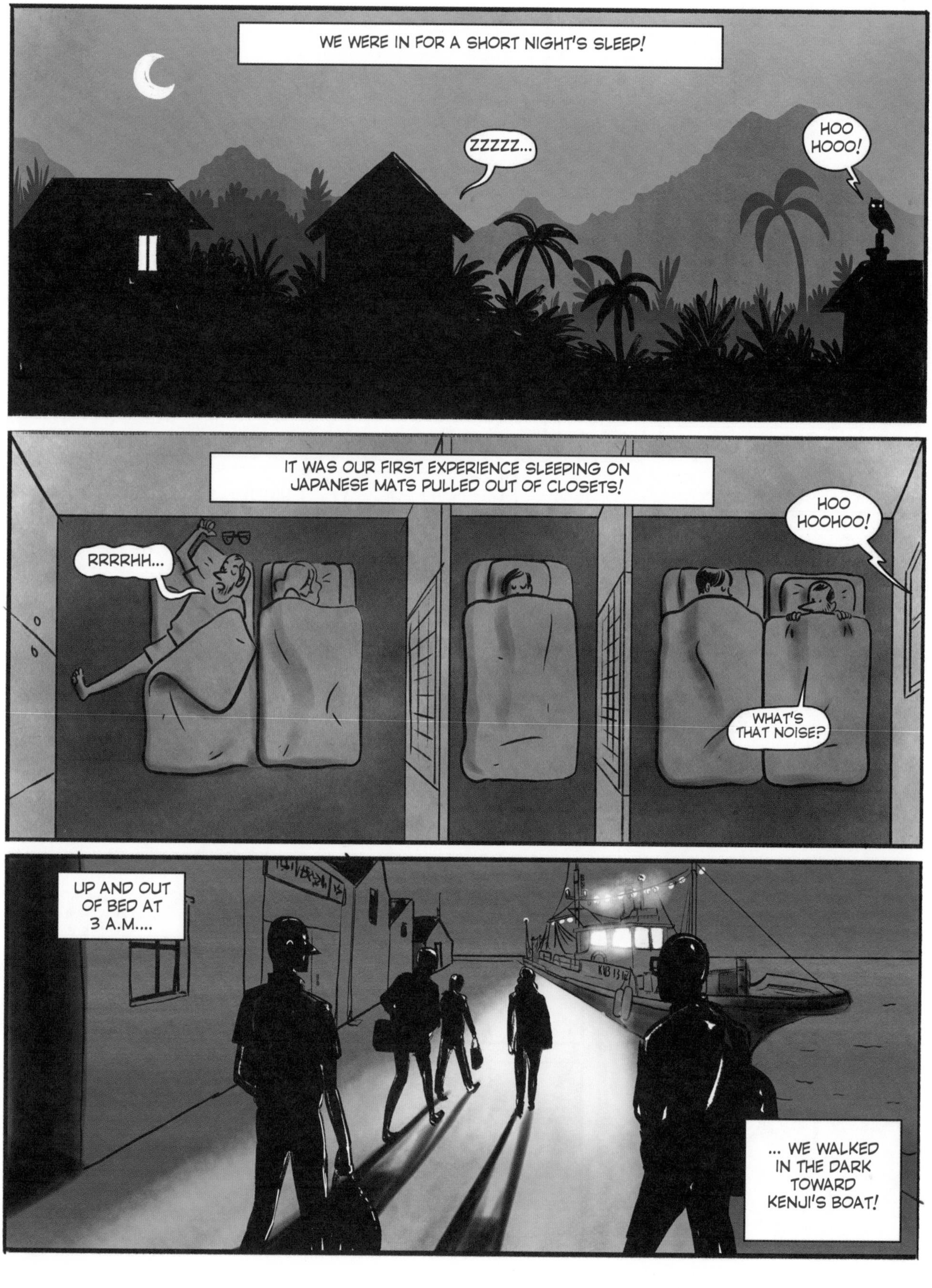
WE WERE IN FOR A SHORT NIGHT'S SLEEP!
ZZZZZ...
HOO HOOO!
IT WAS OUR FIRST EXPERIENCE SLEEPING ON JAPANESE MATS PULLED OUT OF CLOSETS!
RRRRHH...
HOO HOOHOO!
WHAT'S THAT NOISE?
UP AND OUT OF BED AT 3 A.M....
... WE WALKED IN THE DARK TOWARD KENJI'S BOAT!

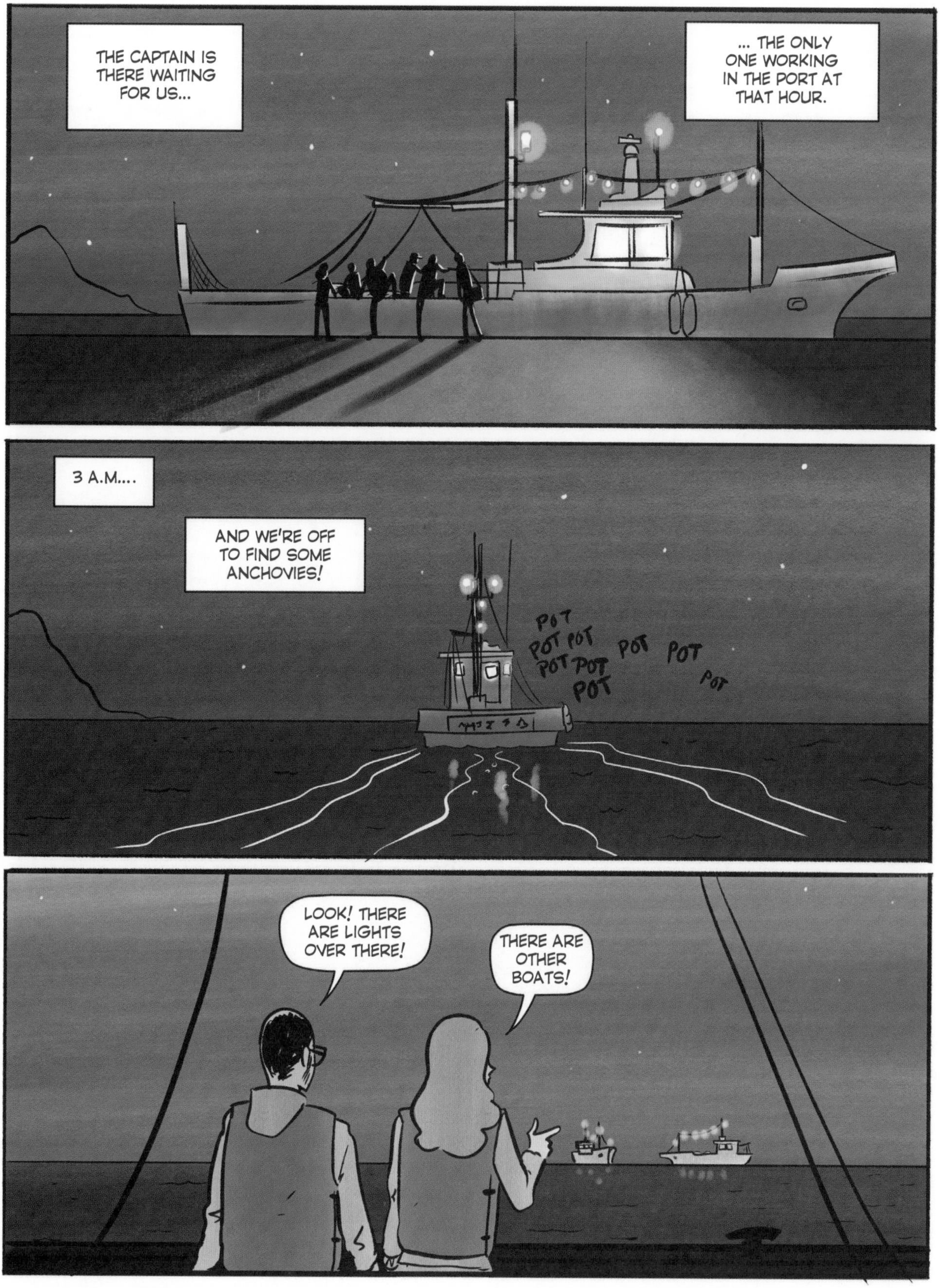

THE CAPTAIN IS THERE WAITING FOR US...
... THE ONLY ONE WORKING IN THE PORT AT THAT HOUR.
3 A.M....
AND WE'RE OFF TO FIND SOME ANCHOVIES!
POT POT POT POT POT POT POT POT POT
LOOK! THERE ARE LIGHTS OVER THERE!
THERE ARE OTHER BOATS!

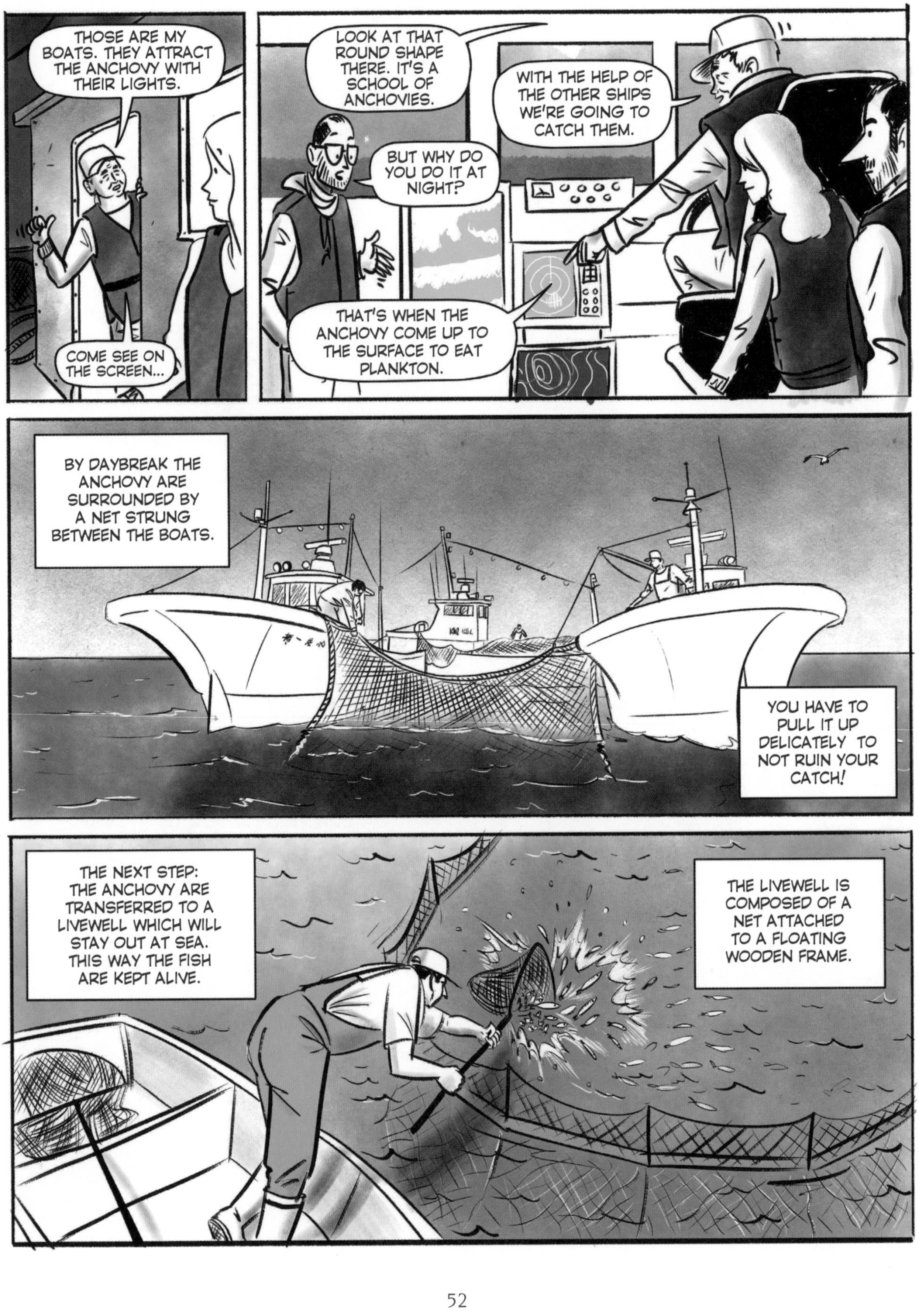
THOSE ARE MY BOATS. THEY ATTRACT THE ANCHOVY WITH THEIR LIGHTS.
COME SEE ON THE SCREEN...
LOOK AT THAT ROUND SHAPE THERE. IT'S A SCHOOL OF ANCHOVIES.
WITH THE HELP OF THE OTHER SHIPS WE'RE GOING TO CATCH THEM.
BUT WHY DO YOU DO IT AT NIGHT?
THAT'S WHEN THE ANCHOVY COME UP TO THE SURFACE TO EAT PLANKTON.
BY DAYBREAK THE ANCHOVY ARE SURROUNDED BY A NET STRUNG BETWEEN THE BOATS.
YOU HAVE TO PULL IT UP DELICATELY TO NOT RUIN YOUR CATCH!
THE NEXT STEP: THE ANCHOVY ARE TRANSFERRED TO A LIVEWELL WHICH WILL STAY OUT AT SEA. THIS WAY THE FISH ARE KEPT ALIVE.
THE LIVEWELL IS COMPOSED OF A NET ATTACHED TO A FLOATING WOODEN FRAME.

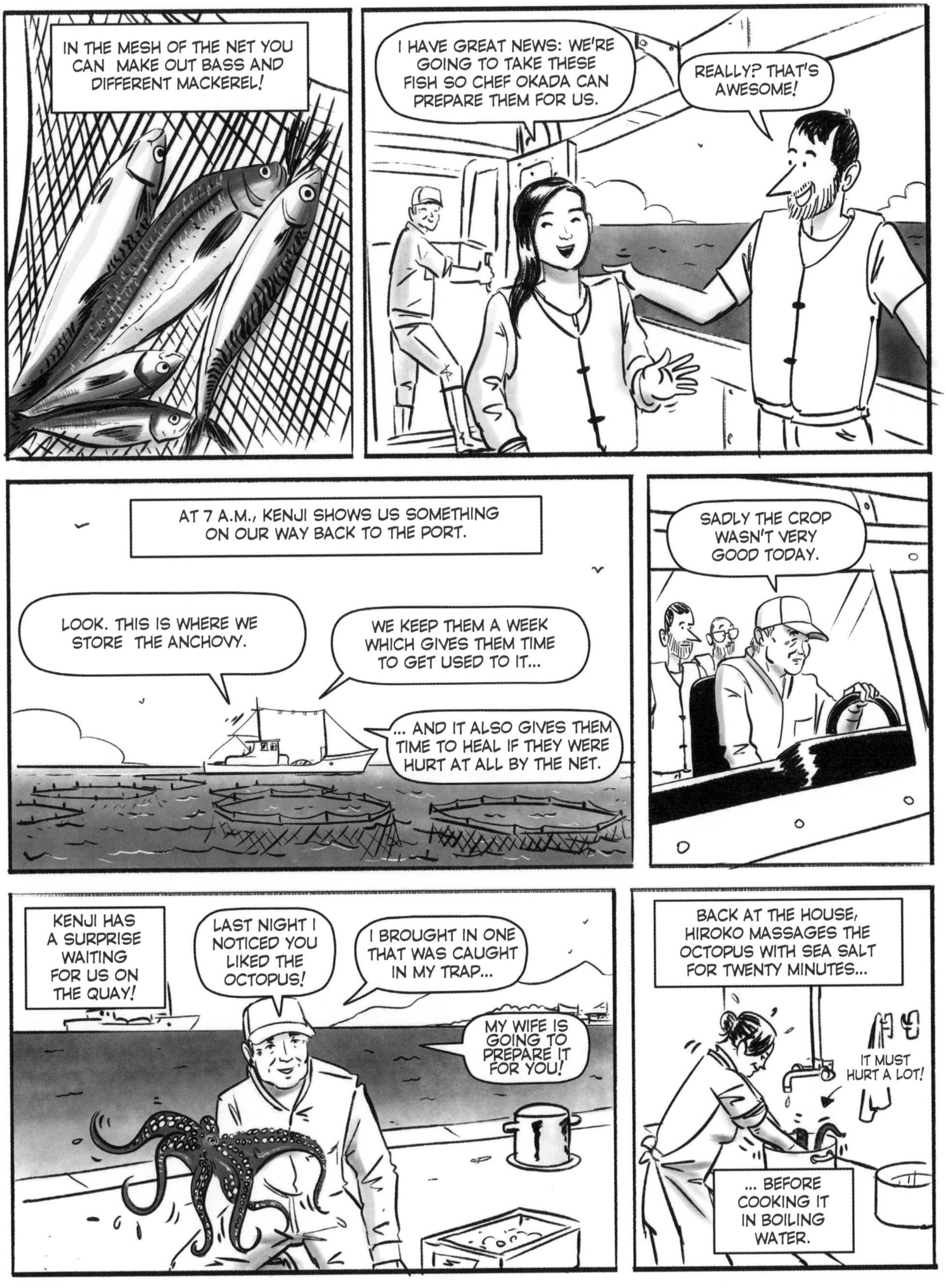
IN THE MESH OF THE NET YOU CAN MAKE OUT BASS AND DIFFERENT MACKEREL!
I HAVE GREAT NEWS: WE'RE GOING TO TAKE THESE FISH SO CHEF OKADA CAN PREPARE THEM FOR US.
REALLY? THAT'S AWESOME!
AT 7 A.M., KENJI SHOWS US SOMETHING ON OUR WAY BACK TO THE PORT.
LOOK. THIS IS WHERE WE STORE THE ANCHOVY.
WE KEEP THEM A WEEK WHICH GIVES THEM TIME TO GET USED TO IT...
... AND IT ALSO GIVES THEM TIME TO HEAL IF THEY WERE HURT AT ALL BY THE NET.
SADLY THE CROP WASN'T VERY GOOD TODAY.
KENJI HAS A SURPRISE WAITING FOR US ON THE QUAY!
LAST NIGHT I NOTICED YOU LIKED THE OCTOPUS!
I BROUGHT IN ONE THAT WAS CAUGHT IN MY TRAP...
MY WIFE IS GOING TO PREPARE IT FOR YOU!
BACK AT THE HOUSE, HIROKO MASSAGES THE OCTOPUS WITH SEA SALT FOR TWENTY MINUTES...
IT MUST HURT A LOT!
... BEFORE COOKING IT IN BOILING WATER.

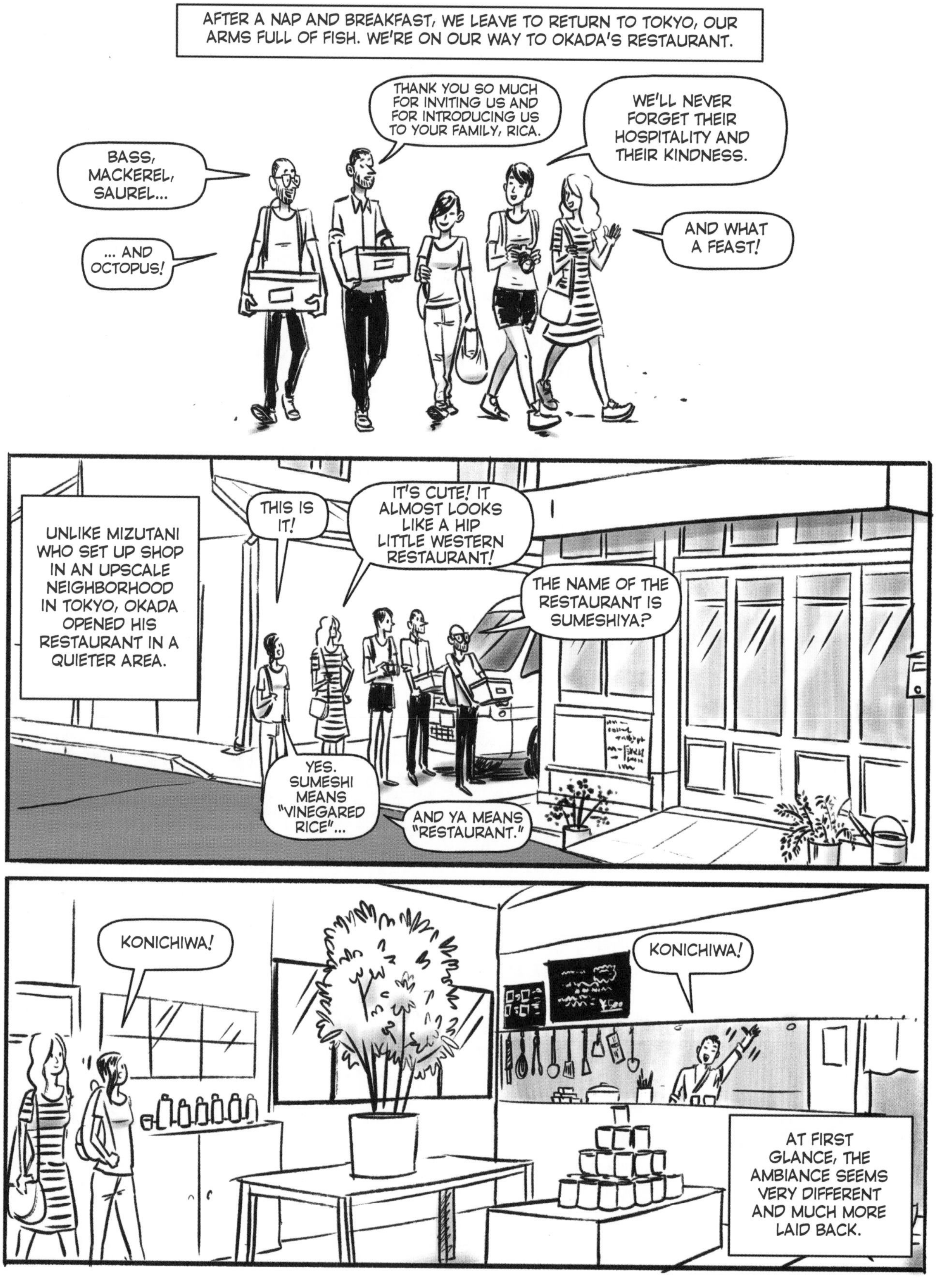
AFTER A NAP AND BREAKFAST, WE LEAVE TO RETURN TO TOKYO, OUR ARMS FULL OF FISH. WE'RE ON OUR WAY TO OKADA'S RESTAURANT.
BASS, MACKEREL, SAUREL...
... AND OCTOPUS!
THANK YOU SO MUCH FOR INVITING US AND FOR INTRODUCING US TO YOUR FAMILY, RICA.
WE'LL NEVER FORGET THEIR HOSPITALITY AND THEIR KINDNESS.
AND WHAT A FEAST!
UNLIKE MIZUTANI WHO SET UP SHOP IN AN UPSCALE NEIGHBORHOOD IN TOKYO, OKADA OPENED HIS RESTAURANT IN A QUIETER AREA.
THIS IS IT!
IT'S CUTE! IT ALMOST LOOKS LIKE A HIP LITTLE WESTERN RESTAURANT!
THE NAME OF THE RESTAURANT IS SUMESHIYA?
YES. SUMESHI MEANS "VINEGARED RICE"...
AND YA MEANS "RESTAURANT."
KONICHIWA!
KONICHIWA!
AT FIRST GLANCE, THE AMBIANCE SEEMS VERY DIFFERENT AND MUCH MORE LAID BACK.

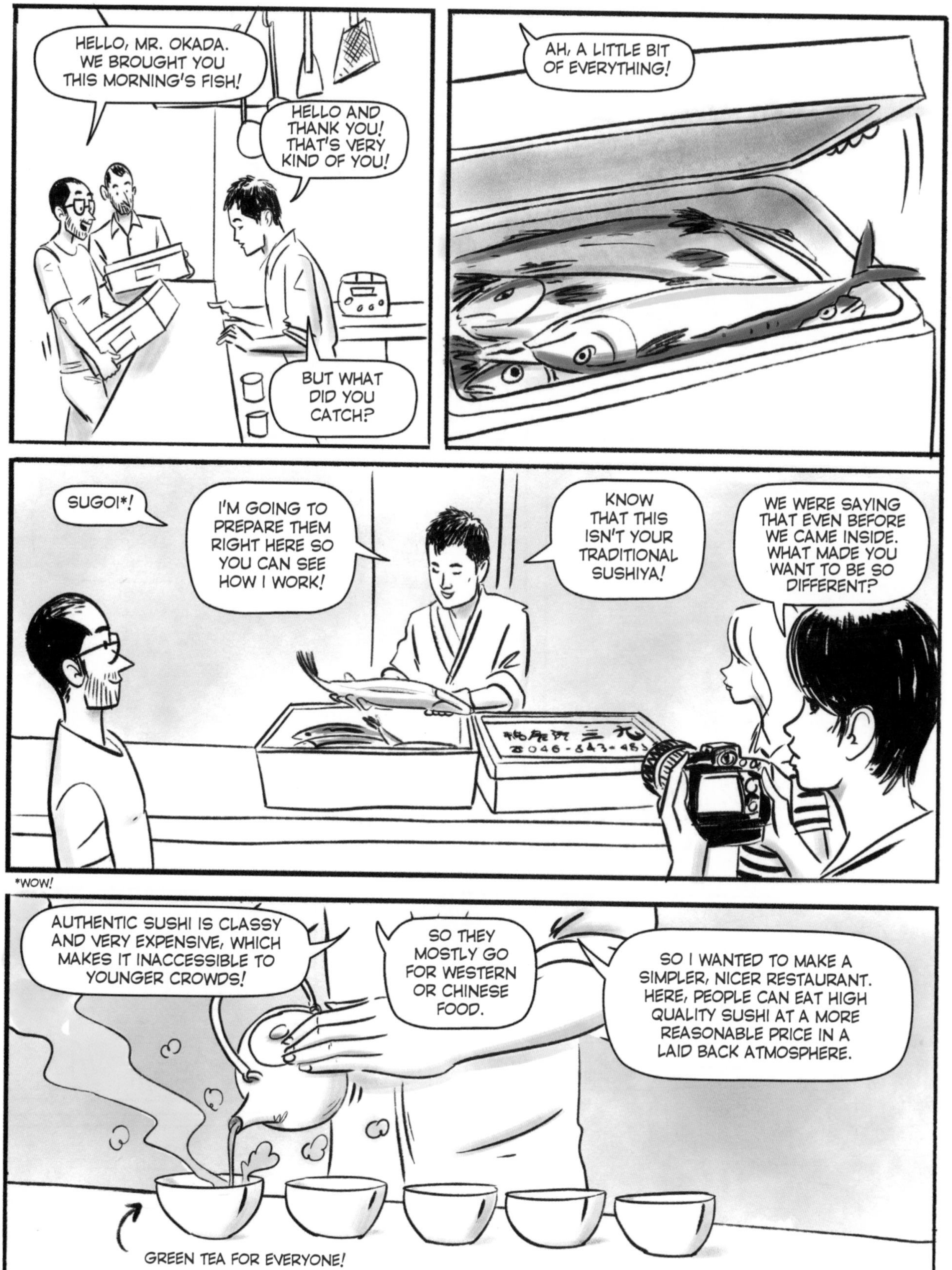
HELLO, MR. OKADA. WE BROUGHT YOU THIS MORNING'S FISH!
HELLO AND THANK YOU! THAT'S VERY KIND OF YOU!
BUT WHAT DID YOU CATCH?
AH, A LITTLE BIT OF EVERYTHING!
SUGOI*!
I'M GOING TO PREPARE THEM RIGHT HERE SO YOU CAN SEE HOW I WORK!
KNOW THAT THIS ISN'T YOUR TRADITIONAL SUSHIYA!
WE WERE SAYING THAT EVEN BEFORE WE CAME INSIDE. WHAT MADE YOU WANT TO BE SO DIFFERENT?
*WOW!
AUTHENTIC SUSHI IS CLASSY AND VERY EXPENSIVE, WHICH MAKES IT INACCESSIBLE TO YOUNGER CROWDS!
SO THEY MOSTLY GO FOR WESTERN OR CHINESE FOOD.
SO I WANTED TO MAKE A SIMPLER, NICER RESTAURANT. HERE, PEOPLE CAN EAT HIGH QUALITY SUSHI AT A MORE REASONABLE PRICE IN A LAID BACK ATMOSPHERE.
GREEN TEA FOR EVERYONE!

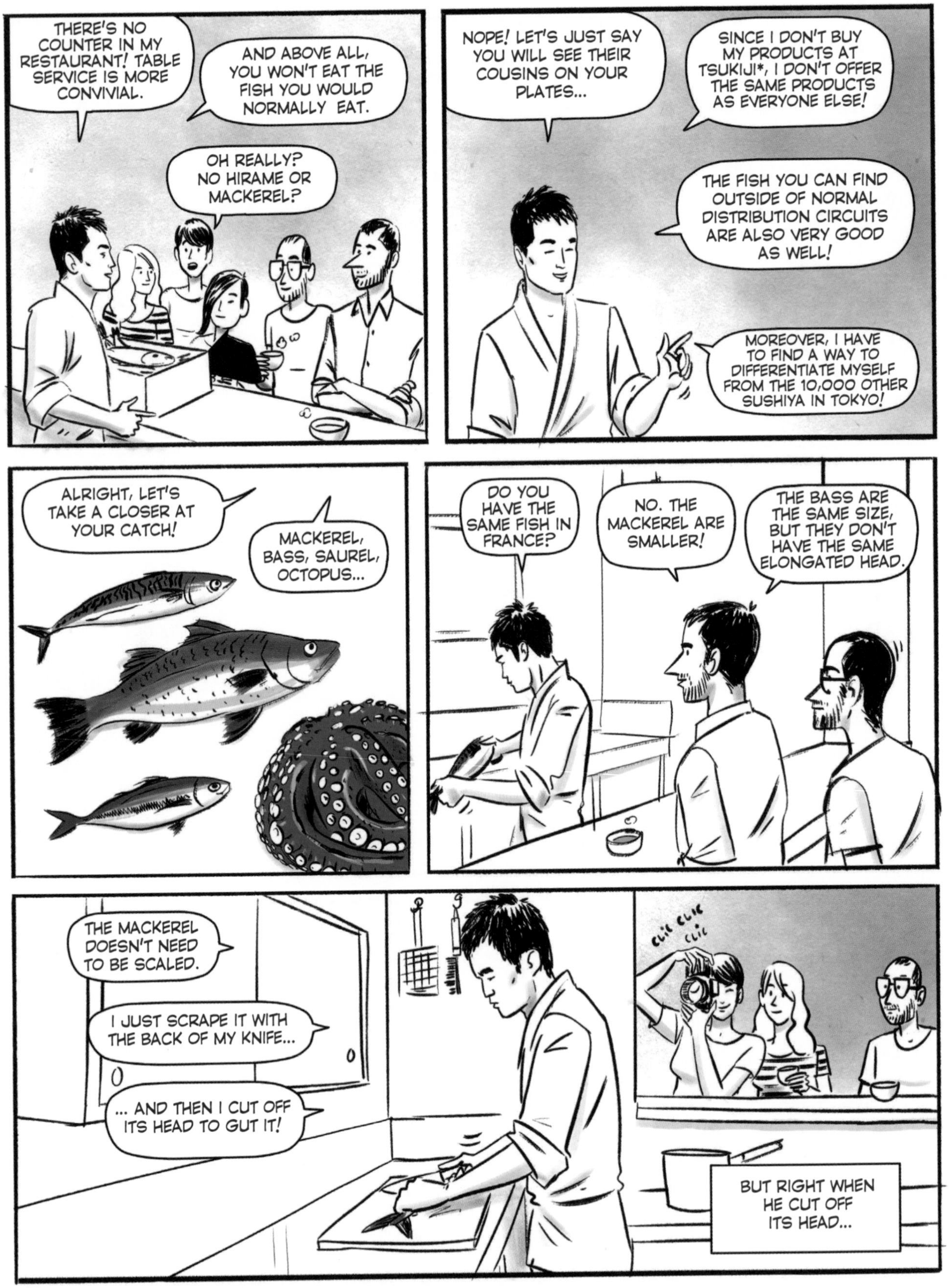
THERE'S NO COUNTER IN MY RESTAURANT! TABLE SERVICE IS MORE CONVIVIAL.
AND ABOVE ALL, YOU WON'T EAT THE FISH YOU WOULD NORMALLY EAT.
OH REALLY? NO HIRAME OR MACKEREL?
NOPE! LET'S JUST SAY YOU WILL SEE THEIR COUSINS ON YOUR PLATES...
SINCE I DON'T BUY MY PRODUCTS AT TSUKIJI*, I DON'T OFFER THE SAME PRODUCTS AS EVERYONE ELSE!
THE FISH YOU CAN FIND OUTSIDE OF NORMAL DISTRIBUTION CIRCUITS ARE ALSO VERY GOOD AS WELL!
MOREOVER, I HAVE TO FIND A WAY TO DIFFERENTIATE MYSELF FROM THE 10,000 OTHER SUSHIYA IN TOKYO!
ALRIGHT, LET'S TAKE A CLOSER AT YOUR CATCH!
MACKEREL, BASS, SAUREL, OCTOPUS...
DO YOU HAVE THE SAME FISH IN FRANCE?
NO. THE MACKEREL ARE SMALLER!
THE BASS ARE THE SAME SIZE, BUT THEY DON'T HAVE THE SAME ELONGATED HEAD.
THE MACKEREL DOESN'T NEED TO BE SCALED.
I JUST SCRAPE IT WITH THE BACK OF MY KNIFE...
... AND THEN I CUT OFF ITS HEAD TO GUT IT!
CLIC CLIC CLIC
BUT RIGHT WHEN HE CUT OFF ITS HEAD...

*NOW REPLACED BY THE TOYOSU MARKET.

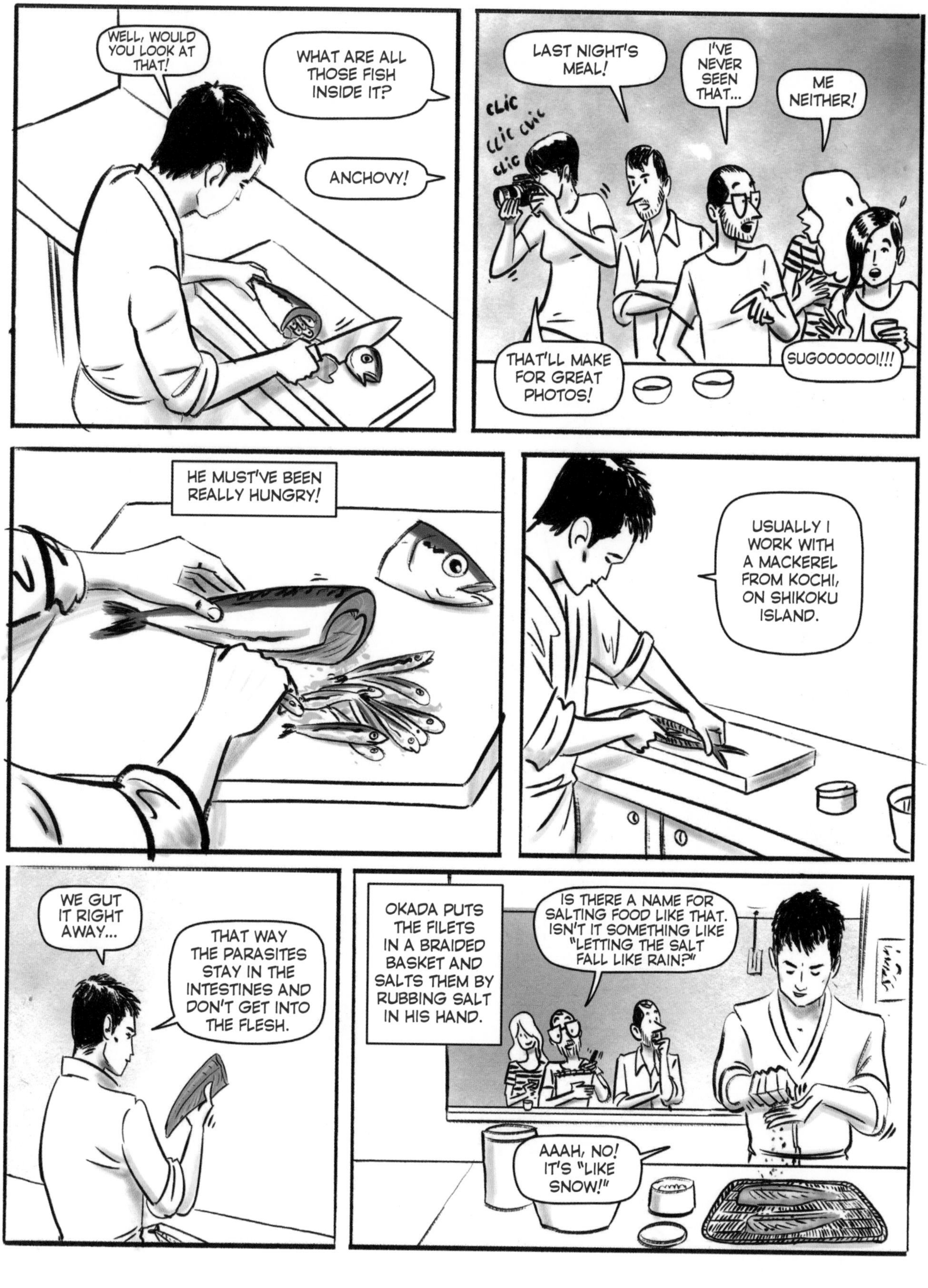
WELL, WOULD YOU LOOK AT THAT!
WHAT ARE ALL THOSE FISH INSIDE IT?
ANCHOVY!
LAST NIGHT'S MEAL!
I'VE NEVER SEEN THAT...
ME NEITHER!
CLIC
CLIC CLIC
CLIC
THAT'LL MAKE FOR GREAT PHOTOS!
SUGOOOOOOI!!!
HE MUST'VE BEEN REALLY HUNGRY!
USUALLY I WORK WITH A MACKEREL FROM KOCHI, ON SHIKOKU ISLAND.
WE GUT IT RIGHT AWAY...
THAT WAY THE PARASITES STAY IN THE INTESTINES AND DON'T GET INTO THE FLESH.
OKADA PUTS THE FILETS IN A BRAIDED BASKET AND SALTS THEM BY RUBBING SALT IN HIS HAND.
IS THERE A NAME FOR SALTING FOOD LIKE THAT. ISN'T IT SOMETHING LIKE "LETTING THE SALT FALL LIKE RAIN?"
AAAH, NO! IT'S "LIKE SNOW!"

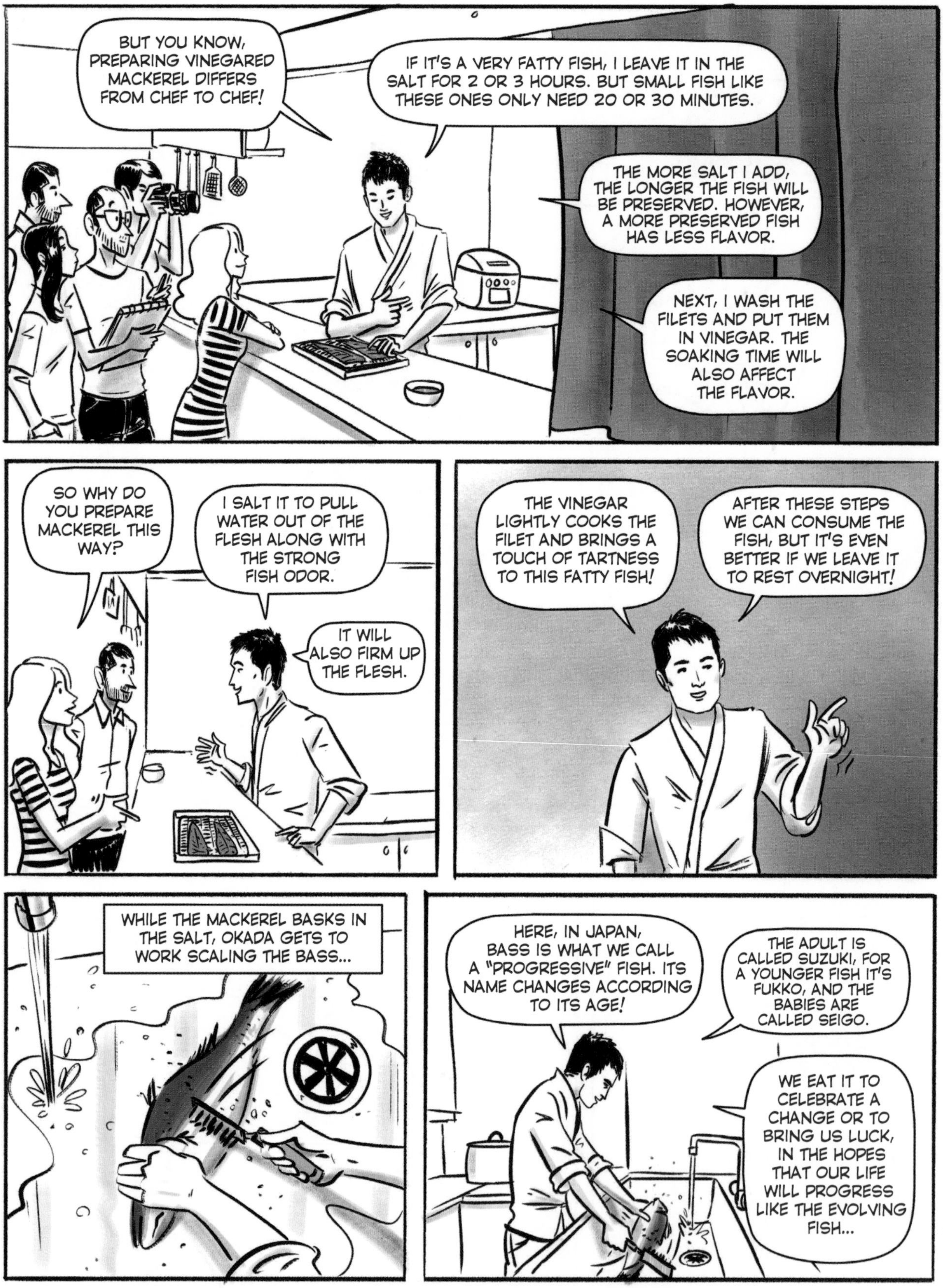
BUT YOU KNOW, PREPARING VINEGARED MACKEREL DIFFERS FROM CHEF TO CHEF!
IF IT'S A VERY FATTY FISH, I LEAVE IT IN THE SALT FOR 2 OR 3 HOURS. BUT SMALL FISH LIKE THESE ONES ONLY NEED 20 OR 30 MINUTES.
THE MORE SALT I ADD, THE LONGER THE FISH WILL BE PRESERVED. HOWEVER, A MORE PRESERVED FISH HAS LESS FLAVOR.
NEXT, I WASH THE FILETS AND PUT THEM IN VINEGAR. THE SOAKING TIME WILL ALSO AFFECT THE FLAVOR.
SO WHY DO YOU PREPARE MACKEREL THIS WAY?
I SALT IT TO PULL WATER OUT OF THE FLESH ALONG WITH THE STRONG FISH ODOR.
IT WILL ALSO FIRM UP THE FLESH.
THE VINEGAR LIGHTLY COOKS THE FILET AND BRINGS A TOUCH OF TARTNESS TO THIS FATTY FISH!
AFTER THESE STEPS WE CAN CONSUME THE FISH, BUT IT'S EVEN BETTER IF WE LEAVE IT TO REST OVERNIGHT!
WHILE THE MACKEREL BASKS IN THE SALT, OKADA GETS TO WORK SCALING THE BASS...
HERE, IN JAPAN, BASS IS WHAT WE CALL A "PROGRESSIVE" FISH. ITS NAME CHANGES ACCORDING TO ITS AGE!
THE ADULT IS CALLED SUZUKI, FOR A YOUNGER FISH IT'S FUKKO, AND THE BABIES ARE CALLED SEIGO.
WE EAT IT TO CELEBRATE A CHANGE OR TO BRING US LUCK, IN THE HOPES THAT OUR LIFE WILL PROGRESS LIKE THE EVOLVING FISH...

AFTER SCALING THE BASS, OKADA PLACES IT ON A GINKO BOARD. FLESH SIDE OUT, HE SKINS THE FILETS BY PASSING THE KNIFE BETWEEN THE SKIN AND THE FLESH BEGINNING WITH THE TAIL.

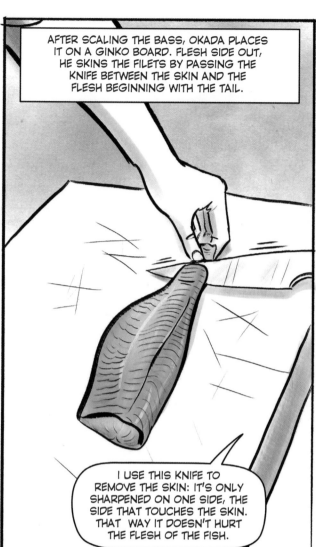

I USE THIS KNIFE TO REMOVE THE SKIN: IT'S ONLY SHARPENED ON ONE SIDE, THE SIDE THAT TOUCHES THE SKIN. THAT WAY IT DOESN'T HURT THE FLESH OF THE FISH.

THE FINAL STEP: REMOVE THE RESIDUE. SINCE IT WON'T BE MARINATED, I PASS IT THROUGH SALTED WATER WITH PLENTY OF ICE. YOU HAVE TO DO THIS STEP QUICKLY SO AS TO AVOID LOSING THE FLAVOR.

SMALL TOWEL FOR WIPING THE FILET

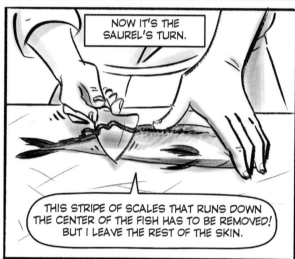

NOW IT'S THE SAUREL'S TURN.

THIS STRIPE OF SCALES THAT RUNS DOWN THE CENTER OF THE FISH HAS TO BE REMOVED! BUT I LEAVE THE REST OF THE SKIN.

AFTER FILETING THIS FISH YOU HAVE TO REMOVE THE BONES. THERE ARE A LOT OF THEM...

TWEEZERS FOR REMOVING FISHBONES

THAT'S WHY WE ALMOST NEVER EAT SAUREL IN FRANCE...

WHAT A SHAME!!!

TO FINISH UP, I REMOVE THE FINE, TRANSLUCID FILM COVERING THE SKIN.

BUT YOU CAN SEE THAT THE CLEANING AND CUTTING TECHNIQUES ARE ALMOST ALWAYS THE SAME...

EVEN THOUGH THE FISH ARE ALL DIFFERENT!

OKADA RETURNS TO THE BASS AND CUTS IT IN SLICES, IN SASHIMI...

SOME THIN, SOME THICKER...

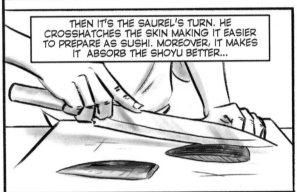

THEN IT'S THE SAUREL'S TURN. HE CROSSHATCHES THE SKIN MAKING IT EASIER TO PREPARE AS SUSHI. MOREOVER, IT MAKES IT ABSORB THE SHOYU BETTER...

... BEFORE LIKEWISE CUTTING IT INTO SASHIMI.

NOW WE'LL TASTE EVERYTHING!

IF THE BASS IS FRESH, IT'S BETTER TO CUT THIN SLICES BECAUSE THE FLESH IS FIRMER. ON THE OTHER HAND, WITH A FISH THAT HAS RESTED FOR 2 OR 3 DAYS, YOU CAN SLICE IT THICKER.

SINCE THE SAUREL IS MORE TENDER, YOU CAN MAKE THICKER SLICES EVEN IF IT WAS JUST CAUGHT.

I SUGGEST YOU TRY IT WITH AND WITHOUT SHOYU SO YOU CAN TASTE THE DIFFERENCE!

THE SAUREL IS DELICIOUS!!!
JUST SOAKED IN A LITTLE BIT OF SOY SAUCE, IT'S SUPERB!
AND TO THINK THAT IN FRANCE WE THROW THE SAUREL AWAY...
REGARDLESS, THE BASS HAS MORE UMAMI THAN THOSE IN FRANCE!
I'M SO JEALOUS... I COULD NEVER EAT SUCH FINE FISH AT HOME...
YOU HAVE TO COME FISHING WITH ME!
WHO WANTS THE LAST SASHIMI?
NOW WE'LL TASTE THESE FISH AS SUSHI!
HOW MUCH RICE DO YOU PUT IN A SUSHI?
AROUND 12 GRAMS, BUT I DON'T WEIGH THEM. I FEEL IT IN MY HAND...
AFTER FORMING THE BALL OF VINEGARED RICE, WHAT WE CALL SHARI, I PUT WASABI ON THE SLICE OF FISH.
YOU HAVE TO AVOID TOUCHING IT TOO MUCH SO AS TO AVOID WARMING IT UP WITH YOUR BODY TEMPERATURE.
THEN I PUT THE NETA* ON THE RICE AND I DELICATELY FORM THE SUSHI!
THE MOST IMPORTANT THING ABOUT MAKING SUSHI ARE THE PREPARATIONS: IT'S 90% OF THE WORK!
TODAY, IN TOKYO, THERE'S A SUSHI SCHOOL WHERE YOU CAN LEARN SUSHI, HOW TO FORM THEM AND CUT THE FISH.
ANYONE CAN GO THROUGH THIS TRAINING IF THEY GO TO THE TROUBLE...
ALTHOUGH THEIR SUSHI IS OFTEN BEAUTIFUL, THESE STUDENTS DON'T LEARN HOW TO LOOK FOR PARASITES, HOW TO PROPERLY PREPARE FISH, HOW TO CONSERVE THEM...
YET IT'S ESSENTIAL THAT THEY UNDERSTAND THEIR PRODUCTS!

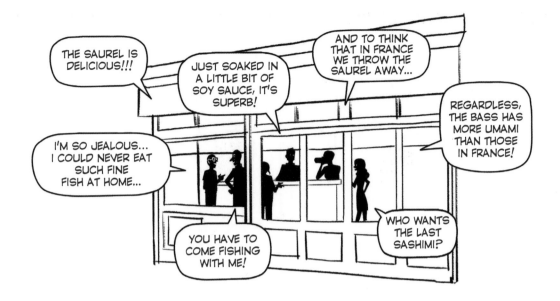

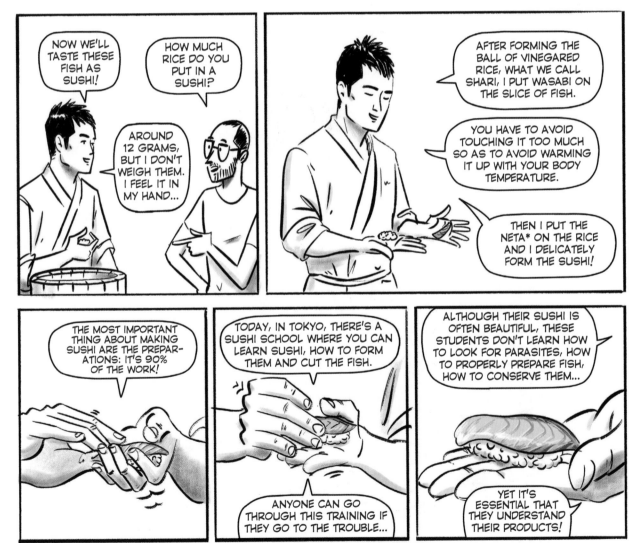

*THE NETA IS THE NAME GIVEN TO ANY INGREDIENT PLACED ON A BALL OF VINEGARED RICE.

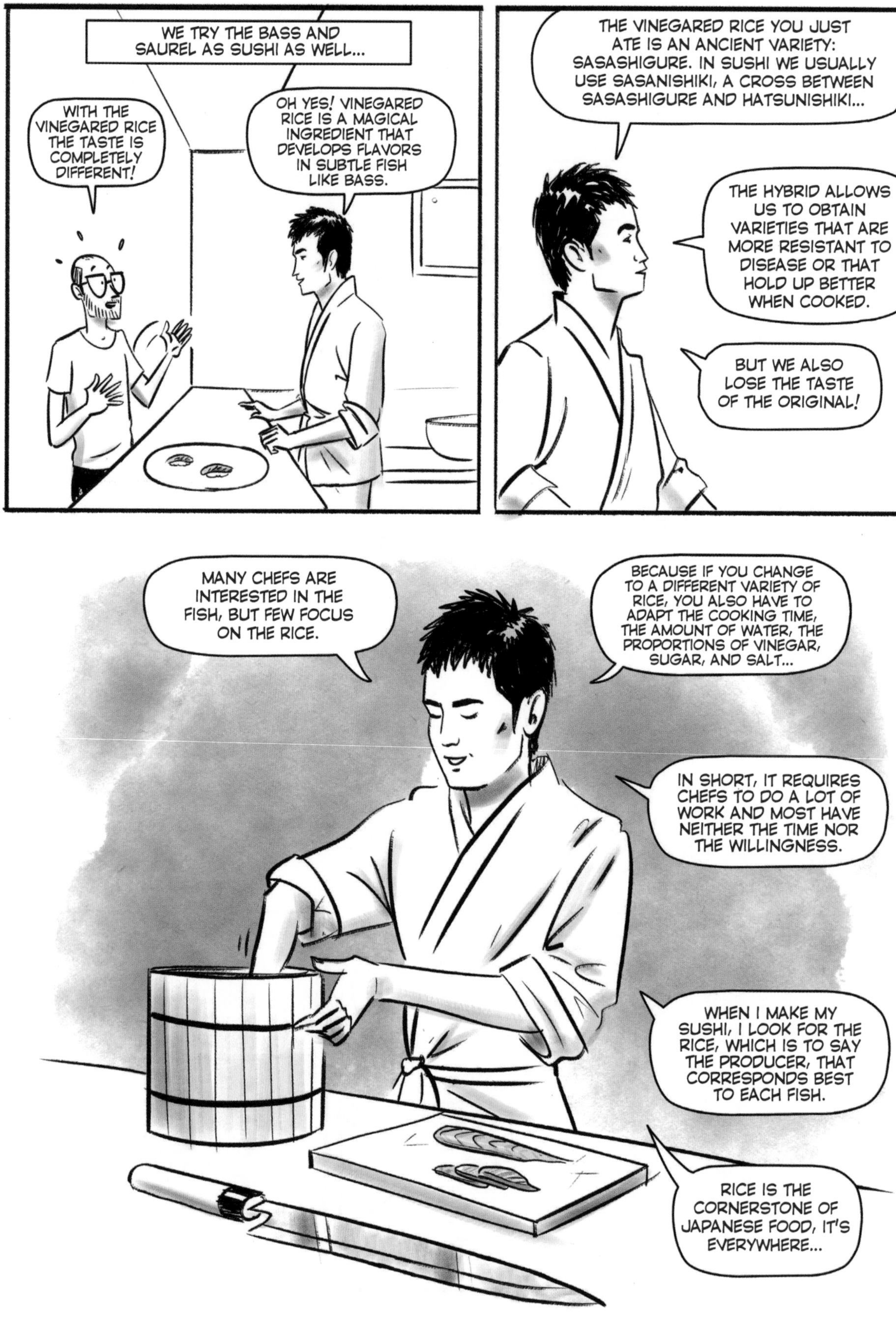
WE TRY THE BASS AND SAUREL AS SUSHI AS WELL...
WITH THE VINEGARED RICE THE TASTE IS COMPLETELY DIFFERENT!
OH YES! VINEGARED RICE IS A MAGICAL INGREDIENT THAT DEVELOPS FLAVORS IN SUBTLE FISH LIKE BASS.
THE VINEGARED RICE YOU JUST ATE IS AN ANCIENT VARIETY: SASASHIGURE. IN SUSHI WE USUALLY USE SASANISHIKI, A CROSS BETWEEN SASASHIGURE AND HATSUNISHIKI...
THE HYBRID ALLOWS US TO OBTAIN VARIETIES THAT ARE MORE RESISTANT TO DISEASE OR THAT HOLD UP BETTER WHEN COOKED.
BUT WE ALSO LOSE THE TASTE OF THE ORIGINAL!
MANY CHEFS ARE INTERESTED IN THE FISH, BUT FEW FOCUS ON THE RICE.
BECAUSE IF YOU CHANGE TO A DIFFERENT VARIETY OF RICE, YOU ALSO HAVE TO ADAPT THE COOKING TIME, THE AMOUNT OF WATER, THE PROPORTIONS OF VINEGAR, SUGAR, AND SALT...
IN SHORT, IT REQUIRES CHEFS TO DO A LOT OF WORK AND MOST HAVE NEITHER THE TIME NOR THE WILLINGNESS.
WHEN I MAKE MY SUSHI, I LOOK FOR THE RICE, WHICH IS TO SAY THE PRODUCER, THAT CORRESPONDS BEST TO EACH FISH.
RICE IS THE CORNERSTONE OF JAPANESE FOOD, IT'S EVERYWHERE...

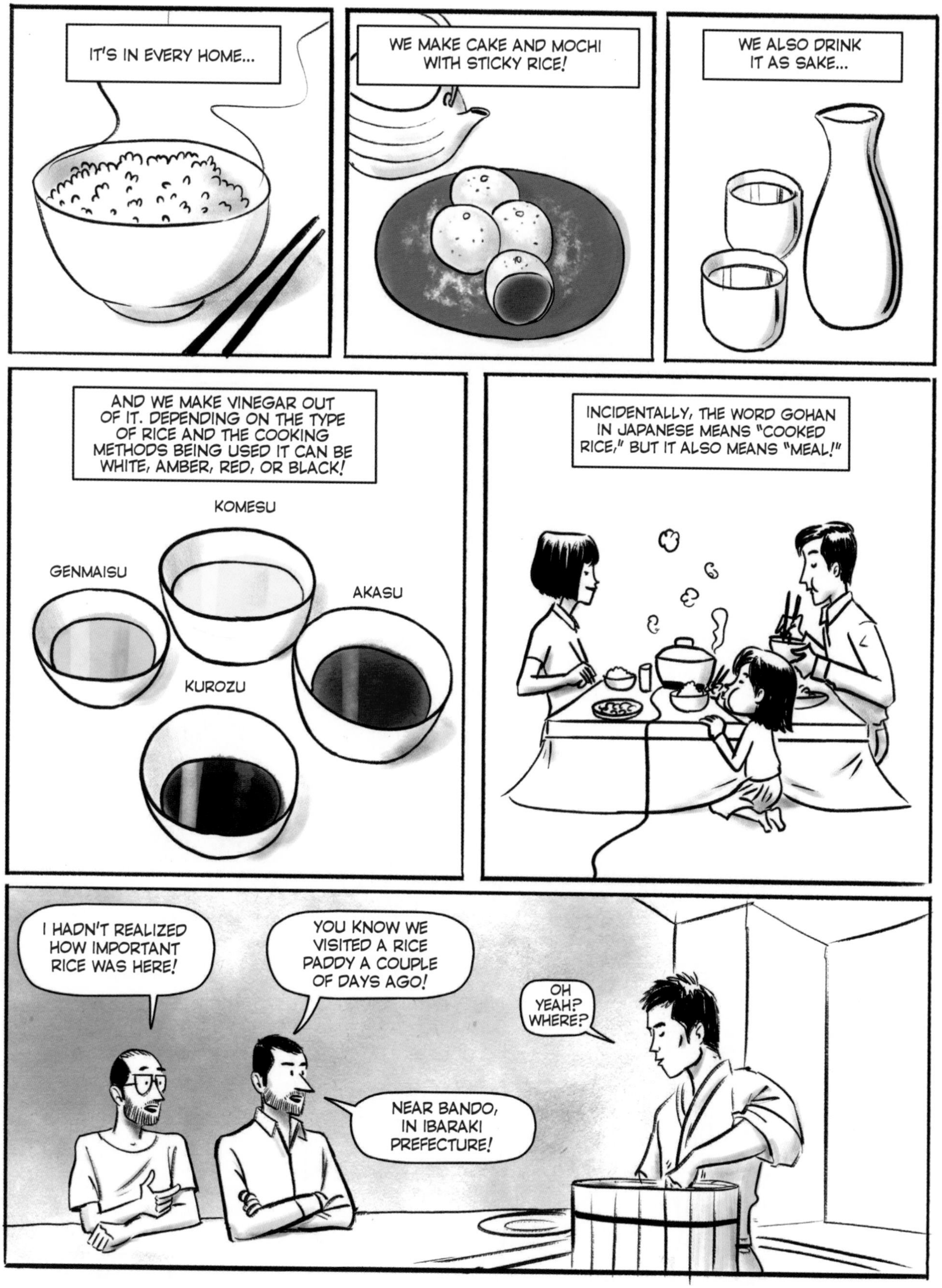
IT'S IN EVERY HOME...
WE MAKE CAKE AND MOCHI WITH STICKY RICE!
WE ALSO DRINK IT AS SAKE...
AND WE MAKE VINEGAR OUT OF IT. DEPENDING ON THE TYPE OF RICE AND THE COOKING METHODS BEING USED IT CAN BE WHITE, AMBER, RED, OR BLACK!
KOMESU
GENMAISU
AKASU
KUROZU
INCIDENTALLY, THE WORD GOHAN IN JAPANESE MEANS "COOKED RICE," BUT IT ALSO MEANS "MEAL!"
I HADN'T REALIZED HOW IMPORTANT RICE WAS HERE!
YOU KNOW WE VISITED A RICE PADDY A COUPLE OF DAYS AGO!
OH YEAH? WHERE?
NEAR BANDO, IN IBARAKI PREFECTURE!

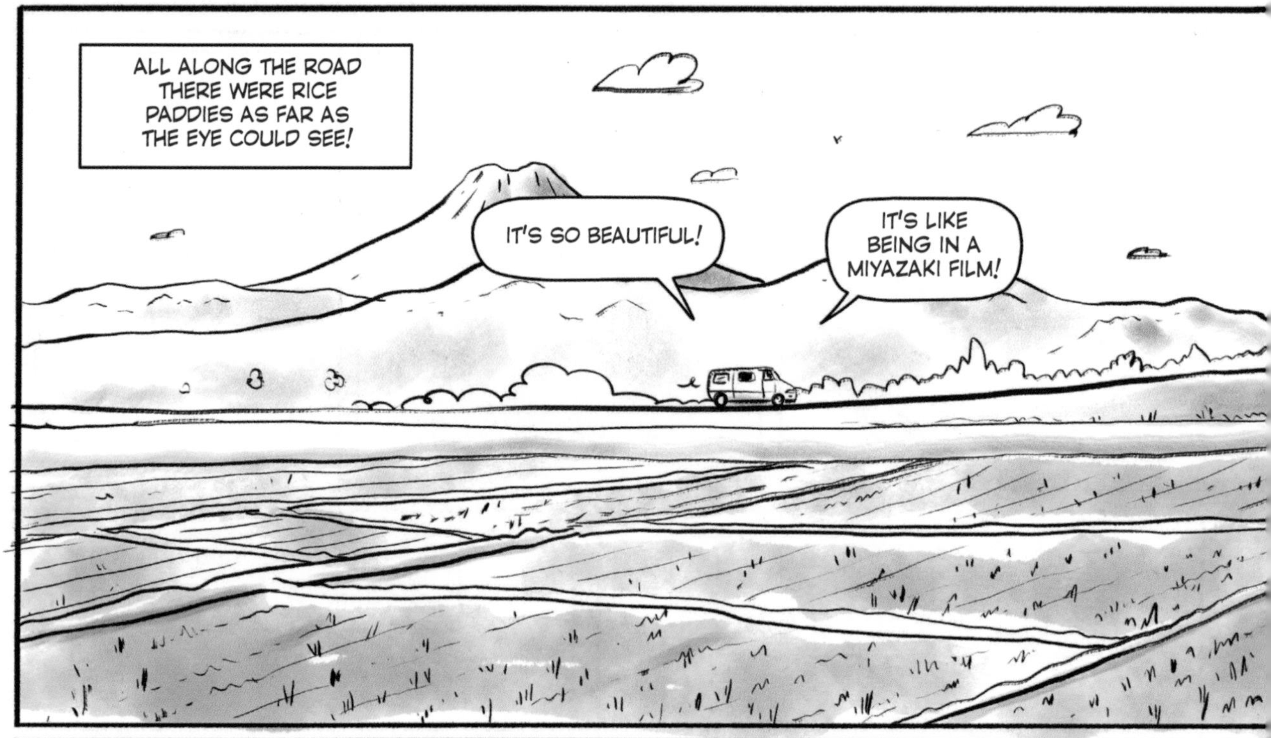
ALL ALONG THE ROAD THERE WERE RICE PADDIES AS FAR AS THE EYE COULD SEE!
IT'S SO BEAUTIFUL!
IT'S LIKE BEING IN A MIYAZAKI FILM!

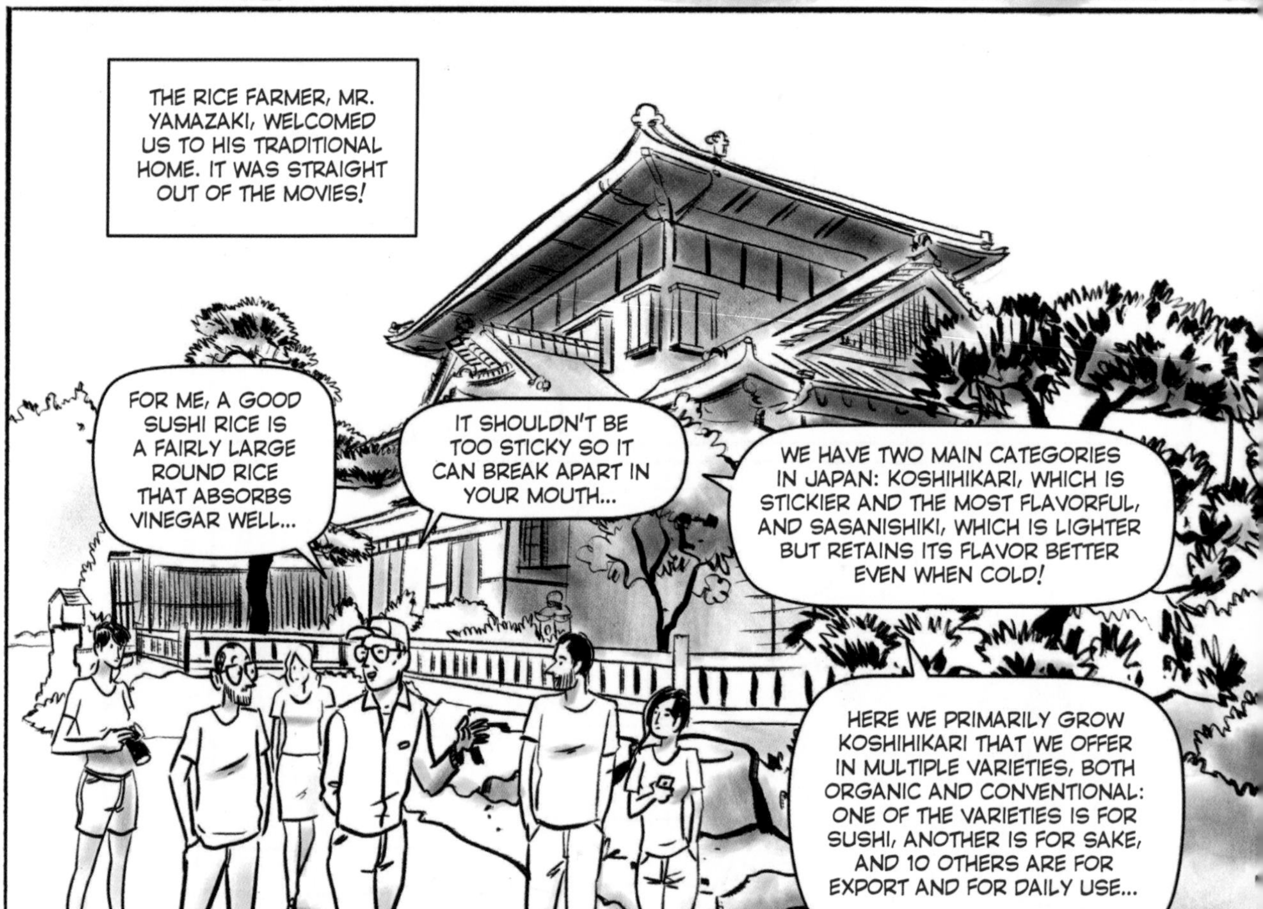
THE RICE FARMER, MR. YAMAZAKI, WELCOMED US TO HIS TRADITIONAL HOME. IT WAS STRAIGHT OUT OF THE MOVIES!
FOR ME, A GOOD SUSHI RICE IS A FAIRLY LARGE ROUND RICE THAT ABSORBS VINEGAR WELL...
IT SHOULDN'T BE TOO STICKY SO IT CAN BREAK APART IN YOUR MOUTH...
WE HAVE TWO MAIN CATEGORIES IN JAPAN: KOSHIHIKARI, WHICH IS STICKIER AND THE MOST FLAVORFUL, AND SASANISHIKI, WHICH IS LIGHTER BUT RETAINS ITS FLAVOR BETTER EVEN WHEN COLD!
HERE WE PRIMARILY GROW KOSHIHIKARI THAT WE OFFER IN MULTIPLE VARIETIES, BOTH ORGANIC AND CONVENTIONAL: ONE OF THE VARIETIES IS FOR SUSHI, ANOTHER IS FOR SAKE, AND 10 OTHERS ARE FOR EXPORT AND FOR DAILY USE...

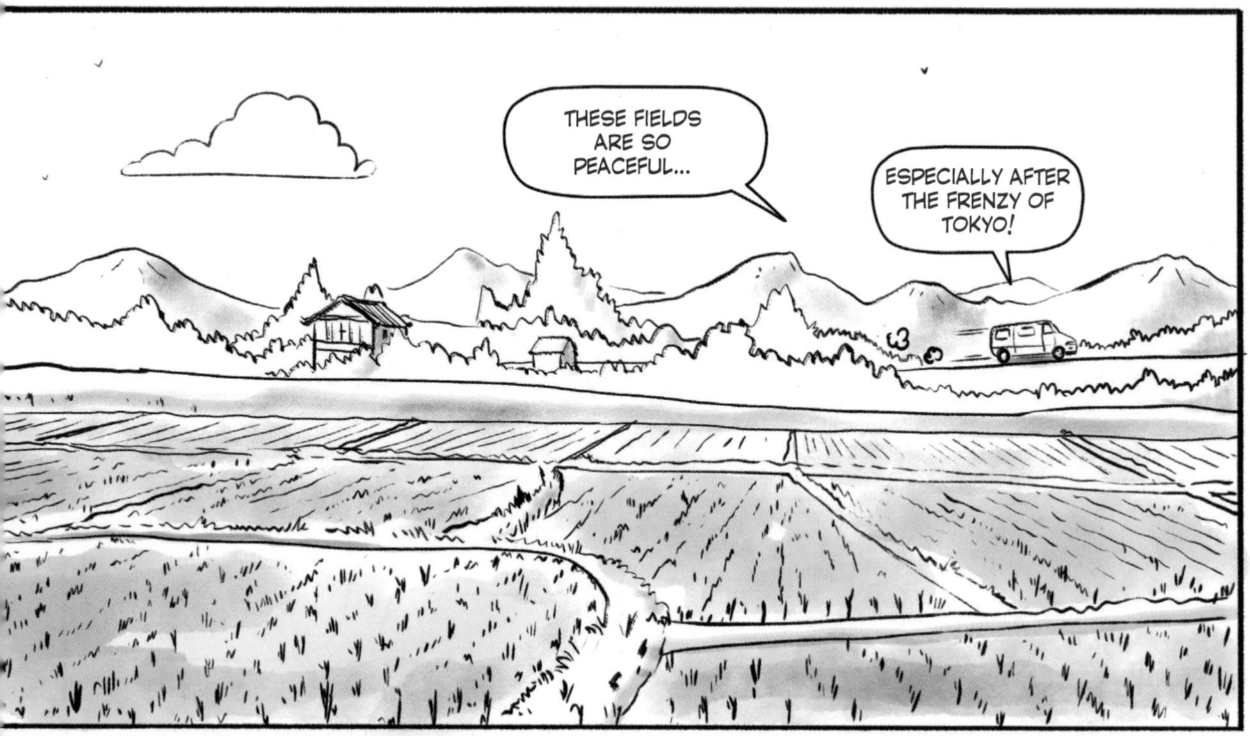
THESE FIELDS ARE SO PEACEFUL...
ESPECIALLY AFTER THE FRENZY OF TOKYO!

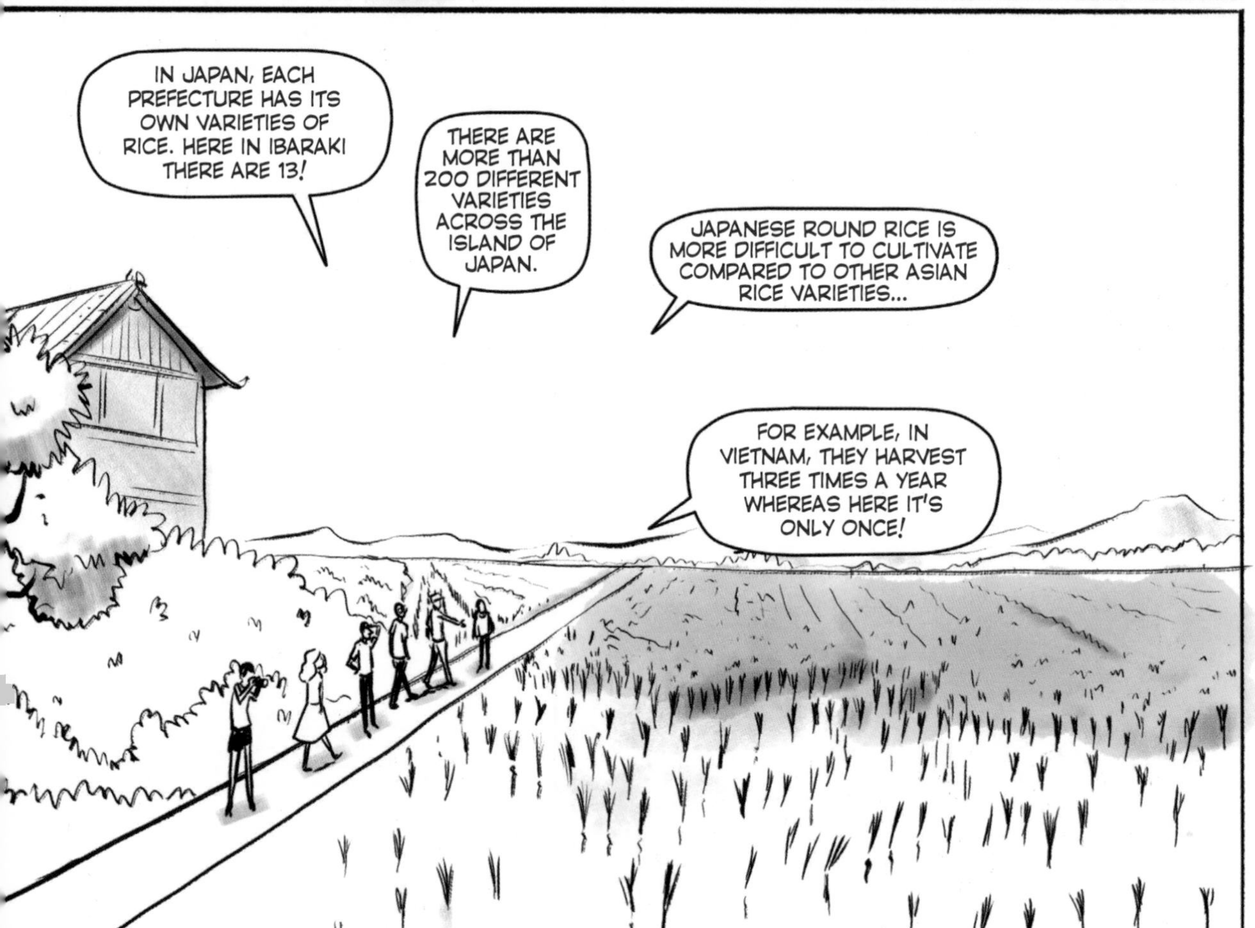
IN JAPAN, EACH PREFECTURE HAS ITS OWN VARIETIES OF RICE. HERE IN IBARAKI THERE ARE 13!
THERE ARE MORE THAN 200 DIFFERENT VARIETIES ACROSS THE ISLAND OF JAPAN.
JAPANESE ROUND RICE IS MORE DIFFICULT TO CULTIVATE COMPARED TO OTHER ASIAN RICE VARIETIES...
FOR EXAMPLE, IN VIETNAM, THEY HARVEST THREE TIMES A YEAR WHEREAS HERE IT'S ONLY ONCE!

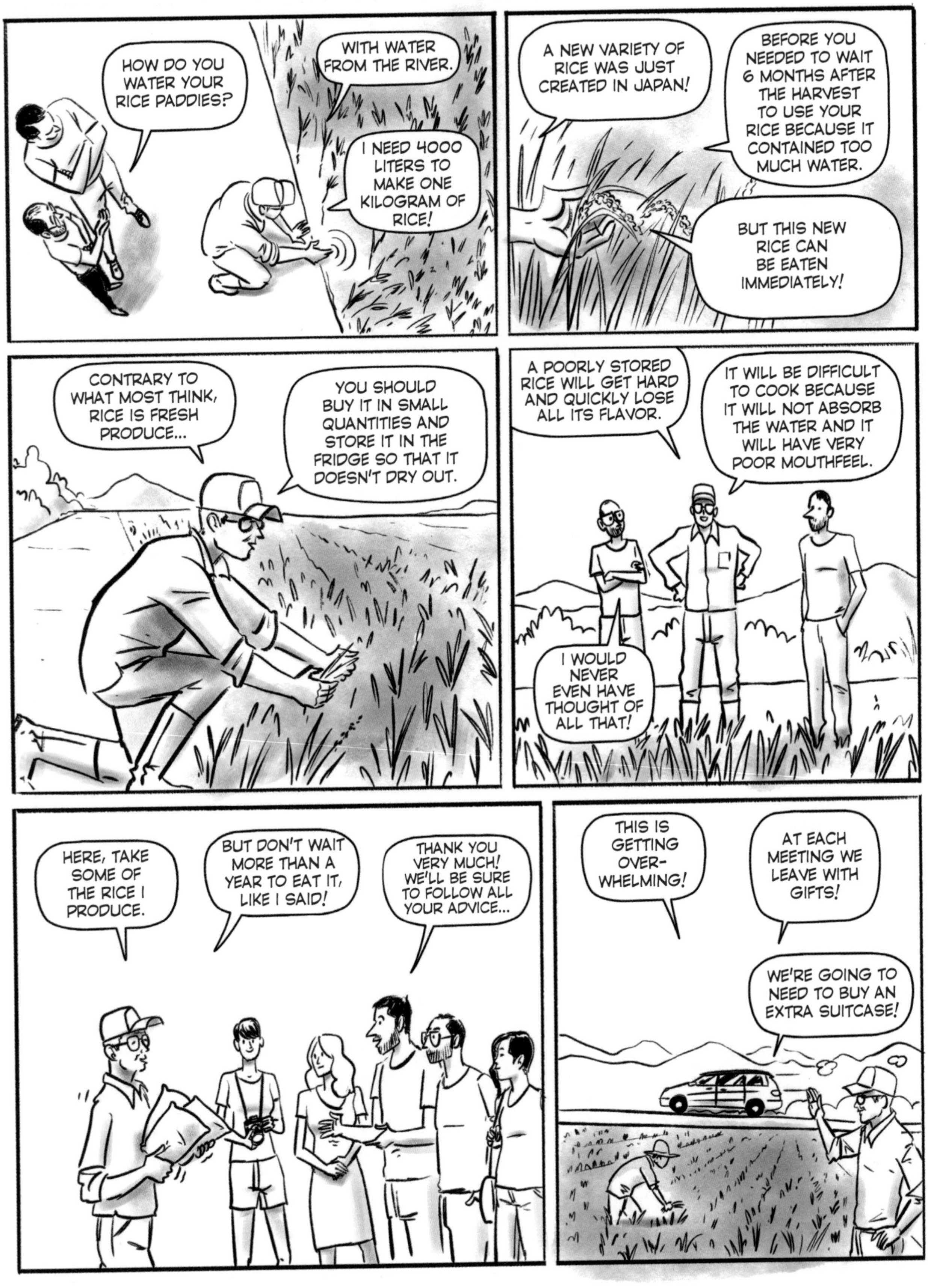
HOW DO YOU WATER YOUR RICE PADDIES?
WITH WATER FROM THE RIVER.
I NEED 4000 LITERS TO MAKE ONE KILOGRAM OF RICE!
A NEW VARIETY OF RICE WAS JUST CREATED IN JAPAN!
BEFORE YOU NEEDED TO WAIT 6 MONTHS AFTER THE HARVEST TO USE YOUR RICE BECAUSE IT CONTAINED TOO MUCH WATER.
BUT THIS NEW RICE CAN BE EATEN IMMEDIATELY!
CONTRARY TO WHAT MOST THINK, RICE IS FRESH PRODUCE...
YOU SHOULD BUY IT IN SMALL QUANTITIES AND STORE IT IN THE FRIDGE SO THAT IT DOESN'T DRY OUT.
A POORLY STORED RICE WILL GET HARD AND QUICKLY LOSE ALL ITS FLAVOR.
IT WILL BE DIFFICULT TO COOK BECAUSE IT WILL NOT ABSORB THE WATER AND IT WILL HAVE VERY POOR MOUTHFEEL.
I WOULD NEVER EVEN HAVE THOUGHT OF ALL THAT!
HERE, TAKE SOME OF THE RICE I PRODUCE.
BUT DON'T WAIT MORE THAN A YEAR TO EAT IT, LIKE I SAID!
THANK YOU VERY MUCH! WE'LL BE SURE TO FOLLOW ALL YOUR ADVICE...
THIS IS GETTING OVER-WHELMING!
AT EACH MEETING WE LEAVE WITH GIFTS!
WE'RE GOING TO NEED TO BUY AN EXTRA SUITCASE!

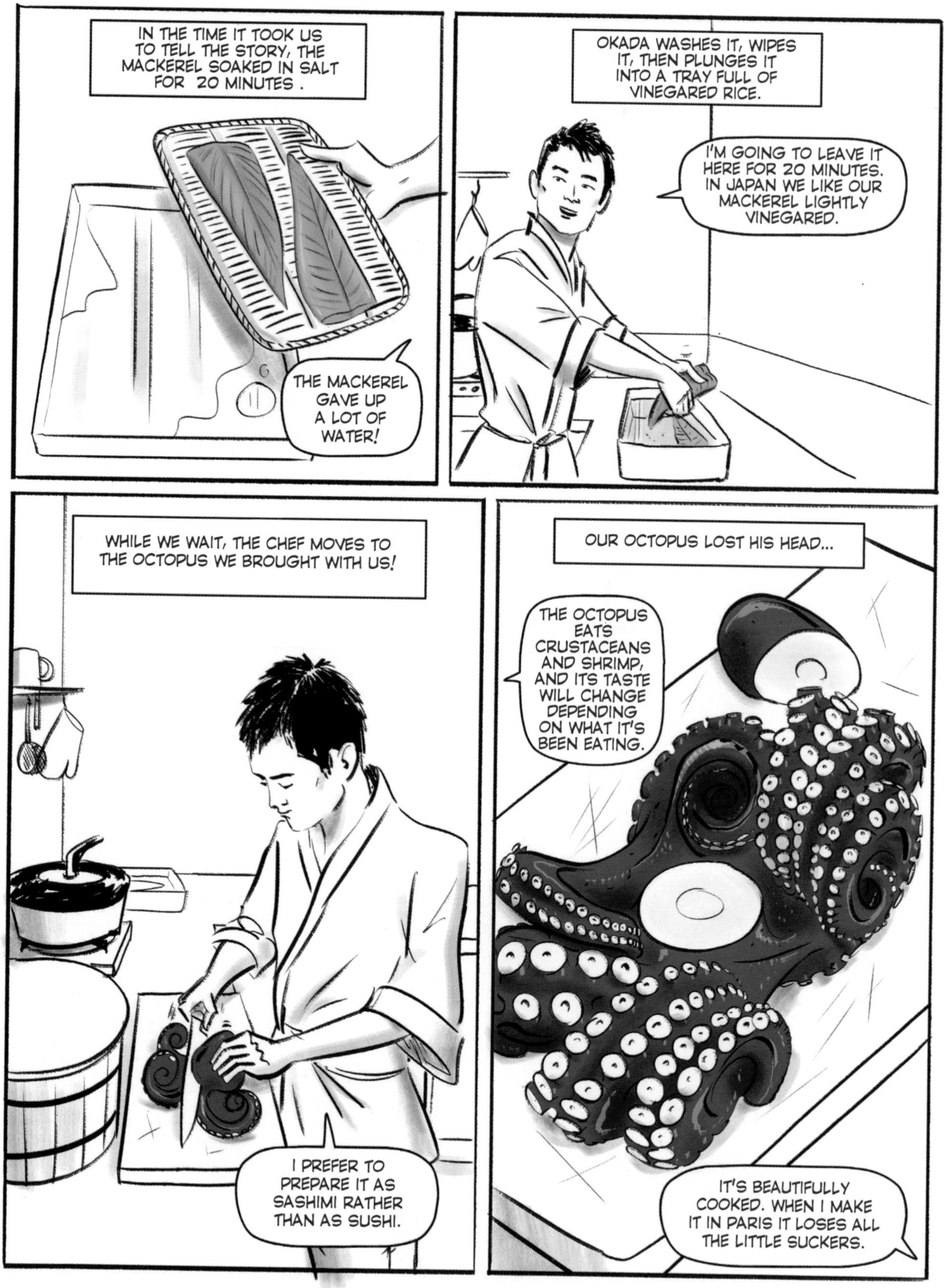

IN THE TIME IT TOOK US TO TELL THE STORY, THE MACKEREL SOAKED IN SALT FOR 20 MINUTES .
THE MACKEREL GAVE UP A LOT OF WATER!
OKADA WASHES IT, WIPES IT, THEN PLUNGES IT INTO A TRAY FULL OF VINEGARED RICE.
I'M GOING TO LEAVE IT HERE FOR 20 MINUTES. IN JAPAN WE LIKE OUR MACKEREL LIGHTLY VINEGARED.
WHILE WE WAIT, THE CHEF MOVES TO THE OCTOPUS WE BROUGHT WITH US!
I PREFER TO PREPARE IT AS SASHIMI RATHER THAN AS SUSHI.
OUR OCTOPUS LOST HIS HEAD...
THE OCTOPUS EATS CRUSTACEANS AND SHRIMP, AND ITS TASTE WILL CHANGE DEPENDING ON WHAT IT'S BEEN EATING.
IT'S BEAUTIFULLY COOKED. WHEN I MAKE IT IN PARIS IT LOSES ALL THE LITTLE SUCKERS.

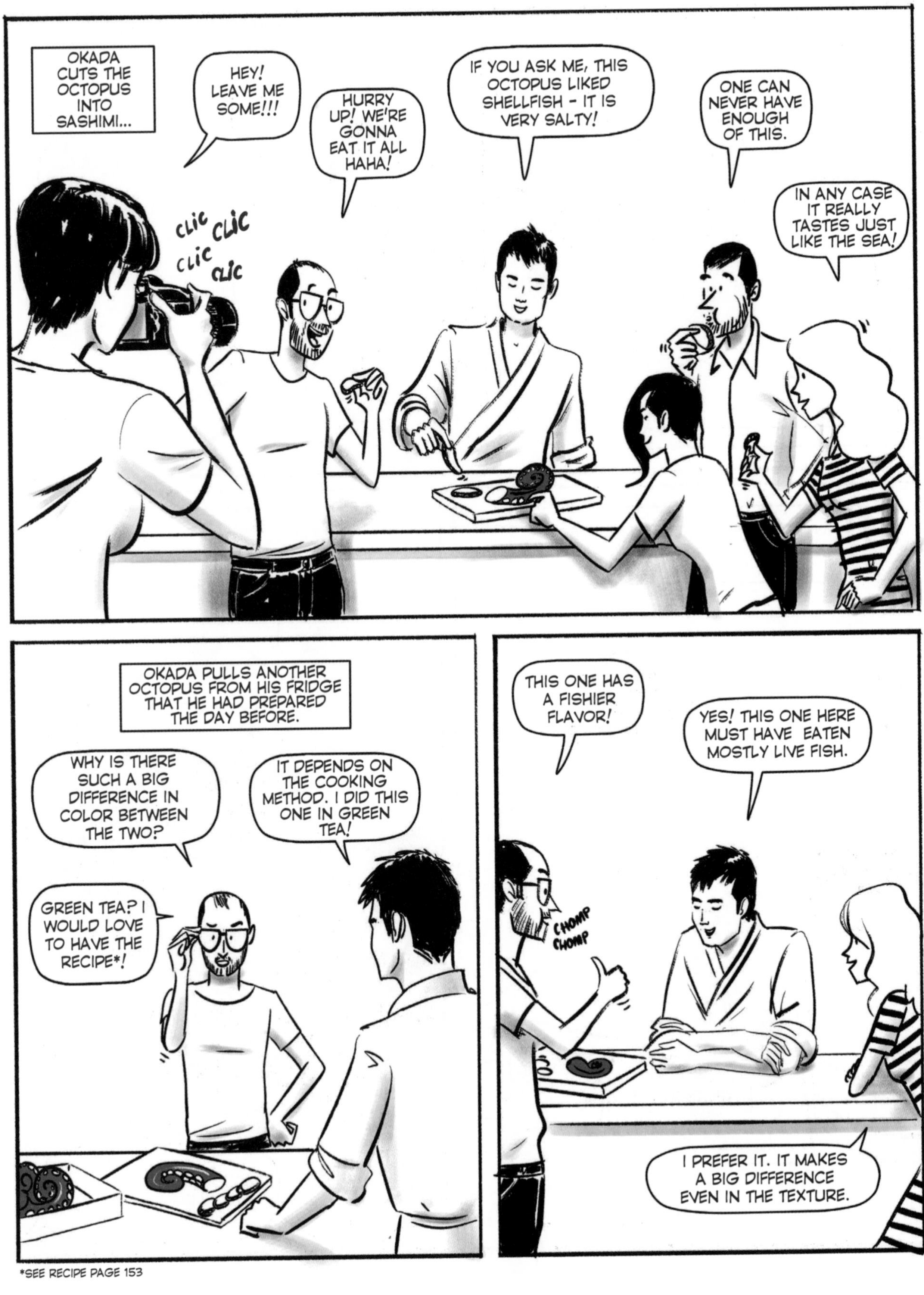
OKADA CUTS THE OCTOPUS INTO SASHIMI...
HEY! LEAVE ME SOME!!!
HURRY UP! WE'RE GONNA EAT IT ALL HAHA!
CLIC CLIC CLIC CLIC
IF YOU ASK ME, THIS OCTOPUS LIKED SHELLFISH - IT IS VERY SALTY!
ONE CAN NEVER HAVE ENOUGH OF THIS.
IN ANY CASE IT REALLY TASTES JUST LIKE THE SEA!
OKADA PULLS ANOTHER OCTOPUS FROM HIS FRIDGE THAT HE HAD PREPARED THE DAY BEFORE.
WHY IS THERE SUCH A BIG DIFFERENCE IN COLOR BETWEEN THE TWO?
IT DEPENDS ON THE COOKING METHOD. I DID THIS ONE IN GREEN TEA!
GREEN TEA? I WOULD LOVE TO HAVE THE RECIPE*!
THIS ONE HAS A FISHIER FLAVOR!
YES! THIS ONE HERE MUST HAVE EATEN MOSTLY LIVE FISH.
CHOMP CHOMP
I PREFER IT. IT MAKES A BIG DIFFERENCE EVEN IN THE TEXTURE.

*SEE RECIPE PAGE 153

FOLLOWING THIS TENTACULAR TASTING, WE'RE FINALLY GOING TO DISCOVER THE MACKEREL MARINATED IN VINEGAR!

IT'S FLESH HAS BEEN WHITENED AFTER BEING "COOKED" BY THE VINEGAR.

AFTER DRAINING AND REMOVING THE BONES, OKADA BEGINS CUTTING...

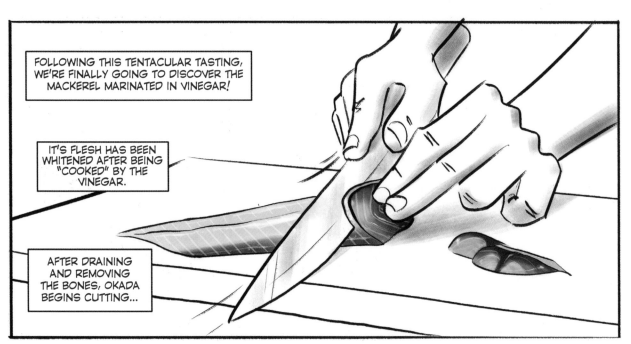

OH! WE WON'T BE ABLE TO TASTE IT!

OH REALLY? WHY NOT?

I FOUND A SMALL PARASITE, AN ANISAKIS...

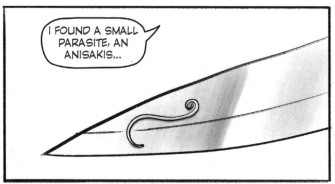

IS IT DEAD?

NO, ALIVE...

IF WE REMOVE THE PARASITE CAN WE EAT THE FISH?

NO. THERE ARE STILL THE EGGS AND SOME PEOPLE ARE ALLERGIC.

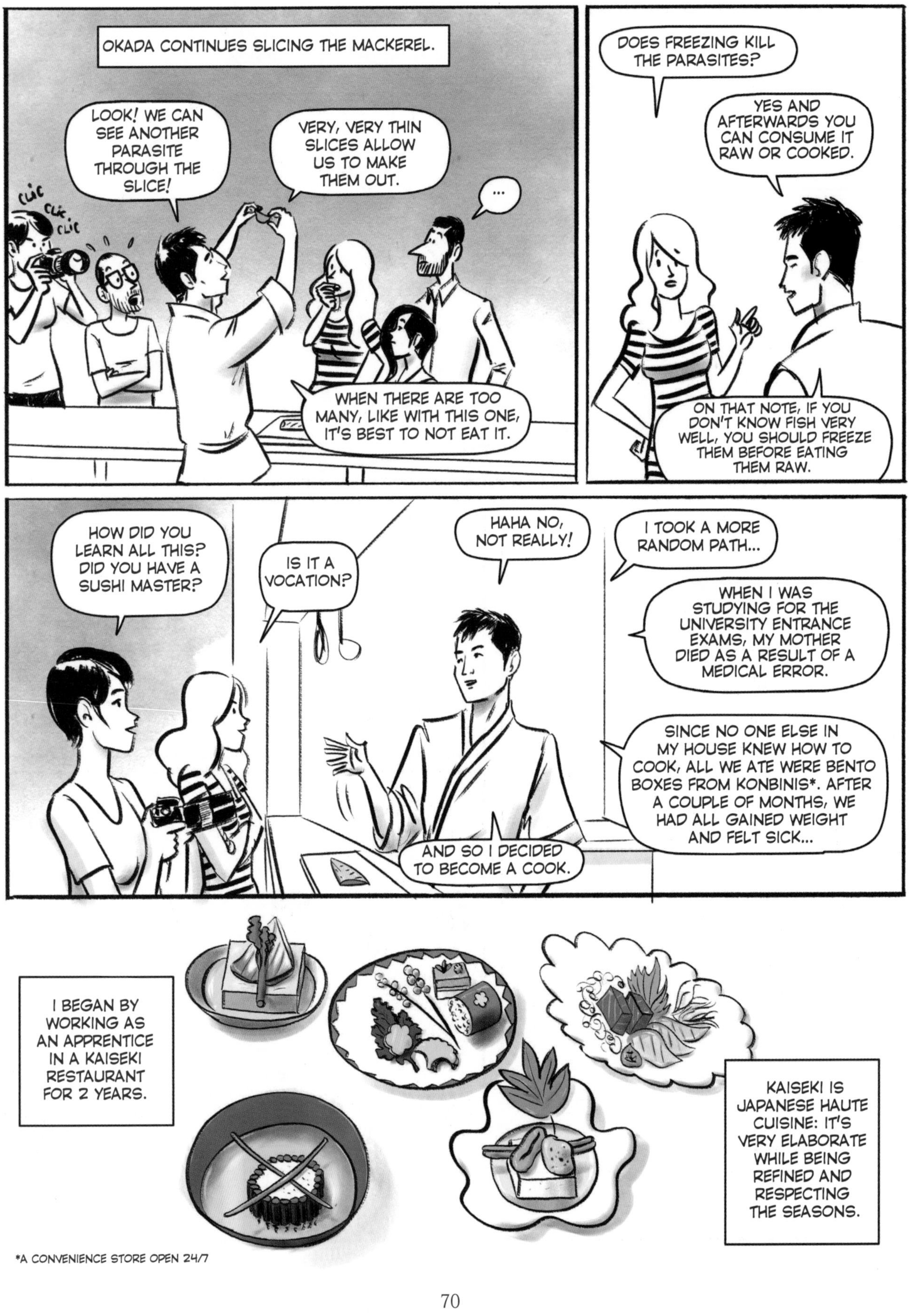
OKADA CONTINUES SLICING THE MACKEREL.
CLIC CLIC CLIC
LOOK! WE CAN SEE ANOTHER PARASITE THROUGH THE SLICE!
VERY, VERY THIN SLICES ALLOW US TO MAKE THEM OUT.
...
WHEN THERE ARE TOO MANY, LIKE WITH THIS ONE, IT'S BEST TO NOT EAT IT.
DOES FREEZING KILL THE PARASITES?
YES AND AFTERWARDS YOU CAN CONSUME IT RAW OR COOKED.
ON THAT NOTE, IF YOU DON'T KNOW FISH VERY WELL, YOU SHOULD FREEZE THEM BEFORE EATING THEM RAW.
HOW DID YOU LEARN ALL THIS? DID YOU HAVE A SUSHI MASTER?
IS IT A VOCATION?
HAHA NO, NOT REALLY!
I TOOK A MORE RANDOM PATH...
WHEN I WAS STUDYING FOR THE UNIVERSITY ENTRANCE EXAMS, MY MOTHER DIED AS A RESULT OF A MEDICAL ERROR.
SINCE NO ONE ELSE IN MY HOUSE KNEW HOW TO COOK, ALL WE ATE WERE BENTO BOXES FROM KONBINIS*. AFTER A COUPLE OF MONTHS, WE HAD ALL GAINED WEIGHT AND FELT SICK...
AND SO I DECIDED TO BECOME A COOK.
I BEGAN BY WORKING AS AN APPRENTICE IN A KAISEKI RESTAURANT FOR 2 YEARS.
KAISEKI IS JAPANESE HAUTE CUISINE: IT'S VERY ELABORATE WHILE BEING REFINED AND RESPECTING THE SEASONS.

*A CONVENIENCE STORE OPEN 24/7

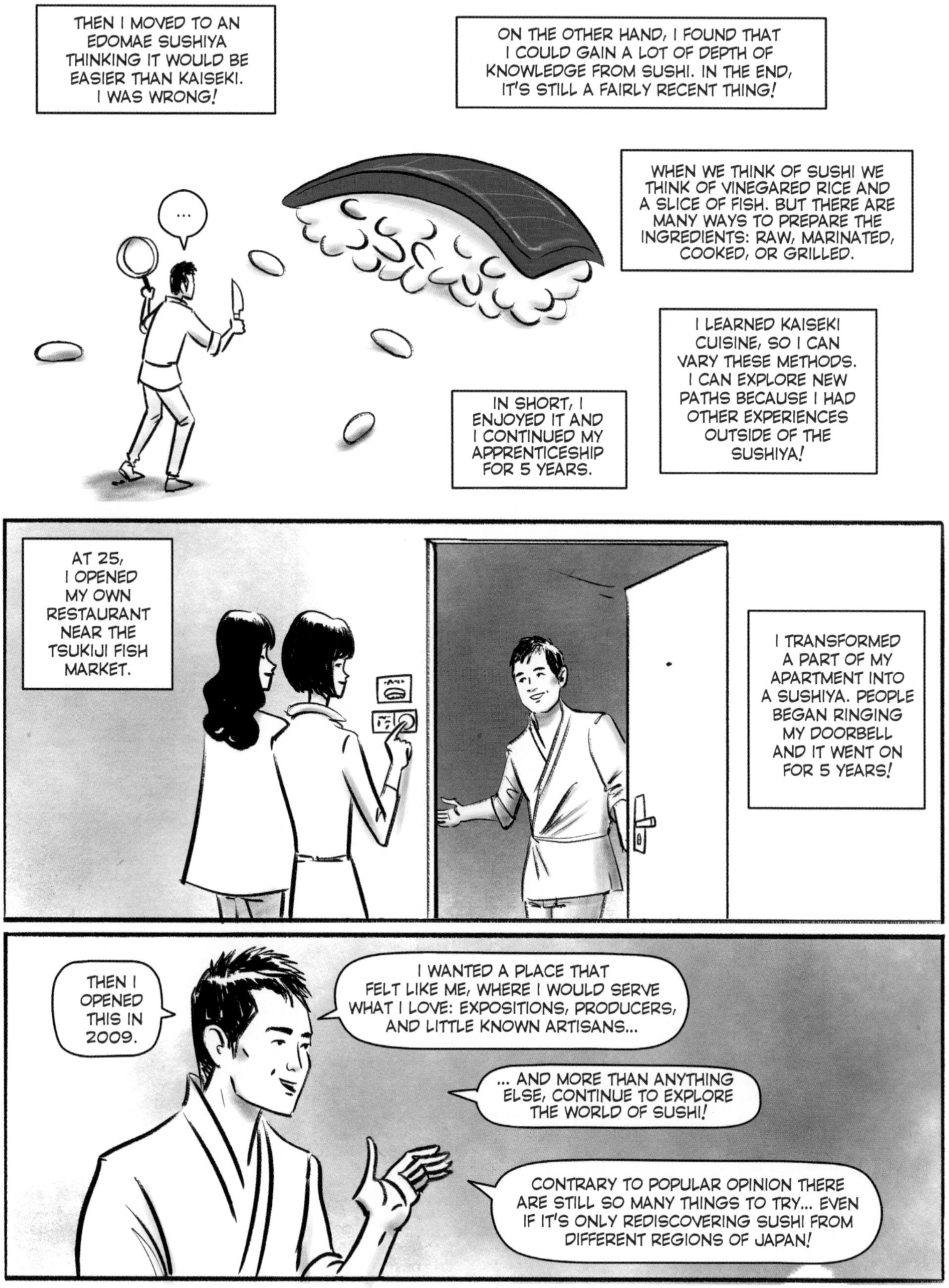
THEN I MOVED TO AN EDOMAE SUSHIYA THINKING IT WOULD BE EASIER THAN KAISEKI. I WAS WRONG!
ON THE OTHER HAND, I FOUND THAT I COULD GAIN A LOT OF DEPTH OF KNOWLEDGE FROM SUSHI. IN THE END, IT'S STILL A FAIRLY RECENT THING!
...
WHEN WE THINK OF SUSHI WE THINK OF VINEGARED RICE AND A SLICE OF FISH. BUT THERE ARE MANY WAYS TO PREPARE THE INGREDIENTS: RAW, MARINATED, COOKED, OR GRILLED.
I LEARNED KAISEKI CUISINE, SO I CAN VARY THESE METHODS. I CAN EXPLORE NEW PATHS BECAUSE I HAD OTHER EXPERIENCES OUTSIDE OF THE SUSHIYA!
IN SHORT, I ENJOYED IT AND I CONTINUED MY APPRENTICESHIP FOR 5 YEARS.
AT 25, I OPENED MY OWN RESTAURANT NEAR THE TSUKIJI FISH MARKET.
I TRANSFORMED A PART OF MY APARTMENT INTO A SUSHIYA. PEOPLE BEGAN RINGING MY DOORBELL AND IT WENT ON FOR 5 YEARS!
THEN I OPENED THIS IN 2009.
I WANTED A PLACE THAT FELT LIKE ME, WHERE I WOULD SERVE WHAT I LOVE: EXPOSITIONS, PRODUCERS, AND LITTLE KNOWN ARTISANS...
... AND MORE THAN ANYTHING ELSE, CONTINUE TO EXPLORE THE WORLD OF SUSHI!
CONTRARY TO POPULAR OPINION THERE ARE STILL SO MANY THINGS TO TRY... EVEN IF IT'S ONLY REDISCOVERING SUSHI FROM DIFFERENT REGIONS OF JAPAN!

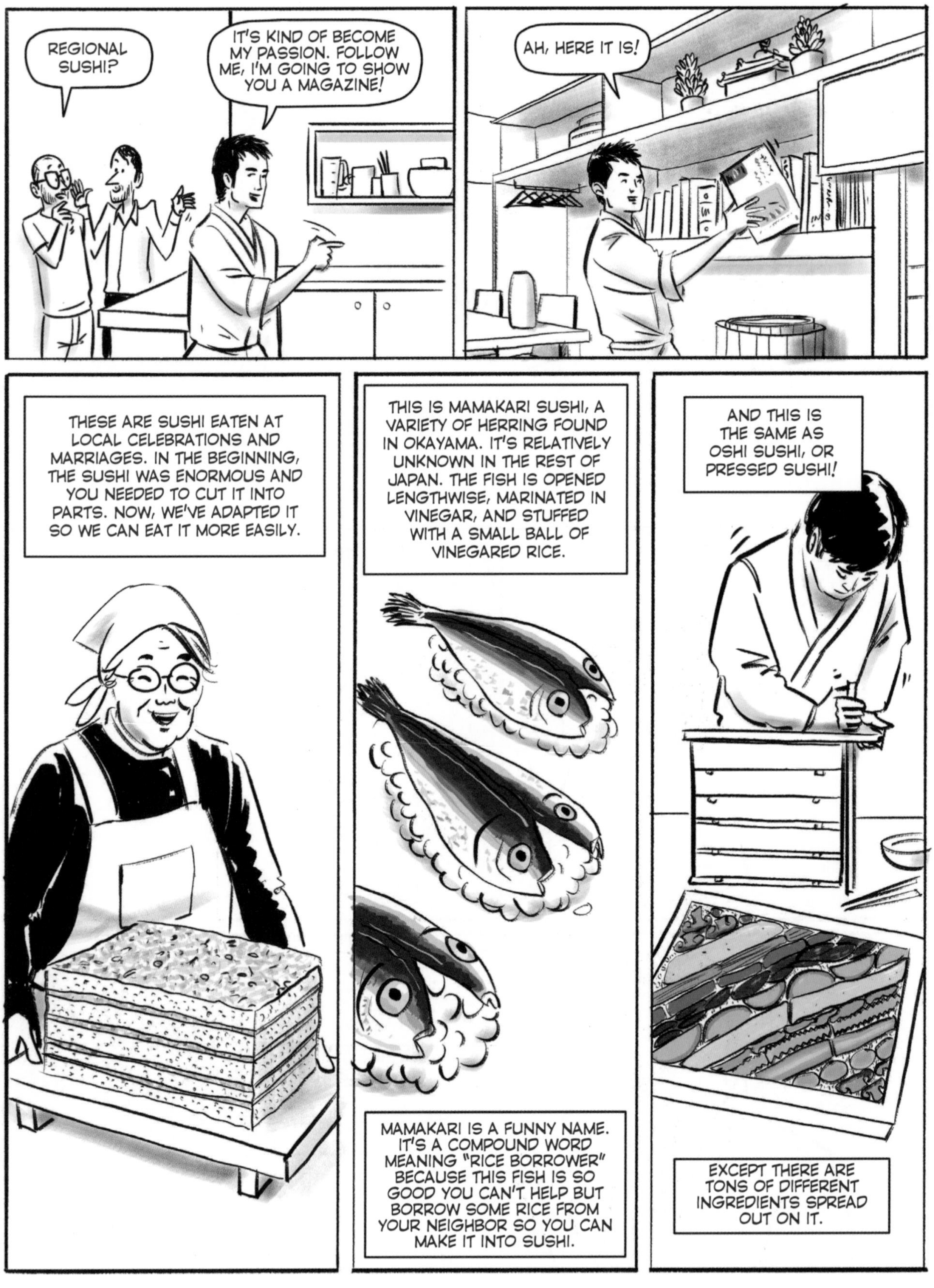
REGIONAL SUSHI?
IT'S KIND OF BECOME MY PASSION. FOLLOW ME, I'M GOING TO SHOW YOU A MAGAZINE!
AH, HERE IT IS!
THESE ARE SUSHI EATEN AT LOCAL CELEBRATIONS AND MARRIAGES. IN THE BEGINNING, THE SUSHI WAS ENORMOUS AND YOU NEEDED TO CUT IT INTO PARTS. NOW, WE'VE ADAPTED IT SO WE CAN EAT IT MORE EASILY.
THIS IS MAMAKARI SUSHI, A VARIETY OF HERRING FOUND IN OKAYAMA. IT'S RELATIVELY UNKNOWN IN THE REST OF JAPAN. THE FISH IS OPENED LENGTHWISE, MARINATED IN VINEGAR, AND STUFFED WITH A SMALL BALL OF VINEGARED RICE.
MAMAKARI IS A FUNNY NAME. IT'S A COMPOUND WORD MEANING "RICE BORROWER" BECAUSE THIS FISH IS SO GOOD YOU CAN'T HELP BUT BORROW SOME RICE FROM YOUR NEIGHBOR SO YOU CAN MAKE IT INTO SUSHI.
AND THIS IS THE SAME AS OSHI SUSHI, OR PRESSED SUSHI!
EXCEPT THERE ARE TONS OF DIFFERENT INGREDIENTS SPREAD OUT ON IT.

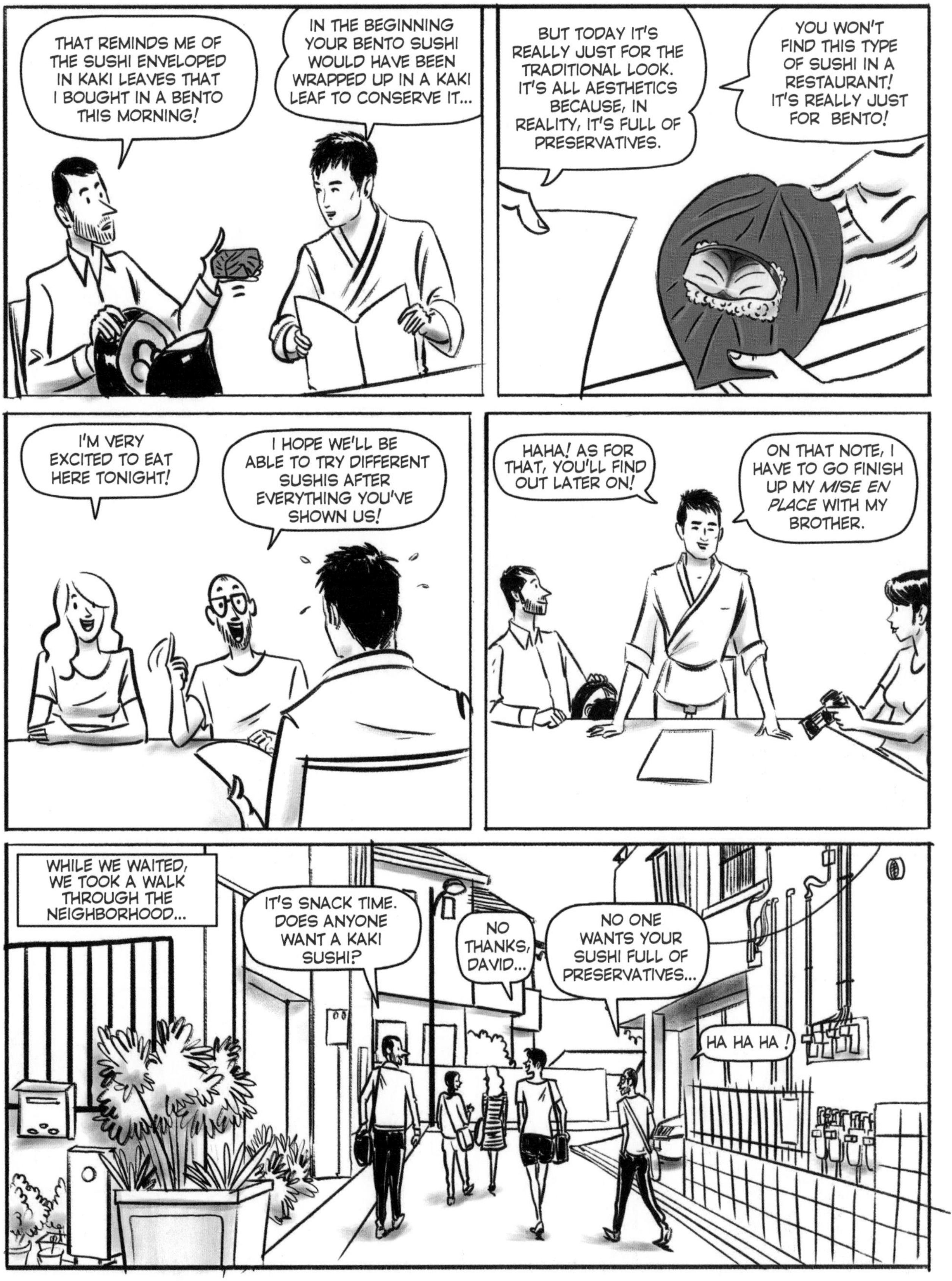
THAT REMINDS ME OF THE SUSHI ENVELOPED IN KAKI LEAVES THAT I BOUGHT IN A BENTO THIS MORNING!
IN THE BEGINNING YOUR BENTO SUSHI WOULD HAVE BEEN WRAPPED UP IN A KAKI LEAF TO CONSERVE IT...
BUT TODAY IT'S REALLY JUST FOR THE TRADITIONAL LOOK. IT'S ALL AESTHETICS BECAUSE, IN REALITY, IT'S FULL OF PRESERVATIVES.
YOU WON'T FIND THIS TYPE OF SUSHI IN A RESTAURANT! IT'S REALLY JUST FOR BENTO!
I'M VERY EXCITED TO EAT HERE TONIGHT!
I HOPE WE'LL BE ABLE TO TRY DIFFERENT SUSHIS AFTER EVERYTHING YOU'VE SHOWN US!
HAHA! AS FOR THAT, YOU'LL FIND OUT LATER ON!
ON THAT NOTE, I HAVE TO GO FINISH UP MY *MISE EN PLACE* WITH MY BROTHER.
WHILE WE WAITED, WE TOOK A WALK THROUGH THE NEIGHBORHOOD...
IT'S SNACK TIME. DOES ANYONE WANT A KAKI SUSHI?
NO THANKS, DAVID...
NO ONE WANTS YOUR SUSHI FULL OF PRESERVATIVES...
HA HA HA!

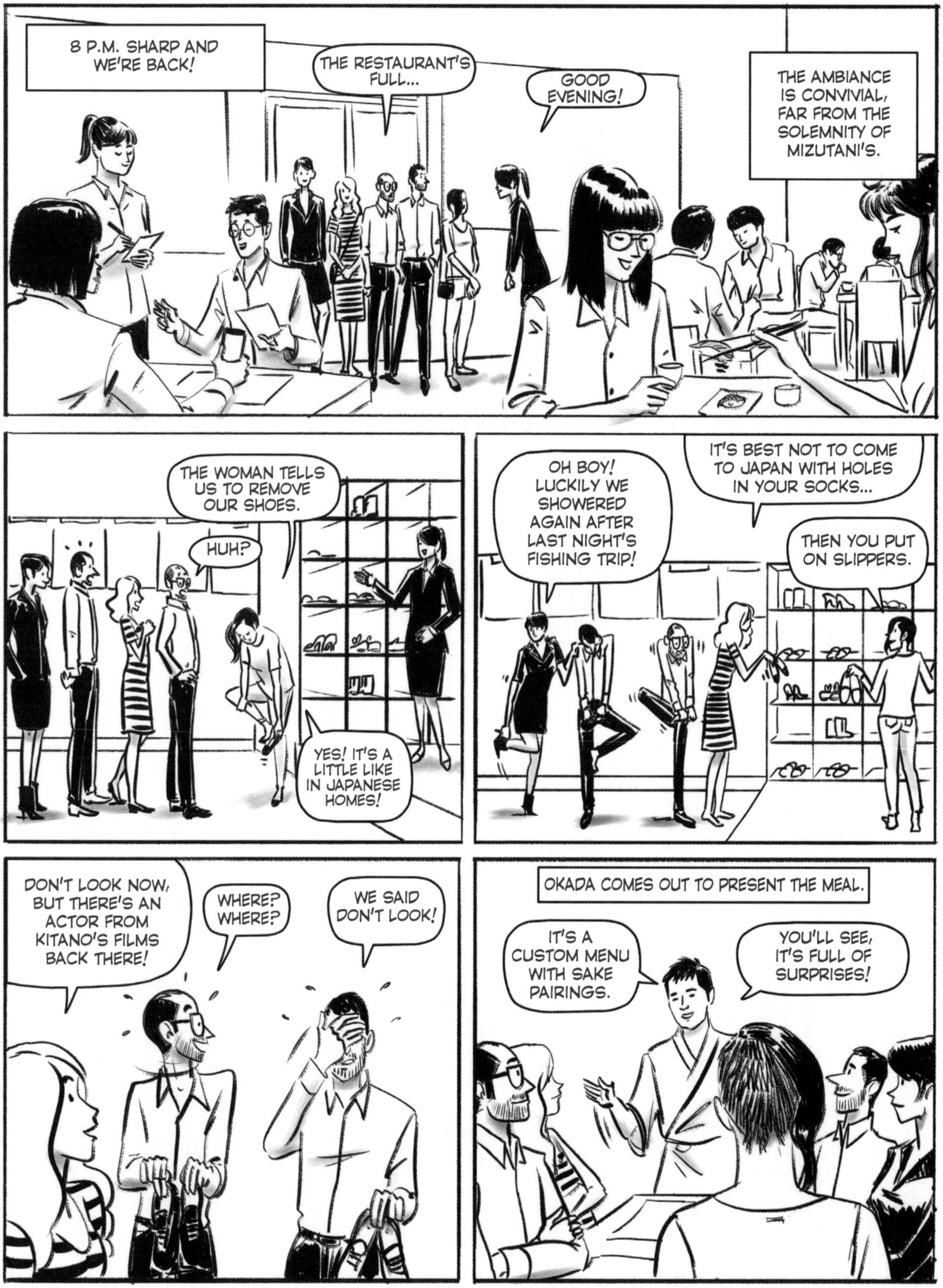
8 P.M. SHARP AND WE'RE BACK!
THE RESTAURANT'S FULL...
GOOD EVENING!
THE AMBIANCE IS CONVIVIAL, FAR FROM THE SOLEMNITY OF MIZUTANI'S.
THE WOMAN TELLS US TO REMOVE OUR SHOES.
HUH?
YES! IT'S A LITTLE LIKE IN JAPANESE HOMES!
OH BOY! LUCKILY WE SHOWERED AGAIN AFTER LAST NIGHT'S FISHING TRIP!
IT'S BEST NOT TO COME TO JAPAN WITH HOLES IN YOUR SOCKS...
THEN YOU PUT ON SLIPPERS.
DON'T LOOK NOW, BUT THERE'S AN ACTOR FROM KITANO'S FILMS BACK THERE!
WHERE? WHERE?
WE SAID DON'T LOOK!
OKADA COMES OUT TO PRESENT THE MEAL.
IT'S A CUSTOM MENU WITH SAKE PAIRINGS.
YOU'LL SEE, IT'S FULL OF SURPRISES!

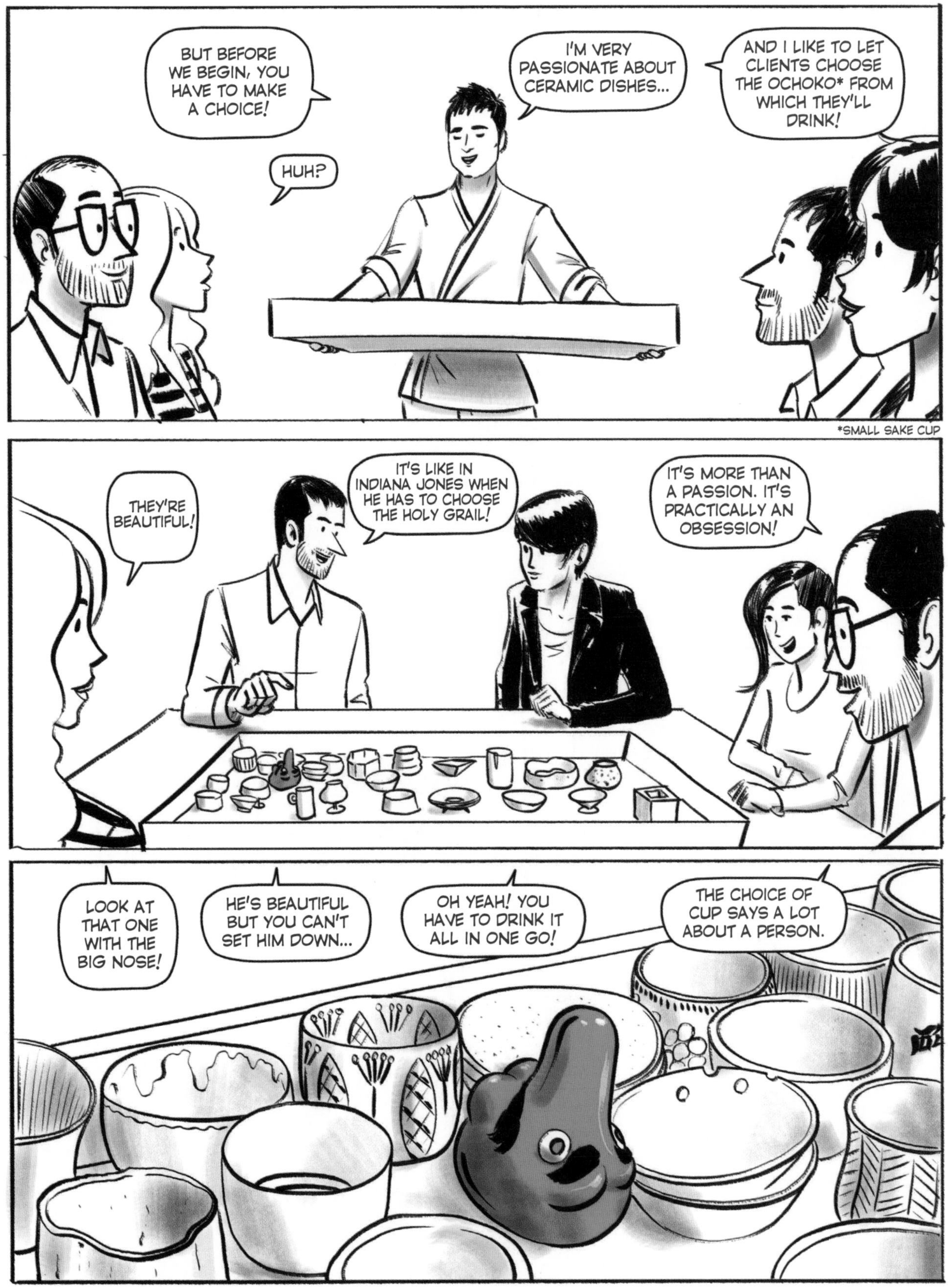
BUT BEFORE WE BEGIN, YOU HAVE TO MAKE A CHOICE!
HUH?
I'M VERY PASSIONATE ABOUT CERAMIC DISHES...
AND I LIKE TO LET CLIENTS CHOOSE THE OCHOKO* FROM WHICH THEY'LL DRINK!
THEY'RE BEAUTIFUL!
IT'S LIKE IN INDIANA JONES WHEN HE HAS TO CHOOSE THE HOLY GRAIL!
IT'S MORE THAN A PASSION. IT'S PRACTICALLY AN OBSESSION!
LOOK AT THAT ONE WITH THE BIG NOSE!
HE'S BEAUTIFUL BUT YOU CAN'T SET HIM DOWN...
OH YEAH! YOU HAVE TO DRINK IT ALL IN ONE GO!
THE CHOICE OF CUP SAYS A LOT ABOUT A PERSON.

*SMALL SAKE CUP

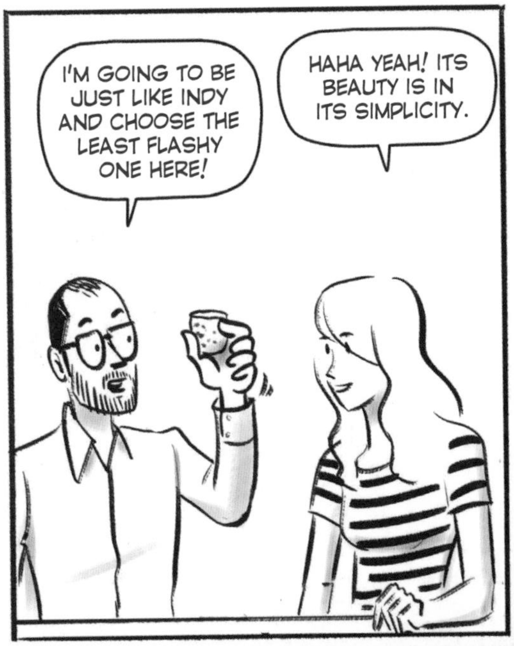
I'M GOING TO BE JUST LIKE INDY AND CHOOSE THE LEAST FLASHY ONE HERE!
HAHA YEAH! ITS BEAUTY IS IN ITS SIMPLICITY.

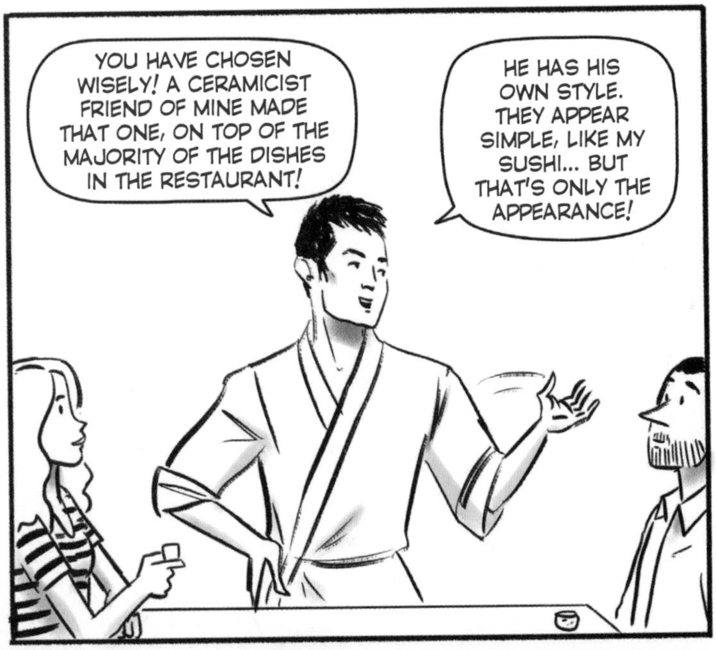
YOU HAVE CHOSEN WISELY! A CERAMICIST FRIEND OF MINE MADE THAT ONE, ON TOP OF THE MAJORITY OF THE DISHES IN THE RESTAURANT!
HE HAS HIS OWN STYLE. THEY APPEAR SIMPLE, LIKE MY SUSHI... BUT THAT'S ONLY THE APPEARANCE!

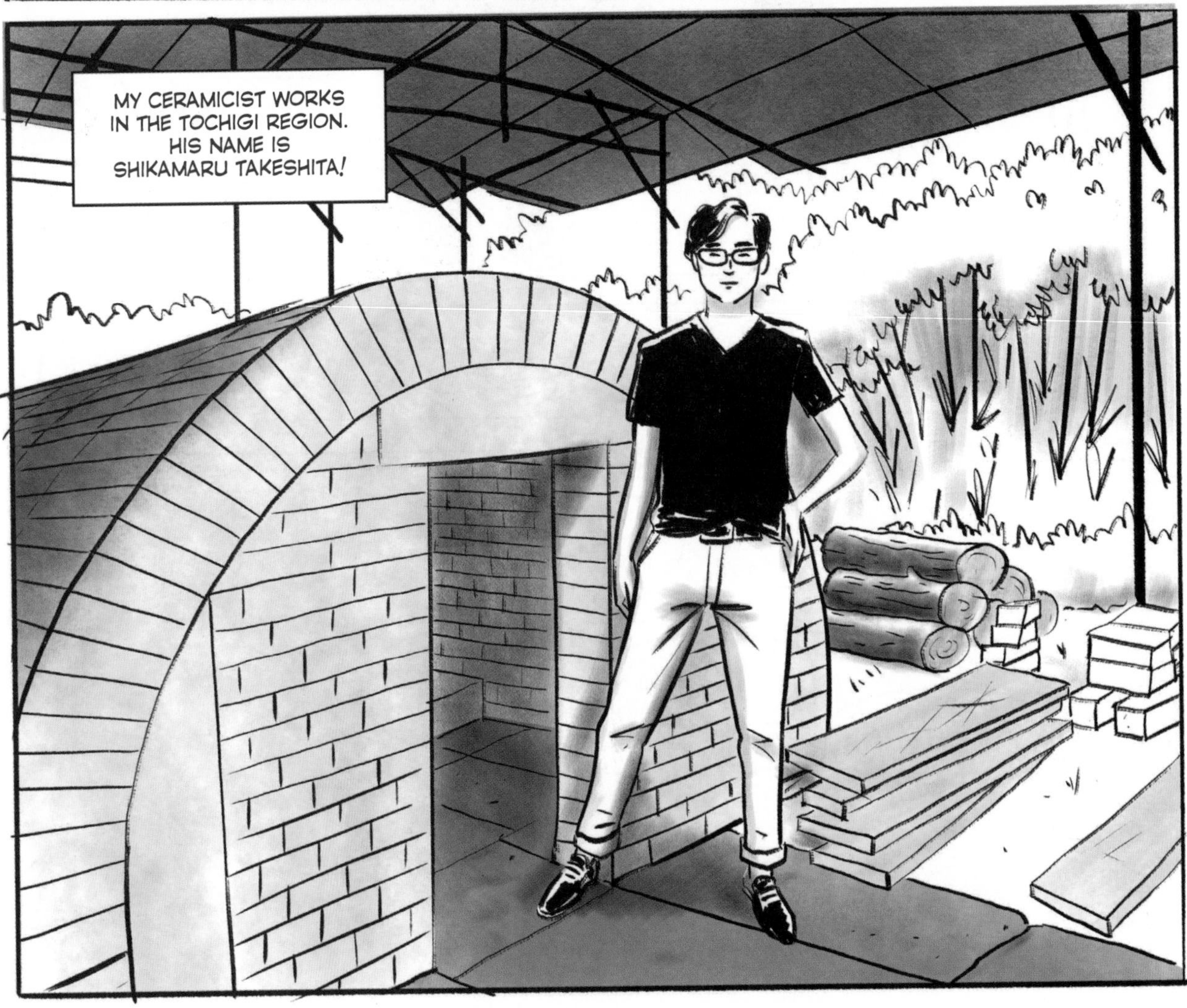
MY CERAMICIST WORKS IN THE TOCHIGI REGION. HIS NAME IS SHIKAMARU TAKESHITA!

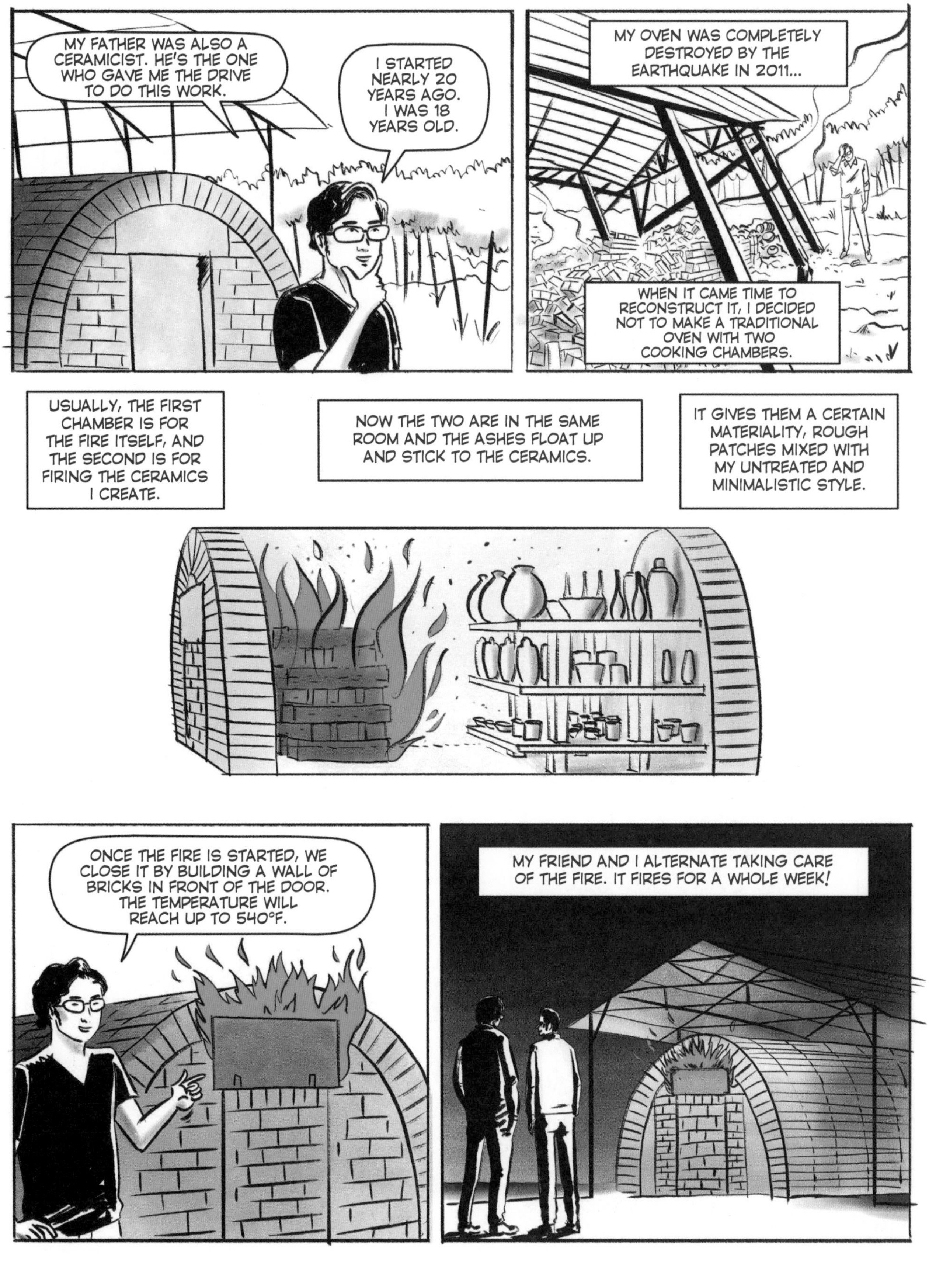
MY FATHER WAS ALSO A CERAMICIST. HE'S THE ONE WHO GAVE ME THE DRIVE TO DO THIS WORK.
I STARTED NEARLY 20 YEARS AGO. I WAS 18 YEARS OLD.
MY OVEN WAS COMPLETELY DESTROYED BY THE EARTHQUAKE IN 2011...
WHEN IT CAME TIME TO RECONSTRUCT IT, I DECIDED NOT TO MAKE A TRADITIONAL OVEN WITH TWO COOKING CHAMBERS.
USUALLY, THE FIRST CHAMBER IS FOR THE FIRE ITSELF, AND THE SECOND IS FOR FIRING THE CERAMICS I CREATE.
NOW THE TWO ARE IN THE SAME ROOM AND THE ASHES FLOAT UP AND STICK TO THE CERAMICS.
IT GIVES THEM A CERTAIN MATERIALITY, ROUGH PATCHES MIXED WITH MY UNTREATED AND MINIMALISTIC STYLE.
ONCE THE FIRE IS STARTED, WE CLOSE IT BY BUILDING A WALL OF BRICKS IN FRONT OF THE DOOR. THE TEMPERATURE WILL REACH UP TO 540°F.
MY FRIEND AND I ALTERNATE TAKING CARE OF THE FIRE. IT FIRES FOR A WHOLE WEEK!

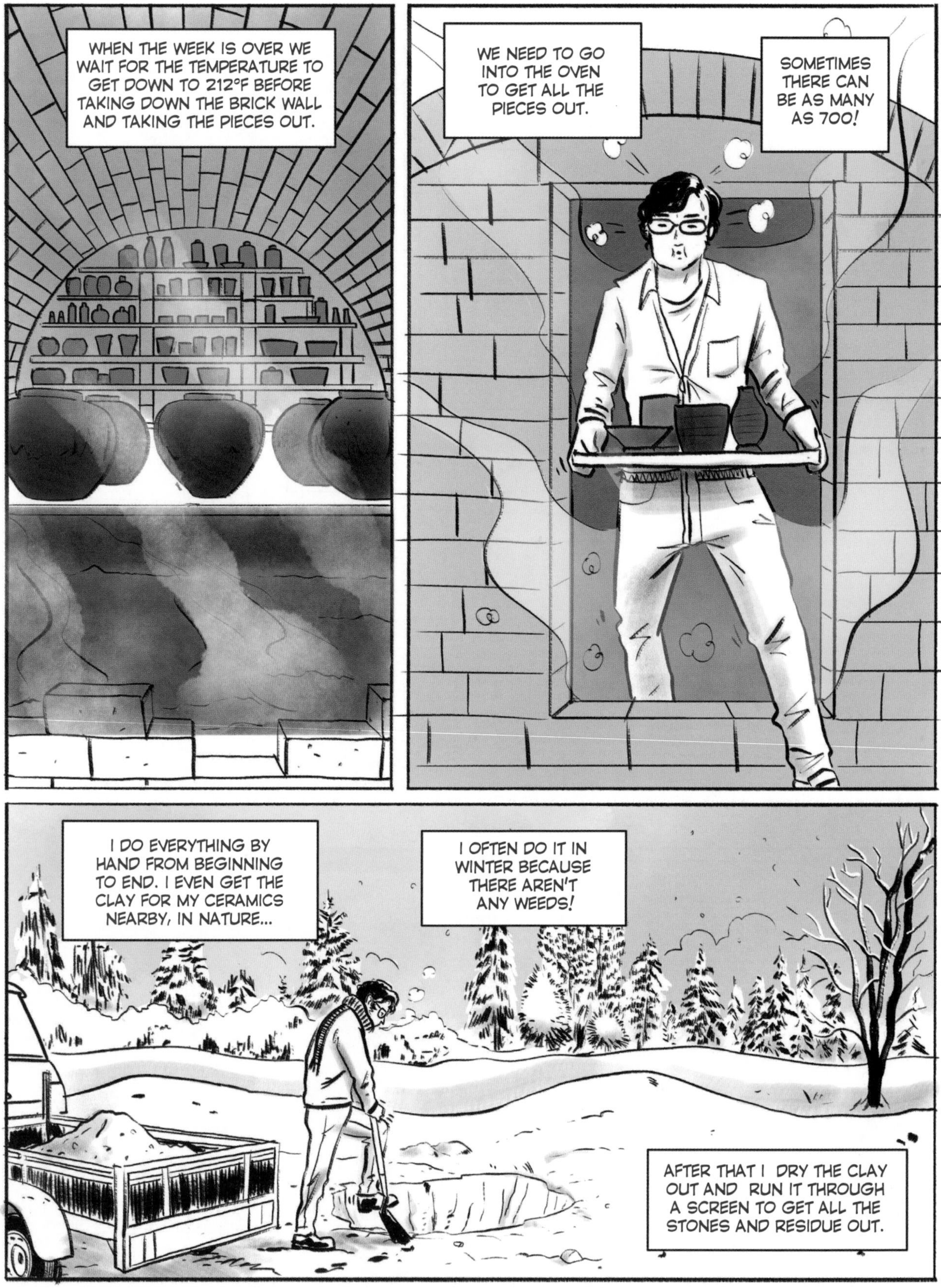
WHEN THE WEEK IS OVER WE WAIT FOR THE TEMPERATURE TO GET DOWN TO 212°F BEFORE TAKING DOWN THE BRICK WALL AND TAKING THE PIECES OUT.
WE NEED TO GO INTO THE OVEN TO GET ALL THE PIECES OUT.
SOMETIMES THERE CAN BE AS MANY AS 700!
I DO EVERYTHING BY HAND FROM BEGINNING TO END. I EVEN GET THE CLAY FOR MY CERAMICS NEARBY, IN NATURE...
I OFTEN DO IT IN WINTER BECAUSE THERE AREN'T ANY WEEDS!
AFTER THAT I DRY THE CLAY OUT AND RUN IT THROUGH A SCREEN TO GET ALL THE STONES AND RESIDUE OUT.

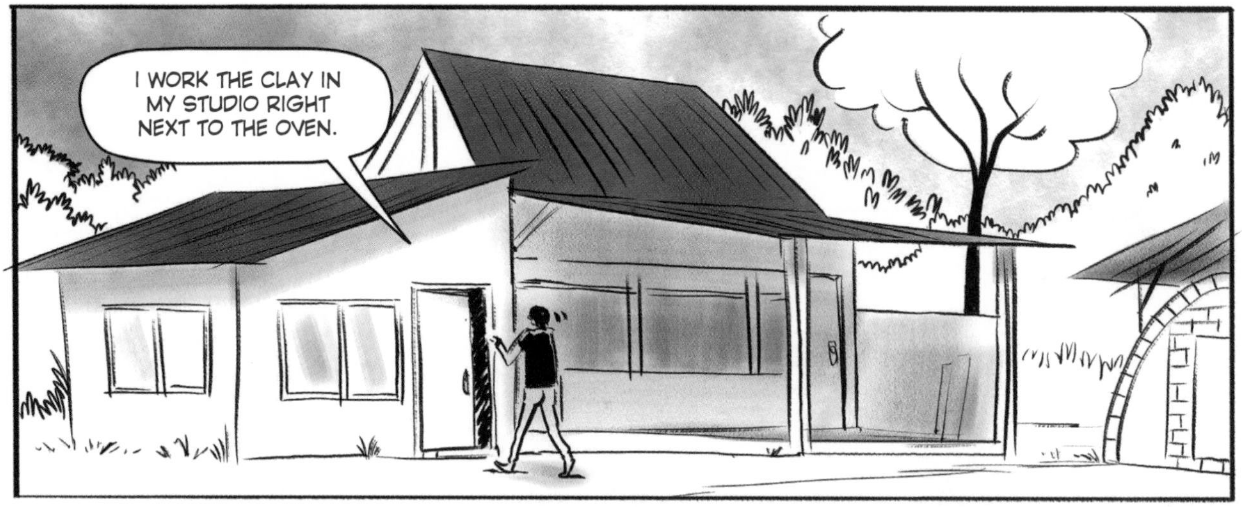
I WORK THE CLAY IN MY STUDIO RIGHT NEXT TO THE OVEN.

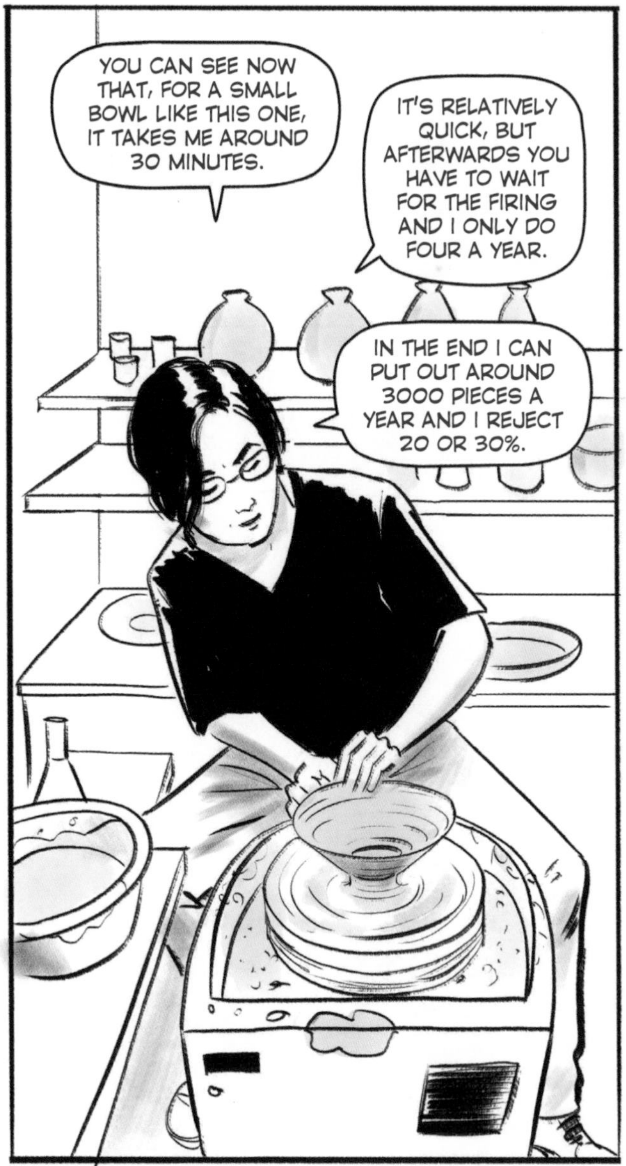
YOU CAN SEE NOW THAT, FOR A SMALL BOWL LIKE THIS ONE, IT TAKES ME AROUND 30 MINUTES.
IT'S RELATIVELY QUICK, BUT AFTERWARDS YOU HAVE TO WAIT FOR THE FIRING AND I ONLY DO FOUR A YEAR.
IN THE END I CAN PUT OUT AROUND 3000 PIECES A YEAR AND I REJECT 20 OR 30%.

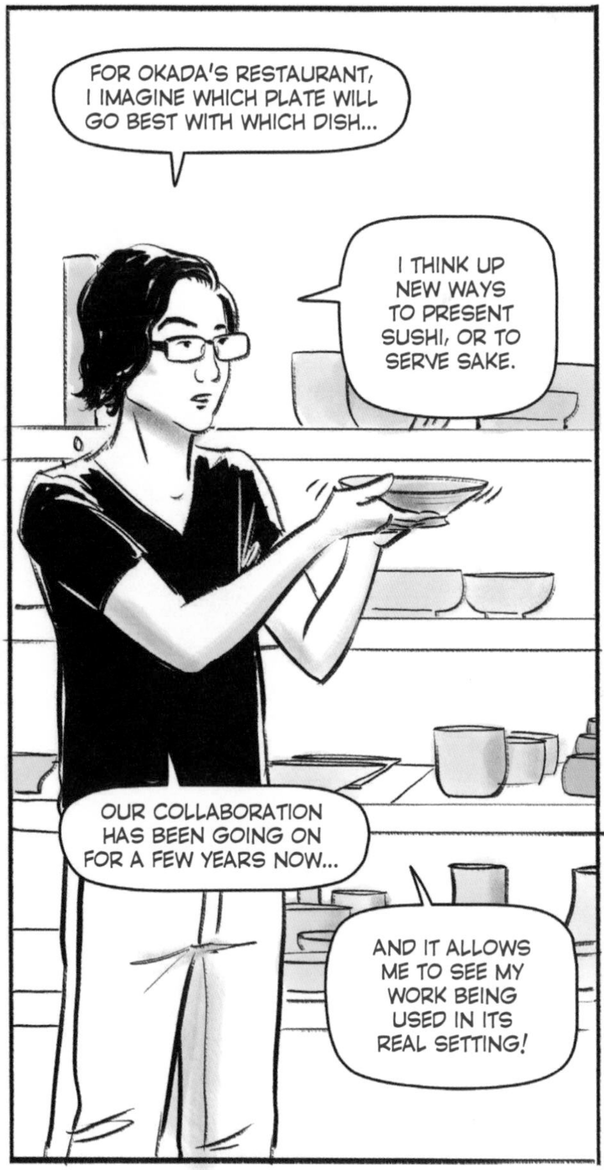
FOR OKADA'S RESTAURANT, I IMAGINE WHICH PLATE WILL GO BEST WITH WHICH DISH...
I THINK UP NEW WAYS TO PRESENT SUSHI, OR TO SERVE SAKE.
OUR COLLABORATION HAS BEEN GOING ON FOR A FEW YEARS NOW...
AND IT ALLOWS ME TO SEE MY WORK BEING USED IN ITS REAL SETTING!

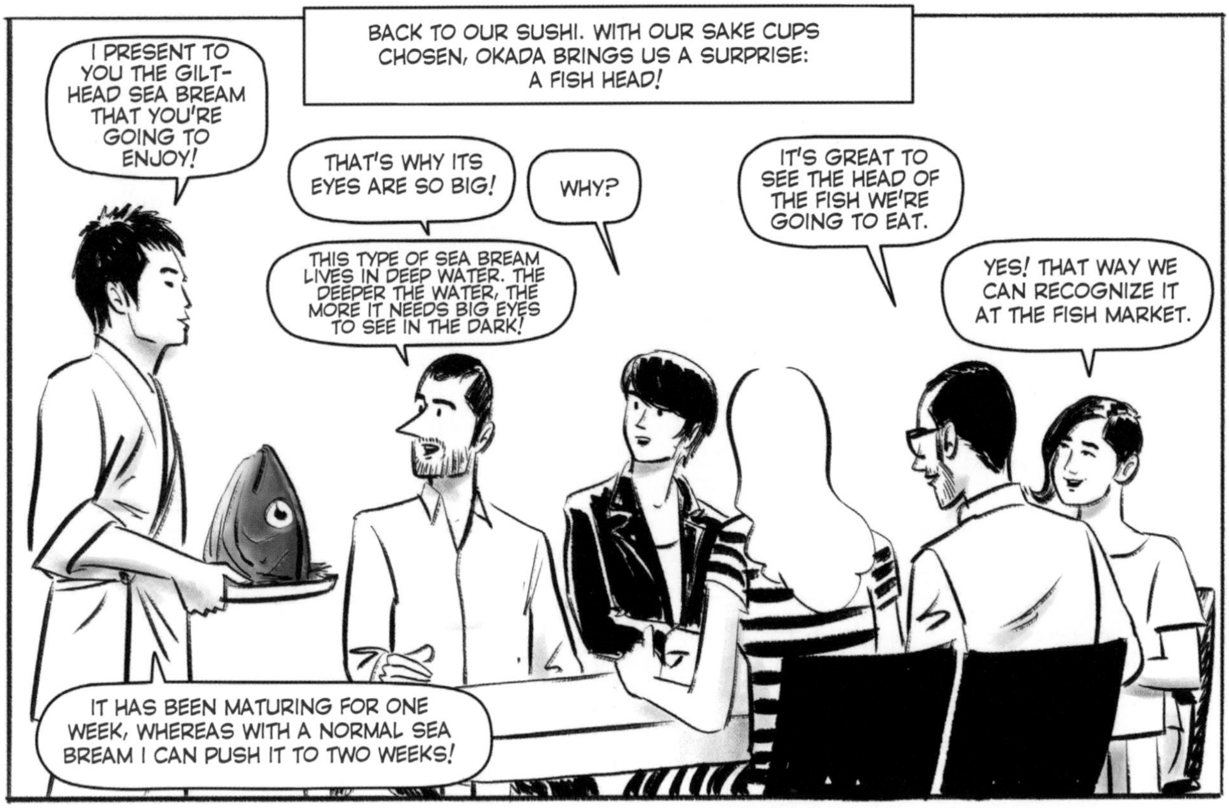
BACK TO OUR SUSHI. WITH OUR SAKE CUPS CHOSEN, OKADA BRINGS US A SURPRISE: A FISH HEAD!
I PRESENT TO YOU THE GILT-HEAD SEA BREAM THAT YOU'RE GOING TO ENJOY!
THAT'S WHY ITS EYES ARE SO BIG!
WHY?
THIS TYPE OF SEA BREAM LIVES IN DEEP WATER. THE DEEPER THE WATER, THE MORE IT NEEDS BIG EYES TO SEE IN THE DARK!
IT'S GREAT TO SEE THE HEAD OF THE FISH WE'RE GOING TO EAT.
YES! THAT WAY WE CAN RECOGNIZE IT AT THE FISH MARKET.
IT HAS BEEN MATURING FOR ONE WEEK, WHEREAS WITH A NORMAL SEA BREAM I CAN PUSH IT TO TWO WEEKS!

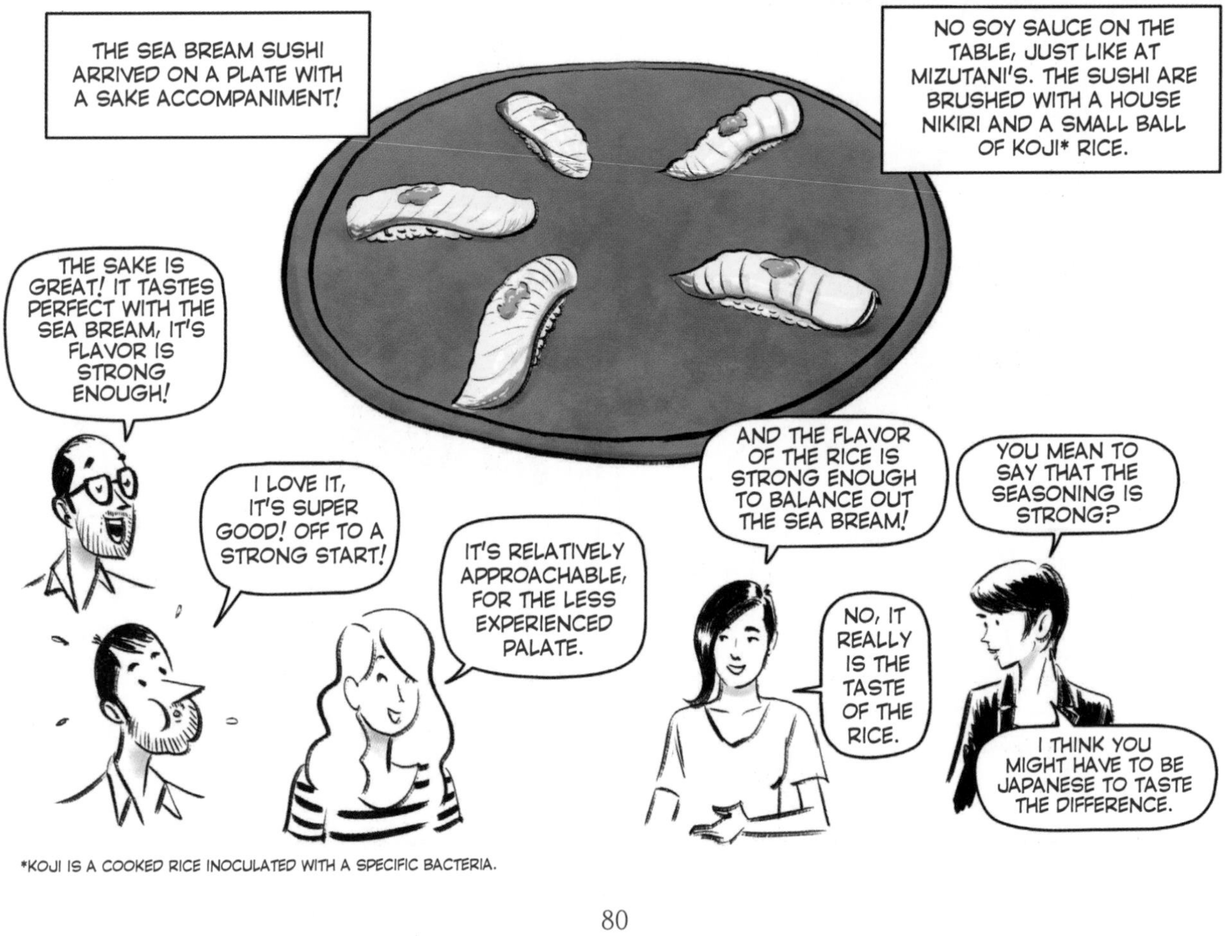
THE SEA BREAM SUSHI ARRIVED ON A PLATE WITH A SAKE ACCOMPANIMENT!
NO SOY SAUCE ON THE TABLE, JUST LIKE AT MIZUTANI'S. THE SUSHI ARE BRUSHED WITH A HOUSE NIKIRI AND A SMALL BALL OF KOJI* RICE.
THE SAKE IS GREAT! IT TASTES PERFECT WITH THE SEA BREAM, IT'S FLAVOR IS STRONG ENOUGH!
I LOVE IT, IT'S SUPER GOOD! OFF TO A STRONG START!
IT'S RELATIVELY APPROACHABLE, FOR THE LESS EXPERIENCED PALATE.
AND THE FLAVOR OF THE RICE IS STRONG ENOUGH TO BALANCE OUT THE SEA BREAM!
YOU MEAN TO SAY THAT THE SEASONING IS STRONG?
NO, IT REALLY IS THE TASTE OF THE RICE.
I THINK YOU MIGHT HAVE TO BE JAPANESE TO TASTE THE DIFFERENCE.

*KOJI IS A COOKED RICE INOCULATED WITH A SPECIFIC BACTERIA.

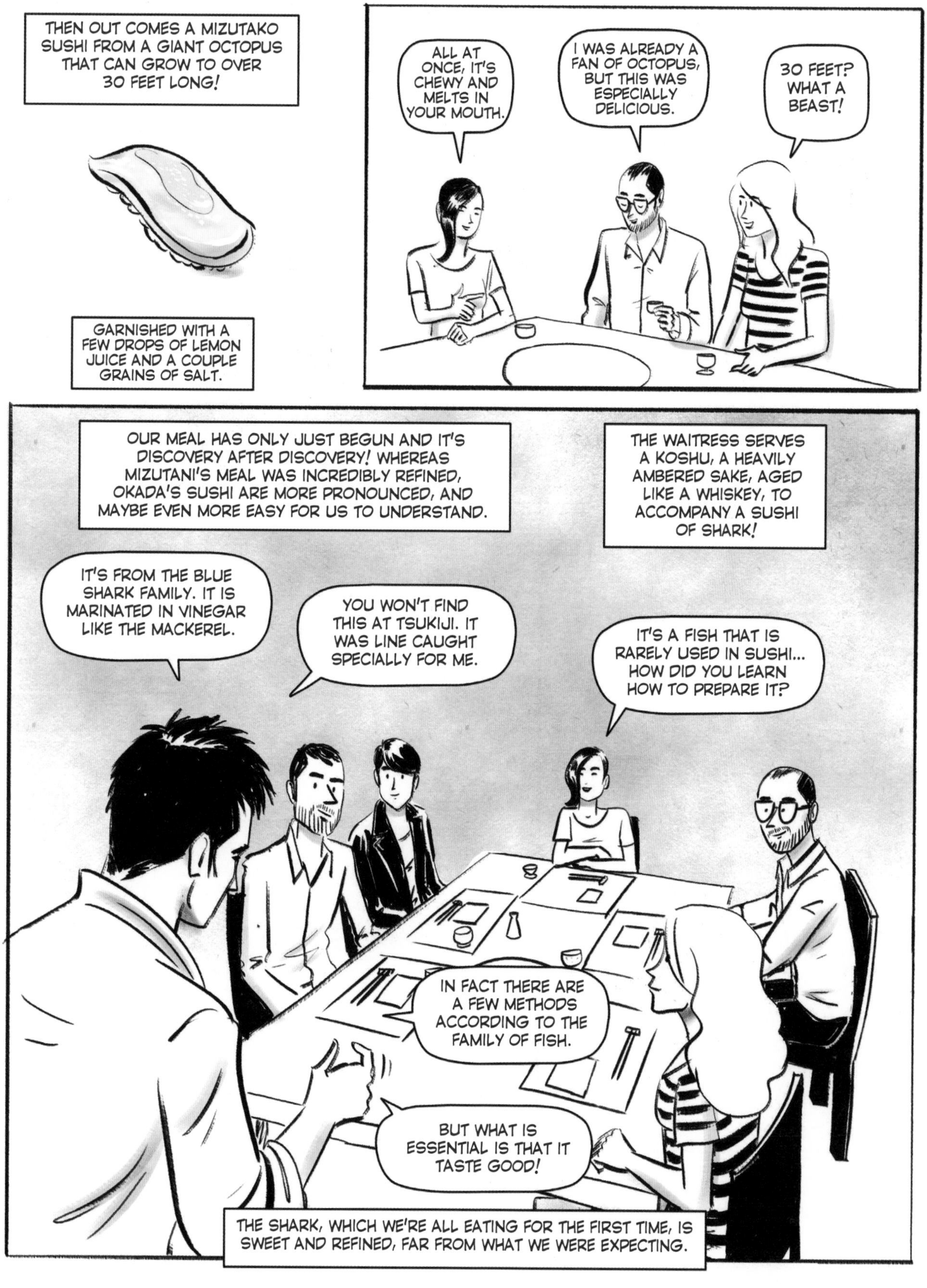
THEN OUT COMES A MIZUTAKO SUSHI FROM A GIANT OCTOPUS THAT CAN GROW TO OVER 30 FEET LONG!
GARNISHED WITH A FEW DROPS OF LEMON JUICE AND A COUPLE GRAINS OF SALT.
ALL AT ONCE, IT'S CHEWY AND MELTS IN YOUR MOUTH.
I WAS ALREADY A FAN OF OCTOPUS, BUT THIS WAS ESPECIALLY DELICIOUS.
30 FEET? WHAT A BEAST!
OUR MEAL HAS ONLY JUST BEGUN AND IT'S DISCOVERY AFTER DISCOVERY! WHEREAS MIZUTANI'S MEAL WAS INCREDIBLY REFINED, OKADA'S SUSHI ARE MORE PRONOUNCED, AND MAYBE EVEN MORE EASY FOR US TO UNDERSTAND.
THE WAITRESS SERVES A KOSHU, A HEAVILY AMBERED SAKE, AGED LIKE A WHISKEY, TO ACCOMPANY A SUSHI OF SHARK!
IT'S FROM THE BLUE SHARK FAMILY. IT IS MARINATED IN VINEGAR LIKE THE MACKEREL.
YOU WON'T FIND THIS AT TSUKIJI. IT WAS LINE CAUGHT SPECIALLY FOR ME.
IT'S A FISH THAT IS RARELY USED IN SUSHI... HOW DID YOU LEARN HOW TO PREPARE IT?
IN FACT THERE ARE A FEW METHODS ACCORDING TO THE FAMILY OF FISH.
BUT WHAT IS ESSENTIAL IS THAT IT TASTE GOOD!
THE SHARK, WHICH WE'RE ALL EATING FOR THE FIRST TIME, IS SWEET AND REFINED, FAR FROM WHAT WE WERE EXPECTING.

THE CHEF RETURNS HOLDING A "SWORD" FROM A SWORDFISH.

MANY FISHERMEN ARE INJURED OR DIE FROM THIS POINTY BEAK.

THE PROBLEM IS THAT AS SOON AS YOU HAVE IT ON THE END OF YOUR LINE, THE SWORDFISH JUMPS ALL OVER THE PLACE. IT CAN JUMP REALLY FAR!

SOMETIMES IT FALLS INTO THE BOAT. THAT'S WHEN IT BECOMES DANGEROUS!

TO ACCOMPANY THE SWORDFISH SUSHI, THEY SERVE US A NIGORIZAKE, AN UNFILTERED SAKE WHICH MAKES IT MILKY!

I'VE NEVER TASTED SO MANY GOOD AND DIFFERENT SAKE!

ME NEITHER!

THEY'RE NOTHING LIKE WHAT I'VE HAD AT HOME...

JAPANESE SAKE RESEMBLES MUCH MORE CLOSELY THE DIVERSITY OF THE WINES OF FRANCE AND RANGES FROM 12 TO 17 PERCENT ALCOHOL.

ANOTHER FISH I HAD NEVER TASTED AS SUSHI...

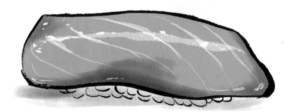

THE SWORDFISH'S STRIATED FLESH IS MARINATED FOR SEVERAL HOURS IN A NIKIRI SHOYU* SAUCE, THE SAME ONE THE CHEF USES TO SEASON THE OTHER FISH RIGHT BEFORE HE SERVES THEM.

*SAUCE MADE UP OF SHOYU, MIRIN, AND SAKE.

AMIDST SUSHI, SAKE, AND FISH HEADS, THE MEAL CONTINUES!

A VISUAL MARVEL: A SUSHI OF AKOYA PEARL OYSTER MARINATED IN MISO AND TAMARI. THIS MOLLUSK PRODUCES JAPAN'S MOST BEAUTIFUL PEARLS.

NEXT, A KING MACKEREL SUSHI.

THE FISH IS GRILLED WITH A BLOWTORCH AND SERVED WITH AN UNPASTEURIZED SAKE.

I LOVE THAT LIGHTLY GRILLED FLAVOR.

AND IT'S SO DIFFERENT FROM THE MACKEREL SUSHI I KNOW.

AND IT'S PAIRED PERFECTLY WITH THE SAKE!

THE CHEF BRINGS OUT A CURIOUS PLATTER...

I LOVE TRYING NEW THINGS!

HERE ARE STRIPED MARLIN SUSHI BURGERS WITH MUSHROOMS, LETTUCE, AND FIG JAM.

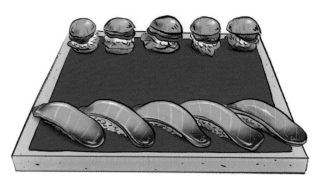

THEN I MARINATE IT IN A MIX OF SOY SAUCE AND MIRIN.

TO MAKE IT I POUR BOILING WATER ON THE FILET TO COOK THE OUTSIDE AND TO TIGHTEN THE PROTEINS.

ON THE OTHER SIDE, STRIPED MARLIN SUSHI.

IT'S THE SAME FISH BUT PREPARED AS YUSHIMO ZUKE!

IT GIVES US A LIGHT TASTE OF THE MARINADE AND THE FLASH COOKING KEEPS THE SAUCE FROM PENETRATING INSIDE THE FIBERS.

NOW YOU DRINK THIS SAKE WITH THESE SUSHI...

GREAT! MORE SAKE!

MY GOODNESS MORE SAKE!

83

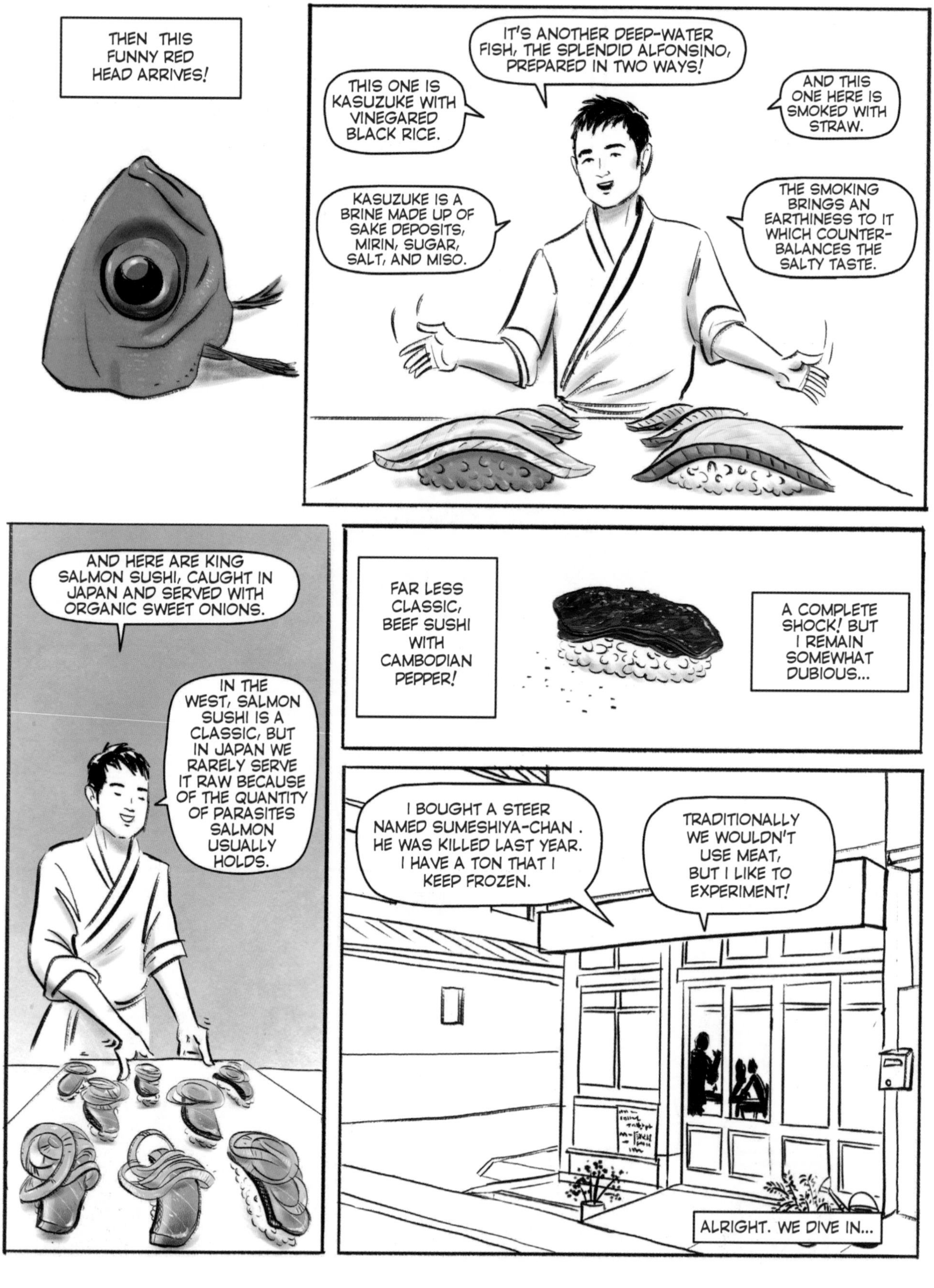
THEN THIS FUNNY RED HEAD ARRIVES!
IT'S ANOTHER DEEP-WATER FISH, THE SPLENDID ALFONSINO, PREPARED IN TWO WAYS!
THIS ONE IS KASUZUKE WITH VINEGARED BLACK RICE.
AND THIS ONE HERE IS SMOKED WITH STRAW.
KASUZUKE IS A BRINE MADE UP OF SAKE DEPOSITS, MIRIN, SUGAR, SALT, AND MISO.
THE SMOKING BRINGS AN EARTHINESS TO IT WHICH COUNTER-BALANCES THE SALTY TASTE.
AND HERE ARE KING SALMON SUSHI, CAUGHT IN JAPAN AND SERVED WITH ORGANIC SWEET ONIONS.
IN THE WEST, SALMON SUSHI IS A CLASSIC, BUT IN JAPAN WE RARELY SERVE IT RAW BECAUSE OF THE QUANTITY OF PARASITES SALMON USUALLY HOLDS.
FAR LESS CLASSIC, BEEF SUSHI WITH CAMBODIAN PEPPER!
A COMPLETE SHOCK! BUT I REMAIN SOMEWHAT DUBIOUS...
I BOUGHT A STEER NAMED SUMESHIYA-CHAN . HE WAS KILLED LAST YEAR. I HAVE A TON THAT I KEEP FROZEN.
TRADITIONALLY WE WOULDN'T USE MEAT, BUT I LIKE TO EXPERIMENT!
ALRIGHT. WE DIVE IN...

THE MEAT IS GRILLED ON TOP WITH STRONGLY PERFUMED MILLED PEPPER!

SO WHAT DO YOU THINK?

...

YUM

YUM

CAN I HAVE YOURS?

CONTINUING ON IN THE SERIES OF OUT OF WACK SUSHI, WE GET ROLL-YOUR-OWN MAKI.

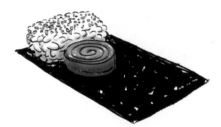

KANPYO MAKI. KANPYO IS SQUASH CUT INTO STRIPS AND DRIED. OKADA CURED IT FOR A LONG TIME IN A MIX OF SHOYU, SUGAR, SAKE, AND MIRIN.

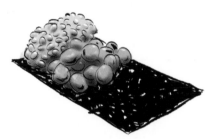

NATTO MAKI. QUITE UNIQUE TO OUR WESTERN PALATES. FERMENTED SOYBEANS WITH A GLUEY TEXTURE AND A -SLIGHTLY TOO- STRONG TASTE OF CHEESE...

IF THE CHEF ROLLED THE MAKI, BY THE TIME HE GOT TO THE TABLE THE NORI WOULD HAVE SOFTENED...

THIS WAY IT STAYS CRUNCHY, WHICH IS GREAT!

HOW DO YOU ROLL IT UP?

NO NEED TO ROLL. YOU JUST FOLD IT WITH YOUR FINGERS LIKE THIS!

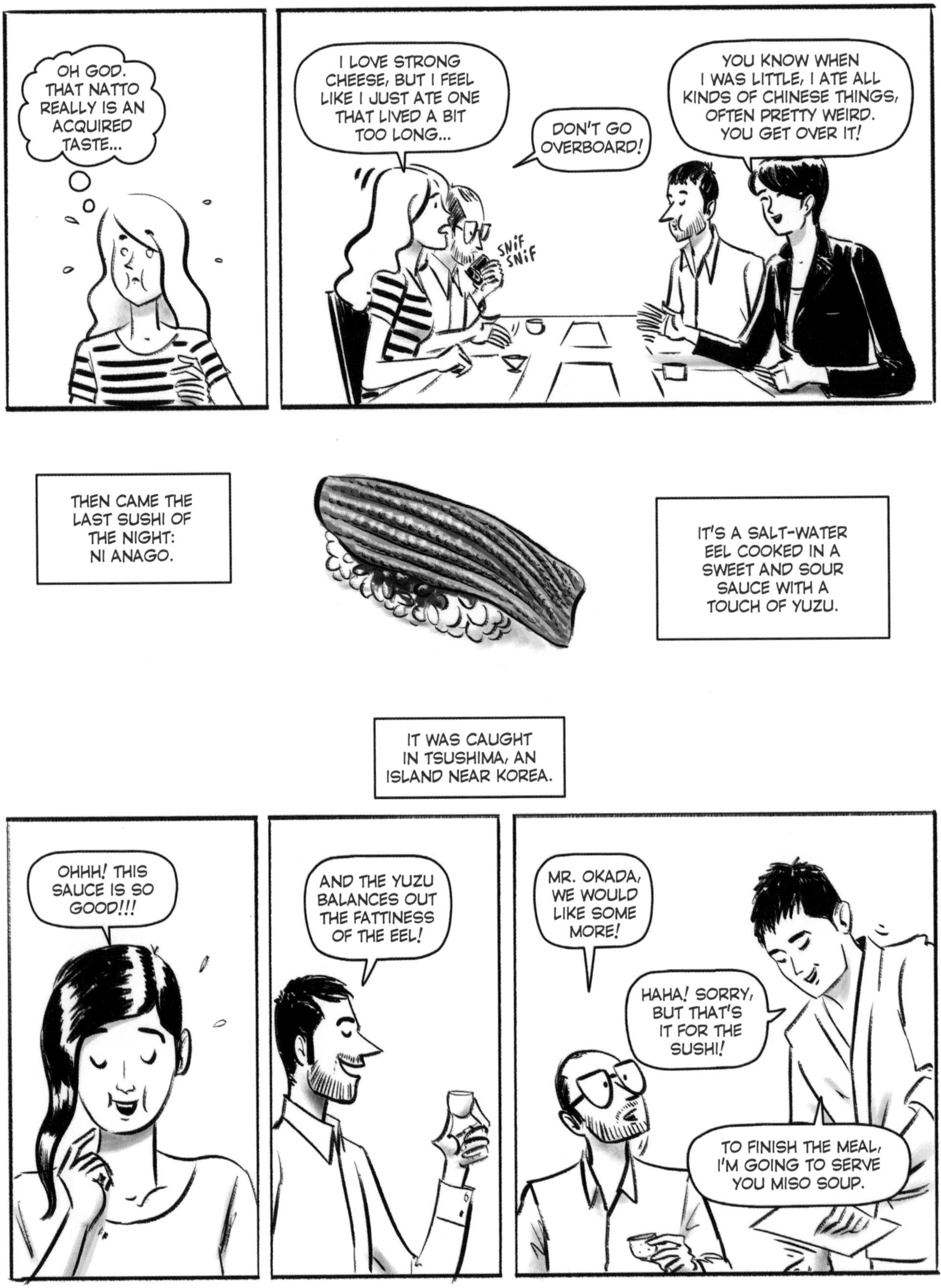
OH GOD. THAT NATTO REALLY IS AN ACQUIRED TASTE...
I LOVE STRONG CHEESE, BUT I FEEL LIKE I JUST ATE ONE THAT LIVED A BIT TOO LONG...
DON'T GO OVERBOARD!
SNIF SNIF
YOU KNOW WHEN I WAS LITTLE, I ATE ALL KINDS OF CHINESE THINGS, OFTEN PRETTY WEIRD. YOU GET OVER IT!
THEN CAME THE LAST SUSHI OF THE NIGHT: NI ANAGO.
IT'S A SALT-WATER EEL COOKED IN A SWEET AND SOUR SAUCE WITH A TOUCH OF YUZU.
IT WAS CAUGHT IN TSUSHIMA, AN ISLAND NEAR KOREA.
OHHH! THIS SAUCE IS SO GOOD!!!
AND THE YUZU BALANCES OUT THE FATTINESS OF THE EEL!
MR. OKADA, WE WOULD LIKE SOME MORE!
HAHA! SORRY, BUT THAT'S IT FOR THE SUSHI!
TO FINISH THE MEAL, I'M GOING TO SERVE YOU MISO SOUP.

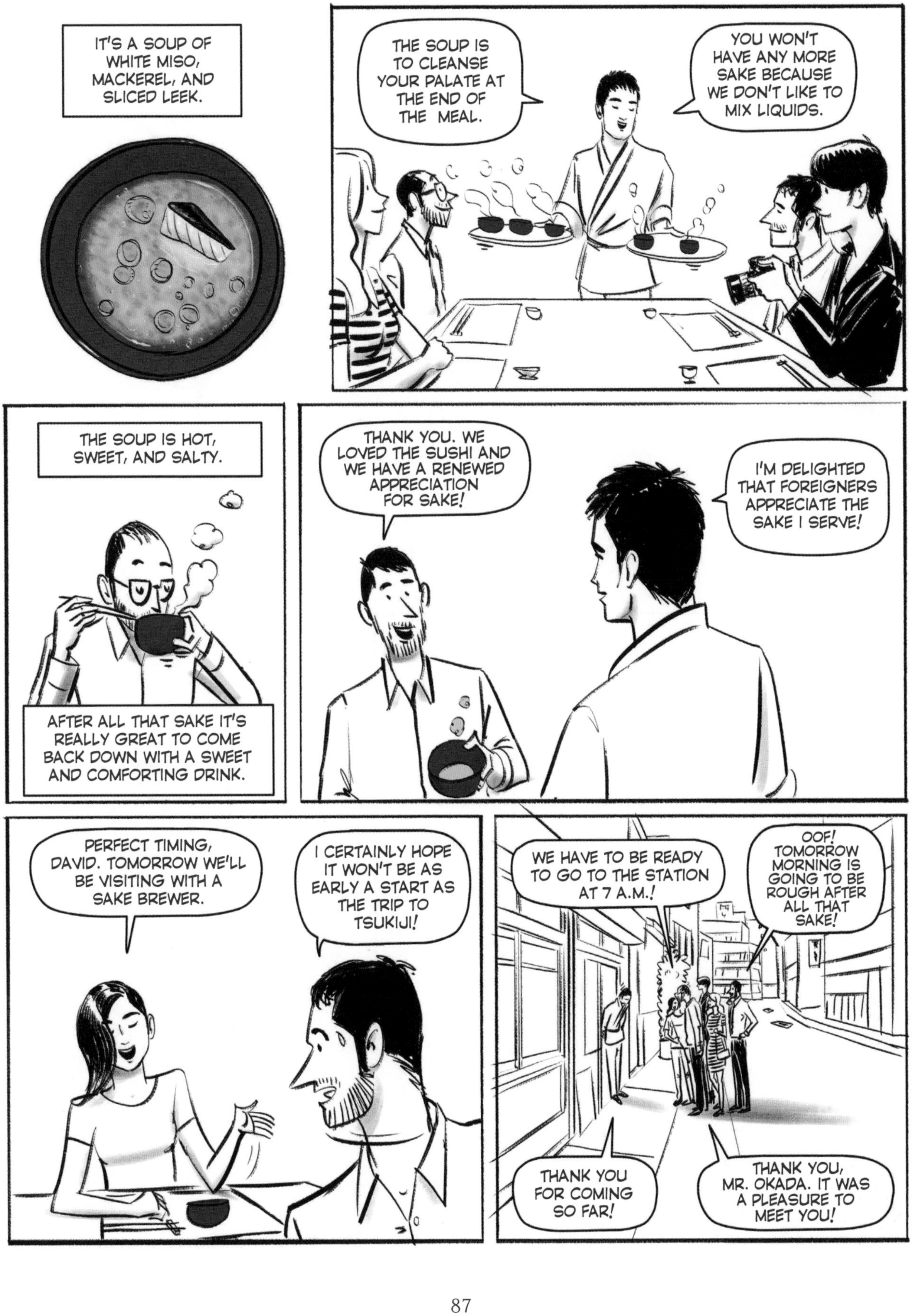
IT'S A SOUP OF WHITE MISO, MACKEREL, AND SLICED LEEK.
THE SOUP IS TO CLEANSE YOUR PALATE AT THE END OF THE MEAL.
YOU WON'T HAVE ANY MORE SAKE BECAUSE WE DON'T LIKE TO MIX LIQUIDS.
THE SOUP IS HOT, SWEET, AND SALTY.
AFTER ALL THAT SAKE IT'S REALLY GREAT TO COME BACK DOWN WITH A SWEET AND COMFORTING DRINK.
THANK YOU. WE LOVED THE SUSHI AND WE HAVE A RENEWED APPRECIATION FOR SAKE!
I'M DELIGHTED THAT FOREIGNERS APPRECIATE THE SAKE I SERVE!
PERFECT TIMING, DAVID. TOMORROW WE'LL BE VISITING WITH A SAKE BREWER.
I CERTAINLY HOPE IT WON'T BE AS EARLY A START AS THE TRIP TO TSUKIJI!
WE HAVE TO BE READY TO GO TO THE STATION AT 7 A.M.!
OOF! TOMORROW MORNING IS GOING TO BE ROUGH AFTER ALL THAT SAKE!
THANK YOU FOR COMING SO FAR!
THANK YOU, MR. OKADA. IT WAS A PLEASURE TO MEET YOU!

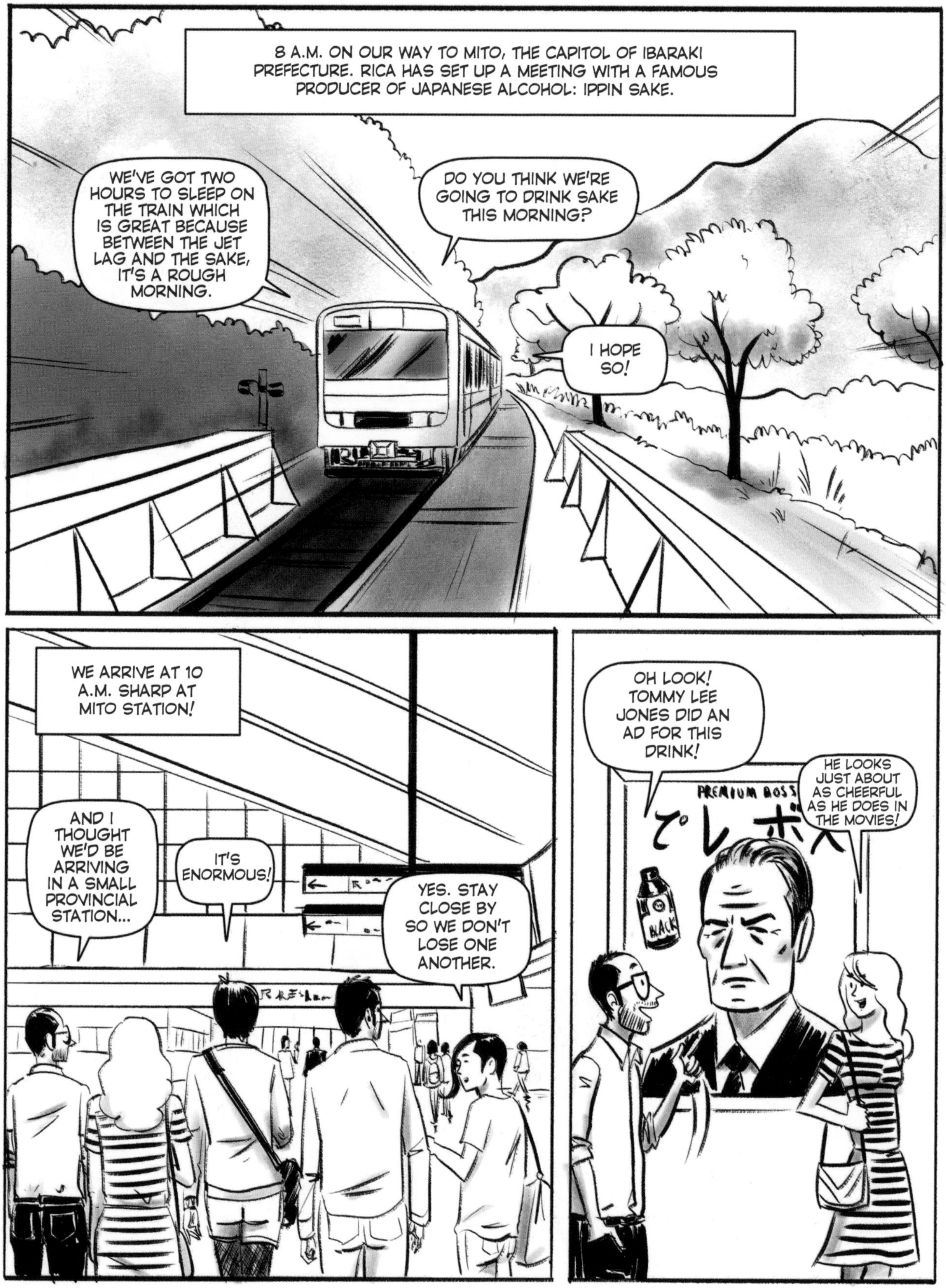
8 A.M. ON OUR WAY TO MITO, THE CAPITOL OF IBARAKI PREFECTURE. RICA HAS SET UP A MEETING WITH A FAMOUS PRODUCER OF JAPANESE ALCOHOL: IPPIN SAKE.
WE'VE GOT TWO HOURS TO SLEEP ON THE TRAIN WHICH IS GREAT BECAUSE BETWEEN THE JET LAG AND THE SAKE, IT'S A ROUGH MORNING.
DO YOU THINK WE'RE GOING TO DRINK SAKE THIS MORNING?
I HOPE SO!
WE ARRIVE AT 10 A.M. SHARP AT MITO STATION!
AND I THOUGHT WE'D BE ARRIVING IN A SMALL PROVINCIAL STATION...
IT'S ENORMOUS!
YES. STAY CLOSE BY SO WE DON'T LOSE ONE ANOTHER.
OH LOOK! TOMMY LEE JONES DID AN AD FOR THIS DRINK!
HE LOOKS JUST ABOUT AS CHEERFUL AS HE DOES IN THE MOVIES!
PREMIUM BOSS
BLACK

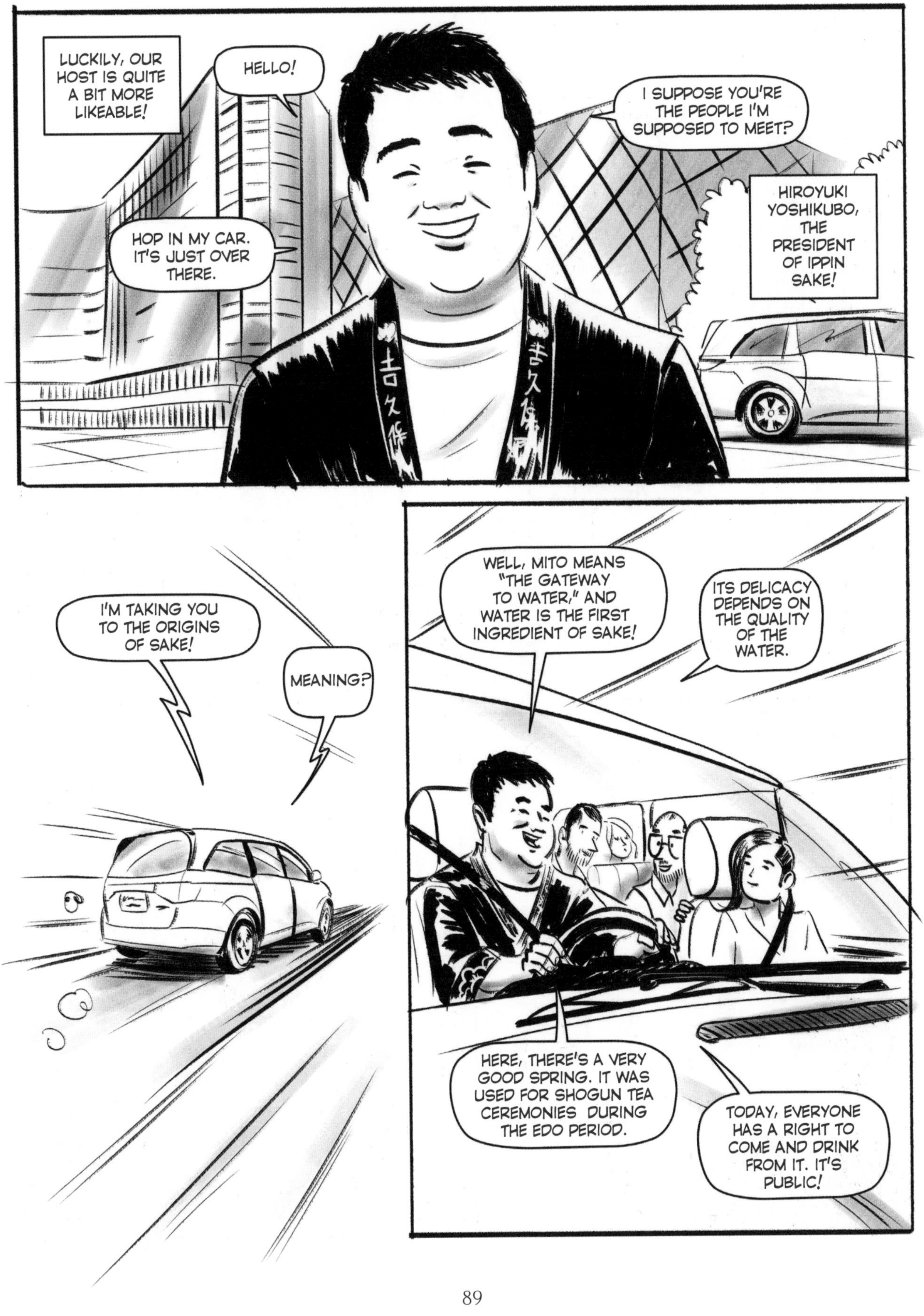
LUCKILY, OUR HOST IS QUITE A BIT MORE LIKEABLE!
HELLO!
I SUPPOSE YOU'RE THE PEOPLE I'M SUPPOSED TO MEET?
HIROYUKI YOSHIKUBO, THE PRESIDENT OF IPPIN SAKE!
HOP IN MY CAR. IT'S JUST OVER THERE.
I'M TAKING YOU TO THE ORIGINS OF SAKE!
MEANING?
WELL, MITO MEANS "THE GATEWAY TO WATER," AND WATER IS THE FIRST INGREDIENT OF SAKE!
ITS DELICACY DEPENDS ON THE QUALITY OF THE WATER.
HERE, THERE'S A VERY GOOD SPRING. IT WAS USED FOR SHOGUN TEA CEREMONIES DURING THE EDO PERIOD.
TODAY, EVERYONE HAS A RIGHT TO COME AND DRINK FROM IT. IT'S PUBLIC!

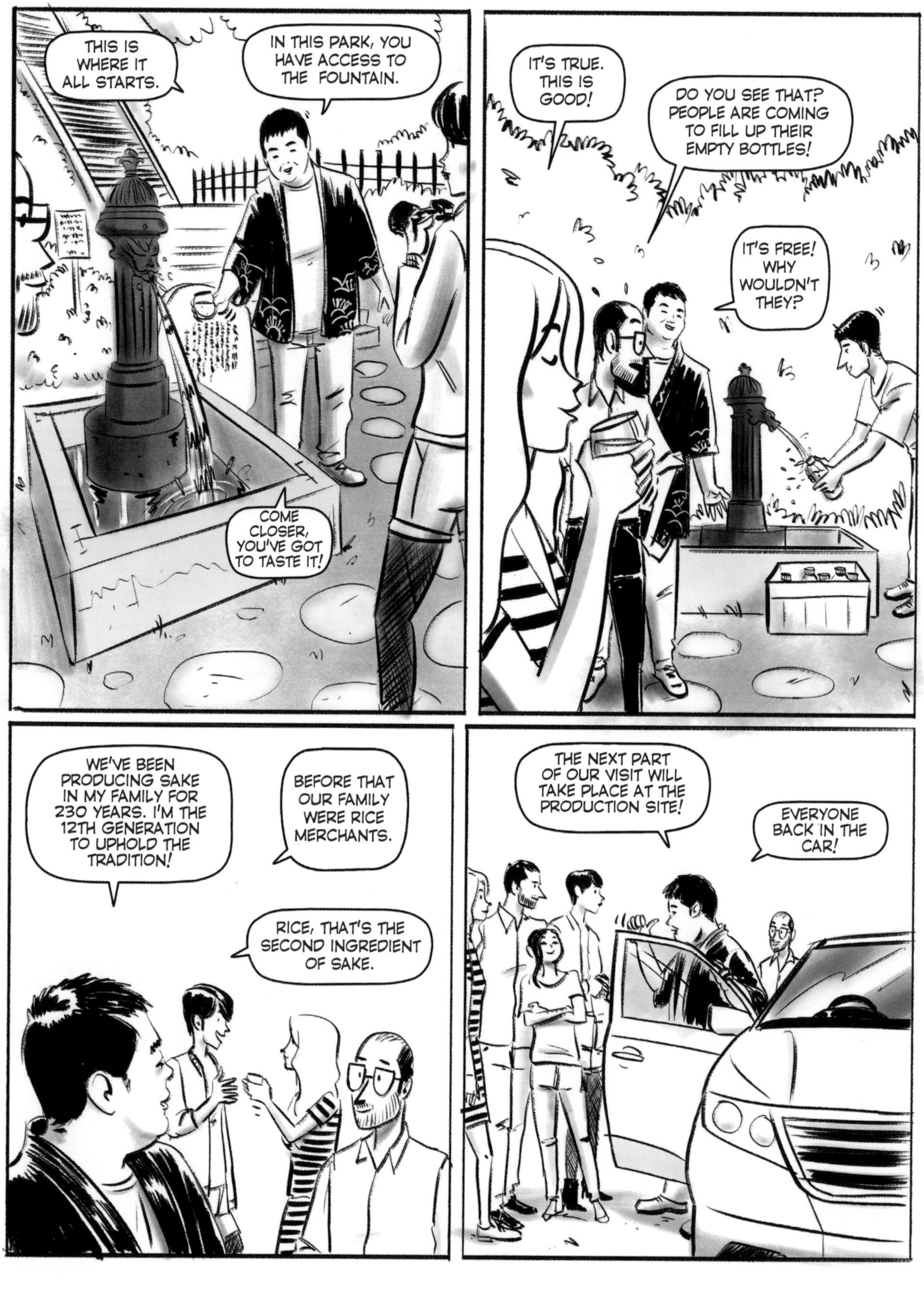
THIS IS WHERE IT ALL STARTS.
IN THIS PARK, YOU HAVE ACCESS TO THE FOUNTAIN.
COME CLOSER, YOU'VE GOT TO TASTE IT!
IT'S TRUE. THIS IS GOOD!
DO YOU SEE THAT? PEOPLE ARE COMING TO FILL UP THEIR EMPTY BOTTLES!
IT'S FREE! WHY WOULDN'T THEY?
WE'VE BEEN PRODUCING SAKE IN MY FAMILY FOR 230 YEARS. I'M THE 12TH GENERATION TO UPHOLD THE TRADITION!
BEFORE THAT OUR FAMILY WERE RICE MERCHANTS.
RICE, THAT'S THE SECOND INGREDIENT OF SAKE.
THE NEXT PART OF OUR VISIT WILL TAKE PLACE AT THE PRODUCTION SITE!
EVERYONE BACK IN THE CAR!

I'VE BEEN WORKING HERE FOR 20 YEARS.

WELCOME TO IPPIN SAKE!

THE DIFFERENT STEPS OF SAKE PRODUCTION ALL TAKE PLACE IN THESE BUILDINGS.

WE PUT OUT 500,000 BOTTLES PER YEAR!

WE'VE EVEN RECEIVED THE GOLD MEDAL FOR BEST SAKE TWICE.

JAPANESE SAKE IS A DRINK OF AROUND 15 PERCENT ALCOHOL MADE WITH RICE THAT WE THEN STEAM AND FERMENT.

AND LIKE I SAID, IT'S QUALITY DEPENDS ON THE WATER BUT ALSO ON THE RICE IT'S POLISHING.

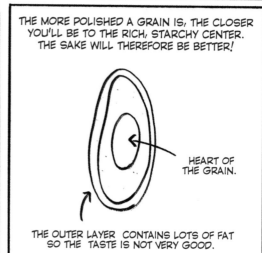

THE MORE POLISHED A GRAIN IS, THE CLOSER YOU'LL BE TO THE RICH, STARCHY CENTER. THE SAKE WILL THEREFORE BE BETTER!

HEART OF THE GRAIN.

THE OUTER LAYER CONTAINS LOTS OF FAT SO THE TASTE IS NOT VERY GOOD.

FOR OUR BEST SAKE WE POLISH 65% OF THE GRAIN AWAY SO THERE'S ONLY 35% OF THE RICE GRAIN LEFT. THIS IS A PRETTY LONG STEP THAT TAKES US THREE DAYS.

AND ONE IMPORTANT THING: WE MAKE SAKE IN WINTER. IN SEPTEMBER, WE HARVEST THE RICE, AND WE MAKE SAKE FROM OCTOBER THROUGH TO APRIL.

THE HEAT IN THE SUMMER IS NOT GOOD FOR SAKE PRODUCTION.

TRADITIONAL SAKE BARRELS.

LET'S GO INSIDE. YOU'RE GOING TO SEE THE PROCESS.

The Stages of

1) Polishing

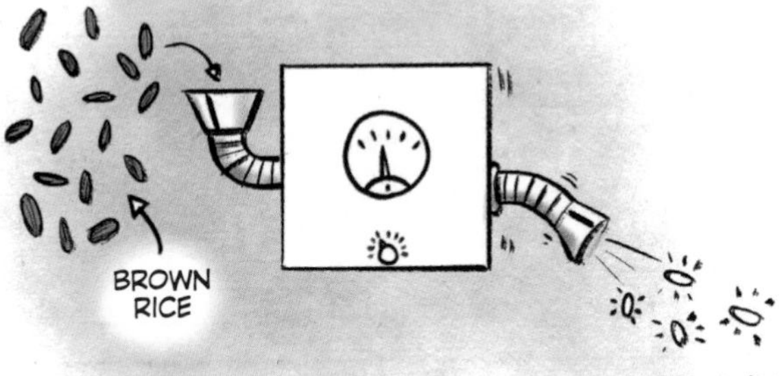
BROWN RICE

AS SOON AS IT ARRIVES AT THE BREWERY IT IS PASSED THROUGH MACHINES THAT WILL USE FRICTION TO POLISH IT. AFTER THE POLISHING, THE GRAIN IS VERY DRY. YOU NEED TO LEAVE IT TO REST THREE WEEKS SO IT CAN RECUPERATE HUMIDITY FROM THE AMBIENT AIR AROUND IT.

2) Washing

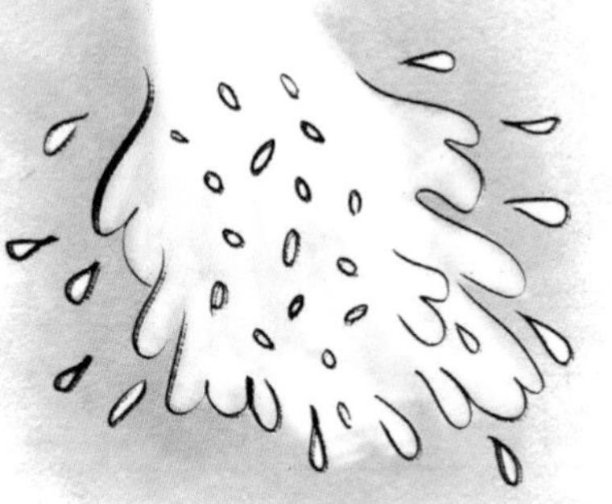

NEXT STEP: IT IS WASHED IN SPRING WATER TO REMOVE ANY RESIDUE FROM THE POLISHING. THE MORE POLISHED THE GRAIN IS, THE QUICKER IT ABSORBS WATER, SO THE SOAKING IS VERY SHORT.

5) Fermentation

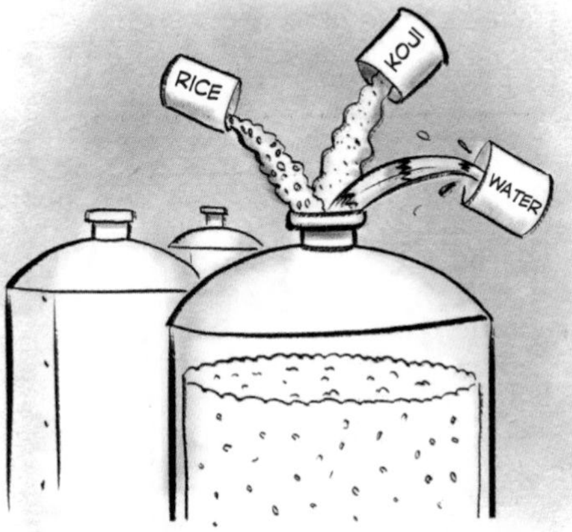
RICE
KOJI
WATER

IN LARGE VATS, YOU MIX UP WHAT IS CALLED THE "SAKE MOTHER." IT'S THE KOJI WITH THE REST OF THE COOKED RICE, WATER, YEAST, AND, USUALLY, LACTIC ACIDS. THE KOJI TRANSFORMS THE STARCH INTO SUGAR AND THE YEAST TRANSFORMS THE SUGAR INTO ALCOHOL. THE WHOLE THING FORMS A SORT OF SOUP THAT WE LEAVE TO FERMENT FOR A MONTH.

6) Pressing

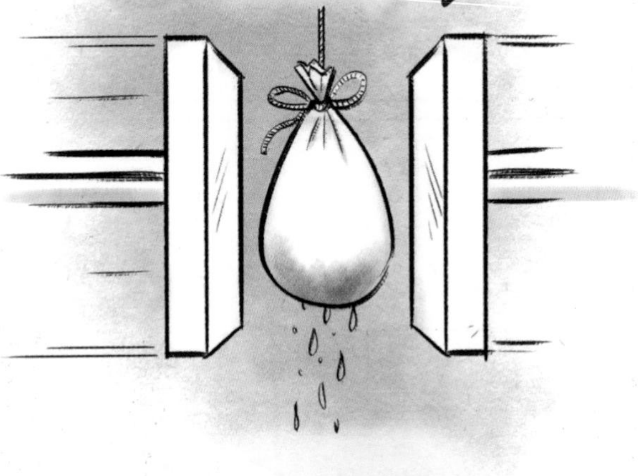

AT THE END OF THE FERMENTATION STAGE THE SAKE IS ALMOST READY. THE RICE IS PUT IN BAGS AND PRESSED TO EXTRACT THE SAKE. WHAT REMAINS—THE DECOMPOSED RICE PARTICLES—IS CALLED SAKE KASU, OR "SAKE DREGS." IT'S VERY POPULAR AMONG CHEFS, AS WE SAW WITH CHEF OKADA.

Making Sake

3) Steaming

THEN WE SLOWLY STEAM THE RICE WITH SPRING WATER TO PREPARE IT FOR THE FERMENTATION PROCESS. ONCE IT'S COOKED, THE RICE HAS A VERY PARTICULAR CONSISTENCY: TENDER ON THE INSIDE, FIRM ON THE OUTSIDE.

4) Koji

AROUND 30% OF THE RICE IS TRANSFERRED TO THE KOJIMURO FOR A FEW DAYS. THE KOJIMURO IS A SPECIAL CLIMATE-CONTROLLED ROOM. THERE, THE RICE IS SEEDED BY HAND ON A LARGE TABLE BEFORE BEING DUSTED WITH ASPERGILLUS ORYZAE, A FUNGUS THAT WILL TRANSFORM THE STARCH OF THE RICE INTO SUGAR. THE RESULT IS CALLED KOJI.

7) Filtration

WE'VE COME TO THE LAST STEP: THE SAKE IS FILTERED, PASTEURIZED, AND AGED IN VATS FOR SIX MONTHS. THERE ARE ALSO SAKES WHICH ARE UNFILTERED, UNPASTEURIZED, OR BOTH.

8) Bottling

FROM THE DAY IT IS BOTTLED, THE SAKE SHOULD BE CONSUMED WITHIN A YEAR. CONSERVED ANY LONGER AND IT BEGINS TO LOSE ITS FLAVOR. IT'S DELICATE AND SHOULD BE STORED IN A DARK PLACE WHERE THE TEMPERATURE IS CONSISTENTLY COOL.

NOW, VERY BROADLY, I'M GOING TO WALK YOU THROUGH SOME OF THE DIFFERENT VARIETIES.

SUPERIOR SAKES ARE RANKED BY THE QUALITY OF RICE USED, ITS POLISHING RATE, AND THE QUANTITY OF ALCOHOL THAT IS ADDED, OR NOT ADDED.

Honjozo Sakes

WITH ADDED ALCOHOL

Junmai Sakes

WITHOUT ADDED ALCOHOL

70% RICE POLISHING RATE

60% RICE POLISHING RATE

50% RICE POLISHING RATE

Honjozo

IT'S A JUNMAI TO WHICH THE BREWER ADDS A LITTLE BIT OF DISTILLED ALCOHOL RIGHT BEFORE FILTRATION. IT ACCENTUATES THE FLAVORS. IT IS THE MOST CONSUMED PREMIUM SAKE.

Junmai

THIS NATURAL SAKE, WITHOUT ADDED ALCOHOL, HAS AN UNMARKED RICE POLISHING RATE, BUT IT'S OFTEN HIGH, WHICH IS WHERE IT GETS ITS PRONOUNCED GRAINY TASTE.

Ginjong

IT'S PRODUCED WITH RICE POLISHED TO 40% WHICH MAKES IT MORE DELICATE WITH VERY FLORAL NOTES.

Junmai Ginjo

A JUNMAI GINJO WILL HAVE MORE FLAVOR THAN A SIMPLE JUNMAI. A STRONG AROMA OF RICE WILL BE PRESENT.

Dainginjo

AN EXTENSION OF GINJO MADE WITH RICE POLISHED TO 50%. IT'S THE FINEST AND MOST HIGH-END OF THE PREMIUM SAKES. IT IS VERY REFINED AND HAS COMPLEX FLAVORS.

Junmai Dainginjo

A VERY COMPLEX SAKE, FINE WITH VERY PRONOUNCED AROMAS. IT IS OFTEN DRY.

Namazake

THIS DESIGNATES ALL UNPASTEURIZED SAKE IN ANY CATEGORY. BECAUSE IT'S MORE DELICATE, IT SHOULD BE KEPT COLD AND CONSUMED SOON AFTER OPENING IT.

Nigori

THIS OTHER NAME TAKES INTO ACCOUNT ALL THE UNFILTERED SAKES REGARDLESS OF CATEGORY. NIGORI MEANS "MURKY": THIS SAKE, AS IT HAPPENS, IS OFTEN MILKY AND OFF-WHITE.

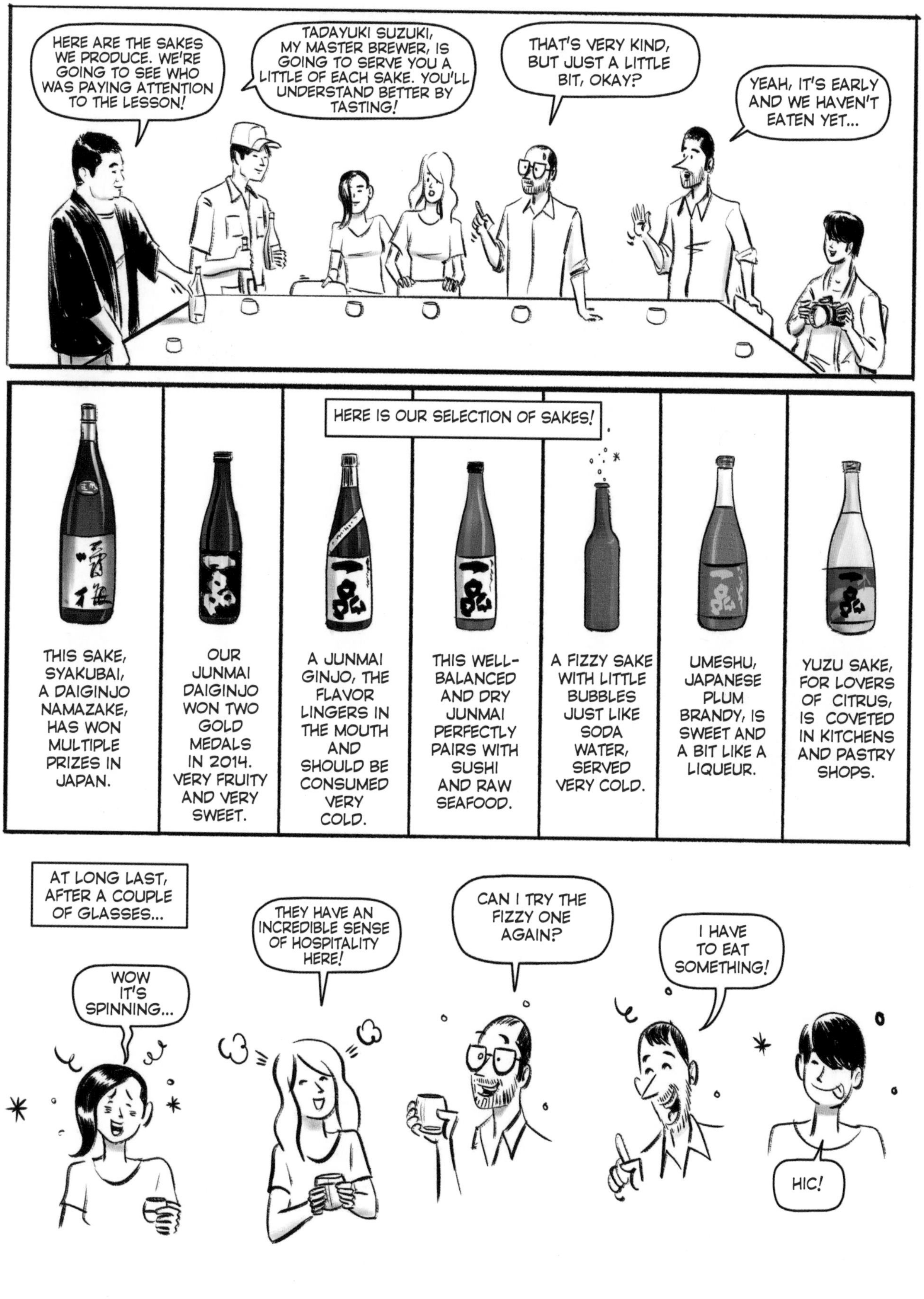
HERE ARE THE SAKES WE PRODUCE. WE'RE GOING TO SEE WHO WAS PAYING ATTENTION TO THE LESSON!
TADAYUKI SUZUKI, MY MASTER BREWER, IS GOING TO SERVE YOU A LITTLE OF EACH SAKE. YOU'LL UNDERSTAND BETTER BY TASTING!
THAT'S VERY KIND, BUT JUST A LITTLE BIT, OKAY?
YEAH, IT'S EARLY AND WE HAVEN'T EATEN YET...
HERE IS OUR SELECTION OF SAKES!
THIS SAKE, SYAKUBAI, A DAIGINJO NAMAZAKE, HAS WON MULTIPLE PRIZES IN JAPAN.
OUR JUNMAI DAIGINJO WON TWO GOLD MEDALS IN 2014. VERY FRUITY AND VERY SWEET.
A JUNMAI GINJO, THE FLAVOR LINGERS IN THE MOUTH AND SHOULD BE CONSUMED VERY COLD.
THIS WELL-BALANCED AND DRY JUNMAI PERFECTLY PAIRS WITH SUSHI AND RAW SEAFOOD.
A FIZZY SAKE WITH LITTLE BUBBLES JUST LIKE SODA WATER, SERVED VERY COLD.
UMESHU, JAPANESE PLUM BRANDY, IS SWEET AND A BIT LIKE A LIQUEUR.
YUZU SAKE, FOR LOVERS OF CITRUS, IS COVETED IN KITCHENS AND PASTRY SHOPS.
AT LONG LAST, AFTER A COUPLE OF GLASSES...
WOW IT'S SPINNING...
THEY HAVE AN INCREDIBLE SENSE OF HOSPITALITY HERE!
CAN I TRY THE FIZZY ONE AGAIN?
I HAVE TO EAT SOMETHING!
HIC!

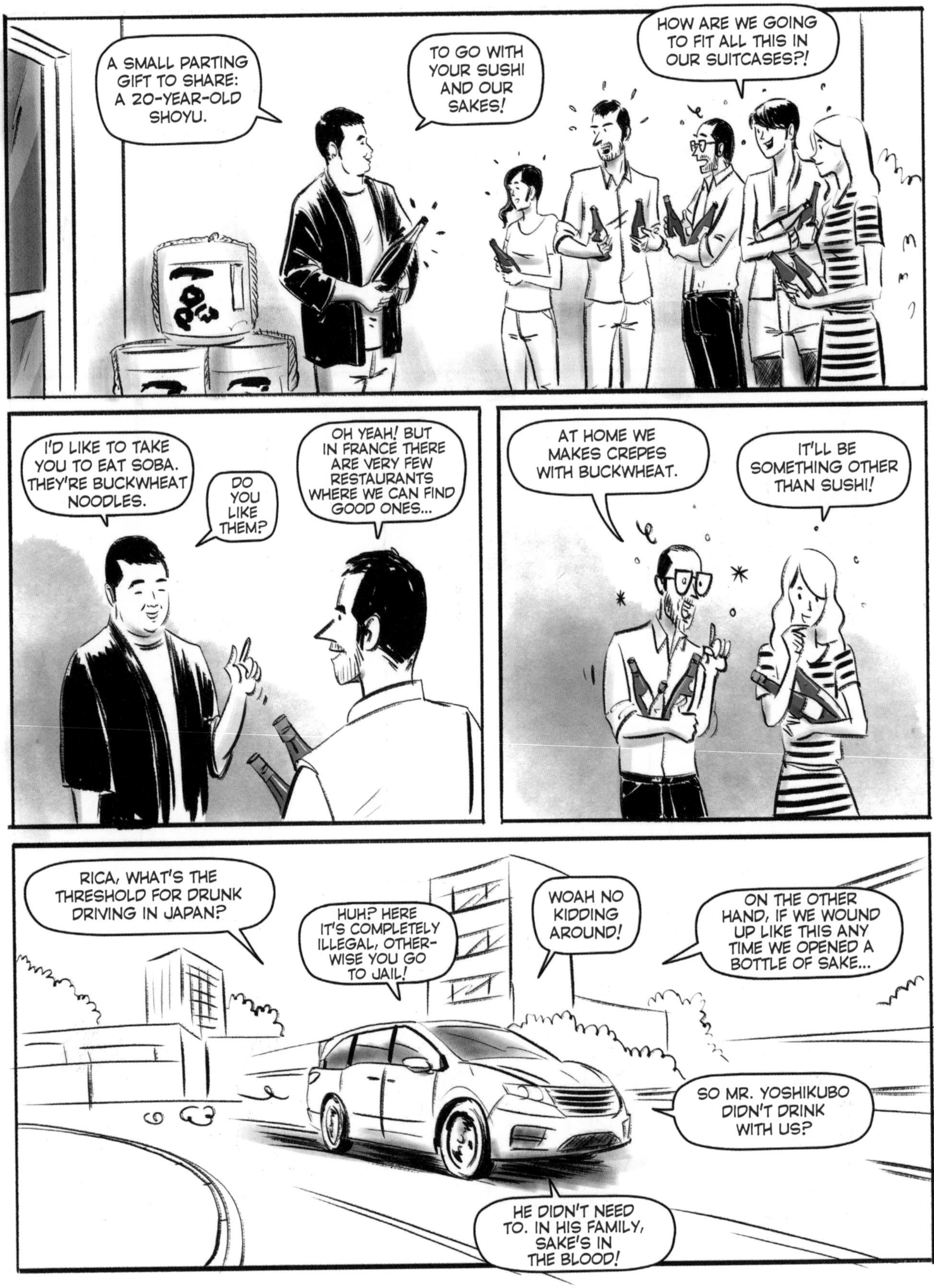
A SMALL PARTING GIFT TO SHARE: A 20-YEAR-OLD SHOYU.
TO GO WITH YOUR SUSHI AND OUR SAKES!
HOW ARE WE GOING TO FIT ALL THIS IN OUR SUITCASES?!
I'D LIKE TO TAKE YOU TO EAT SOBA. THEY'RE BUCKWHEAT NOODLES.
DO YOU LIKE THEM?
OH YEAH! BUT IN FRANCE THERE ARE VERY FEW RESTAURANTS WHERE WE CAN FIND GOOD ONES...
AT HOME WE MAKES CREPES WITH BUCKWHEAT.
IT'LL BE SOMETHING OTHER THAN SUSHI!
RICA, WHAT'S THE THRESHOLD FOR DRUNK DRIVING IN JAPAN?
HUH? HERE IT'S COMPLETELY ILLEGAL, OTHER-WISE YOU GO TO JAIL!
WOAH NO KIDDING AROUND!
ON THE OTHER HAND, IF WE WOUND UP LIKE THIS ANY TIME WE OPENED A BOTTLE OF SAKE...
SO MR. YOSHIKUBO DIDN'T DRINK WITH US?
HE DIDN'T NEED TO. IN HIS FAMILY, SAKE'S IN THE BLOOD!

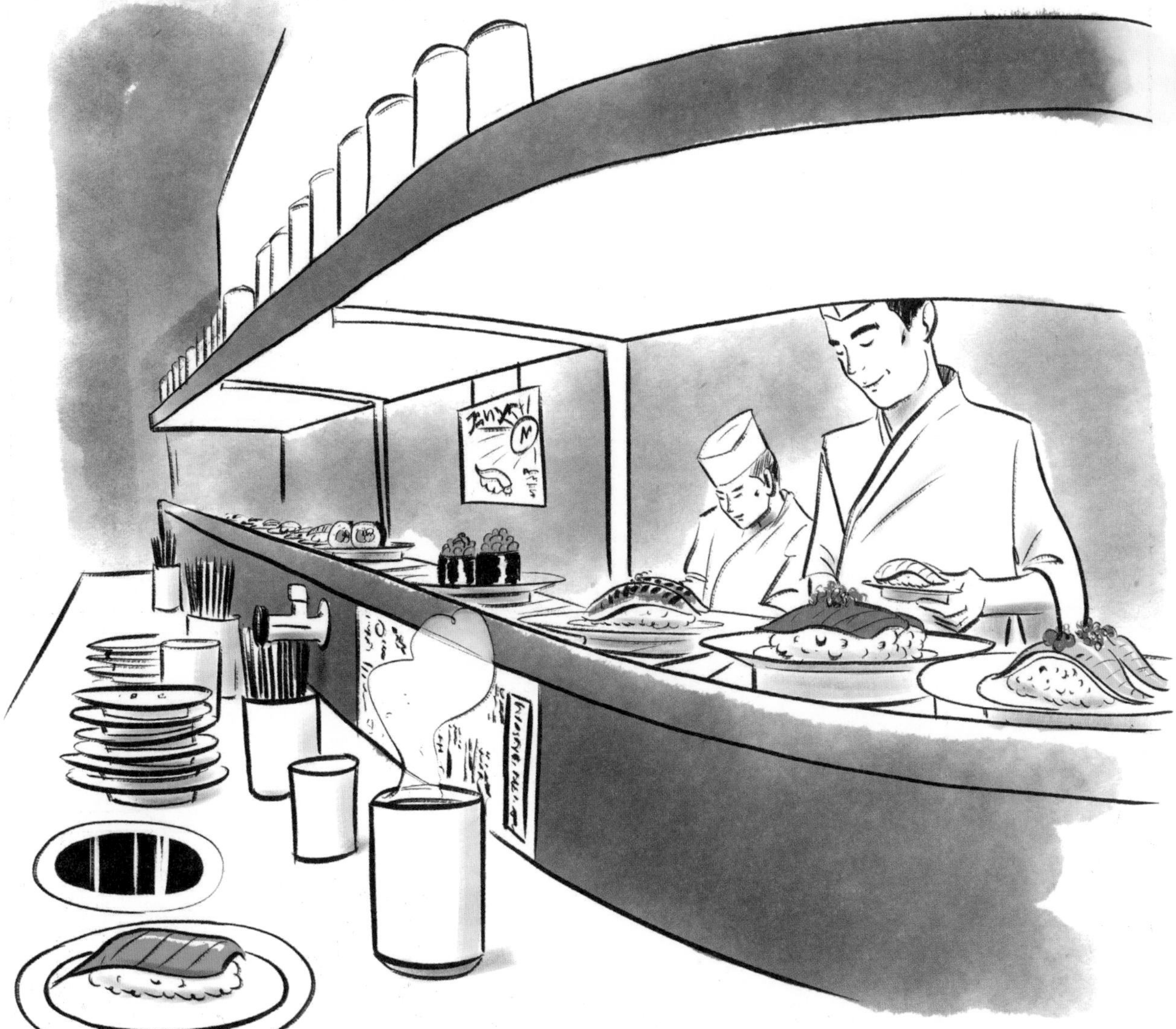

Everyday Sushi

JAPANESE SUSHI ISN'T JUST FOR FANCY RESTAURANTS AND GOURMETS. IT HAS BEEN WIDELY POPULARIZED AND IS EATEN IN VERY ACCESSIBLE RESTAURANTS AND EVEN AT HOME, IN SIMPLIFIED FORMS.

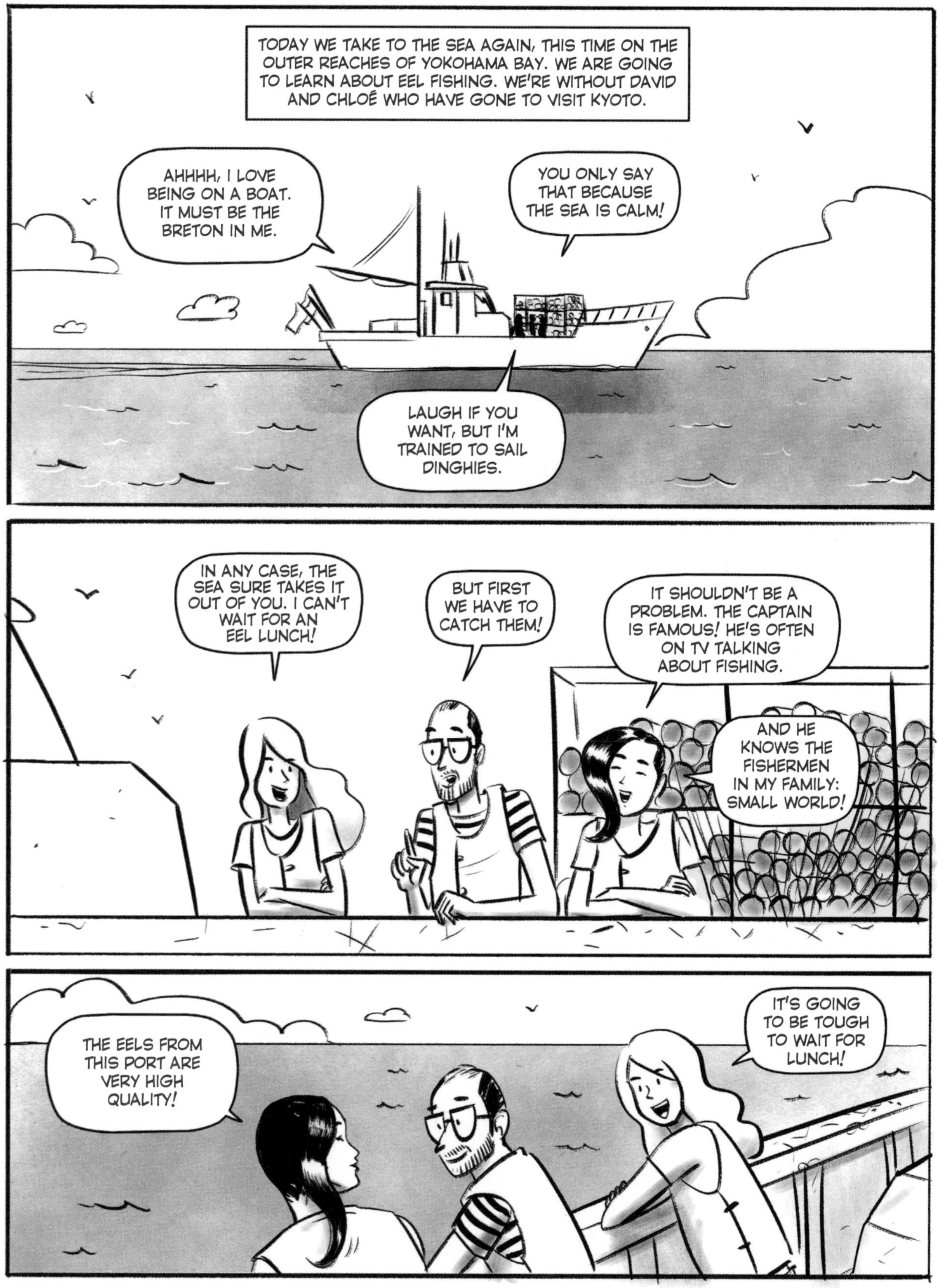
TODAY WE TAKE TO THE SEA AGAIN, THIS TIME ON THE OUTER REACHES OF YOKOHAMA BAY. WE ARE GOING TO LEARN ABOUT EEL FISHING. WE'RE WITHOUT DAVID AND CHLOÉ WHO HAVE GONE TO VISIT KYOTO.
AHHHH, I LOVE BEING ON A BOAT. IT MUST BE THE BRETON IN ME.
YOU ONLY SAY THAT BECAUSE THE SEA IS CALM!
LAUGH IF YOU WANT, BUT I'M TRAINED TO SAIL DINGHIES.
IN ANY CASE, THE SEA SURE TAKES IT OUT OF YOU. I CAN'T WAIT FOR AN EEL LUNCH!
BUT FIRST WE HAVE TO CATCH THEM!
IT SHOULDN'T BE A PROBLEM. THE CAPTAIN IS FAMOUS! HE'S OFTEN ON TV TALKING ABOUT FISHING.
AND HE KNOWS THE FISHERMEN IN MY FAMILY: SMALL WORLD!
THE EELS FROM THIS PORT ARE VERY HIGH QUALITY!
IT'S GOING TO BE TOUGH TO WAIT FOR LUNCH!

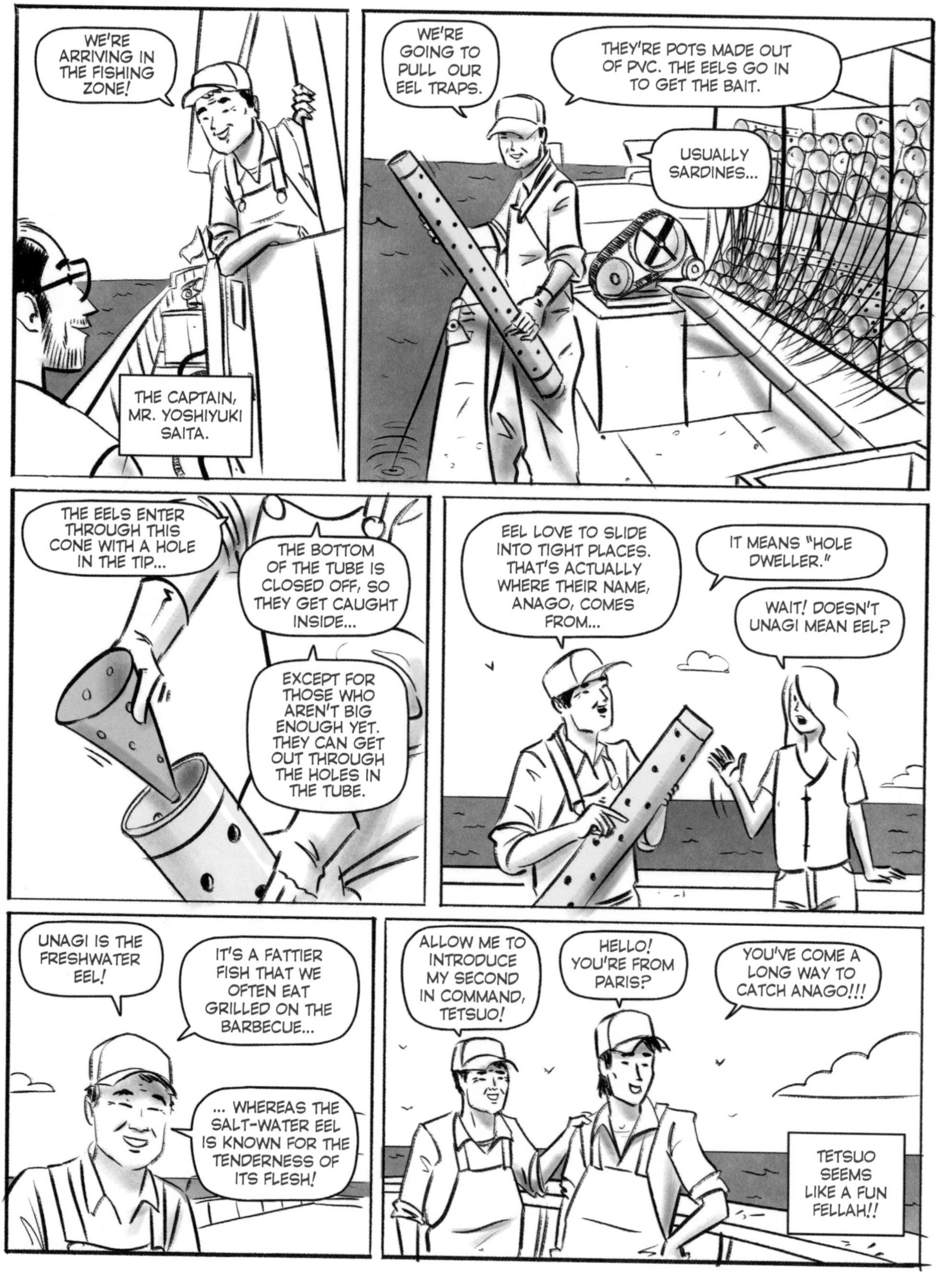
WE'RE ARRIVING IN THE FISHING ZONE!
THE CAPTAIN, MR. YOSHIYUKI SAITA.
WE'RE GOING TO PULL OUR EEL TRAPS.
THEY'RE POTS MADE OUT OF PVC. THE EELS GO IN TO GET THE BAIT.
USUALLY SARDINES...
THE EELS ENTER THROUGH THIS CONE WITH A HOLE IN THE TIP...
THE BOTTOM OF THE TUBE IS CLOSED OFF, SO THEY GET CAUGHT INSIDE...
EXCEPT FOR THOSE WHO AREN'T BIG ENOUGH YET. THEY CAN GET OUT THROUGH THE HOLES IN THE TUBE.
EEL LOVE TO SLIDE INTO TIGHT PLACES. THAT'S ACTUALLY WHERE THEIR NAME, ANAGO, COMES FROM...
IT MEANS "HOLE DWELLER."
WAIT! DOESN'T UNAGI MEAN EEL?
UNAGI IS THE FRESHWATER EEL!
IT'S A FATTIER FISH THAT WE OFTEN EAT GRILLED ON THE BARBECUE...
... WHEREAS THE SALT-WATER EEL IS KNOWN FOR THE TENDERNESS OF ITS FLESH!
ALLOW ME TO INTRODUCE MY SECOND IN COMMAND, TETSUO!
HELLO! YOU'RE FROM PARIS?
YOU'VE COME A LONG WAY TO CATCH ANAGO!!!
TETSUO SEEMS LIKE A FUN FELLAH!!

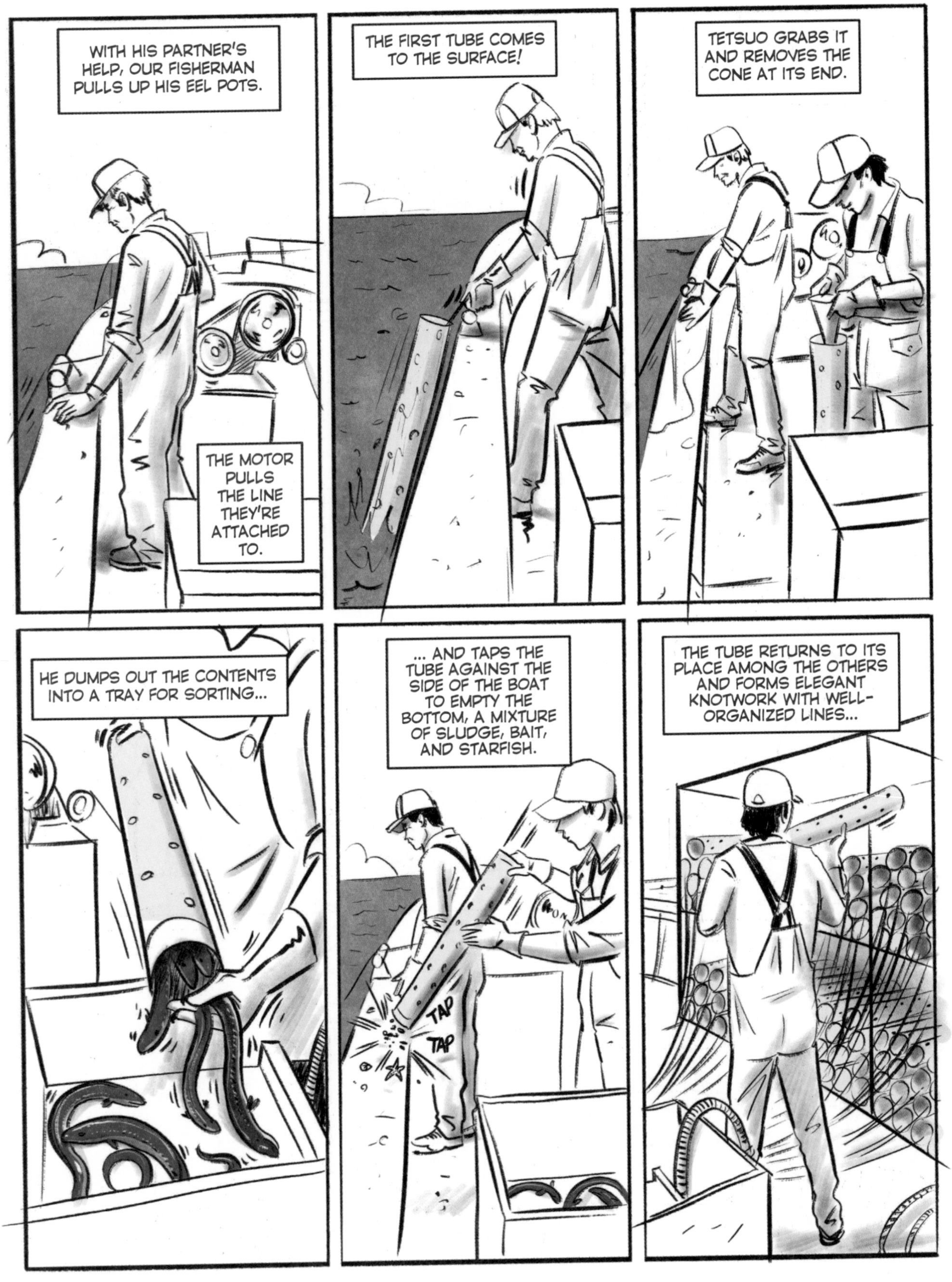
WITH HIS PARTNER'S HELP, OUR FISHERMAN PULLS UP HIS EEL POTS.
THE MOTOR PULLS THE LINE THEY'RE ATTACHED TO.
THE FIRST TUBE COMES TO THE SURFACE!
TETSUO GRABS IT AND REMOVES THE CONE AT ITS END.
HE DUMPS OUT THE CONTENTS INTO A TRAY FOR SORTING...
... AND TAPS THE TUBE AGAINST THE SIDE OF THE BOAT TO EMPTY THE BOTTOM, A MIXTURE OF SLUDGE, BAIT, AND STARFISH.
TAP
TAP
THE TUBE RETURNS TO ITS PLACE AMONG THE OTHERS AND FORMS ELEGANT KNOTWORK WITH WELL-ORGANIZED LINES...

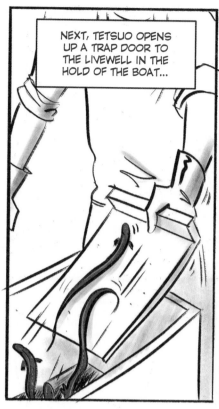

NEXT, TETSUO OPENS UP A TRAP DOOR TO THE LIVEWELL IN THE HOLD OF THE BOAT...

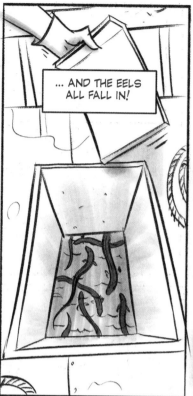

... AND THE EELS ALL FALL IN!

THAT WAY WE KEEP THEM ALIVE!

SO THAT'S HOW THEY MAKE IT TO TSUKIJI ALIVE!

AFTER A FEW HOURS AT SEA WE RETURN TO THE PORT.

MRS. TANEMURA IS WAITING FOR US. SHE'S A SPECIALIST AT COOKING EEL!

WE SUPPLY FISH FOR HER RESTAURANT!

YOU WON'T EAT ANYTHING FRESHER ANYWHERE ELSE!

SHE PICKS US UP IN HER "KEI CAR," ONE OF THE LITTLE JAPANESE CARS WE SEE EVERYWHERE HERE.

WE'RE HEADED TO HER HOME, WHICH IS ALSO HER RESTAURANT, WITH THE EELS IN THE TRUNK.

AT HER HOUSE WE OBSERVE THE RATHER BARBARIC PREPARATION OF THESE FISH.

CRRR

SHE TAKES ONE AND MAKES A NOTCH BEHIND ITS HEAD. THE ANAGO STOPS MOVING.

THEN TO FIX IT TO HER CUTTING BOARD SHE STABS A PICK INTO ITS HEAD...

I OPEN IT FROM THE BACK BECAUSE THAT'S THE TRADITIONAL METHOD IN THE TOKYO REGION, WHEREAS IN OSAKA YOU OPEN IT BY THE STOMACH.

SOUND LIKE AIR WHOOSHING IN

SSHHHHHH!

THERE WERE A LOT OF SAMURAI IN TOKYO. OPENING THE FISH BY ITS STOMACH REMINDED THEM TOO MUCH OF HARA-KIRI, RITUALISTIC SUICIDE...

IN OSAKA, WHICH IS A CITY OF MERCHANTS, THEY PREFER THE SAYING "HARA WO WATTE HANASU," WHICH MEANS: "SPEAK WITH YOUR BELLY OPEN."

WITH THOSE CUTS MADE LENGTHWISE, THE VISCERA ARE REMOVED.

MAKE AN INCISION ALL ALONG THE SPINE...

I PULL IT UP...

... AND I KEEP IT SO I CAN FRY IT!

WITH ITS HEAD REMOVED, THE EEL IS READ TO BE COOKED!

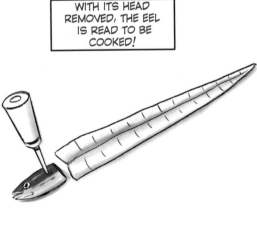

WHILE WE'RE WAITING FOR OUR EEL, WE HAVE A SEAT IN THE SMALL LIVING ROOM.

THE APPETIZER NEARLY BEATS US TO THE TABLE: ANAGO SASHIMI!

RICA EXPLAINS THAT EATING RAW EEL IS VERY RARE BECAUSE YOU NEED TO HAVE JUST CAUGHT IT.

THE TEXTURE IS COMPELLING, THE TASTE, SUBTLE!

MUNCH MUNCH

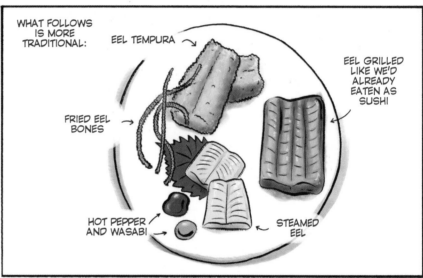

WHAT FOLLOWS IS MORE TRADITIONAL:

EEL TEMPURA

FRIED EEL BONES

EEL GRILLED LIKE WE'D ALREADY EATEN AS SUSHI

HOT PEPPER AND WASABI

STEAMED EEL

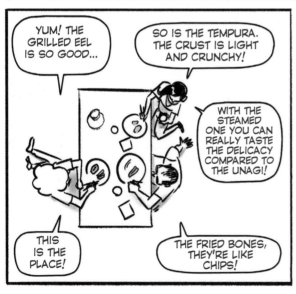

YUM! THE GRILLED EEL IS SO GOOD...

SO IS THE TEMPURA. THE CRUST IS LIGHT AND CRUNCHY!

WITH THE STEAMED ONE YOU CAN REALLY TASTE THE DELICACY COMPARED TO THE UNAGI!

THIS IS THE PLACE!

THE FRIED BONES, THEY'RE LIKE CHIPS!

IT'S SO NICE TO EAT ON THE GROUND! YOU CAN KEEL OVER WHEN YOU'RE TIRED!

IT REMINDS ME OF OUR LITTLE APARTMENT NEAR THE GARE DE LYON...

WE ALWAYS ATE AT THE COFFEE TABLE!

DON'T FALL ASLEEP, FRANCKIE! IT'S NOT VERY POLITE!

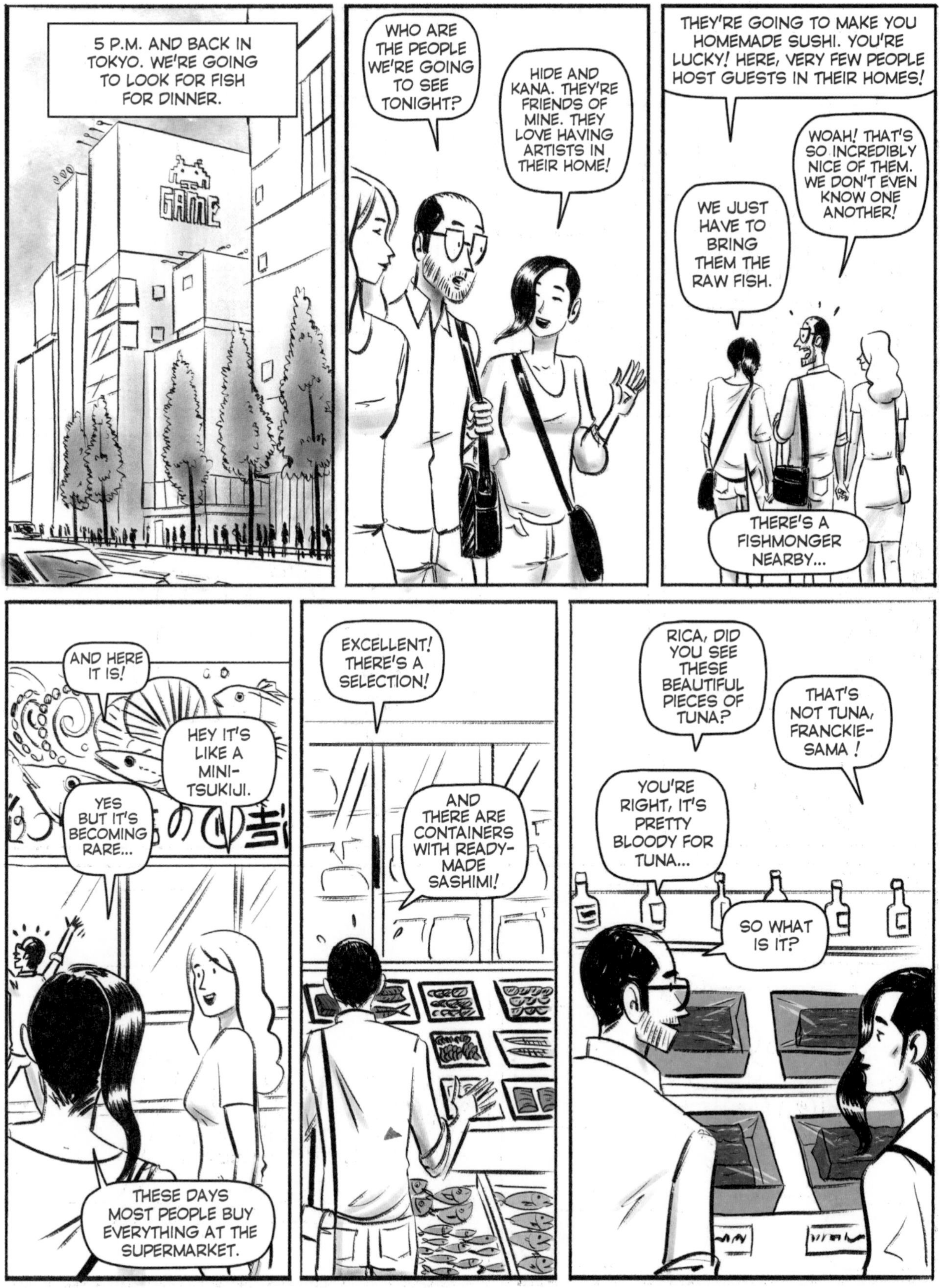
5 P.M. AND BACK IN TOKYO. WE'RE GOING TO LOOK FOR FISH FOR DINNER.
GAME
WHO ARE THE PEOPLE WE'RE GOING TO SEE TONIGHT?
HIDE AND KANA. THEY'RE FRIENDS OF MINE. THEY LOVE HAVING ARTISTS IN THEIR HOME!
THEY'RE GOING TO MAKE YOU HOMEMADE SUSHI. YOU'RE LUCKY! HERE, VERY FEW PEOPLE HOST GUESTS IN THEIR HOMES!
WOAH! THAT'S SO INCREDIBLY NICE OF THEM. WE DON'T EVEN KNOW ONE ANOTHER!
WE JUST HAVE TO BRING THEM THE RAW FISH.
THERE'S A FISHMONGER NEARBY...
AND HERE IT IS!
HEY IT'S LIKE A MINI-TSUKIJI.
YES BUT IT'S BECOMING RARE...
THESE DAYS MOST PEOPLE BUY EVERYTHING AT THE SUPERMARKET.
EXCELLENT! THERE'S A SELECTION!
AND THERE ARE CONTAINERS WITH READY-MADE SASHIMI!
RICA, DID YOU SEE THESE BEAUTIFUL PIECES OF TUNA?
THAT'S NOT TUNA, FRANCKIE-SAMA !
YOU'RE RIGHT, IT'S PRETTY BLOODY FOR TUNA...
SO WHAT IS IT?

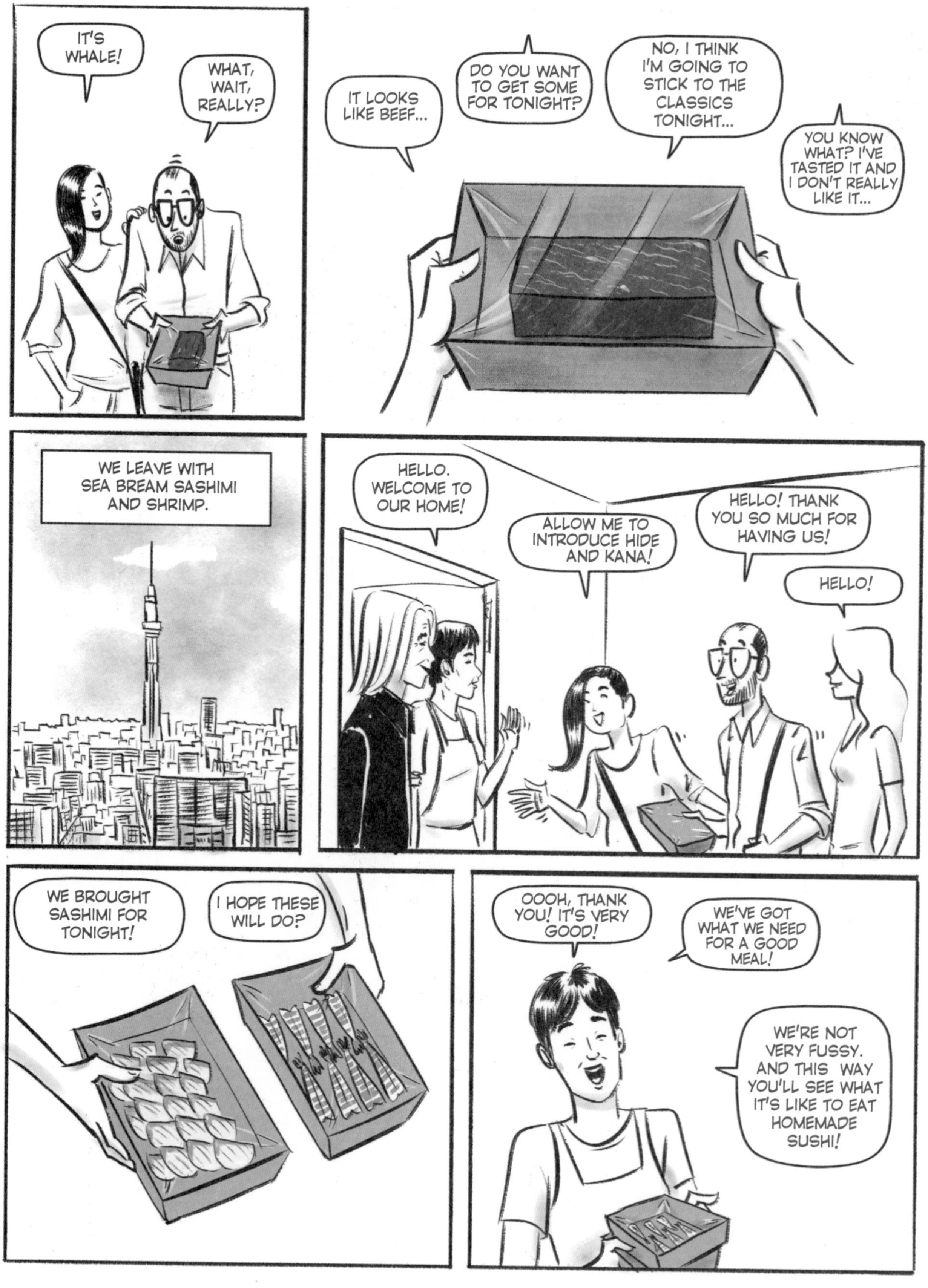
IT'S WHALE!
WHAT, WAIT, REALLY?
IT LOOKS LIKE BEEF...
DO YOU WANT TO GET SOME FOR TONIGHT?
NO, I THINK I'M GOING TO STICK TO THE CLASSICS TONIGHT...
YOU KNOW WHAT? I'VE TASTED IT AND I DON'T REALLY LIKE IT...
WE LEAVE WITH SEA BREAM SASHIMI AND SHRIMP.
HELLO. WELCOME TO OUR HOME!
ALLOW ME TO INTRODUCE HIDE AND KANA!
HELLO! THANK YOU SO MUCH FOR HAVING US!
HELLO!
WE BROUGHT SASHIMI FOR TONIGHT!
I HOPE THESE WILL DO?
OOOH, THANK YOU! IT'S VERY GOOD!
WE'VE GOT WHAT WE NEED FOR A GOOD MEAL!
WE'RE NOT VERY FUSSY. AND THIS WAY YOU'LL SEE WHAT IT'S LIKE TO EAT HOMEMADE SUSHI!

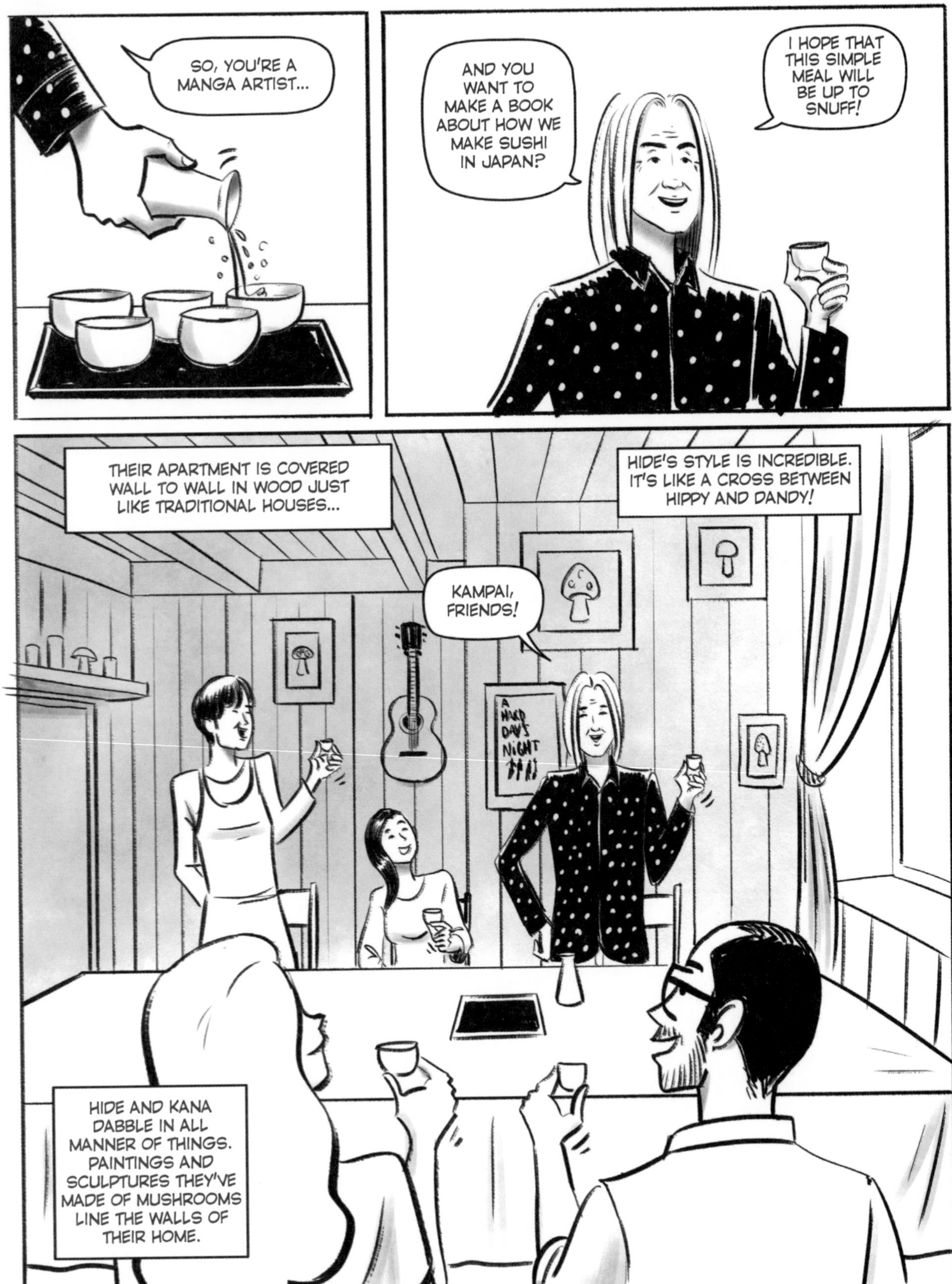
SO, YOU'RE A MANGA ARTIST...
AND YOU WANT TO MAKE A BOOK ABOUT HOW WE MAKE SUSHI IN JAPAN?
I HOPE THAT THIS SIMPLE MEAL WILL BE UP TO SNUFF!
THEIR APARTMENT IS COVERED WALL TO WALL IN WOOD JUST LIKE TRADITIONAL HOUSES...
HIDE'S STYLE IS INCREDIBLE. IT'S LIKE A CROSS BETWEEN HIPPY AND DANDY!
KAMPAI, FRIENDS!
A HARD DAY'S NIGHT
HIDE AND KANA DABBLE IN ALL MANNER OF THINGS. PAINTINGS AND SCULPTURES THEY'VE MADE OF MUSHROOMS LINE THE WALLS OF THEIR HOME.

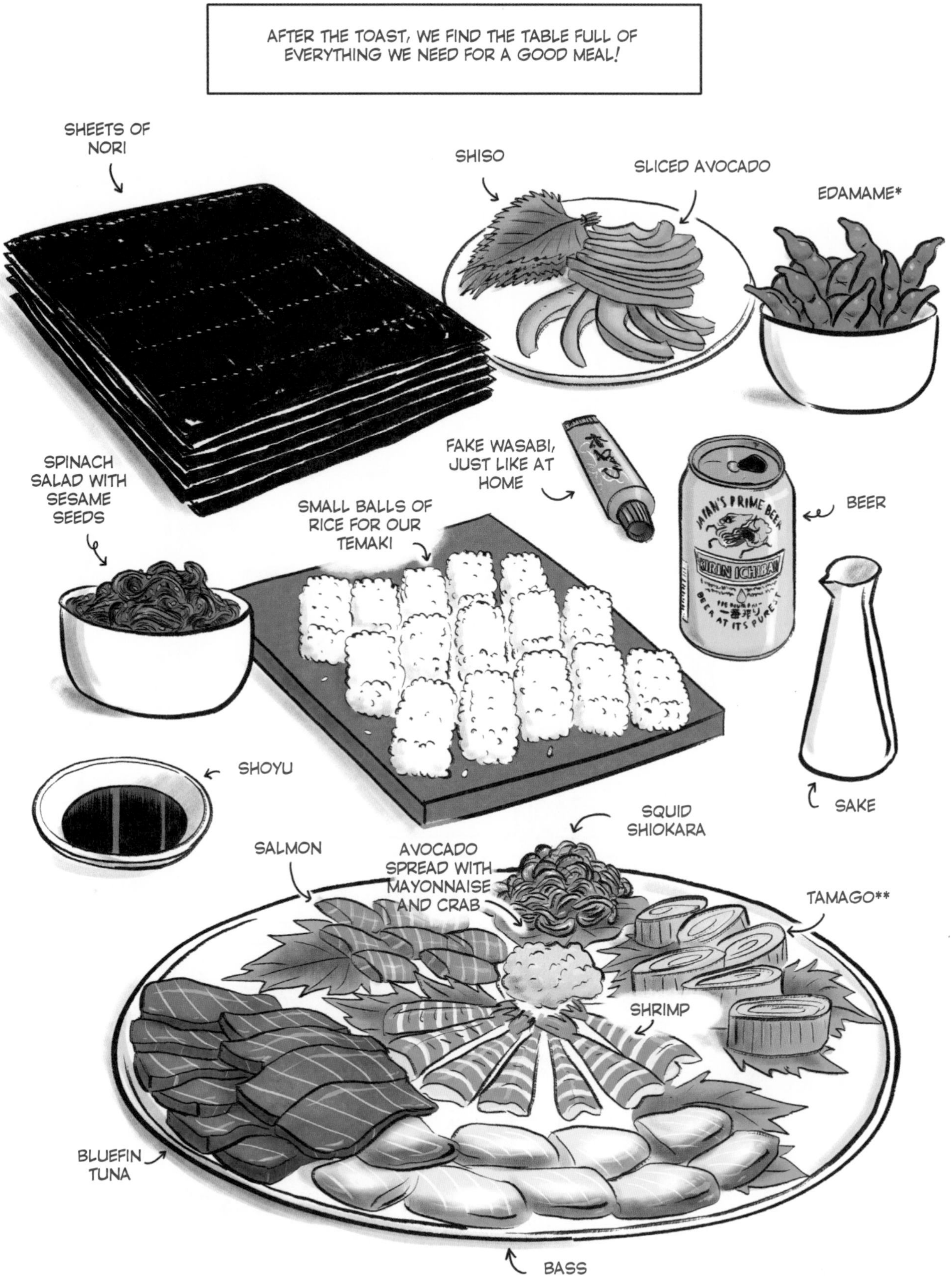
AFTER THE TOAST, WE FIND THE TABLE FULL OF EVERYTHING WE NEED FOR A GOOD MEAL!
SHEETS OF NORI
SHISO
SLICED AVOCADO
EDAMAME*
SPINACH SALAD WITH SESAME SEEDS
FAKE WASABI, JUST LIKE AT HOME
SMALL BALLS OF RICE FOR OUR TEMAKI
JAPAN'S PRIME BEER
KIRIN ICHIBAN
BEER AT ITS PUREST
BEER
SHOYU
SAKE
SQUID SHIOKARA
SALMON
AVOCADO SPREAD WITH MAYONNAISE AND CRAB
TAMAGO**
SHRIMP
BLUEFIN TUNA
BASS

*EDAMAME: BOILED SOYBEANS IN THEIR SHELLS, SALTED. **TAMAGO: JAPANESE OMELET

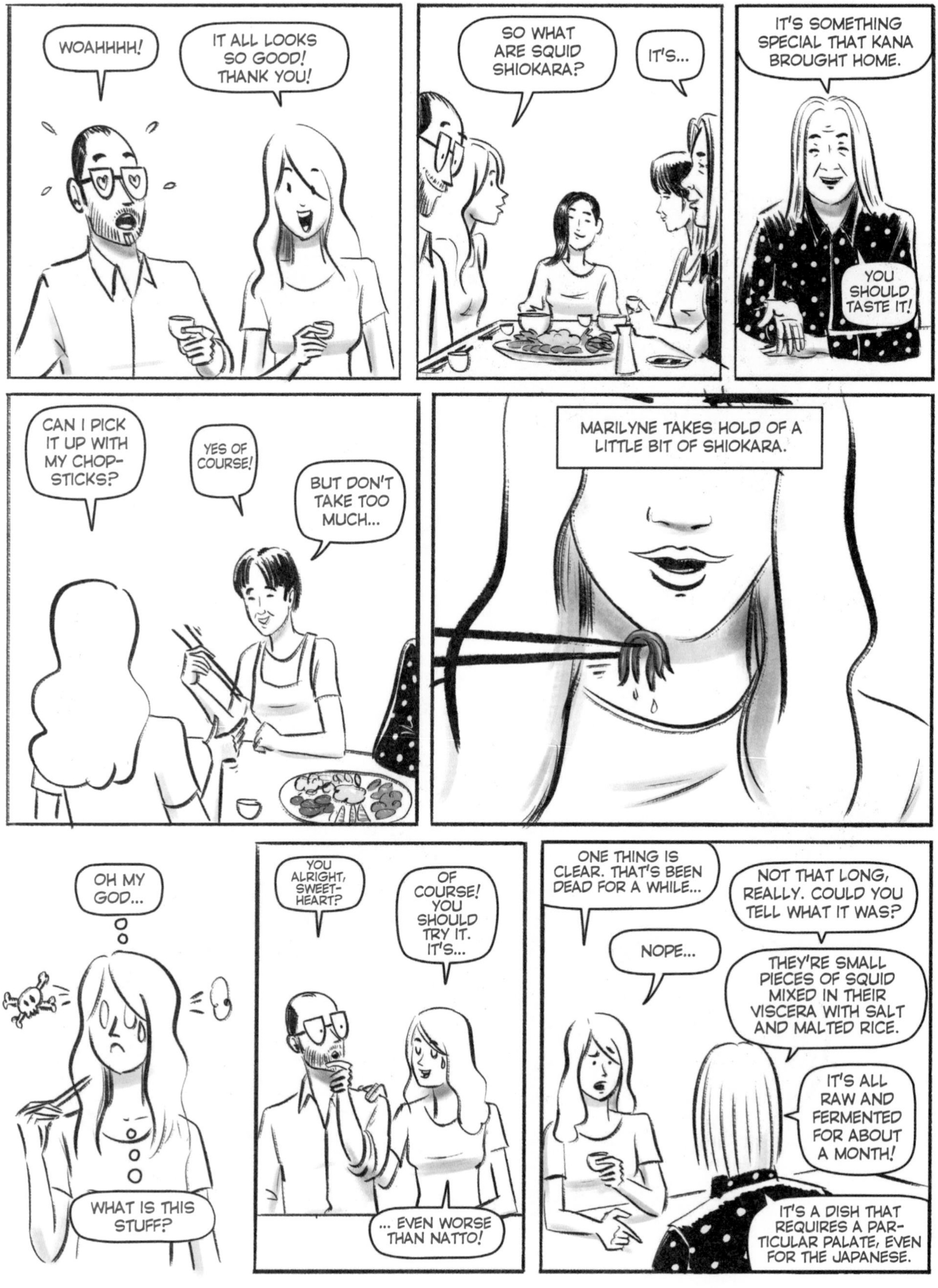
WOAHHHH!
IT ALL LOOKS SO GOOD! THANK YOU!
SO WHAT ARE SQUID SHIOKARA?
IT'S...
IT'S SOMETHING SPECIAL THAT KANA BROUGHT HOME.
YOU SHOULD TASTE IT!
CAN I PICK IT UP WITH MY CHOP-STICKS?
YES OF COURSE!
BUT DON'T TAKE TOO MUCH...
MARILYNE TAKES HOLD OF A LITTLE BIT OF SHIOKARA.
OH MY GOD...
WHAT IS THIS STUFF?
YOU ALRIGHT, SWEET-HEART?
OF COURSE! YOU SHOULD TRY IT. IT'S...
... EVEN WORSE THAN NATTO!
ONE THING IS CLEAR. THAT'S BEEN DEAD FOR A WHILE...
NOT THAT LONG, REALLY. COULD YOU TELL WHAT IT WAS?
NOPE...
THEY'RE SMALL PIECES OF SQUID MIXED IN THEIR VISCERA WITH SALT AND MALTED RICE.
IT'S ALL RAW AND FERMENTED FOR ABOUT A MONTH!
IT'S A DISH THAT REQUIRES A PAR-TICULAR PALATE, EVEN FOR THE JAPANESE.

HIDE RECOMMENDS WE TRY THE SHIOKARA IN A TEMAKI WITH OTHER INGREDIENTS, AS A SEASONING.

YOU REMEMBER TEMAKI? IT'S THE SMALL CONE OF NORI FULL OF WHATEVER YOU WANT TO PUT IN IT.

AHEM... THIS IS MY VERSION...

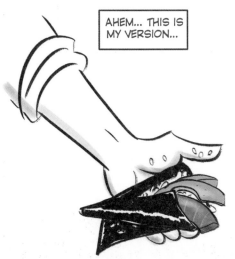

HERE'S THE TEXTBOOK WAY TO ROLL THEM!

CUT A SHEET OF NORI IN TWO AND SPREAD A SMALL LAYER OF RICE ON ONE HALF.

PLACE SOME OF THE FILLINGS ON THE RICE AND TAKE THE LOWER RIGHT-HAND CORNER...

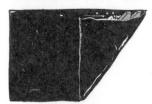

... AND FOLD IT OVER TOWARDS THE CENTER OF THE SHEET OF NORI.

TAKE THE HALF ON THE RIGHT, FOLD IT, AND THEN FOLD IT BACK OVER ON THE FINAL REMAINING PART.

IF YOU'RE GOOD AT ORIGAMI, THIS IS WHAT IT SHOULD LOOK LIKE!

IT'S ALL SO GOOD AND THE NORI IS VERY CRUNCHY!

IT'S THANKS TO TWO THINGS!

FIRSTLY, THE QUALITY OF THE NORI. WE GOT SOME OF THE BEST IN JAPAN!

SECONDLY, IN A MAKI, THE RICE IS IN CONTACT WITH THE WHOLE SURFACE OF THE SHEET OF SEAWEED WHICH SOFTENS THE NORI.

HERE, SINCE THERE IS ONLY A SMALL PART COVERED BY THE RICE, THE SEAWEED RETAINS ITS TEXTURE!

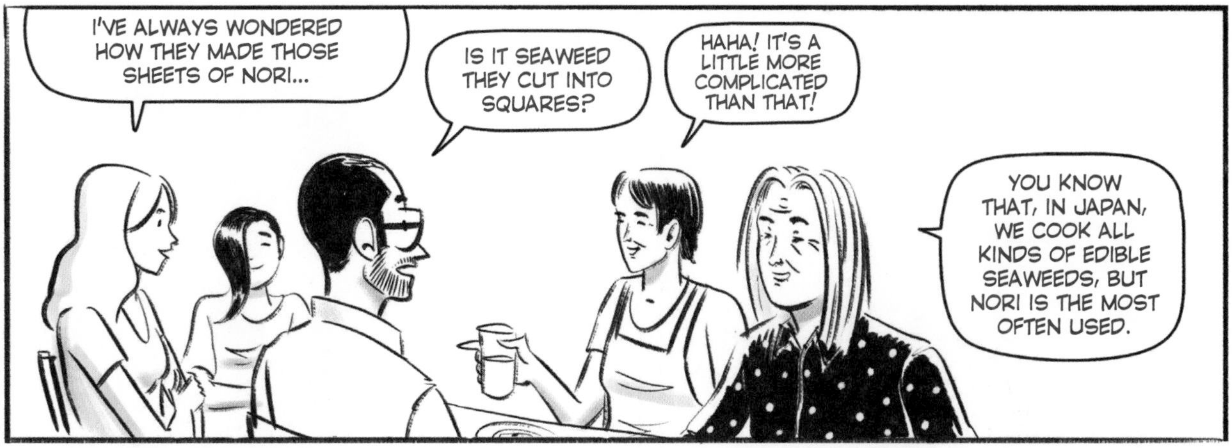
I'VE ALWAYS WONDERED HOW THEY MADE THOSE SHEETS OF NORI...
IS IT SEAWEED THEY CUT INTO SQUARES?
HAHA! IT'S A LITTLE MORE COMPLICATED THAN THAT!
YOU KNOW THAT, IN JAPAN, WE COOK ALL KINDS OF EDIBLE SEAWEEDS, BUT NORI IS THE MOST OFTEN USED.

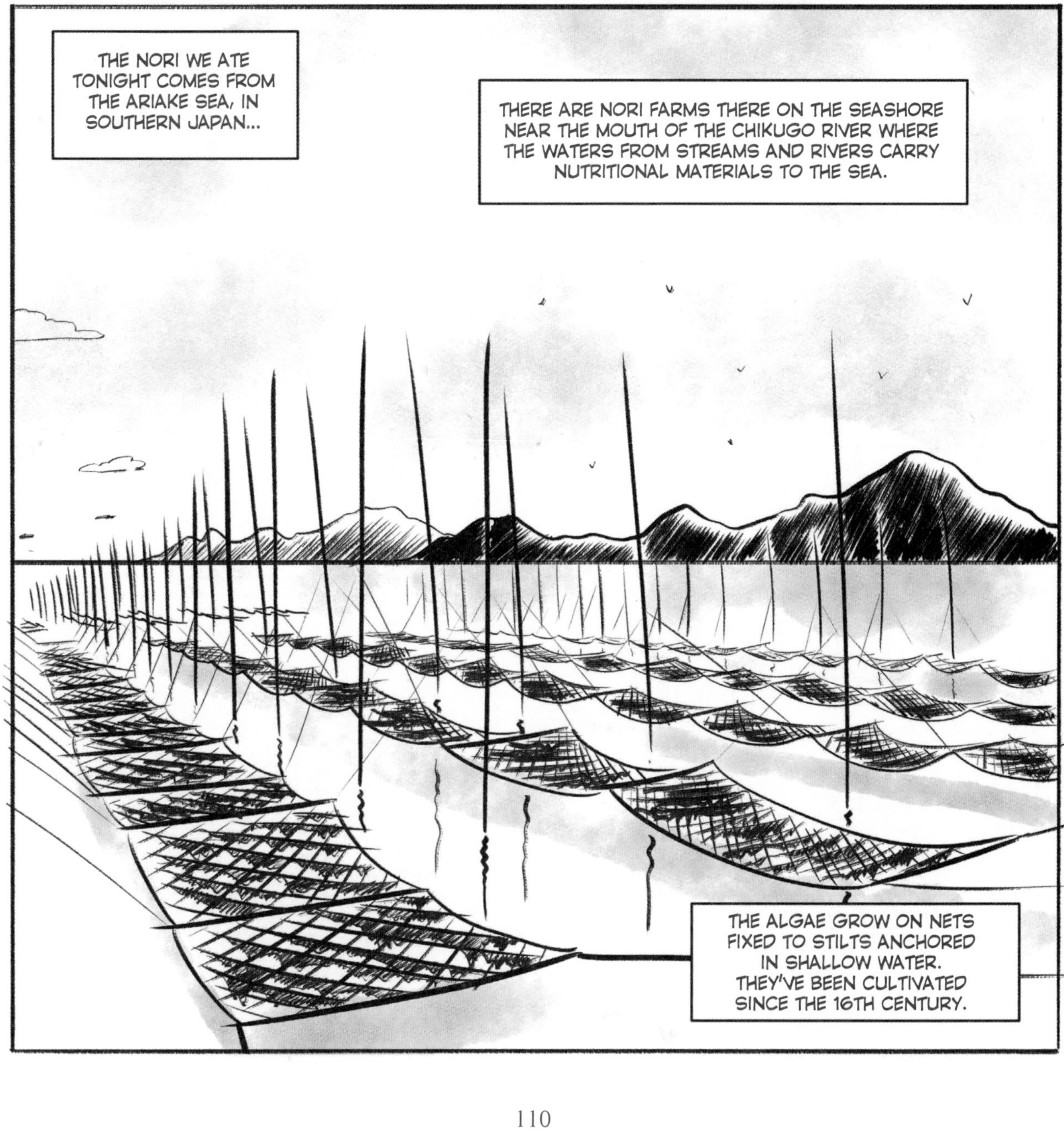
THE NORI WE ATE TONIGHT COMES FROM THE ARIAKE SEA, IN SOUTHERN JAPAN...
THERE ARE NORI FARMS THERE ON THE SEASHORE NEAR THE MOUTH OF THE CHIKUGO RIVER WHERE THE WATERS FROM STREAMS AND RIVERS CARRY NUTRITIONAL MATERIALS TO THE SEA.
THE ALGAE GROW ON NETS FIXED TO STILTS ANCHORED IN SHALLOW WATER. THEY'VE BEEN CULTIVATED SINCE THE 16TH CENTURY.

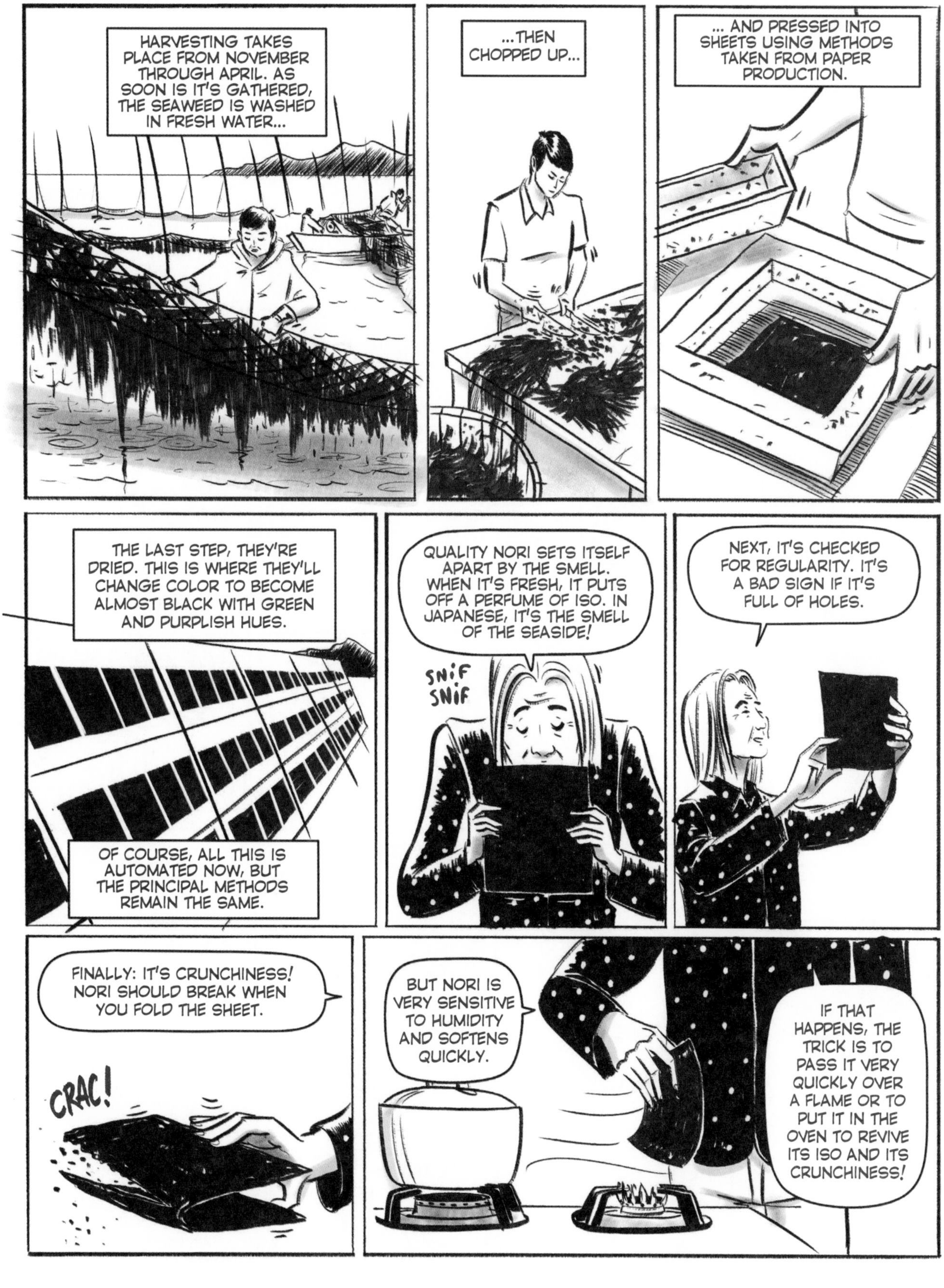
HARVESTING TAKES PLACE FROM NOVEMBER THROUGH APRIL. AS SOON IS IT'S GATHERED, THE SEAWEED IS WASHED IN FRESH WATER...
...THEN CHOPPED UP...
... AND PRESSED INTO SHEETS USING METHODS TAKEN FROM PAPER PRODUCTION.
THE LAST STEP, THEY'RE DRIED. THIS IS WHERE THEY'LL CHANGE COLOR TO BECOME ALMOST BLACK WITH GREEN AND PURPLISH HUES.
OF COURSE, ALL THIS IS AUTOMATED NOW, BUT THE PRINCIPAL METHODS REMAIN THE SAME.
QUALITY NORI SETS ITSELF APART BY THE SMELL. WHEN IT'S FRESH, IT PUTS OFF A PERFUME OF ISO. IN JAPANESE, IT'S THE SMELL OF THE SEASIDE!
SNIF SNIF
NEXT, IT'S CHECKED FOR REGULARITY. IT'S A BAD SIGN IF IT'S FULL OF HOLES.
FINALLY: IT'S CRUNCHINESS! NORI SHOULD BREAK WHEN YOU FOLD THE SHEET.
CRAC!
BUT NORI IS VERY SENSITIVE TO HUMIDITY AND SOFTENS QUICKLY.
IF THAT HAPPENS, THE TRICK IS TO PASS IT VERY QUICKLY OVER A FLAME OR TO PUT IT IN THE OVEN TO REVIVE ITS ISO AND ITS CRUNCHINESS!

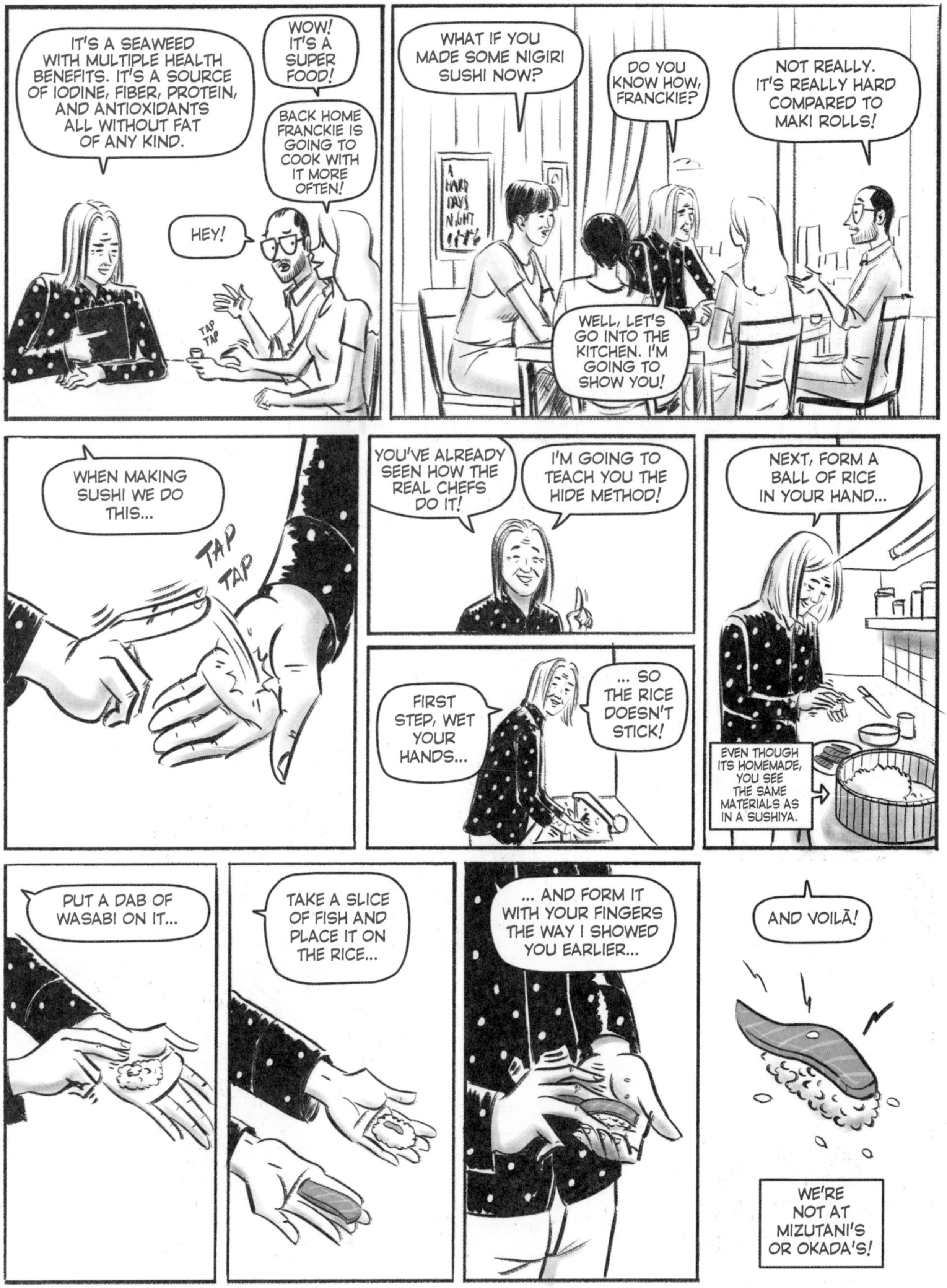
IT'S A SEAWEED WITH MULTIPLE HEALTH BENEFITS. IT'S A SOURCE OF IODINE, FIBER, PROTEIN, AND ANTIOXIDANTS ALL WITHOUT FAT OF ANY KIND.
WOW! IT'S A SUPER FOOD!
BACK HOME FRANCKIE IS GOING TO COOK WITH IT MORE OFTEN!
HEY!
TAP TAP
WHAT IF YOU MADE SOME NIGIRI SUSHI NOW?
DO YOU KNOW HOW, FRANCKIE?
NOT REALLY. IT'S REALLY HARD COMPARED TO MAKI ROLLS!
WELL, LET'S GO INTO THE KITCHEN. I'M GOING TO SHOW YOU!
WHEN MAKING SUSHI WE DO THIS...
TAP TAP
YOU'VE ALREADY SEEN HOW THE REAL CHEFS DO IT!
I'M GOING TO TEACH YOU THE HIDE METHOD!
FIRST STEP, WET YOUR HANDS...
... SO THE RICE DOESN'T STICK!
NEXT, FORM A BALL OF RICE IN YOUR HAND...
EVEN THOUGH ITS HOMEMADE, YOU SEE THE SAME MATERIALS AS IN A SUSHIYA.
PUT A DAB OF WASABI ON IT...
TAKE A SLICE OF FISH AND PLACE IT ON THE RICE...
... AND FORM IT WITH YOUR FINGERS THE WAY I SHOWED YOU EARLIER...
AND VOILÃ!
WE'RE NOT AT MIZUTANI'S OR OKADA'S!

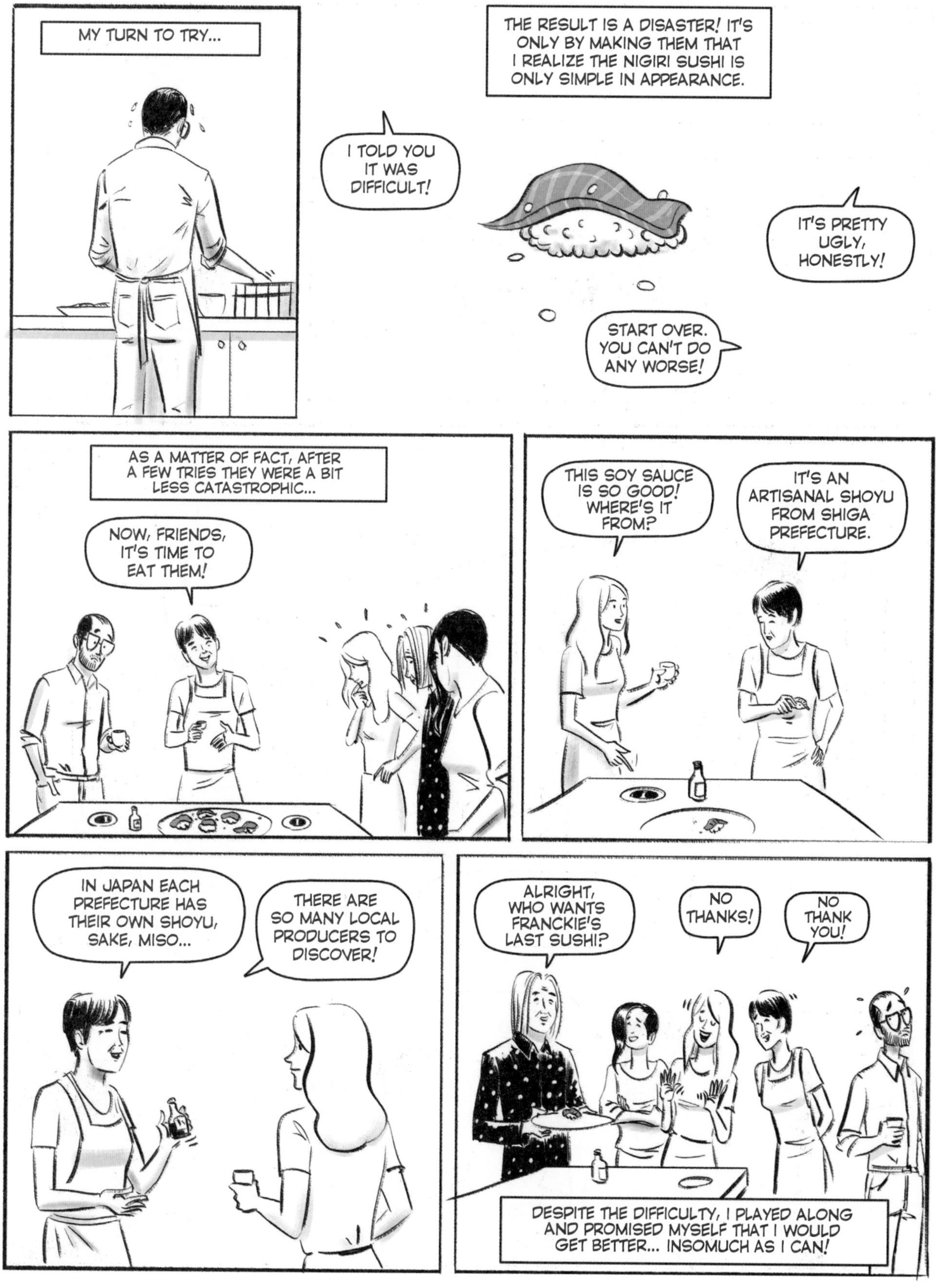

MY TURN TO TRY...
THE RESULT IS A DISASTER! IT'S ONLY BY MAKING THEM THAT I REALIZE THE NIGIRI SUSHI IS ONLY SIMPLE IN APPEARANCE.
I TOLD YOU IT WAS DIFFICULT!
IT'S PRETTY UGLY, HONESTLY!
START OVER. YOU CAN'T DO ANY WORSE!
AS A MATTER OF FACT, AFTER A FEW TRIES THEY WERE A BIT LESS CATASTROPHIC...
NOW, FRIENDS, IT'S TIME TO EAT THEM!
THIS SOY SAUCE IS SO GOOD! WHERE'S IT FROM?
IT'S AN ARTISANAL SHOYU FROM SHIGA PREFECTURE.
IN JAPAN EACH PREFECTURE HAS THEIR OWN SHOYU, SAKE, MISO...
THERE ARE SO MANY LOCAL PRODUCERS TO DISCOVER!
ALRIGHT, WHO WANTS FRANCKIE'S LAST SUSHI?
NO THANKS!
NO THANK YOU!
DESPITE THE DIFFICULTY, I PLAYED ALONG AND PROMISED MYSELF THAT I WOULD GET BETTER... INSOMUCH AS I CAN!

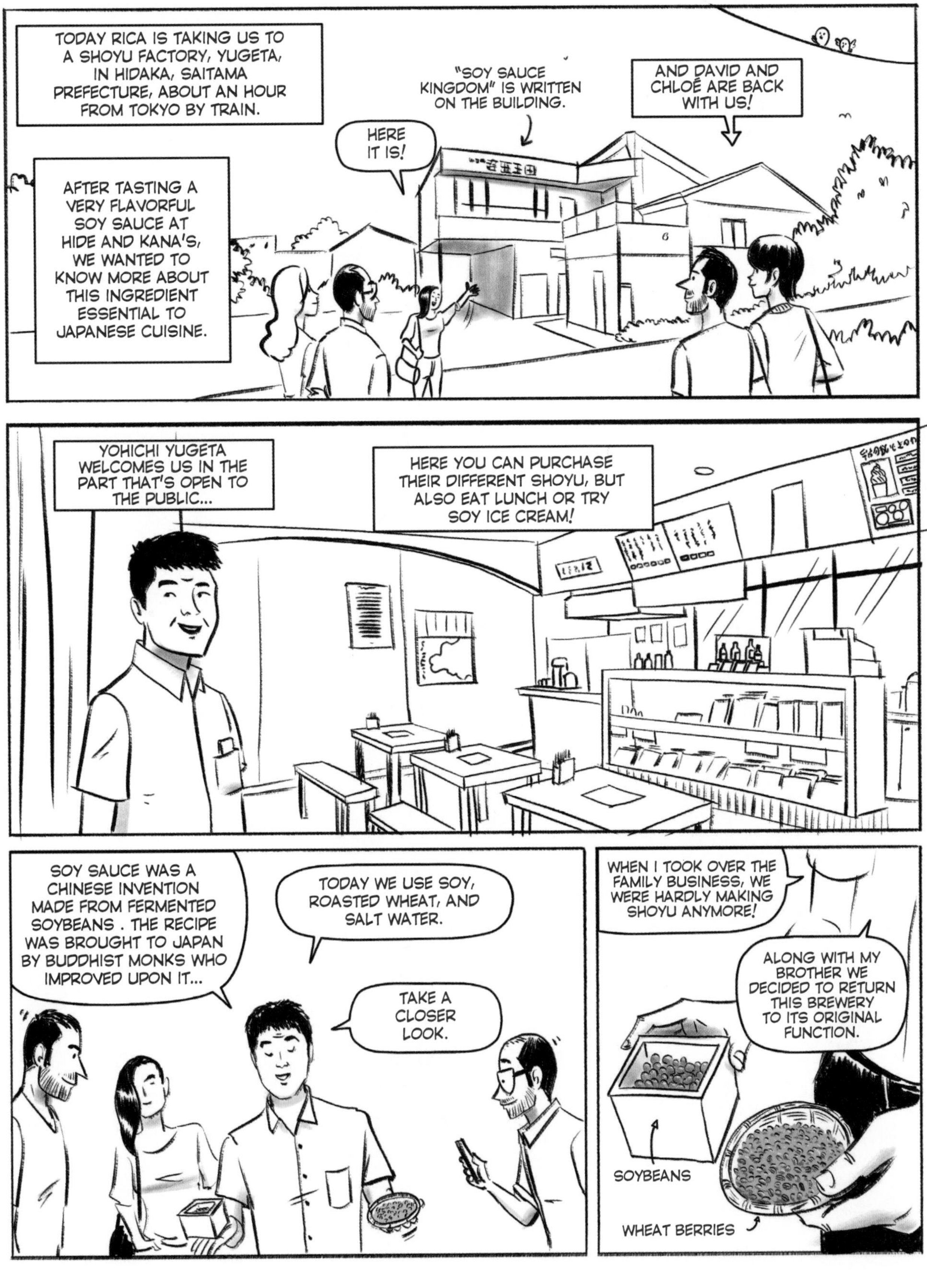

TODAY RICA IS TAKING US TO A SHOYU FACTORY, YUGETA, IN HIDAKA, SAITAMA PREFECTURE, ABOUT AN HOUR FROM TOKYO BY TRAIN.
AFTER TASTING A VERY FLAVORFUL SOY SAUCE AT HIDE AND KANA'S, WE WANTED TO KNOW MORE ABOUT THIS INGREDIENT ESSENTIAL TO JAPANESE CUISINE.
HERE IT IS!
"SOY SAUCE KINGDOM" IS WRITTEN ON THE BUILDING.
AND DAVID AND CHLOÉ ARE BACK WITH US!
YOHICHI YUGETA WELCOMES US IN THE PART THAT'S OPEN TO THE PUBLIC...
HERE YOU CAN PURCHASE THEIR DIFFERENT SHOYU, BUT ALSO EAT LUNCH OR TRY SOY ICE CREAM!
SOY SAUCE WAS A CHINESE INVENTION MADE FROM FERMENTED SOYBEANS . THE RECIPE WAS BROUGHT TO JAPAN BY BUDDHIST MONKS WHO IMPROVED UPON IT...
TODAY WE USE SOY, ROASTED WHEAT, AND SALT WATER.
TAKE A CLOSER LOOK.
WHEN I TOOK OVER THE FAMILY BUSINESS, WE WERE HARDLY MAKING SHOYU ANYMORE!
ALONG WITH MY BROTHER WE DECIDED TO RETURN THIS BREWERY TO ITS ORIGINAL FUNCTION.
SOYBEANS
WHEAT BERRIES

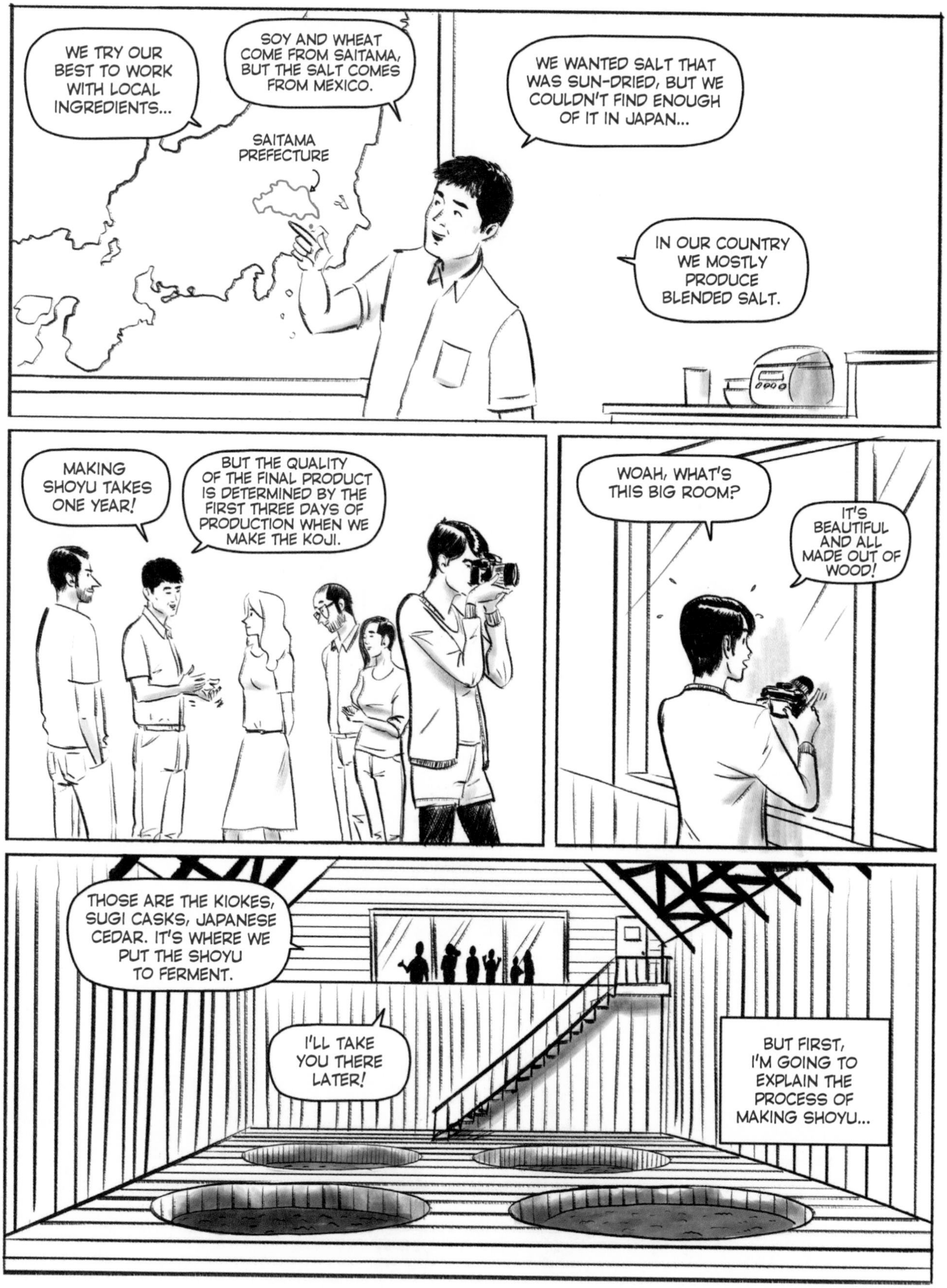
WE TRY OUR BEST TO WORK WITH LOCAL INGREDIENTS...
SOY AND WHEAT COME FROM SAITAMA, BUT THE SALT COMES FROM MEXICO.
SAITAMA PREFECTURE
WE WANTED SALT THAT WAS SUN-DRIED, BUT WE COULDN'T FIND ENOUGH OF IT IN JAPAN...
IN OUR COUNTRY WE MOSTLY PRODUCE BLENDED SALT.
MAKING SHOYU TAKES ONE YEAR!
BUT THE QUALITY OF THE FINAL PRODUCT IS DETERMINED BY THE FIRST THREE DAYS OF PRODUCTION WHEN WE MAKE THE KOJI.
WOAH, WHAT'S THIS BIG ROOM?
IT'S BEAUTIFUL AND ALL MADE OUT OF WOOD!
THOSE ARE THE KIOKES, SUGI CASKS, JAPANESE CEDAR. IT'S WHERE WE PUT THE SHOYU TO FERMENT.
I'LL TAKE YOU THERE LATER!
BUT FIRST, I'M GOING TO EXPLAIN THE PROCESS OF MAKING SHOYU...

THE SOYBEANS SOAK FOR 10 HOURS OR SO IN SPRING WATER BEFORE BEING STEAMED IN A VAT FOR AN HOUR.

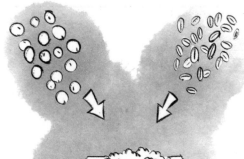

THE WHEAT (EQUAL TO THE QUANTITY OF SOY) IS ROASTED AT 572°F FOR A FEW MINUTES, THEN GROUND.

YOU SPREAD THE STEAMED SOYBEANS AND THE ROASTED AND GROUND WHEAT ON A TABLE IN A SPECIAL ROOM CALLED THE KOJI MURO (THE "KOJI ROOM").

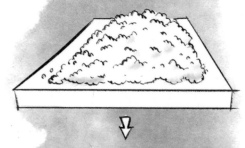

THIS MIXTURE IS SOWN WITH ASPERGILLUS, THE MICROSCOPIC FUNGUS YOU USE TO MAKE SAKE. THE END RESULT IS KOJI.

THE KOJI IS DILUTED IN SALT WATER AND FERMENTED IN CYPRUS CASKS.

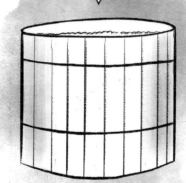

THIS MIXTURE IS CALLED MOROMI AND IT'S DURING ITS YEAR OF AGING THAT IT WILL BECOME SOY SAUCE.

YOU TRANSFER THE CONTENTS OF THE VATS IN BAGS ONLY TO PRESS THEM TO EXTRACT THE LIQUID.

WHAT REMAINS IN THE BAGS IS USED FOR ANIMAL FEED.

BEFORE BOTTLING, THE SHOYU IS LEFT TO DECANT TO REMOVE ANY IMPURITIES FROM THE SOY SAUCE.

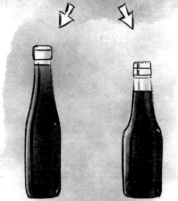

AN OPTIONAL LAST STEP, THE SAUCE IS PASTEURIZED. JUST LIKE FOR SAKE, THERE IS UNPASTEURIZED SHOYU!

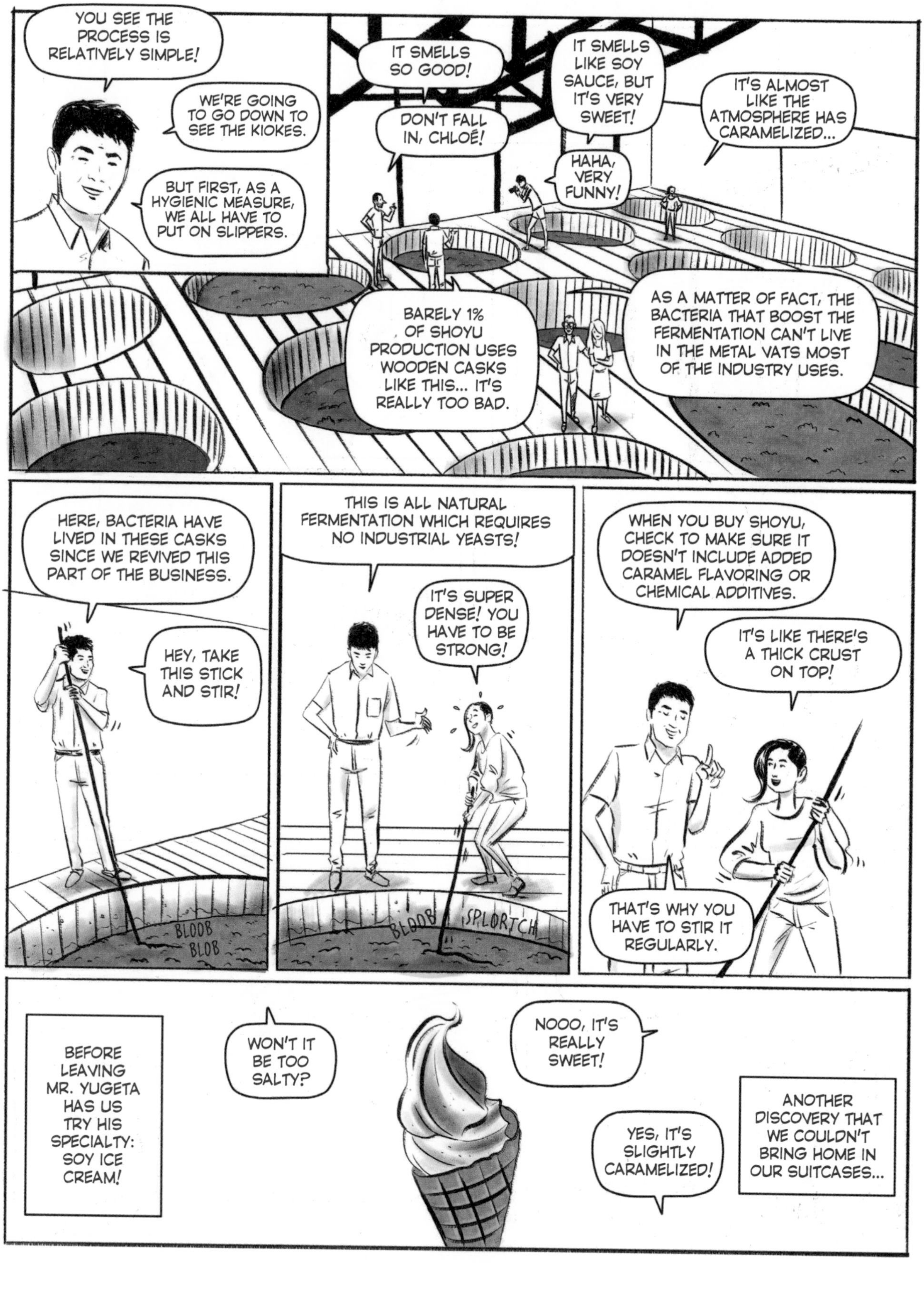
YOU SEE THE PROCESS IS RELATIVELY SIMPLE!
WE'RE GOING TO GO DOWN TO SEE THE KIOKES.
BUT FIRST, AS A HYGIENIC MEASURE, WE ALL HAVE TO PUT ON SLIPPERS.
IT SMELLS SO GOOD!
DON'T FALL IN, CHLOÉ!
IT SMELLS LIKE SOY SAUCE, BUT IT'S VERY SWEET!
HAHA, VERY FUNNY!
IT'S ALMOST LIKE THE ATMOSPHERE HAS CARAMELIZED...
BARELY 1% OF SHOYU PRODUCTION USES WOODEN CASKS LIKE THIS... IT'S REALLY TOO BAD.
AS A MATTER OF FACT, THE BACTERIA THAT BOOST THE FERMENTATION CAN'T LIVE IN THE METAL VATS MOST OF THE INDUSTRY USES.
HERE, BACTERIA HAVE LIVED IN THESE CASKS SINCE WE REVIVED THIS PART OF THE BUSINESS.
HEY, TAKE THIS STICK AND STIR!
BLOOB
BLOB
THIS IS ALL NATURAL FERMENTATION WHICH REQUIRES NO INDUSTRIAL YEASTS!
IT'S SUPER DENSE! YOU HAVE TO BE STRONG!
BLOOB
SPLORTCH
WHEN YOU BUY SHOYU, CHECK TO MAKE SURE IT DOESN'T INCLUDE ADDED CARAMEL FLAVORING OR CHEMICAL ADDITIVES.
IT'S LIKE THERE'S A THICK CRUST ON TOP!
THAT'S WHY YOU HAVE TO STIR IT REGULARLY.
BEFORE LEAVING MR. YUGETA HAS US TRY HIS SPECIALTY: SOY ICE CREAM!
WON'T IT BE TOO SALTY?
NOOO, IT'S REALLY SWEET!
YES, IT'S SLIGHTLY CARAMELIZED!
ANOTHER DISCOVERY THAT WE COULDN'T BRING HOME IN OUR SUITCASES...

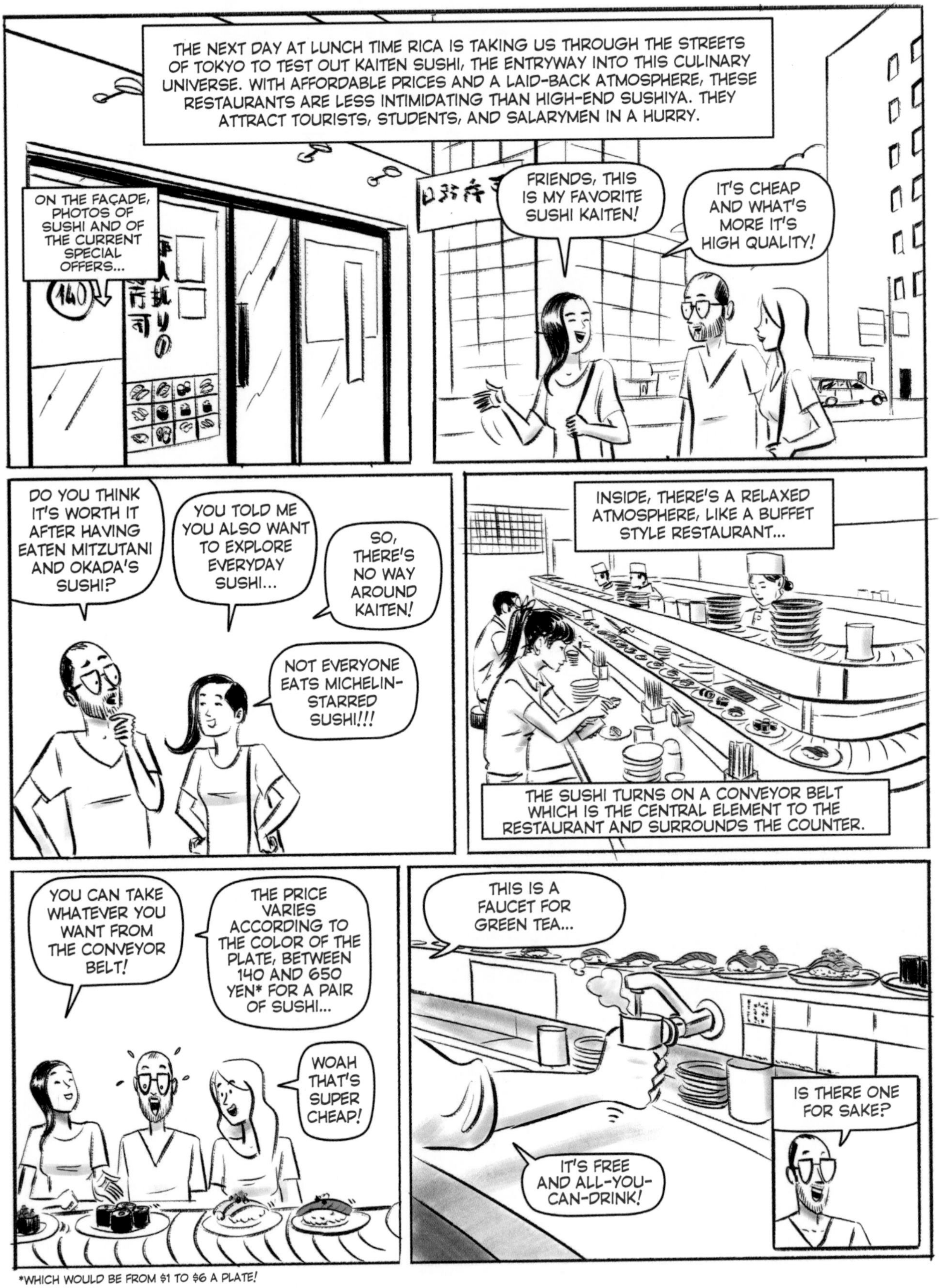
THE NEXT DAY AT LUNCH TIME RICA IS TAKING US THROUGH THE STREETS OF TOKYO TO TEST OUT KAITEN SUSHI, THE ENTRYWAY INTO THIS CULINARY UNIVERSE. WITH AFFORDABLE PRICES AND A LAID-BACK ATMOSPHERE, THESE RESTAURANTS ARE LESS INTIMIDATING THAN HIGH-END SUSHIYA. THEY ATTRACT TOURISTS, STUDENTS, AND SALARYMEN IN A HURRY.
ON THE FAÇADE, PHOTOS OF SUSHI AND OF THE CURRENT SPECIAL OFFERS...
140
FRIENDS, THIS IS MY FAVORITE SUSHI KAITEN!
IT'S CHEAP AND WHAT'S MORE IT'S HIGH QUALITY!
DO YOU THINK IT'S WORTH IT AFTER HAVING EATEN MITZUTANI AND OKADA'S SUSHI?
YOU TOLD ME YOU ALSO WANT TO EXPLORE EVERYDAY SUSHI...
SO, THERE'S NO WAY AROUND KAITEN!
NOT EVERYONE EATS MICHELIN-STARRED SUSHI!!!
INSIDE, THERE'S A RELAXED ATMOSPHERE, LIKE A BUFFET STYLE RESTAURANT...
THE SUSHI TURNS ON A CONVEYOR BELT WHICH IS THE CENTRAL ELEMENT TO THE RESTAURANT AND SURROUNDS THE COUNTER.
YOU CAN TAKE WHATEVER YOU WANT FROM THE CONVEYOR BELT!
THE PRICE VARIES ACCORDING TO THE COLOR OF THE PLATE, BETWEEN 140 AND 650 YEN* FOR A PAIR OF SUSHI...
WOAH THAT'S SUPER CHEAP!
THIS IS A FAUCET FOR GREEN TEA...
IT'S FREE AND ALL-YOU-CAN-DRINK!
IS THERE ONE FOR SAKE?

*WHICH WOULD BE FROM $1 TO $6 A PLATE!

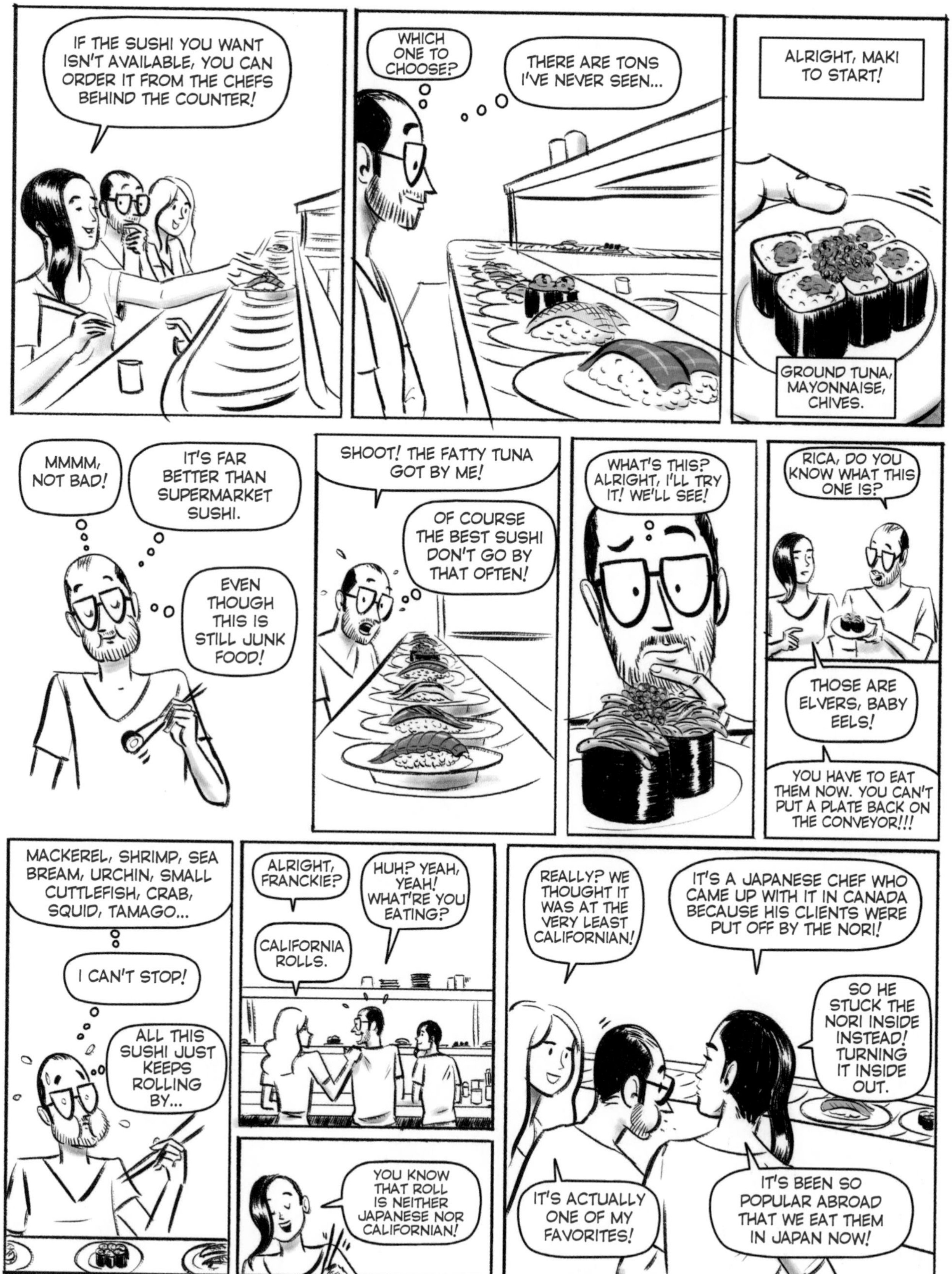
IF THE SUSHI YOU WANT ISN'T AVAILABLE, YOU CAN ORDER IT FROM THE CHEFS BEHIND THE COUNTER!
WHICH ONE TO CHOOSE?
THERE ARE TONS I'VE NEVER SEEN...
ALRIGHT, MAKI TO START!
GROUND TUNA, MAYONNAISE, CHIVES.
MMMM, NOT BAD!
IT'S FAR BETTER THAN SUPERMARKET SUSHI.
EVEN THOUGH THIS IS STILL JUNK FOOD!
SHOOT! THE FATTY TUNA GOT BY ME!
OF COURSE THE BEST SUSHI DON'T GO BY THAT OFTEN!
WHAT'S THIS? ALRIGHT, I'LL TRY IT! WE'LL SEE!
RICA, DO YOU KNOW WHAT THIS ONE IS?
THOSE ARE ELVERS, BABY EELS!
YOU HAVE TO EAT THEM NOW. YOU CAN'T PUT A PLATE BACK ON THE CONVEYOR!!!
MACKEREL, SHRIMP, SEA BREAM, URCHIN, SMALL CUTTLEFISH, CRAB, SQUID, TAMAGO...
I CAN'T STOP!
ALL THIS SUSHI JUST KEEPS ROLLING BY...
ALRIGHT, FRANCKIE?
HUH? YEAH, YEAH! WHAT'RE YOU EATING?
CALIFORNIA ROLLS.
YOU KNOW THAT ROLL IS NEITHER JAPANESE NOR CALIFORNIAN!
REALLY? WE THOUGHT IT WAS AT THE VERY LEAST CALIFORNIAN!
IT'S A JAPANESE CHEF WHO CAME UP WITH IT IN CANADA BECAUSE HIS CLIENTS WERE PUT OFF BY THE NORI!
SO HE STUCK THE NORI INSIDE INSTEAD! TURNING IT INSIDE OUT.
IT'S ACTUALLY ONE OF MY FAVORITES!
IT'S BEEN SO POPULAR ABROAD THAT WE EAT THEM IN JAPAN NOW!

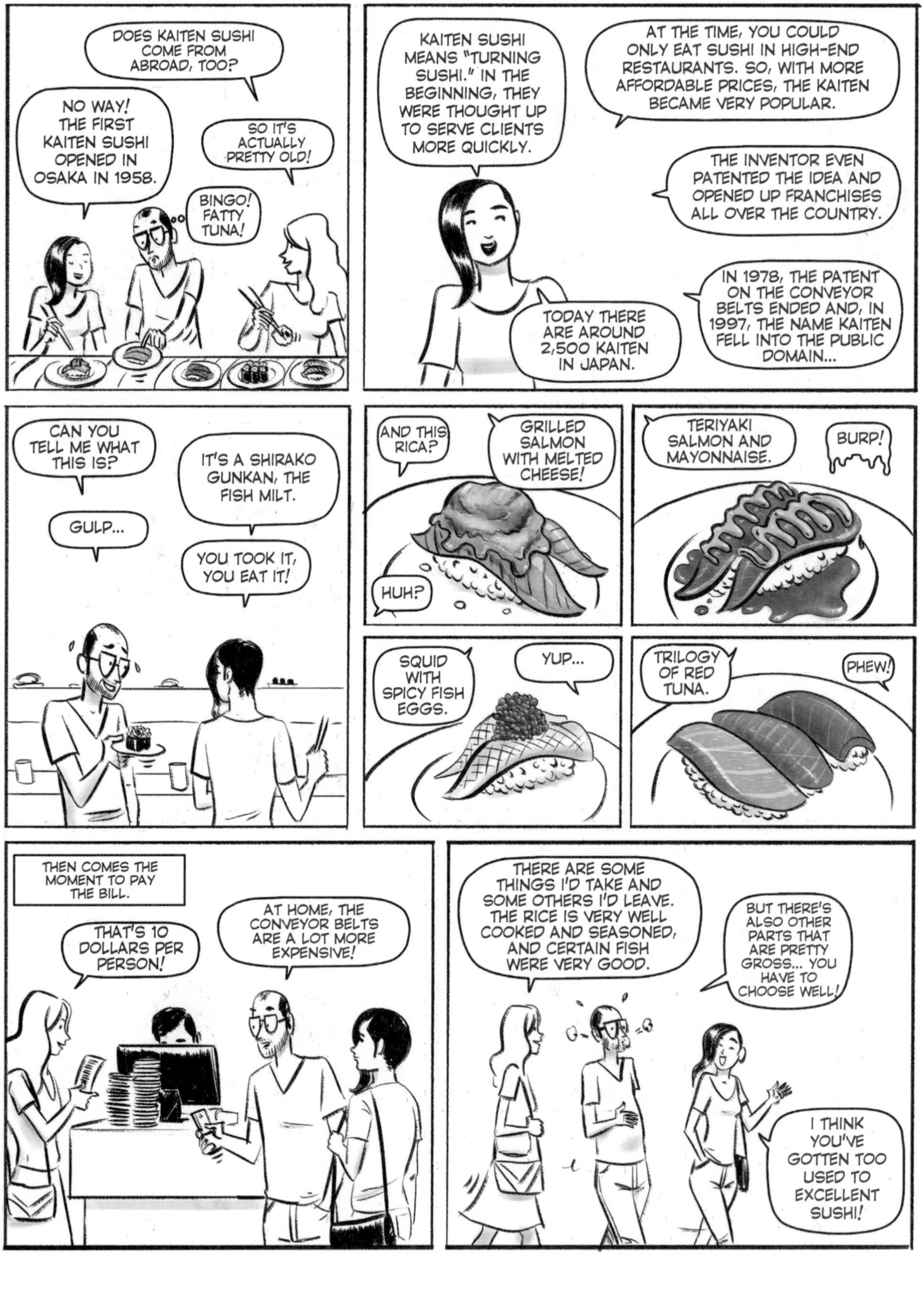
DOES KAITEN SUSHI COME FROM ABROAD, TOO?
NO WAY! THE FIRST KAITEN SUSHI OPENED IN OSAKA IN 1958.
SO IT'S ACTUALLY PRETTY OLD!
BINGO! FATTY TUNA!
KAITEN SUSHI MEANS "TURNING SUSHI." IN THE BEGINNING, THEY WERE THOUGHT UP TO SERVE CLIENTS MORE QUICKLY.
AT THE TIME, YOU COULD ONLY EAT SUSHI IN HIGH-END RESTAURANTS. SO, WITH MORE AFFORDABLE PRICES, THE KAITEN BECAME VERY POPULAR.
THE INVENTOR EVEN PATENTED THE IDEA AND OPENED UP FRANCHISES ALL OVER THE COUNTRY.
IN 1978, THE PATENT ON THE CONVEYOR BELTS ENDED AND, IN 1997, THE NAME KAITEN FELL INTO THE PUBLIC DOMAIN...
TODAY THERE ARE AROUND 2,500 KAITEN IN JAPAN.
CAN YOU TELL ME WHAT THIS IS?
IT'S A SHIRAKO GUNKAN, THE FISH MILT.
GULP...
YOU TOOK IT, YOU EAT IT!
AND THIS RICA?
GRILLED SALMON WITH MELTED CHEESE!
HUH?
TERIYAKI SALMON AND MAYONNAISE.
BURP!
SQUID WITH SPICY FISH EGGS.
YUP...
TRILOGY OF RED TUNA.
PHEW!
THEN COMES THE MOMENT TO PAY THE BILL.
THAT'S 10 DOLLARS PER PERSON!
AT HOME, THE CONVEYOR BELTS ARE A LOT MORE EXPENSIVE!
THERE ARE SOME THINGS I'D TAKE AND SOME OTHERS I'D LEAVE. THE RICE IS VERY WELL COOKED AND SEASONED, AND CERTAIN FISH WERE VERY GOOD.
BUT THERE'S ALSO OTHER PARTS THAT ARE PRETTY GROSS... YOU HAVE TO CHOOSE WELL!
I THINK YOU'VE GOTTEN TOO USED TO EXCELLENT SUSHI!

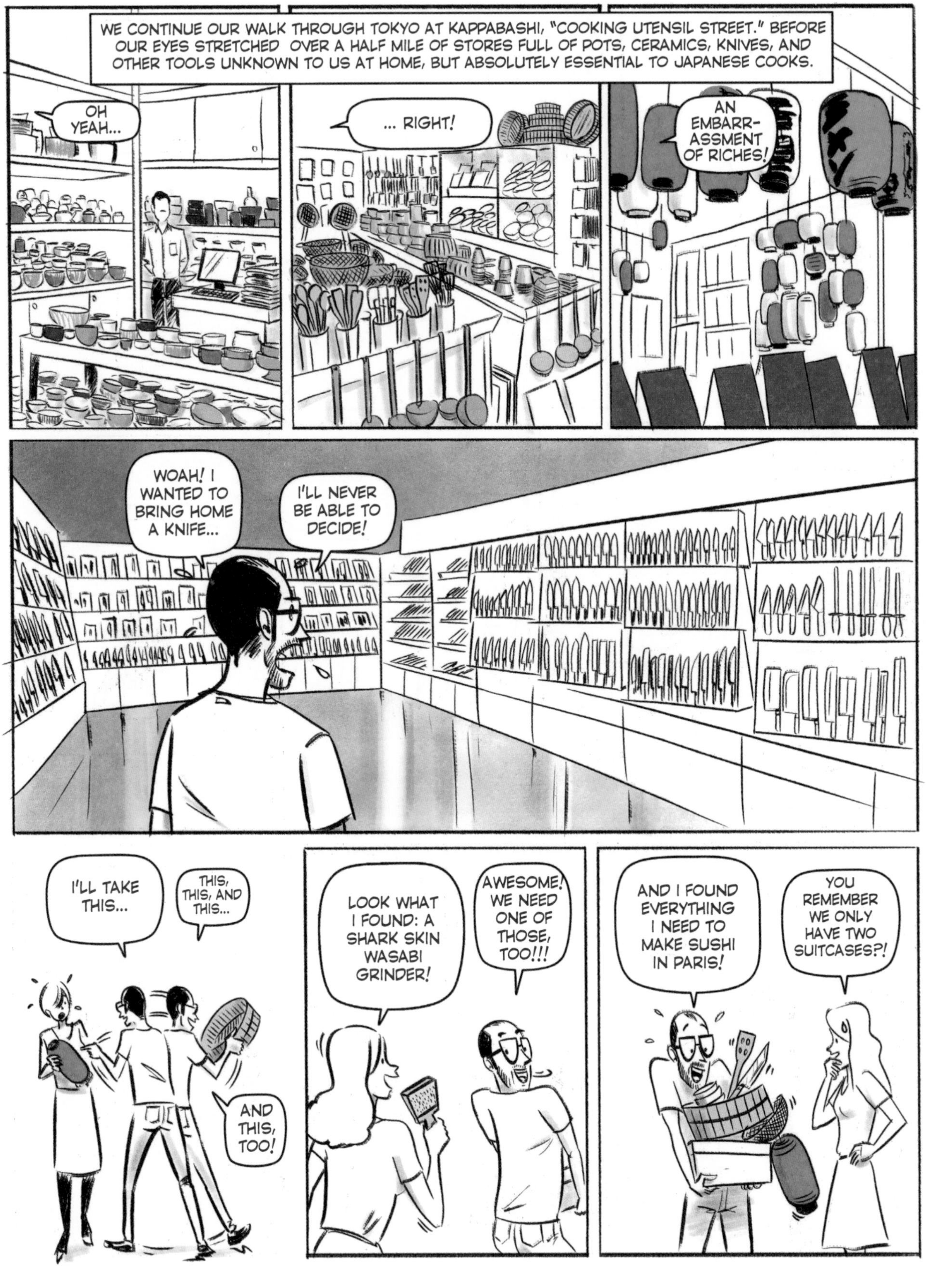
WE CONTINUE OUR WALK THROUGH TOKYO AT KAPPABASHI, "COOKING UTENSIL STREET." BEFORE OUR EYES STRETCHED OVER A HALF MILE OF STORES FULL OF POTS, CERAMICS, KNIVES, AND OTHER TOOLS UNKNOWN TO US AT HOME, BUT ABSOLUTELY ESSENTIAL TO JAPANESE COOKS.
OH YEAH...
... RIGHT!
AN EMBARR-ASSMENT OF RICHES!
WOAH! I WANTED TO BRING HOME A KNIFE...
I'LL NEVER BE ABLE TO DECIDE!
I'LL TAKE THIS...
THIS, THIS, AND THIS...
AND THIS, TOO!
LOOK WHAT I FOUND: A SHARK SKIN WASABI GRINDER!
AWESOME! WE NEED ONE OF THOSE, TOO!!!
AND I FOUND EVERYTHING I NEED TO MAKE SUSHI IN PARIS!
YOU REMEMBER WE ONLY HAVE TWO SUITCASES?!

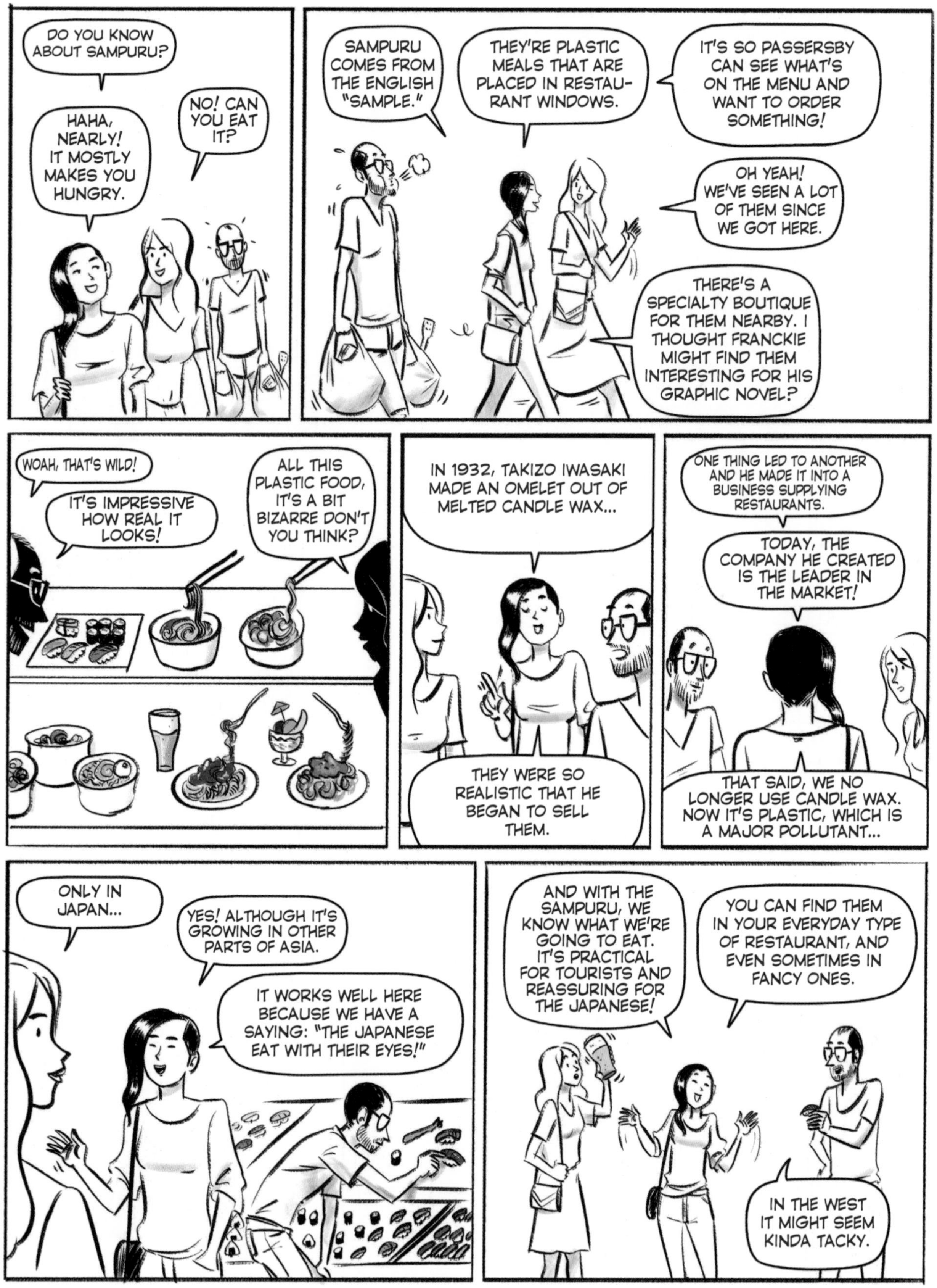
DO YOU KNOW ABOUT SAMPURU?
NO! CAN YOU EAT IT?
HAHA, NEARLY! IT MOSTLY MAKES YOU HUNGRY.
SAMPURU COMES FROM THE ENGLISH "SAMPLE."
THEY'RE PLASTIC MEALS THAT ARE PLACED IN RESTAU-RANT WINDOWS.
IT'S SO PASSERSBY CAN SEE WHAT'S ON THE MENU AND WANT TO ORDER SOMETHING!
OH YEAH! WE'VE SEEN A LOT OF THEM SINCE WE GOT HERE.
THERE'S A SPECIALTY BOUTIQUE FOR THEM NEARBY. I THOUGHT FRANCKIE MIGHT FIND THEM INTERESTING FOR HIS GRAPHIC NOVEL?
WOAH, THAT'S WILD!
IT'S IMPRESSIVE HOW REAL IT LOOKS!
ALL THIS PLASTIC FOOD, IT'S A BIT BIZARRE DON'T YOU THINK?
IN 1932, TAKIZO IWASAKI MADE AN OMELET OUT OF MELTED CANDLE WAX...
THEY WERE SO REALISTIC THAT HE BEGAN TO SELL THEM.
ONE THING LED TO ANOTHER AND HE MADE IT INTO A BUSINESS SUPPLYING RESTAURANTS.
TODAY, THE COMPANY HE CREATED IS THE LEADER IN THE MARKET!
THAT SAID, WE NO LONGER USE CANDLE WAX. NOW IT'S PLASTIC, WHICH IS A MAJOR POLLUTANT...
ONLY IN JAPAN...
YES! ALTHOUGH IT'S GROWING IN OTHER PARTS OF ASIA.
IT WORKS WELL HERE BECAUSE WE HAVE A SAYING: "THE JAPANESE EAT WITH THEIR EYES!"
AND WITH THE SAMPURU, WE KNOW WHAT WE'RE GOING TO EAT. IT'S PRACTICAL FOR TOURISTS AND REASSURING FOR THE JAPANESE!
YOU CAN FIND THEM IN YOUR EVERYDAY TYPE OF RESTAURANT, AND EVEN SOMETIMES IN FANCY ONES.
IN THE WEST IT MIGHT SEEM KINDA TACKY.

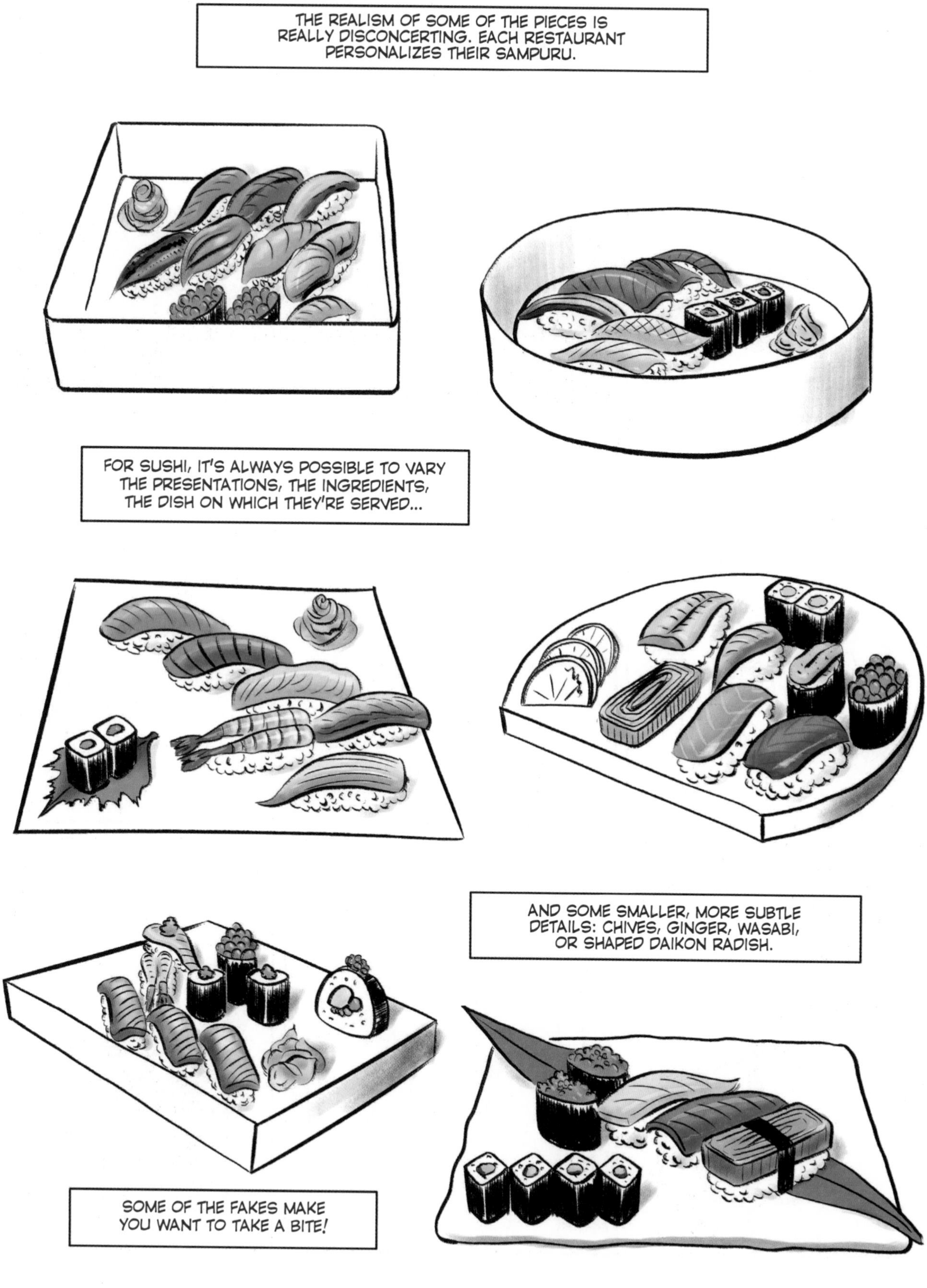
THE REALISM OF SOME OF THE PIECES IS REALLY DISCONCERTING. EACH RESTAURANT PERSONALIZES THEIR SAMPURU.
FOR SUSHI, IT'S ALWAYS POSSIBLE TO VARY THE PRESENTATIONS, THE INGREDIENTS, THE DISH ON WHICH THEY'RE SERVED...
AND SOME SMALLER, MORE SUBTLE DETAILS: CHIVES, GINGER, WASABI, OR SHAPED DAIKON RADISH.
SOME OF THE FAKES MAKE YOU WANT TO TAKE A BITE!

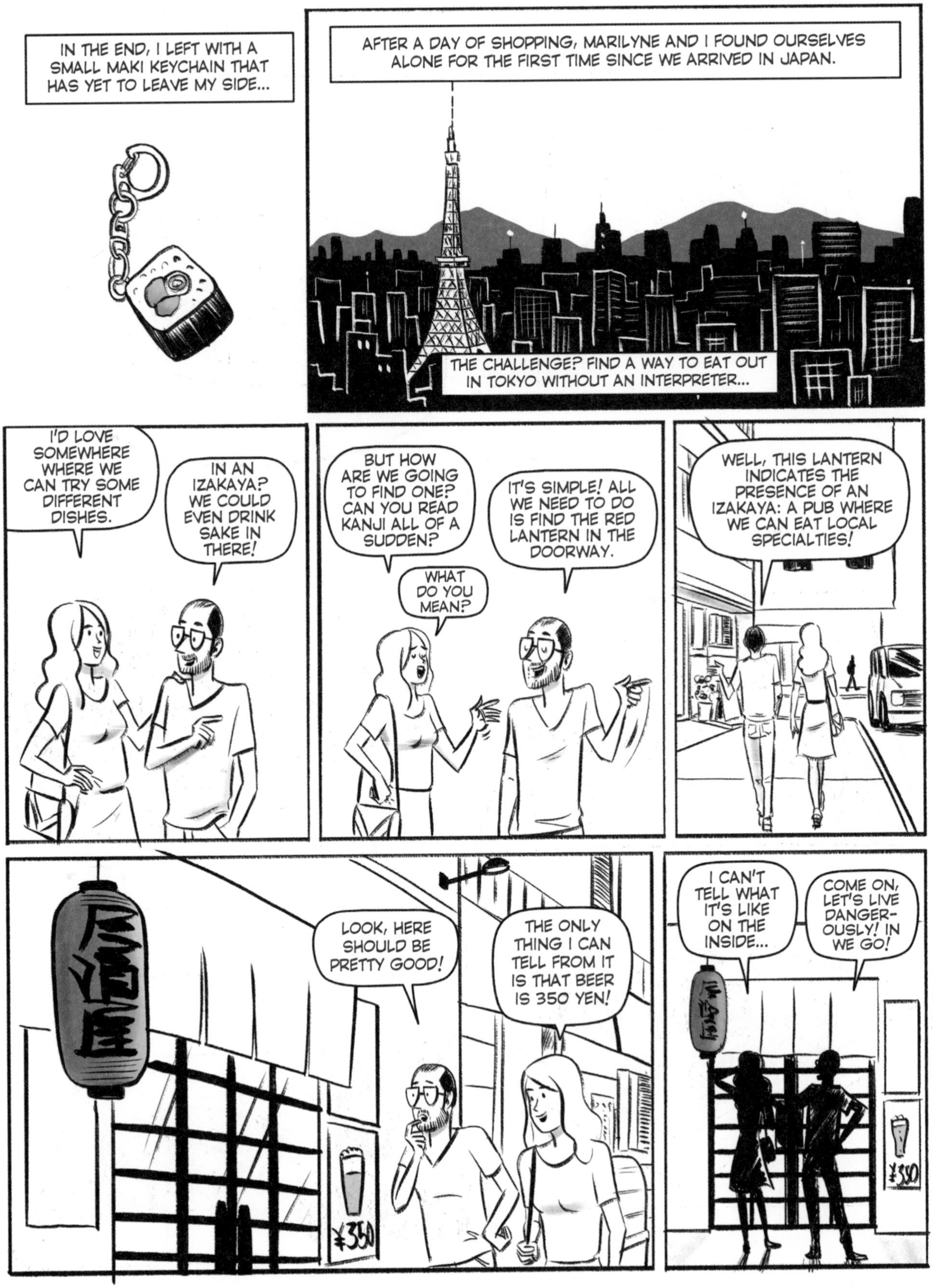
IN THE END, I LEFT WITH A SMALL MAKI KEYCHAIN THAT HAS YET TO LEAVE MY SIDE...
AFTER A DAY OF SHOPPING, MARILYNE AND I FOUND OURSELVES ALONE FOR THE FIRST TIME SINCE WE ARRIVED IN JAPAN.
THE CHALLENGE? FIND A WAY TO EAT OUT IN TOKYO WITHOUT AN INTERPRETER...
I'D LOVE SOMEWHERE WHERE WE CAN TRY SOME DIFFERENT DISHES.
IN AN IZAKAYA? WE COULD EVEN DRINK SAKE IN THERE!
BUT HOW ARE WE GOING TO FIND ONE? CAN YOU READ KANJI ALL OF A SUDDEN?
IT'S SIMPLE! ALL WE NEED TO DO IS FIND THE RED LANTERN IN THE DOORWAY.
WHAT DO YOU MEAN?
WELL, THIS LANTERN INDICATES THE PRESENCE OF AN IZAKAYA: A PUB WHERE WE CAN EAT LOCAL SPECIALTIES!
LOOK, HERE SHOULD BE PRETTY GOOD!
THE ONLY THING I CAN TELL FROM IT IS THAT BEER IS 350 YEN!
¥350
I CAN'T TELL WHAT IT'S LIKE ON THE INSIDE...
COME ON, LET'S LIVE DANGER-OUSLY! IN WE GO!
¥350

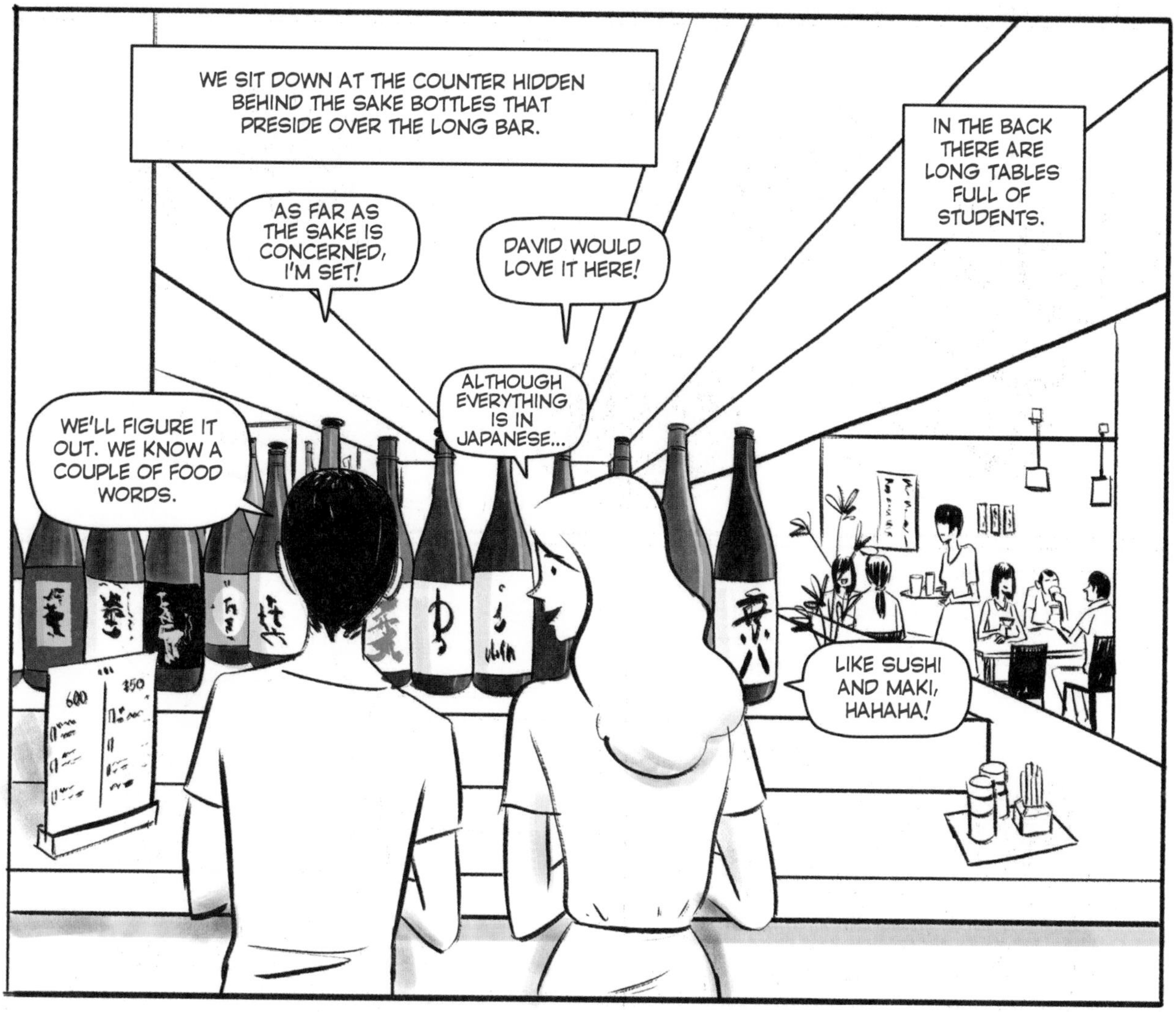
WE SIT DOWN AT THE COUNTER HIDDEN BEHIND THE SAKE BOTTLES THAT PRESIDE OVER THE LONG BAR.
IN THE BACK THERE ARE LONG TABLES FULL OF STUDENTS.
AS FAR AS THE SAKE IS CONCERNED, I'M SET!
DAVID WOULD LOVE IT HERE!
ALTHOUGH EVERYTHING IS IN JAPANESE...
WE'LL FIGURE IT OUT. WE KNOW A COUPLE OF FOOD WORDS.
LIKE SUSHI AND MAKI, HAHAHA!

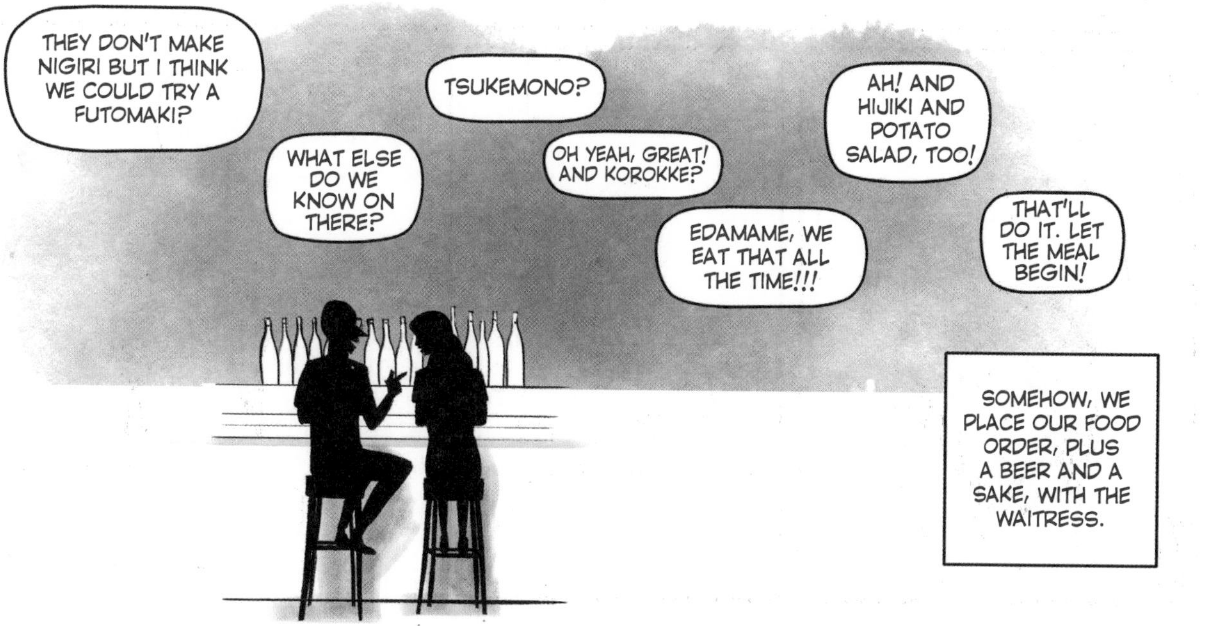
THEY DON'T MAKE NIGIRI BUT I THINK WE COULD TRY A FUTOMAKI?
TSUKEMONO?
WHAT ELSE DO WE KNOW ON THERE?
OH YEAH, GREAT! AND KOROKKE?
AH! AND HIJIKI AND POTATO SALAD, TOO!
EDAMAME, WE EAT THAT ALL THE TIME!!!
THAT'LL DO IT. LET THE MEAL BEGIN!
SOMEHOW, WE PLACE OUR FOOD ORDER, PLUS A BEER AND A SAKE, WITH THE WAITRESS.

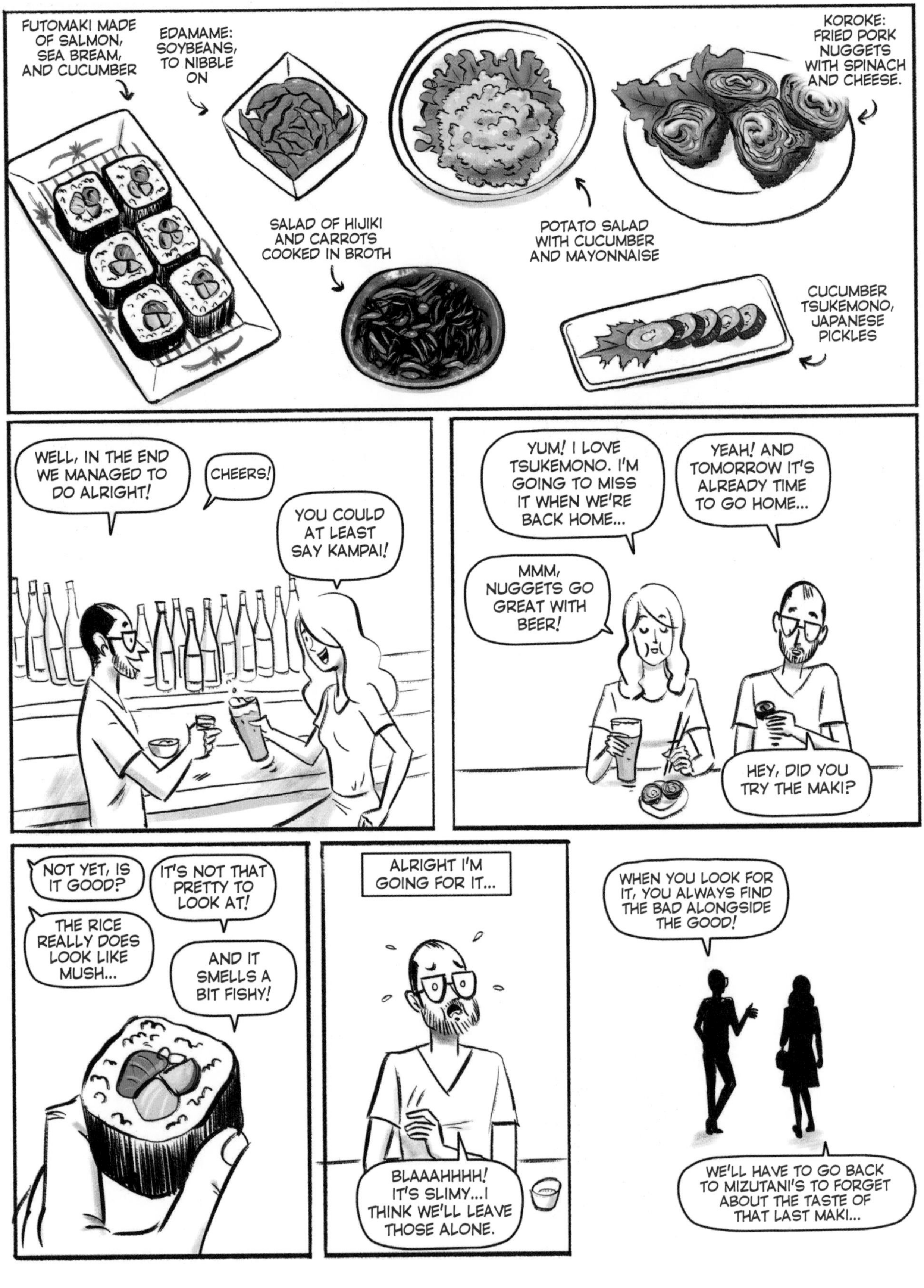
FUTOMAKI MADE OF SALMON, SEA BREAM, AND CUCUMBER
EDAMAME: SOYBEANS, TO NIBBLE ON
KOROKE: FRIED PORK NUGGETS WITH SPINACH AND CHEESE.
SALAD OF HIJIKI AND CARROTS COOKED IN BROTH
POTATO SALAD WITH CUCUMBER AND MAYONNAISE
CUCUMBER TSUKEMONO, JAPANESE PICKLES
WELL, IN THE END WE MANAGED TO DO ALRIGHT!
CHEERS!
YOU COULD AT LEAST SAY KAMPAI!
YUM! I LOVE TSUKEMONO. I'M GOING TO MISS IT WHEN WE'RE BACK HOME...
YEAH! AND TOMORROW IT'S ALREADY TIME TO GO HOME...
MMM, NUGGETS GO GREAT WITH BEER!
HEY, DID YOU TRY THE MAKI?
NOT YET, IS IT GOOD?
IT'S NOT THAT PRETTY TO LOOK AT!
THE RICE REALLY DOES LOOK LIKE MUSH...
AND IT SMELLS A BIT FISHY!
ALRIGHT I'M GOING FOR IT...
BLAAAHHHH! IT'S SLIMY...I THINK WE'LL LEAVE THOSE ALONE.
WHEN YOU LOOK FOR IT, YOU ALWAYS FIND THE BAD ALONGSIDE THE GOOD!
WE'LL HAVE TO GO BACK TO MIZUTANI'S TO FORGET ABOUT THE TASTE OF THAT LAST MAKI...

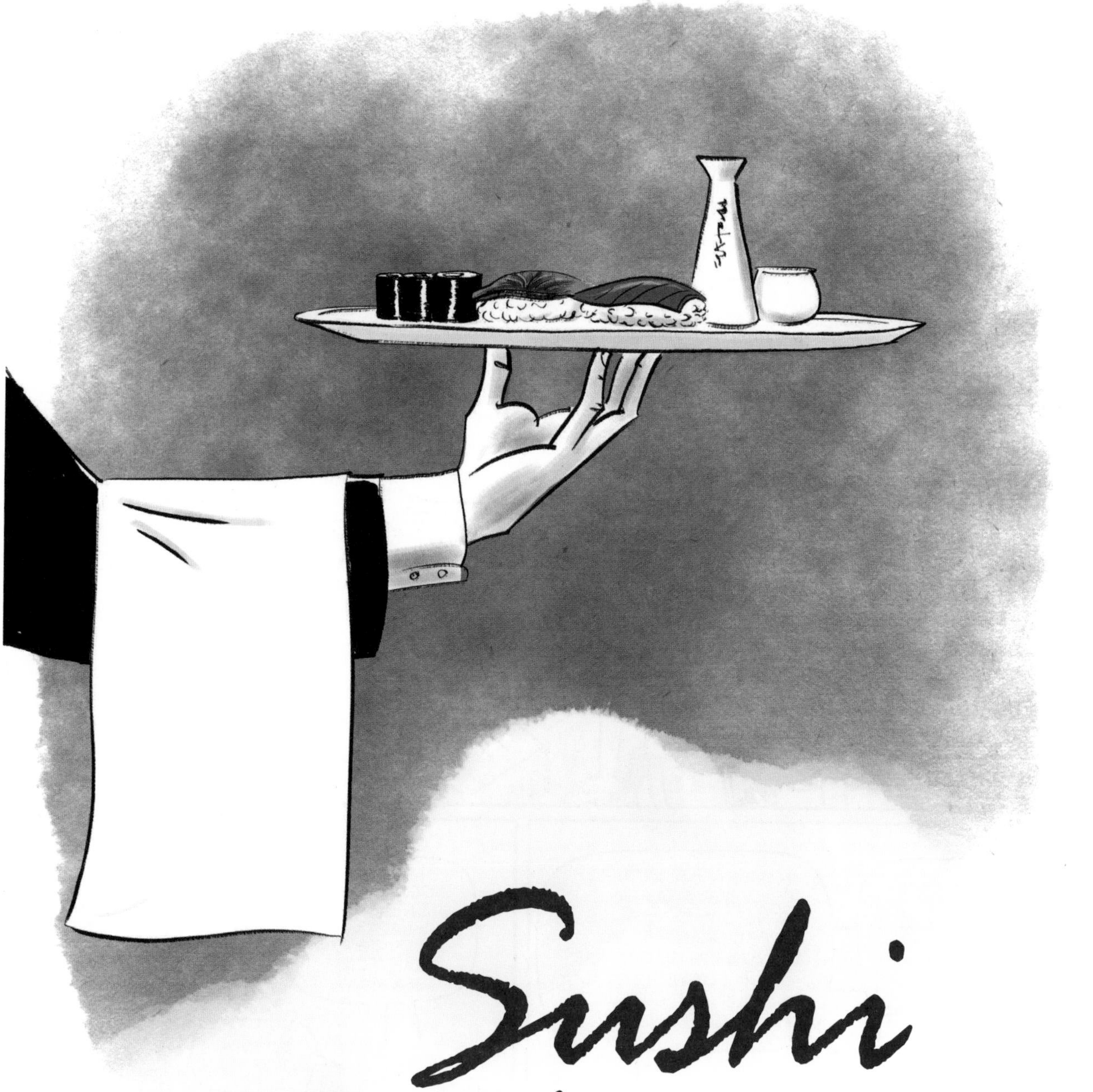

Sushi in France

IN RECENT YEARS, SUSHI HAS SPREAD ACROSS THE GLOBE, INCLUDING FRANCE, A COUNTRY IN WHICH PEOPLE HAVE FALLEN IN LOVE WITH IT. BUT CAN YOU REALLY MAKE AUTHENTIC SUSHI IN THE COUNTRY OF CAMEMBERT? HOW ARE CHEFS GOING ABOUT FINDING INDISPENSABLE INGREDIENTS AND HOW ARE THEY ADAPTING TO LOCAL RESOURCES?

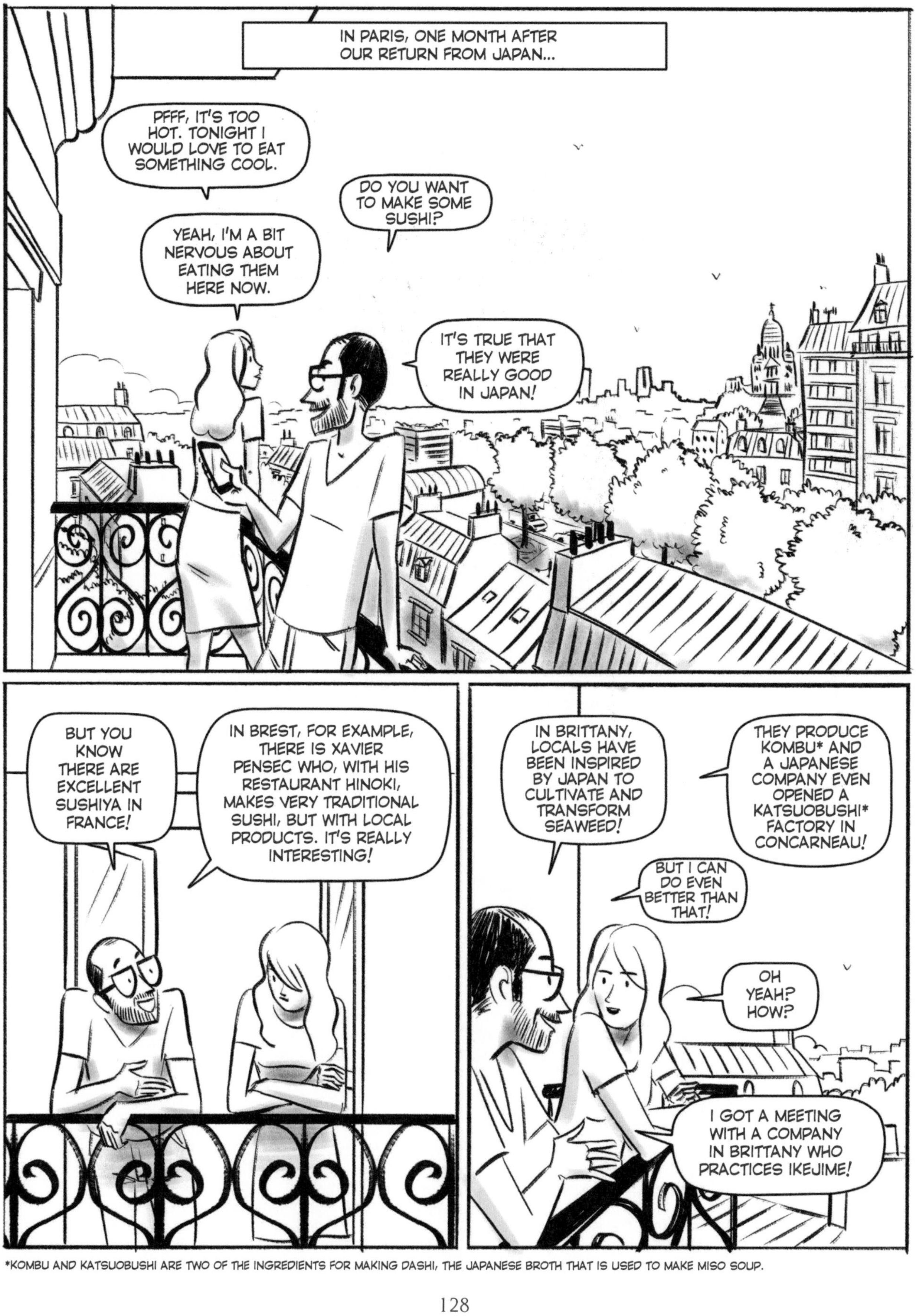
IN PARIS, ONE MONTH AFTER OUR RETURN FROM JAPAN...
PFFF, IT'S TOO HOT. TONIGHT I WOULD LOVE TO EAT SOMETHING COOL.
DO YOU WANT TO MAKE SOME SUSHI?
YEAH, I'M A BIT NERVOUS ABOUT EATING THEM HERE NOW.
IT'S TRUE THAT THEY WERE REALLY GOOD IN JAPAN!
BUT YOU KNOW THERE ARE EXCELLENT SUSHIYA IN FRANCE!
IN BREST, FOR EXAMPLE, THERE IS XAVIER PENSEC WHO, WITH HIS RESTAURANT HINOKI, MAKES VERY TRADITIONAL SUSHI, BUT WITH LOCAL PRODUCTS. IT'S REALLY INTERESTING!
IN BRITTANY, LOCALS HAVE BEEN INSPIRED BY JAPAN TO CULTIVATE AND TRANSFORM SEAWEED!
THEY PRODUCE KOMBU* AND A JAPANESE COMPANY EVEN OPENED A KATSUOBUSHI* FACTORY IN CONCARNEAU!
BUT I CAN DO EVEN BETTER THAN THAT!
OH YEAH? HOW?
I GOT A MEETING WITH A COMPANY IN BRITTANY WHO PRACTICES IKEJIME!

*KOMBU AND KATSUOBUSHI ARE TWO OF THE INGREDIENTS FOR MAKING DASHI, THE JAPANESE BROTH THAT IS USED TO MAKE MISO SOUP.

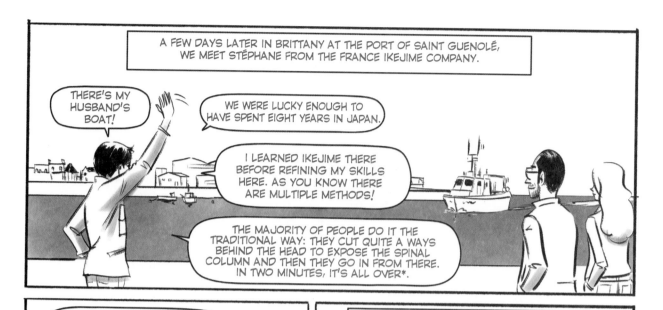

A FEW DAYS LATER IN BRITTANY AT THE PORT OF SAINT GUENOLÉ, WE MEET STÉPHANE FROM THE FRANCE IKEJIME COMPANY.

THERE'S MY HUSBAND'S BOAT!

WE WERE LUCKY ENOUGH TO HAVE SPENT EIGHT YEARS IN JAPAN.

I LEARNED IKEJIME THERE BEFORE REFINING MY SKILLS HERE. AS YOU KNOW THERE ARE MULTIPLE METHODS!

THE MAJORITY OF PEOPLE DO IT THE TRADITIONAL WAY: THEY CUT QUITE A WAYS BEHIND THE HEAD TO EXPOSE THE SPINAL COLUMN AND THEN THEY GO IN FROM THERE. IN TWO MINUTES, IT'S ALL OVER*.

MY WAY, I NEED 25 TO 30 MINUTES PER FISH. I DON'T CUT INTO THE FISH. I MAKE A SMALL HOLE IN THE FOREHEAD AND I PUT A NEEDLE THROUGH IT TO NEUTRALIZE THE NERVOUS SYSTEM.

HANG ON A MINUTE. I'LL BE RIGHT BACK, I'M GOING TO UNLOAD TODAY'S CATCH!

ON THE DOCKET: SEASONAL FISH INCLUDING MACKEREL, RED MULLET, GURNARD, JOHN DORY, ALL BROUGHT ALIVE TO THE QUAY.

THEN THEY'RE TRANSFERRED TO A LIVEWELL IN THE BACK OF A TRUCK...

... THEN BACK TO THE WORKSHOP WHERE THEY'LL FINISH THEIR DAY IN A CALM ENVIRONMENT TO HELP THEM RECOVER FROM THE STRESS OF BEING CAUGHT.

CHEFS WILL TELL YOU THAT A DEER THAT'S BEEN CAUGHT BY DOGS IS OF A LESS QUALITY THAN A DEER THAT'S BEEN SHOT BY A HUNTER IN A BLIND.

IT'S THE SAME FOR FISH! IF THEY'RE STRESSED, THEY'LL TASTE WORSE!

* THAT'S THE METHOD USED BY MIZUTANI'S SUPPLIERS (SEE CHAPTER 1).

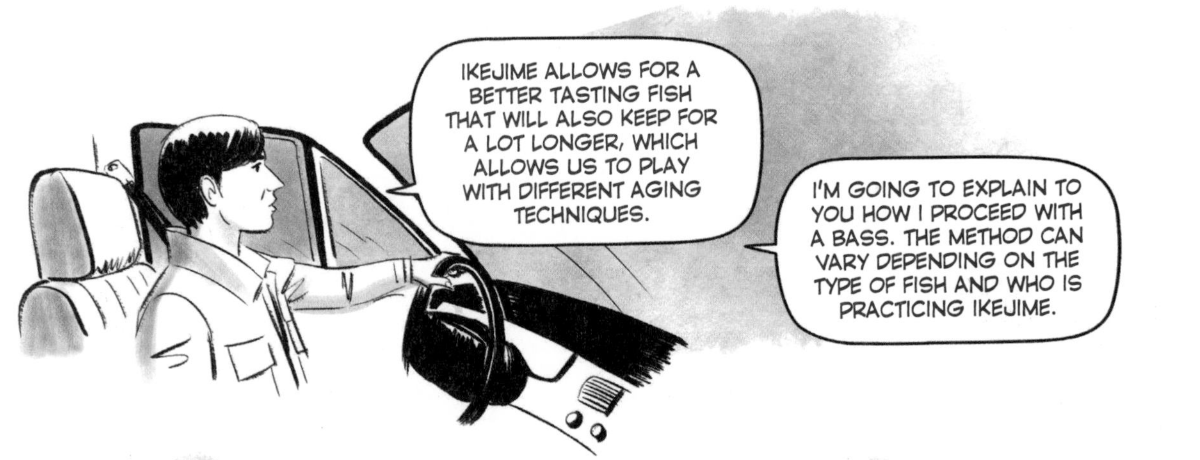
IKEJIME ALLOWS FOR A BETTER TASTING FISH THAT WILL ALSO KEEP FOR A LOT LONGER, WHICH ALLOWS US TO PLAY WITH DIFFERENT AGING TECHNIQUES.
I'M GOING TO EXPLAIN TO YOU HOW I PROCEED WITH A BASS. THE METHOD CAN VARY DEPENDING ON THE TYPE OF FISH AND WHO IS PRACTICING IKEJIME.

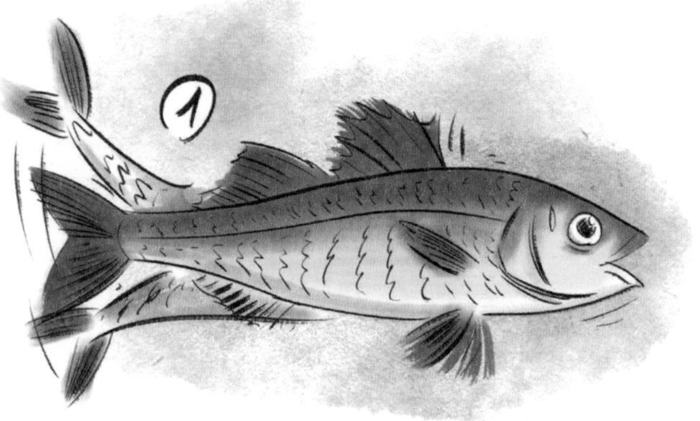
1

WHEN A FISH IS CAUGHT, IT IS IN A STATE OF MAXIMUM STRESS. IT PANICS, STRUGGLES, IT'S DYING A SLOW DEATH AND IS CONSUMING NEARLY ALL ITS ATP* MOLECULES.

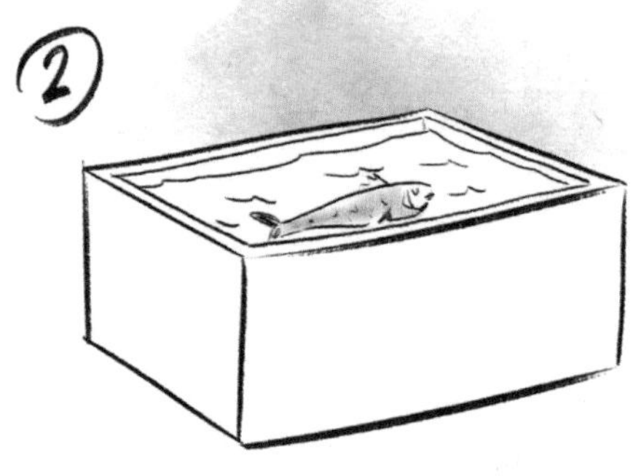
2

THAT'S WHY I LEAVE MY FISH TO REST IN A LIVEWELL. THAT WAY, THEY CALM DOWN, THEY RECONSTITUTE THEIR STOCK OF ATP AND THEY DEVELOP THEIR FLAVOR AGAIN.

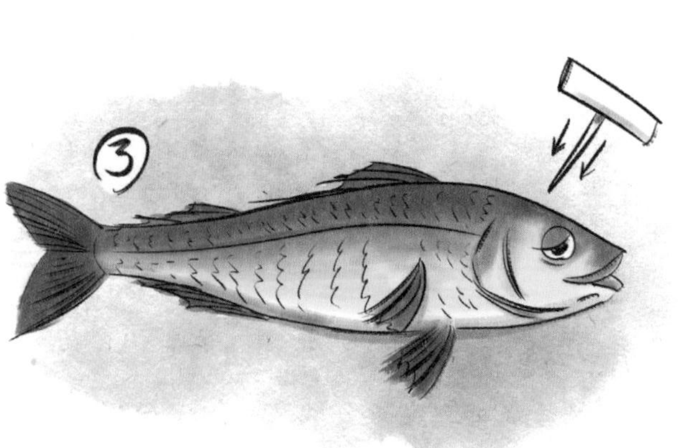
3

WHEN THE FISH HAS HAD A CHANCE TO REST, I APPLY A SUDDEN DEATH TECHNIQUE WITHOUT FIGHTING OR STRESS. I PUT ON GLOVES AND I HOLD THE FISH, COVERING ITS EYES TO CALM IT DOWN QUICKLY. THEN I MAKE A CEREBRAL PERFORATION WITH A POINTED TOOL THAT NEUTRALIZES ITS BRAIN: THE FISH SUFFERS NO MORE.

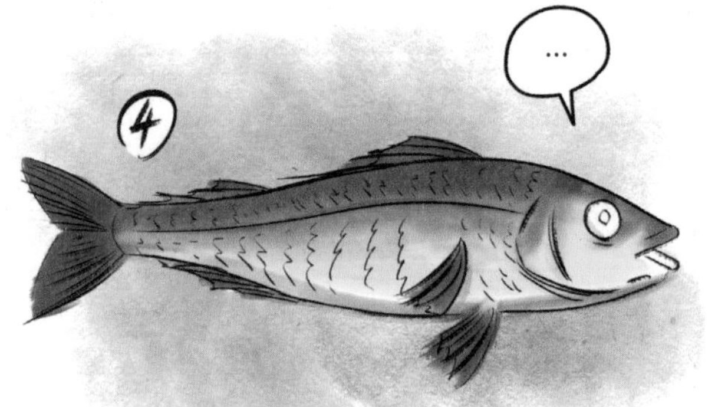
4
...

IT'S BRAIN DEAD: ITS HEART IS STILL PUMPING, BUT THE FISH IS NO LONGER BREATHING. IT'S ESSENTIAL TO DO THIS BEFORE EMPTYING IT OF ITS BLOOD IN THE NEXT STEP.

*ATP IS THE MOLECULE THAT ALLOWS FOR MUSCULAR FUNCTION.

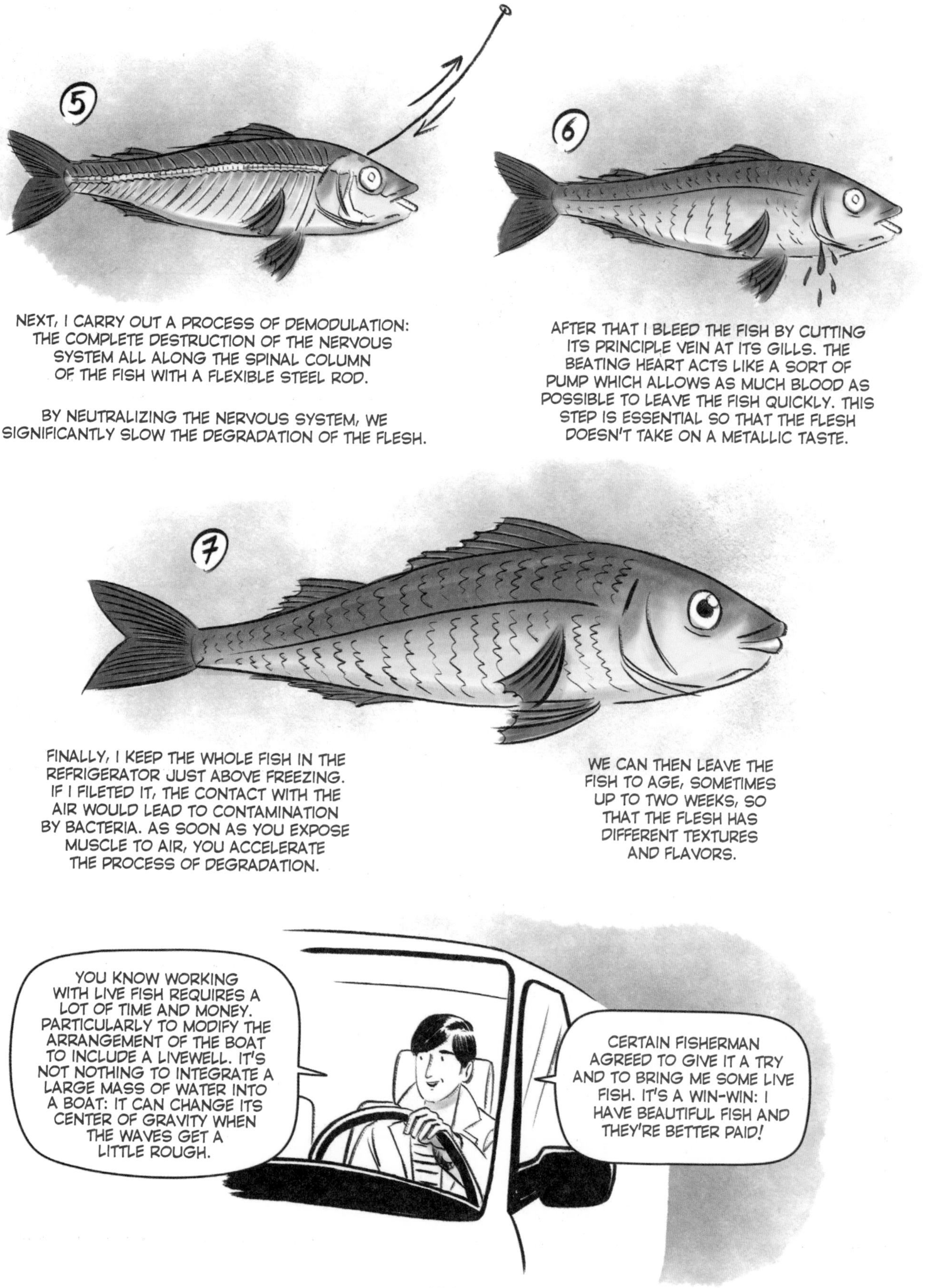
5
NEXT, I CARRY OUT A PROCESS OF DEMODULATION: THE COMPLETE DESTRUCTION OF THE NERVOUS SYSTEM ALL ALONG THE SPINAL COLUMN OF THE FISH WITH A FLEXIBLE STEEL ROD.
BY NEUTRALIZING THE NERVOUS SYSTEM, WE SIGNIFICANTLY SLOW THE DEGRADATION OF THE FLESH.
6
AFTER THAT I BLEED THE FISH BY CUTTING ITS PRINCIPLE VEIN AT ITS GILLS. THE BEATING HEART ACTS LIKE A SORT OF PUMP WHICH ALLOWS AS MUCH BLOOD AS POSSIBLE TO LEAVE THE FISH QUICKLY. THIS STEP IS ESSENTIAL SO THAT THE FLESH DOESN'T TAKE ON A METALLIC TASTE.
7
FINALLY, I KEEP THE WHOLE FISH IN THE REFRIGERATOR JUST ABOVE FREEZING. IF I FILETED IT, THE CONTACT WITH THE AIR WOULD LEAD TO CONTAMINATION BY BACTERIA. AS SOON AS YOU EXPOSE MUSCLE TO AIR, YOU ACCELERATE THE PROCESS OF DEGRADATION.
WE CAN THEN LEAVE THE FISH TO AGE, SOMETIMES UP TO TWO WEEKS, SO THAT THE FLESH HAS DIFFERENT TEXTURES AND FLAVORS.
YOU KNOW WORKING WITH LIVE FISH REQUIRES A LOT OF TIME AND MONEY. PARTICULARLY TO MODIFY THE ARRANGEMENT OF THE BOAT TO INCLUDE A LIVEWELL. IT'S NOT NOTHING TO INTEGRATE A LARGE MASS OF WATER INTO A BOAT: IT CAN CHANGE ITS CENTER OF GRAVITY WHEN THE WAVES GET A LITTLE ROUGH.
CERTAIN FISHERMAN AGREED TO GIVE IT A TRY AND TO BRING ME SOME LIVE FISH. IT'S A WIN-WIN: I HAVE BEAUTIFUL FISH AND THEY'RE BETTER PAID!

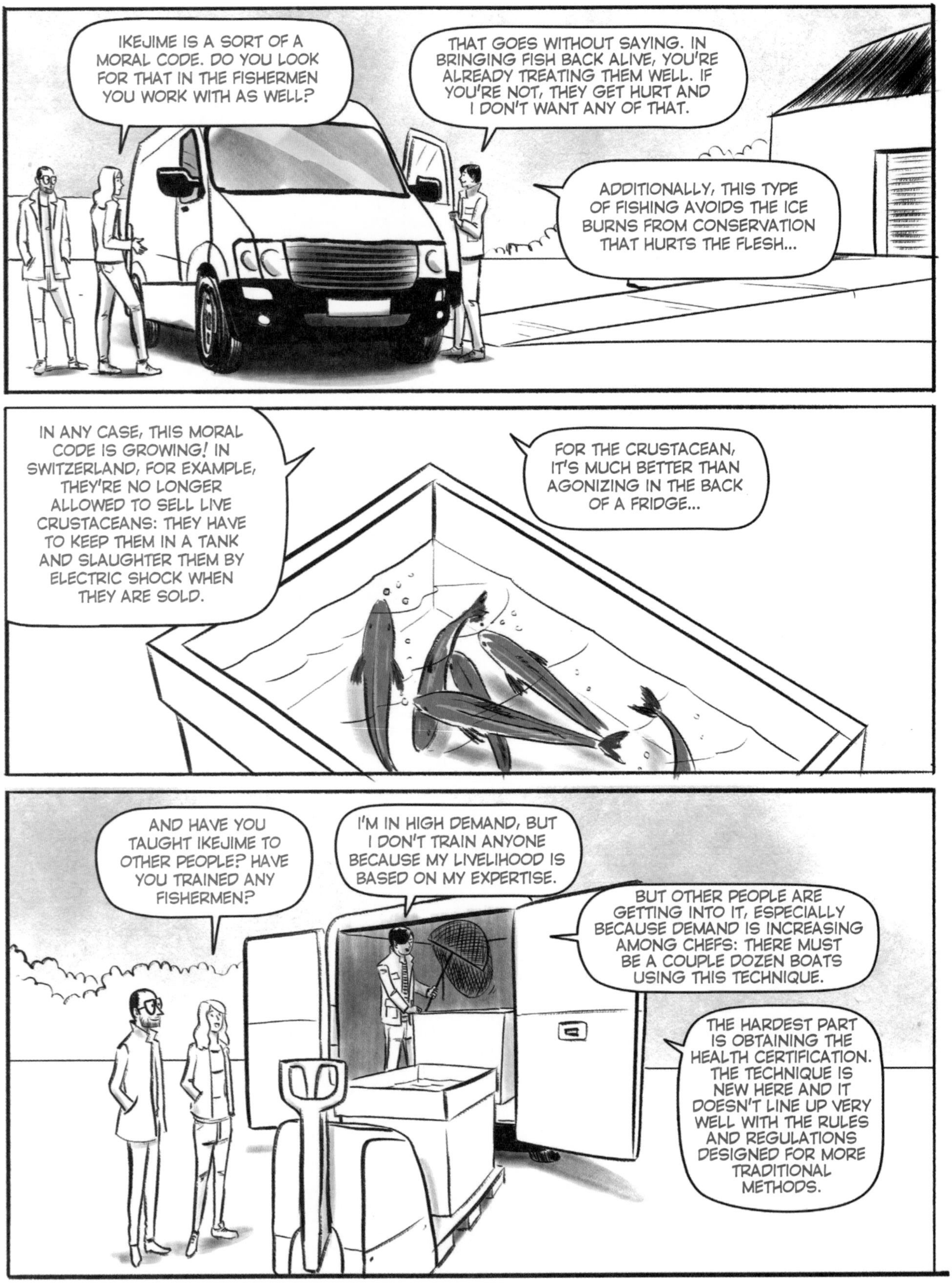
IKEJIME IS A SORT OF A MORAL CODE. DO YOU LOOK FOR THAT IN THE FISHERMEN YOU WORK WITH AS WELL?
THAT GOES WITHOUT SAYING. IN BRINGING FISH BACK ALIVE, YOU'RE ALREADY TREATING THEM WELL. IF YOU'RE NOT, THEY GET HURT AND I DON'T WANT ANY OF THAT.
ADDITIONALLY, THIS TYPE OF FISHING AVOIDS THE ICE BURNS FROM CONSERVATION THAT HURTS THE FLESH...
IN ANY CASE, THIS MORAL CODE IS GROWING! IN SWITZERLAND, FOR EXAMPLE, THEY'RE NO LONGER ALLOWED TO SELL LIVE CRUSTACEANS: THEY HAVE TO KEEP THEM IN A TANK AND SLAUGHTER THEM BY ELECTRIC SHOCK WHEN THEY ARE SOLD.
FOR THE CRUSTACEAN, IT'S MUCH BETTER THAN AGONIZING IN THE BACK OF A FRIDGE...
AND HAVE YOU TAUGHT IKEJIME TO OTHER PEOPLE? HAVE YOU TRAINED ANY FISHERMEN?
I'M IN HIGH DEMAND, BUT I DON'T TRAIN ANYONE BECAUSE MY LIVELIHOOD IS BASED ON MY EXPERTISE.
BUT OTHER PEOPLE ARE GETTING INTO IT, ESPECIALLY BECAUSE DEMAND IS INCREASING AMONG CHEFS: THERE MUST BE A COUPLE DOZEN BOATS USING THIS TECHNIQUE.
THE HARDEST PART IS OBTAINING THE HEALTH CERTIFICATION. THE TECHNIQUE IS NEW HERE AND IT DOESN'T LINE UP VERY WELL WITH THE RULES AND REGULATIONS DESIGNED FOR MORE TRADITIONAL METHODS.

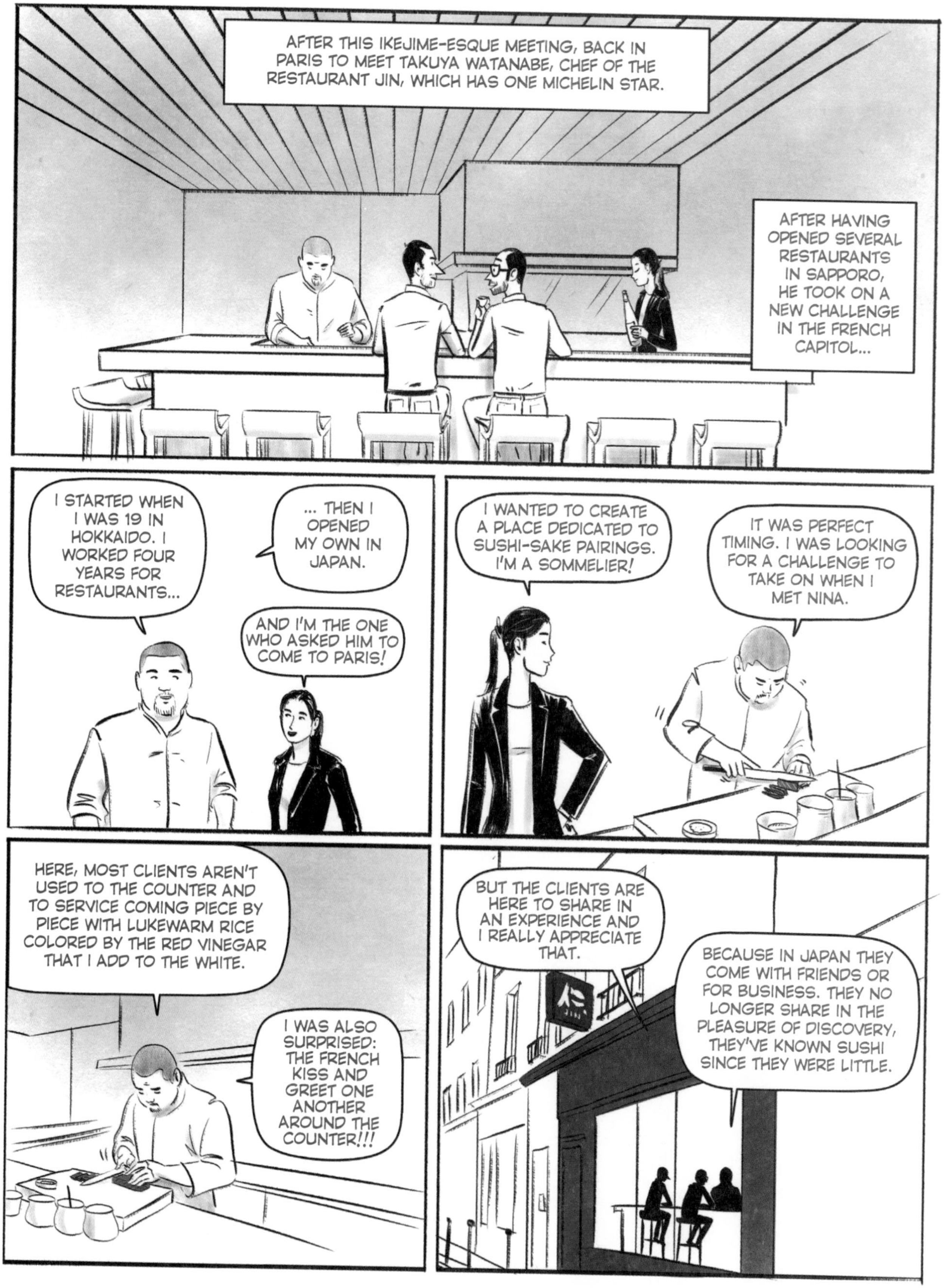
AFTER THIS IKEJIME-ESQUE MEETING, BACK IN PARIS TO MEET TAKUYA WATANABE, CHEF OF THE RESTAURANT JIN, WHICH HAS ONE MICHELIN STAR.
AFTER HAVING OPENED SEVERAL RESTAURANTS IN SAPPORO, HE TOOK ON A NEW CHALLENGE IN THE FRENCH CAPITOL...
I STARTED WHEN I WAS 19 IN HOKKAIDO. I WORKED FOUR YEARS FOR RESTAURANTS...
... THEN I OPENED MY OWN IN JAPAN.
AND I'M THE ONE WHO ASKED HIM TO COME TO PARIS!
I WANTED TO CREATE A PLACE DEDICATED TO SUSHI-SAKE PAIRINGS. I'M A SOMMELIER!
IT WAS PERFECT TIMING. I WAS LOOKING FOR A CHALLENGE TO TAKE ON WHEN I MET NINA.
HERE, MOST CLIENTS AREN'T USED TO THE COUNTER AND TO SERVICE COMING PIECE BY PIECE WITH LUKEWARM RICE COLORED BY THE RED VINEGAR THAT I ADD TO THE WHITE.
I WAS ALSO SURPRISED: THE FRENCH KISS AND GREET ONE ANOTHER AROUND THE COUNTER!!!
BUT THE CLIENTS ARE HERE TO SHARE IN AN EXPERIENCE AND I REALLY APPRECIATE THAT.
BECAUSE IN JAPAN THEY COME WITH FRIENDS OR FOR BUSINESS. THEY NO LONGER SHARE IN THE PLEASURE OF DISCOVERY, THEY'VE KNOWN SUSHI SINCE THEY WERE LITTLE.

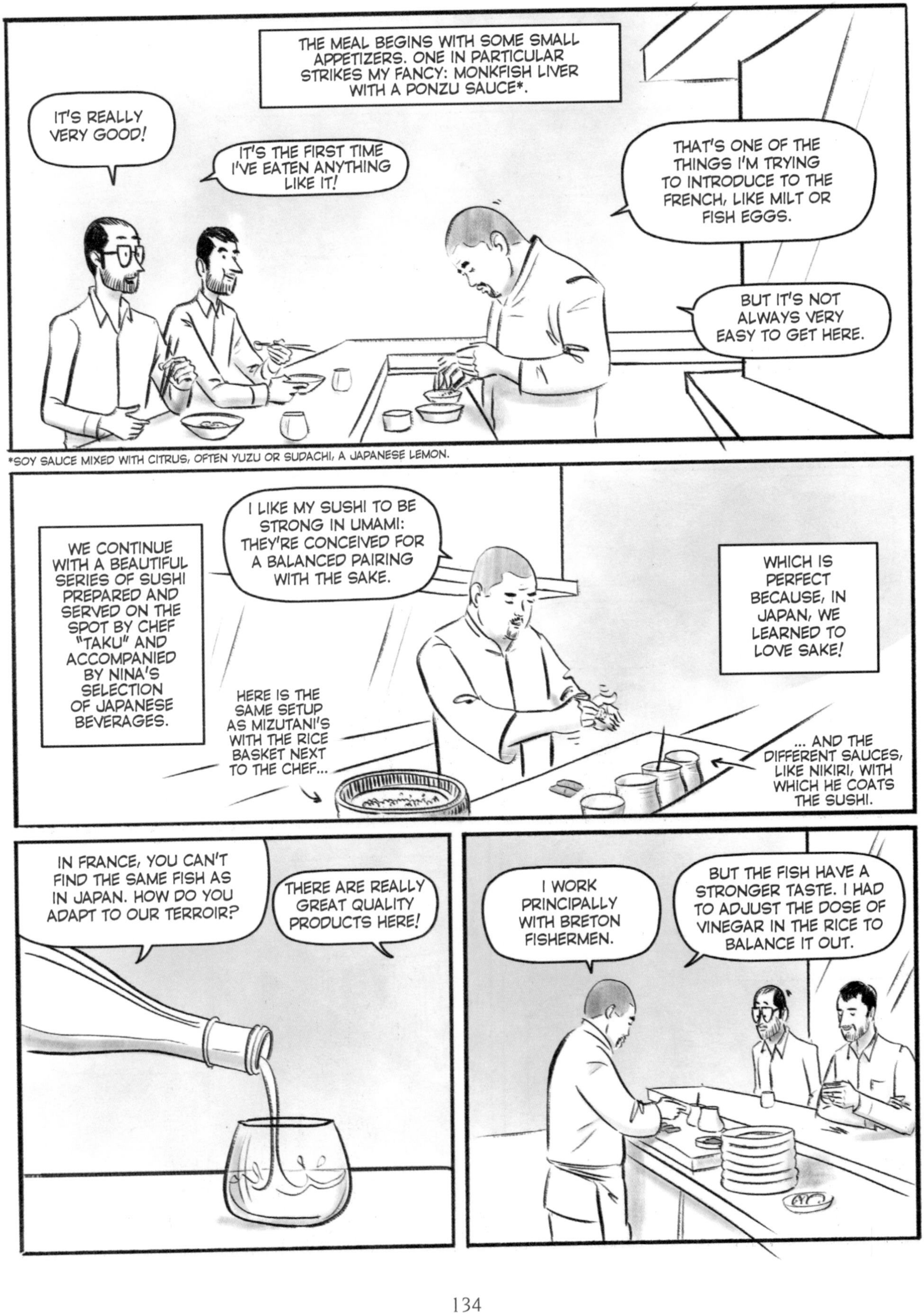
THE MEAL BEGINS WITH SOME SMALL APPETIZERS. ONE IN PARTICULAR STRIKES MY FANCY: MONKFISH LIVER WITH A PONZU SAUCE*.
IT'S REALLY VERY GOOD!
IT'S THE FIRST TIME I'VE EATEN ANYTHING LIKE IT!
THAT'S ONE OF THE THINGS I'M TRYING TO INTRODUCE TO THE FRENCH, LIKE MILT OR FISH EGGS.
BUT IT'S NOT ALWAYS VERY EASY TO GET HERE.
*SOY SAUCE MIXED WITH CITRUS, OFTEN YUZU OR SUDACHI, A JAPANESE LEMON.
WE CONTINUE WITH A BEAUTIFUL SERIES OF SUSHI PREPARED AND SERVED ON THE SPOT BY CHEF "TAKU" AND ACCOMPANIED BY NINA'S SELECTION OF JAPANESE BEVERAGES.
I LIKE MY SUSHI TO BE STRONG IN UMAMI: THEY'RE CONCEIVED FOR A BALANCED PAIRING WITH THE SAKE.
WHICH IS PERFECT BECAUSE, IN JAPAN, WE LEARNED TO LOVE SAKE!
HERE IS THE SAME SETUP AS MIZUTANI'S WITH THE RICE BASKET NEXT TO THE CHEF...
... AND THE DIFFERENT SAUCES, LIKE NIKIRI, WITH WHICH HE COATS THE SUSHI.
IN FRANCE, YOU CAN'T FIND THE SAME FISH AS IN JAPAN. HOW DO YOU ADAPT TO OUR TERROIR?
THERE ARE REALLY GREAT QUALITY PRODUCTS HERE!
I WORK PRINCIPALLY WITH BRETON FISHERMEN.
BUT THE FISH HAVE A STRONGER TASTE. I HAD TO ADJUST THE DOSE OF VINEGAR IN THE RICE TO BALANCE IT OUT.

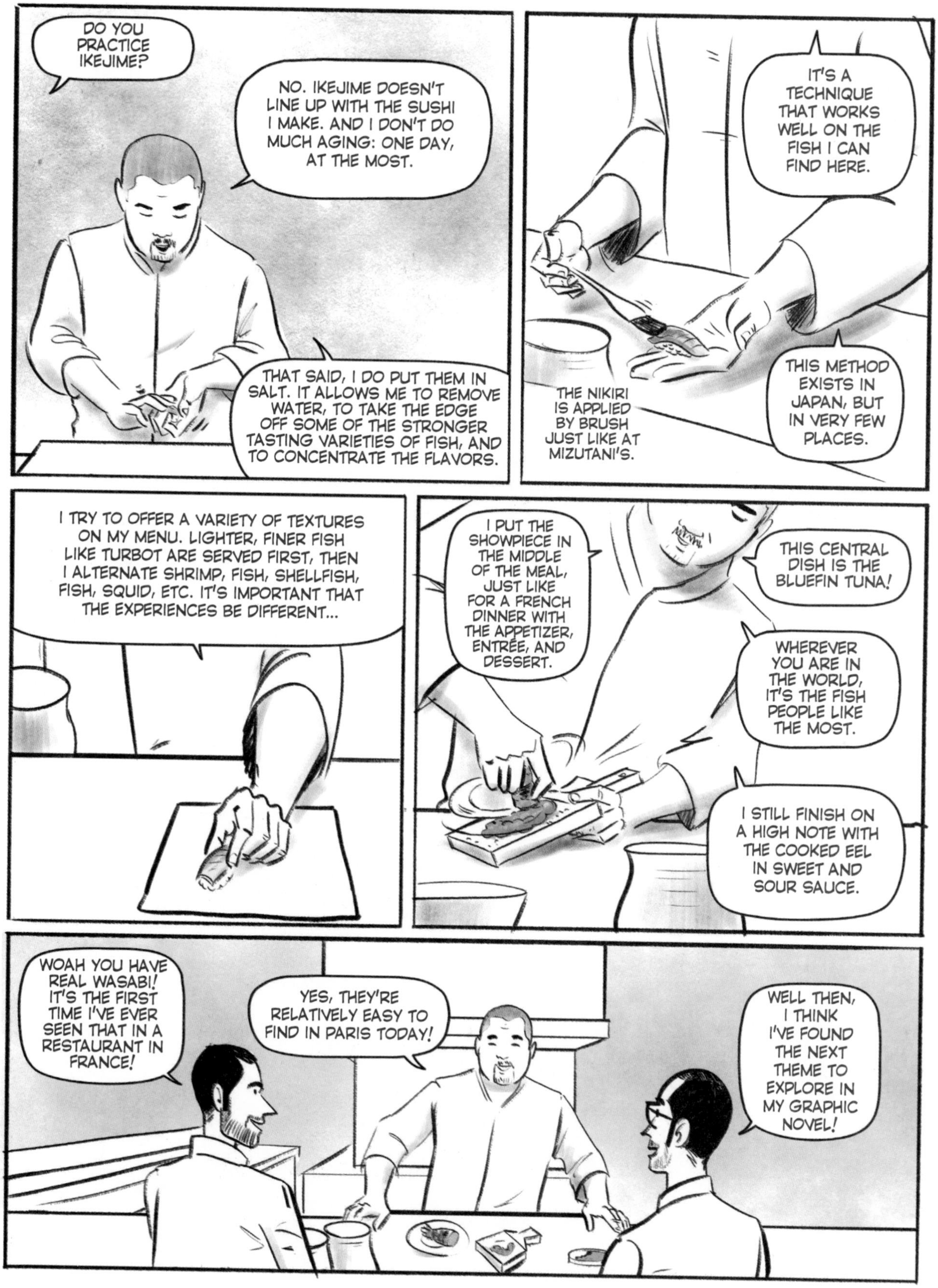
DO YOU PRACTICE IKEJIME?
NO. IKEJIME DOESN'T LINE UP WITH THE SUSHI I MAKE. AND I DON'T DO MUCH AGING: ONE DAY, AT THE MOST.
THAT SAID, I DO PUT THEM IN SALT. IT ALLOWS ME TO REMOVE WATER, TO TAKE THE EDGE OFF SOME OF THE STRONGER TASTING VARIETIES OF FISH, AND TO CONCENTRATE THE FLAVORS.
IT'S A TECHNIQUE THAT WORKS WELL ON THE FISH I CAN FIND HERE.
THE NIKIRI IS APPLIED BY BRUSH JUST LIKE AT MIZUTANI'S.
THIS METHOD EXISTS IN JAPAN, BUT IN VERY FEW PLACES.
I TRY TO OFFER A VARIETY OF TEXTURES ON MY MENU. LIGHTER, FINER FISH LIKE TURBOT ARE SERVED FIRST, THEN I ALTERNATE SHRIMP, FISH, SHELLFISH, FISH, SQUID, ETC. IT'S IMPORTANT THAT THE EXPERIENCES BE DIFFERENT...
I PUT THE SHOWPIECE IN THE MIDDLE OF THE MEAL, JUST LIKE FOR A FRENCH DINNER WITH THE APPETIZER, ENTRÉE, AND DESSERT.
THIS CENTRAL DISH IS THE BLUEFIN TUNA!
WHEREVER YOU ARE IN THE WORLD, IT'S THE FISH PEOPLE LIKE THE MOST.
I STILL FINISH ON A HIGH NOTE WITH THE COOKED EEL IN SWEET AND SOUR SAUCE.
WOAH YOU HAVE REAL WASABI! IT'S THE FIRST TIME I'VE EVER SEEN THAT IN A RESTAURANT IN FRANCE!
YES, THEY'RE RELATIVELY EASY TO FIND IN PARIS TODAY!
WELL THEN, I THINK I'VE FOUND THE NEXT THEME TO EXPLORE IN MY GRAPHIC NOVEL!

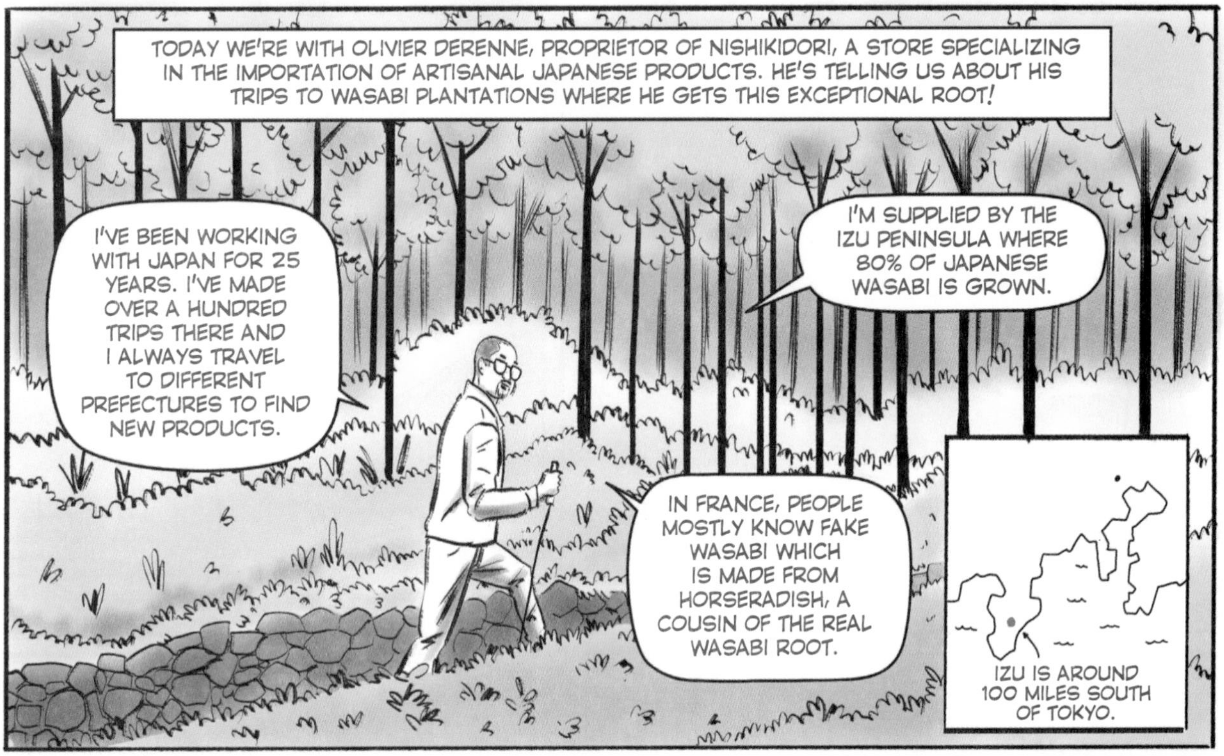
TODAY WE'RE WITH OLIVIER DERENNE, PROPRIETOR OF NISHIKIDORI, A STORE SPECIALIZING IN THE IMPORTATION OF ARTISANAL JAPANESE PRODUCTS. HE'S TELLING US ABOUT HIS TRIPS TO WASABI PLANTATIONS WHERE HE GETS THIS EXCEPTIONAL ROOT!
I'VE BEEN WORKING WITH JAPAN FOR 25 YEARS. I'VE MADE OVER A HUNDRED TRIPS THERE AND I ALWAYS TRAVEL TO DIFFERENT PREFECTURES TO FIND NEW PRODUCTS.
I'M SUPPLIED BY THE IZU PENINSULA WHERE 80% OF JAPANESE WASABI IS GROWN.
IN FRANCE, PEOPLE MOSTLY KNOW FAKE WASABI WHICH IS MADE FROM HORSERADISH, A COUSIN OF THE REAL WASABI ROOT.
IZU IS AROUND 100 MILES SOUTH OF TOKYO.

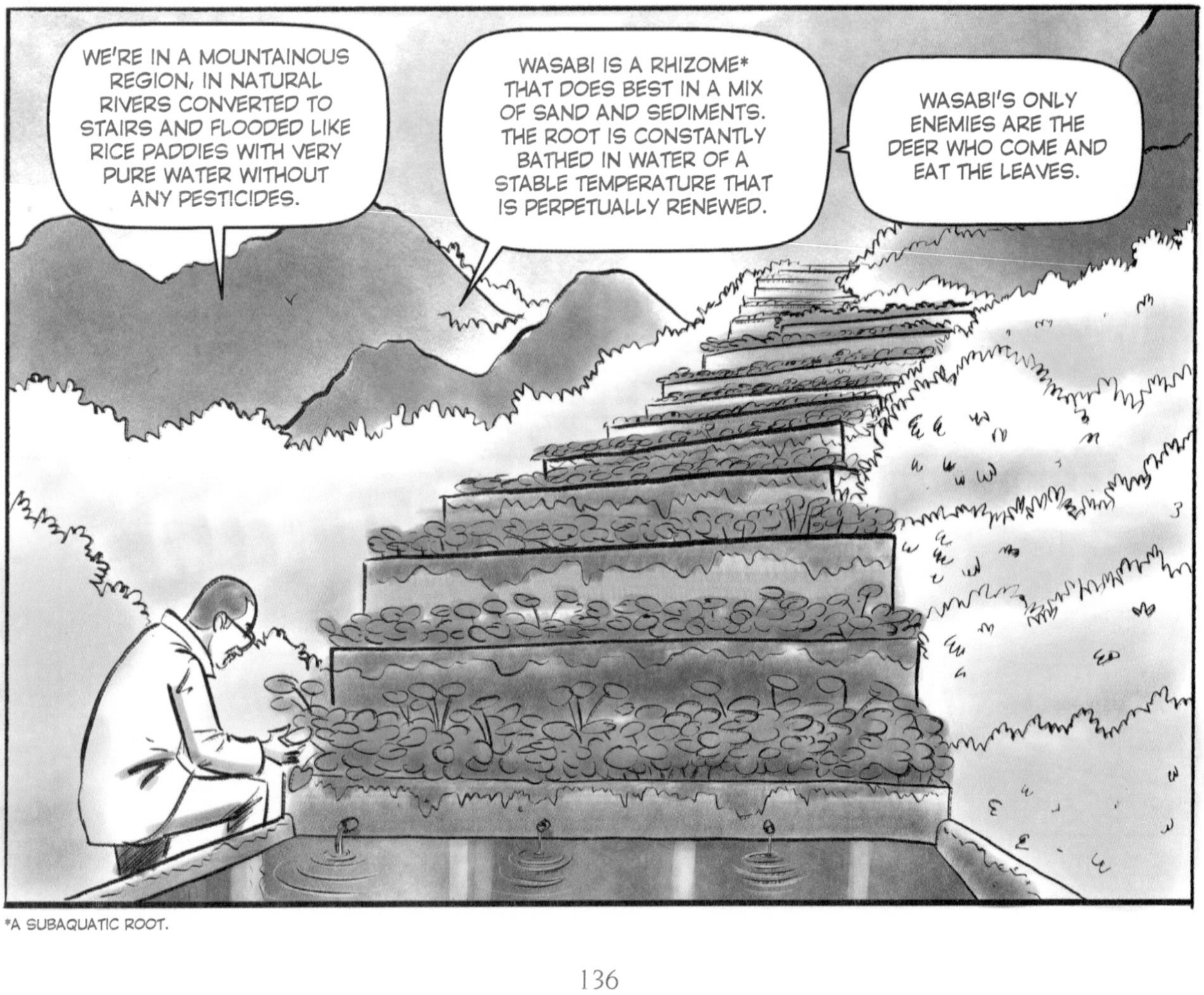
WE'RE IN A MOUNTAINOUS REGION, IN NATURAL RIVERS CONVERTED TO STAIRS AND FLOODED LIKE RICE PADDIES WITH VERY PURE WATER WITHOUT ANY PESTICIDES.
WASABI IS A RHIZOME* THAT DOES BEST IN A MIX OF SAND AND SEDIMENTS. THE ROOT IS CONSTANTLY BATHED IN WATER OF A STABLE TEMPERATURE THAT IS PERPETUALLY RENEWED.
WASABI'S ONLY ENEMIES ARE THE DEER WHO COME AND EAT THE LEAVES.

*A SUBAQUATIC ROOT.

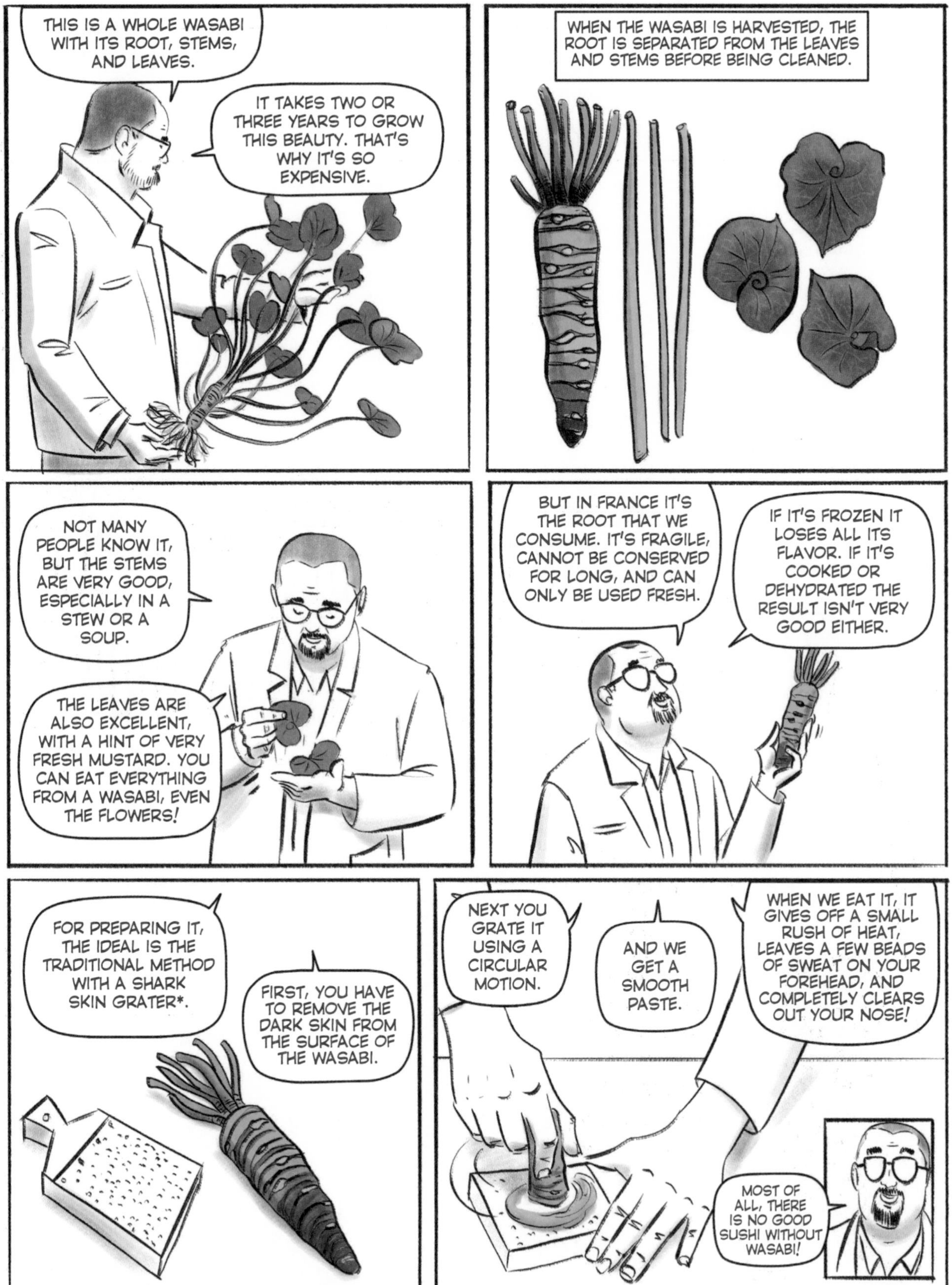
THIS IS A WHOLE WASABI WITH ITS ROOT, STEMS, AND LEAVES.
IT TAKES TWO OR THREE YEARS TO GROW THIS BEAUTY. THAT'S WHY IT'S SO EXPENSIVE.
WHEN THE WASABI IS HARVESTED, THE ROOT IS SEPARATED FROM THE LEAVES AND STEMS BEFORE BEING CLEANED.
NOT MANY PEOPLE KNOW IT, BUT THE STEMS ARE VERY GOOD, ESPECIALLY IN A STEW OR A SOUP.
THE LEAVES ARE ALSO EXCELLENT, WITH A HINT OF VERY FRESH MUSTARD. YOU CAN EAT EVERYTHING FROM A WASABI, EVEN THE FLOWERS!
BUT IN FRANCE IT'S THE ROOT THAT WE CONSUME. IT'S FRAGILE, CANNOT BE CONSERVED FOR LONG, AND CAN ONLY BE USED FRESH.
IF IT'S FROZEN IT LOSES ALL ITS FLAVOR. IF IT'S COOKED OR DEHYDRATED THE RESULT ISN'T VERY GOOD EITHER.
FOR PREPARING IT, THE IDEAL IS THE TRADITIONAL METHOD WITH A SHARK SKIN GRATER*.
FIRST, YOU HAVE TO REMOVE THE DARK SKIN FROM THE SURFACE OF THE WASABI.
NEXT YOU GRATE IT USING A CIRCULAR MOTION.
AND WE GET A SMOOTH PASTE.
WHEN WE EAT IT, IT GIVES OFF A SMALL RUSH OF HEAT, LEAVES A FEW BEADS OF SWEAT ON YOUR FOREHEAD, AND COMPLETELY CLEARS OUT YOUR NOSE!
MOST OF ALL, THERE IS NO GOOD SUSHI WITHOUT WASABI!

*LIKE THE ONE I BOUGHT IN TOKYO.

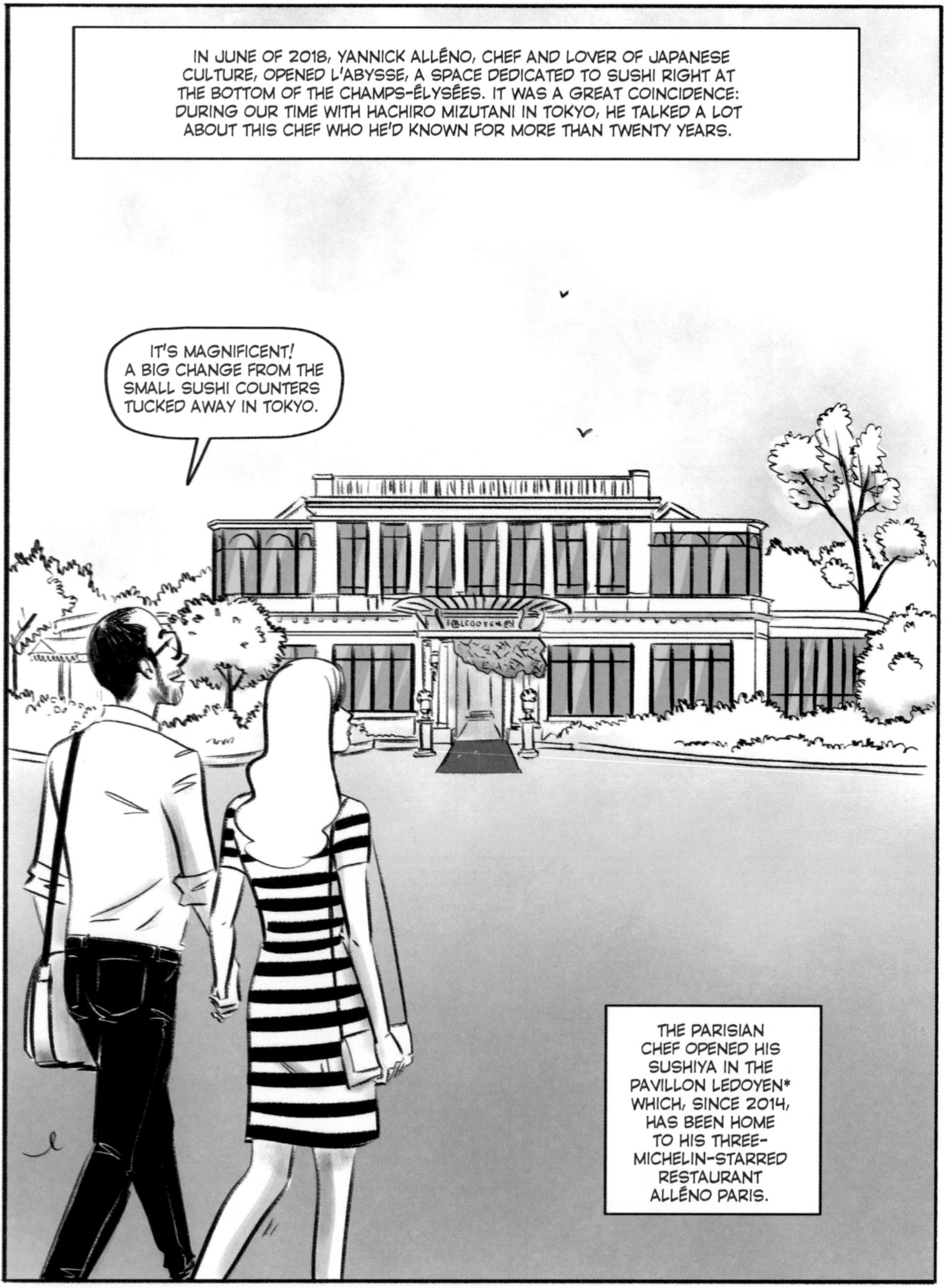
IN JUNE OF 2018, YANNICK ALLÉNO, CHEF AND LOVER OF JAPANESE CULTURE, OPENED L'ABYSSE, A SPACE DEDICATED TO SUSHI RIGHT AT THE BOTTOM OF THE CHAMPS-ÉLYSÉES. IT WAS A GREAT COINCIDENCE: DURING OUR TIME WITH HACHIRO MIZUTANI IN TOKYO, HE TALKED A LOT ABOUT THIS CHEF WHO HE'D KNOWN FOR MORE THAN TWENTY YEARS.
IT'S MAGNIFICENT! A BIG CHANGE FROM THE SMALL SUSHI COUNTERS TUCKED AWAY IN TOKYO.
THE PARISIAN CHEF OPENED HIS SUSHIYA IN THE PAVILLON LEDOYEN* WHICH, SINCE 2014, HAS BEEN HOME TO HIS THREE-MICHELIN-STARRED RESTAURANT ALLÉNO PARIS.

*THIS BUILDING HAS HOUSED VARIOUS RESTAURANTS SINCE THE LATE 18TH CENTURY.

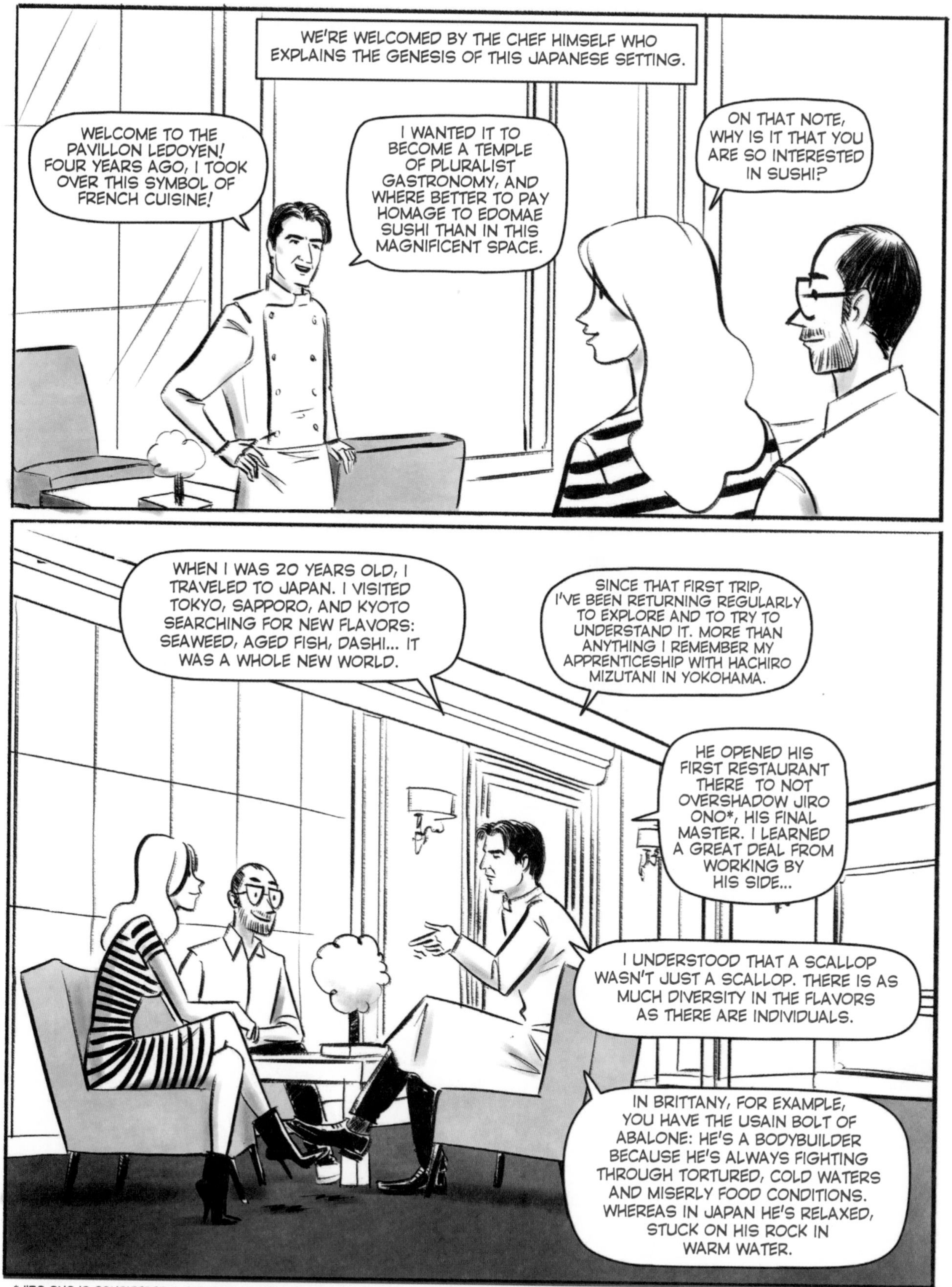
WE'RE WELCOMED BY THE CHEF HIMSELF WHO EXPLAINS THE GENESIS OF THIS JAPANESE SETTING.
WELCOME TO THE PAVILLON LEDOYEN! FOUR YEARS AGO, I TOOK OVER THIS SYMBOL OF FRENCH CUISINE!
I WANTED IT TO BECOME A TEMPLE OF PLURALIST GASTRONOMY, AND WHERE BETTER TO PAY HOMAGE TO EDOMAE SUSHI THAN IN THIS MAGNIFICENT SPACE.
ON THAT NOTE, WHY IS IT THAT YOU ARE SO INTERESTED IN SUSHI?
WHEN I WAS 20 YEARS OLD, I TRAVELED TO JAPAN. I VISITED TOKYO, SAPPORO, AND KYOTO SEARCHING FOR NEW FLAVORS: SEAWEED, AGED FISH, DASHI... IT WAS A WHOLE NEW WORLD.
SINCE THAT FIRST TRIP, I'VE BEEN RETURNING REGULARLY TO EXPLORE AND TO TRY TO UNDERSTAND IT. MORE THAN ANYTHING I REMEMBER MY APPRENTICESHIP WITH HACHIRO MIZUTANI IN YOKOHAMA.
HE OPENED HIS FIRST RESTAURANT THERE TO NOT OVERSHADOW JIRO ONO*, HIS FINAL MASTER. I LEARNED A GREAT DEAL FROM WORKING BY HIS SIDE...
I UNDERSTOOD THAT A SCALLOP WASN'T JUST A SCALLOP. THERE IS AS MUCH DIVERSITY IN THE FLAVORS AS THERE ARE INDIVIDUALS.
IN BRITTANY, FOR EXAMPLE, YOU HAVE THE USAIN BOLT OF ABALONE: HE'S A BODYBUILDER BECAUSE HE'S ALWAYS FIGHTING THROUGH TORTURED, COLD WATERS AND MISERLY FOOD CONDITIONS. WHEREAS IN JAPAN HE'S RELAXED, STUCK ON HIS ROCK IN WARM WATER.

*JIRO ONO IS CONSIDERED THE GRAND MASTER OF SUSHI IN JAPAN. HIS RESTAURANT SUKIYABASHI JIRO IS THE FIRST TO HAVE OBTAINED 3 MICHELIN STARS.

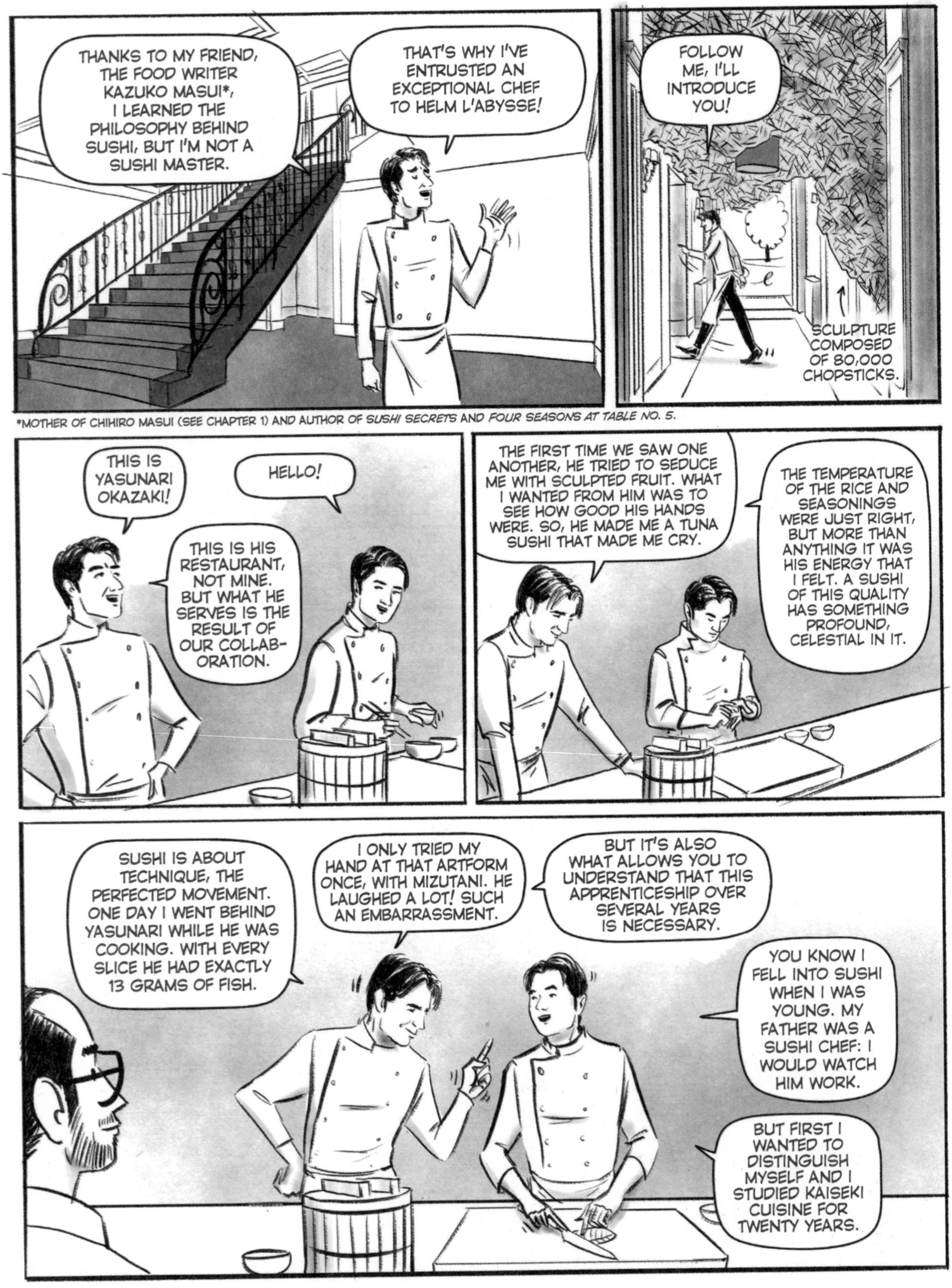
THANKS TO MY FRIEND, THE FOOD WRITER KAZUKO MASUI*, I LEARNED THE PHILOSOPHY BEHIND SUSHI, BUT I'M NOT A SUSHI MASTER.
THAT'S WHY I'VE ENTRUSTED AN EXCEPTIONAL CHEF TO HELM L'ABYSSE!
FOLLOW ME, I'LL INTRODUCE YOU!
SCULPTURE COMPOSED OF 80,000 CHOPSTICKS.
THIS IS YASUNARI OKAZAKI!
HELLO!
THIS IS HIS RESTAURANT, NOT MINE. BUT WHAT HE SERVES IS THE RESULT OF OUR COLLAB-ORATION.
THE FIRST TIME WE SAW ONE ANOTHER, HE TRIED TO SEDUCE ME WITH SCULPTED FRUIT. WHAT I WANTED FROM HIM WAS TO SEE HOW GOOD HIS HANDS WERE. SO, HE MADE ME A TUNA SUSHI THAT MADE ME CRY.
THE TEMPERATURE OF THE RICE AND SEASONINGS WERE JUST RIGHT, BUT MORE THAN ANYTHING IT WAS HIS ENERGY THAT I FELT. A SUSHI OF THIS QUALITY HAS SOMETHING PROFOUND, CELESTIAL IN IT.
SUSHI IS ABOUT TECHNIQUE, THE PERFECTED MOVEMENT. ONE DAY I WENT BEHIND YASUNARI WHILE HE WAS COOKING. WITH EVERY SLICE HE HAD EXACTLY 13 GRAMS OF FISH.
I ONLY TRIED MY HAND AT THAT ARTFORM ONCE, WITH MIZUTANI. HE LAUGHED A LOT! SUCH AN EMBARRASSMENT.
BUT IT'S ALSO WHAT ALLOWS YOU TO UNDERSTAND THAT THIS APPRENTICESHIP OVER SEVERAL YEARS IS NECESSARY.
YOU KNOW I FELL INTO SUSHI WHEN I WAS YOUNG. MY FATHER WAS A SUSHI CHEF: I WOULD WATCH HIM WORK.
BUT FIRST I WANTED TO DISTINGUISH MYSELF AND I STUDIED KAISEKI CUISINE FOR TWENTY YEARS.

*MOTHER OF CHIHIRO MASUI (SEE CHAPTER 1) AND AUTHOR OF *SUSHI SECRETS* AND *FOUR SEASONS AT TABLE NO. 5*.

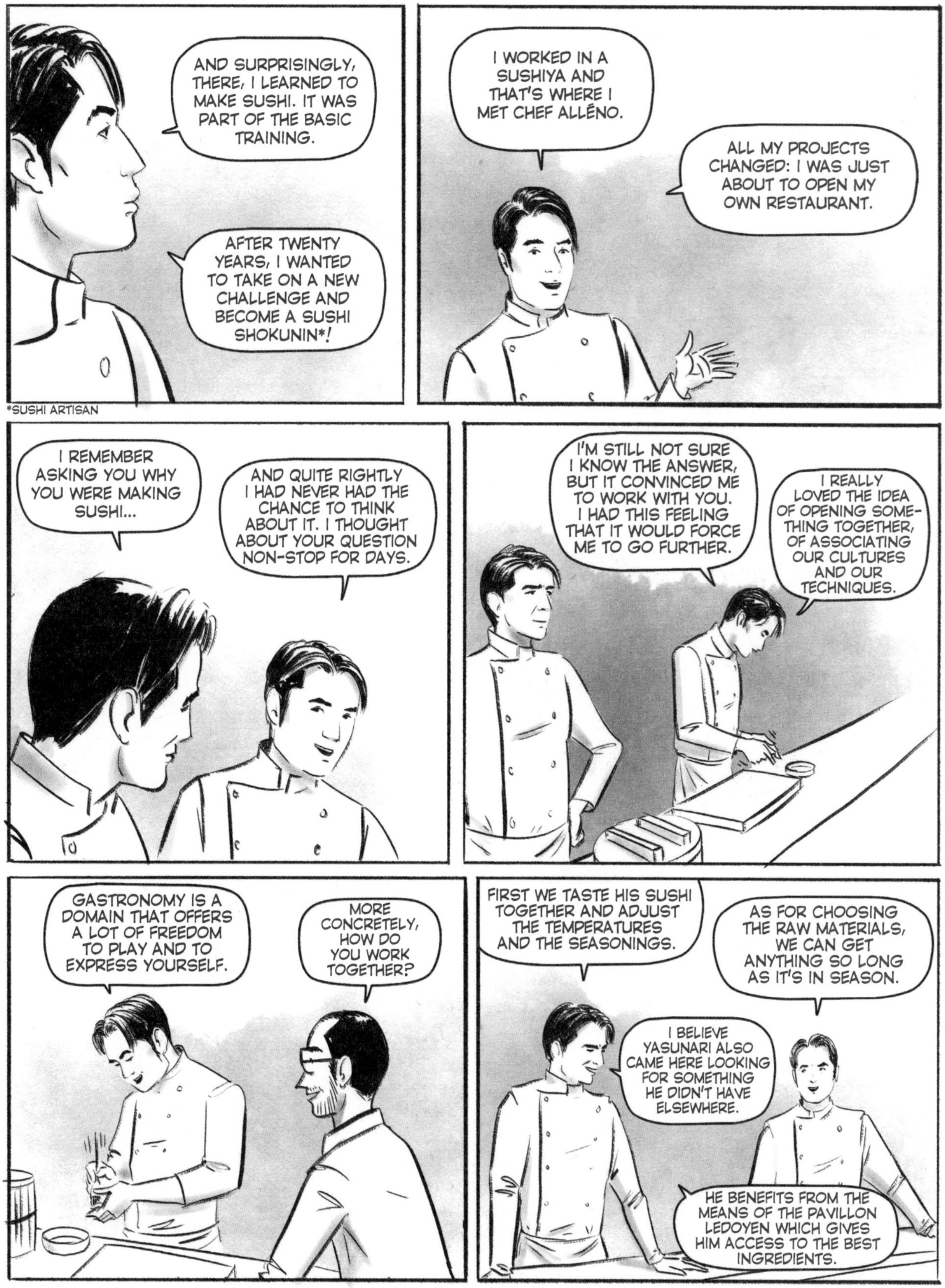
AND SURPRISINGLY, THERE, I LEARNED TO MAKE SUSHI. IT WAS PART OF THE BASIC TRAINING.
AFTER TWENTY YEARS, I WANTED TO TAKE ON A NEW CHALLENGE AND BECOME A SUSHI SHOKUNIN*!
I WORKED IN A SUSHIYA AND THAT'S WHERE I MET CHEF ALLÉNO.
ALL MY PROJECTS CHANGED: I WAS JUST ABOUT TO OPEN MY OWN RESTAURANT.
*SUSHI ARTISAN
I REMEMBER ASKING YOU WHY YOU WERE MAKING SUSHI...
AND QUITE RIGHTLY I HAD NEVER HAD THE CHANCE TO THINK ABOUT IT. I THOUGHT ABOUT YOUR QUESTION NON-STOP FOR DAYS.
I'M STILL NOT SURE I KNOW THE ANSWER, BUT IT CONVINCED ME TO WORK WITH YOU. I HAD THIS FEELING THAT IT WOULD FORCE ME TO GO FURTHER.
I REALLY LOVED THE IDEA OF OPENING SOME-THING TOGETHER, OF ASSOCIATING OUR CULTURES AND OUR TECHNIQUES.
GASTRONOMY IS A DOMAIN THAT OFFERS A LOT OF FREEDOM TO PLAY AND TO EXPRESS YOURSELF.
MORE CONCRETELY, HOW DO YOU WORK TOGETHER?
FIRST WE TASTE HIS SUSHI TOGETHER AND ADJUST THE TEMPERATURES AND THE SEASONINGS.
AS FOR CHOOSING THE RAW MATERIALS, WE CAN GET ANYTHING SO LONG AS IT'S IN SEASON.
I BELIEVE YASUNARI ALSO CAME HERE LOOKING FOR SOMETHING HE DIDN'T HAVE ELSEWHERE.
HE BENEFITS FROM THE MEANS OF THE PAVILLON LEDOYEN WHICH GIVES HIM ACCESS TO THE BEST INGREDIENTS.

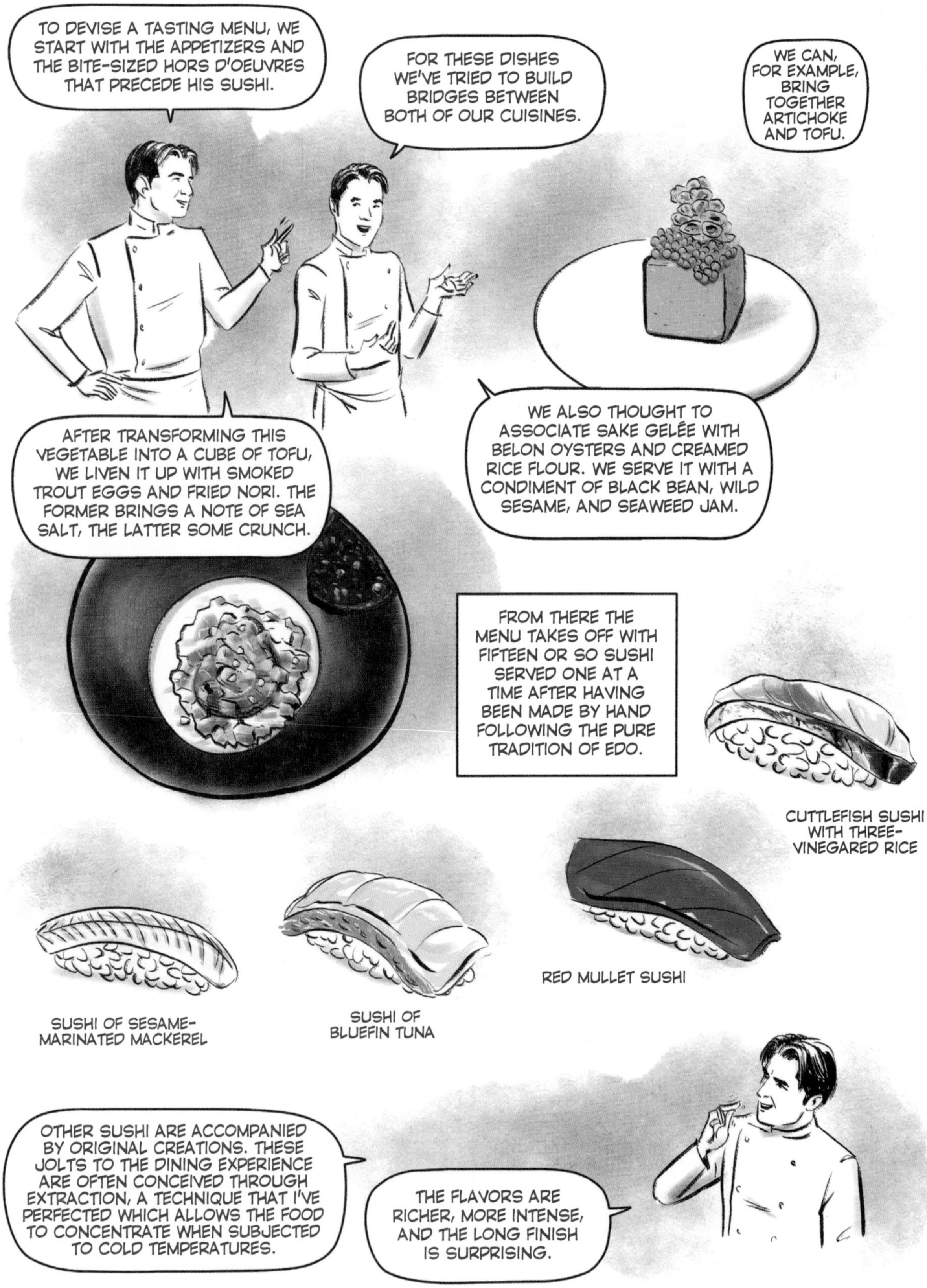
TO DEVISE A TASTING MENU, WE START WITH THE APPETIZERS AND THE BITE-SIZED HORS D'OEUVRES THAT PRECEDE HIS SUSHI.
FOR THESE DISHES WE'VE TRIED TO BUILD BRIDGES BETWEEN BOTH OF OUR CUISINES.
WE CAN, FOR EXAMPLE, BRING TOGETHER ARTICHOKE AND TOFU.
AFTER TRANSFORMING THIS VEGETABLE INTO A CUBE OF TOFU, WE LIVEN IT UP WITH SMOKED TROUT EGGS AND FRIED NORI. THE FORMER BRINGS A NOTE OF SEA SALT, THE LATTER SOME CRUNCH.
WE ALSO THOUGHT TO ASSOCIATE SAKE GELÉE WITH BELON OYSTERS AND CREAMED RICE FLOUR. WE SERVE IT WITH A CONDIMENT OF BLACK BEAN, WILD SESAME, AND SEAWEED JAM.
FROM THERE THE MENU TAKES OFF WITH FIFTEEN OR SO SUSHI SERVED ONE AT A TIME AFTER HAVING BEEN MADE BY HAND FOLLOWING THE PURE TRADITION OF EDO.
CUTTLEFISH SUSHI WITH THREE-VINEGARED RICE
SUSHI OF SESAME-MARINATED MACKEREL
SUSHI OF BLUEFIN TUNA
RED MULLET SUSHI
OTHER SUSHI ARE ACCOMPANIED BY ORIGINAL CREATIONS. THESE JOLTS TO THE DINING EXPERIENCE ARE OFTEN CONCEIVED THROUGH EXTRACTION, A TECHNIQUE THAT I'VE PERFECTED WHICH ALLOWS THE FOOD TO CONCENTRATE WHEN SUBJECTED TO COLD TEMPERATURES.
THE FLAVORS ARE RICHER, MORE INTENSE, AND THE LONG FINISH IS SURPRISING.

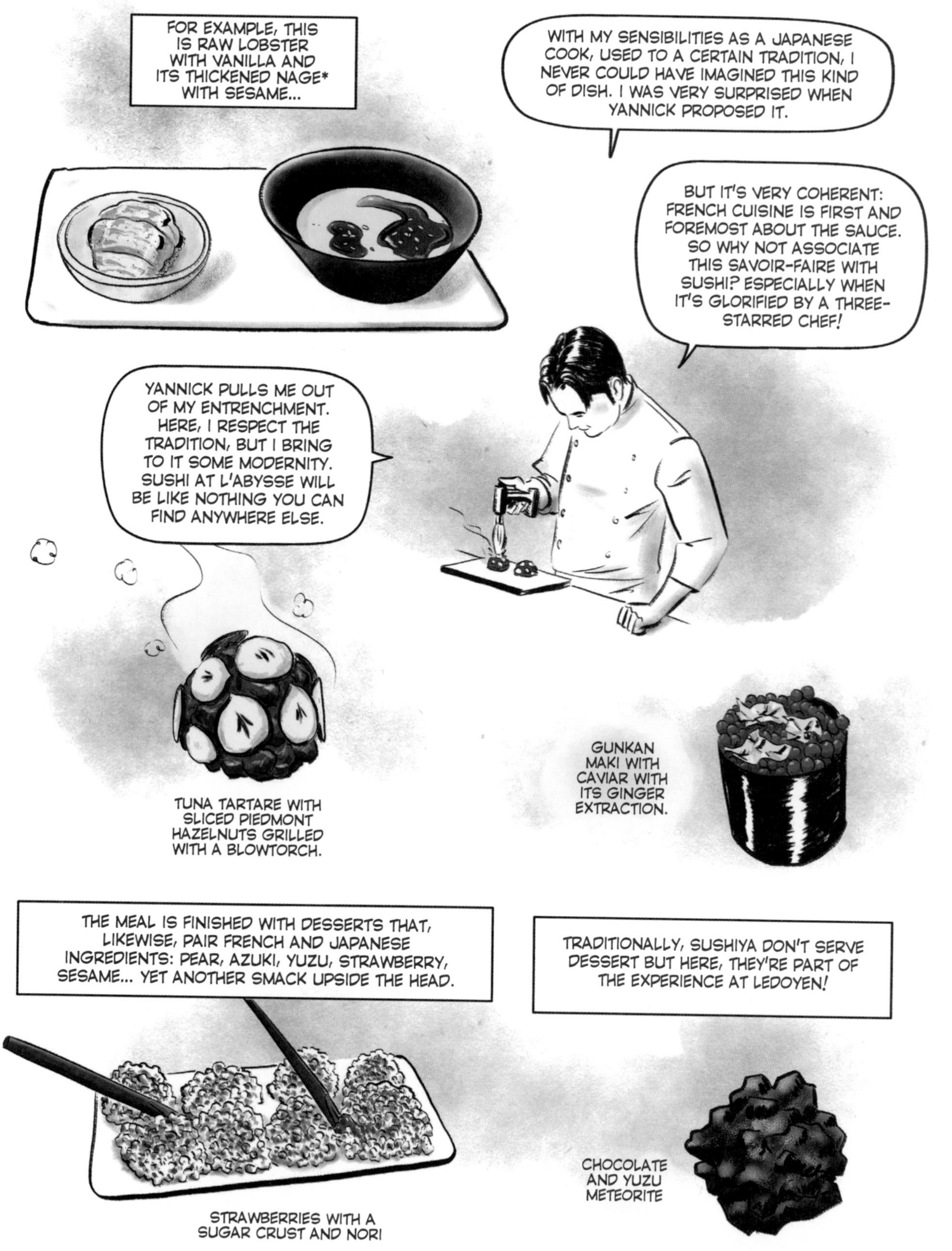

FOR EXAMPLE, THIS IS RAW LOBSTER WITH VANILLA AND ITS THICKENED NAGE* WITH SESAME...
WITH MY SENSIBILITIES AS A JAPANESE COOK, USED TO A CERTAIN TRADITION, I NEVER COULD HAVE IMAGINED THIS KIND OF DISH. I WAS VERY SURPRISED WHEN YANNICK PROPOSED IT.
BUT IT'S VERY COHERENT: FRENCH CUISINE IS FIRST AND FOREMOST ABOUT THE SAUCE. SO WHY NOT ASSOCIATE THIS SAVOIR-FAIRE WITH SUSHI? ESPECIALLY WHEN IT'S GLORIFIED BY A THREE-STARRED CHEF!
YANNICK PULLS ME OUT OF MY ENTRENCHMENT. HERE, I RESPECT THE TRADITION, BUT I BRING TO IT SOME MODERNITY. SUSHI AT L'ABYSSE WILL BE LIKE NOTHING YOU CAN FIND ANYWHERE ELSE.
TUNA TARTARE WITH SLICED PIEDMONT HAZELNUTS GRILLED WITH A BLOWTORCH.
GUNKAN MAKI WITH CAVIAR WITH ITS GINGER EXTRACTION.
THE MEAL IS FINISHED WITH DESSERTS THAT, LIKEWISE, PAIR FRENCH AND JAPANESE INGREDIENTS: PEAR, AZUKI, YUZU, STRAWBERRY, SESAME... YET ANOTHER SMACK UPSIDE THE HEAD.
TRADITIONALLY, SUSHIYA DON'T SERVE DESSERT BUT HERE, THEY'RE PART OF THE EXPERIENCE AT LEDOYEN!
STRAWBERRIES WITH A SUGAR CRUST AND NORI
CHOCOLATE AND YUZU METEORITE

*NAGE IS AN AROMATIC LIQUID, OFTENTIMES A STOCK, IN WHICH YOU COOK FISH OR SHELLFISH.

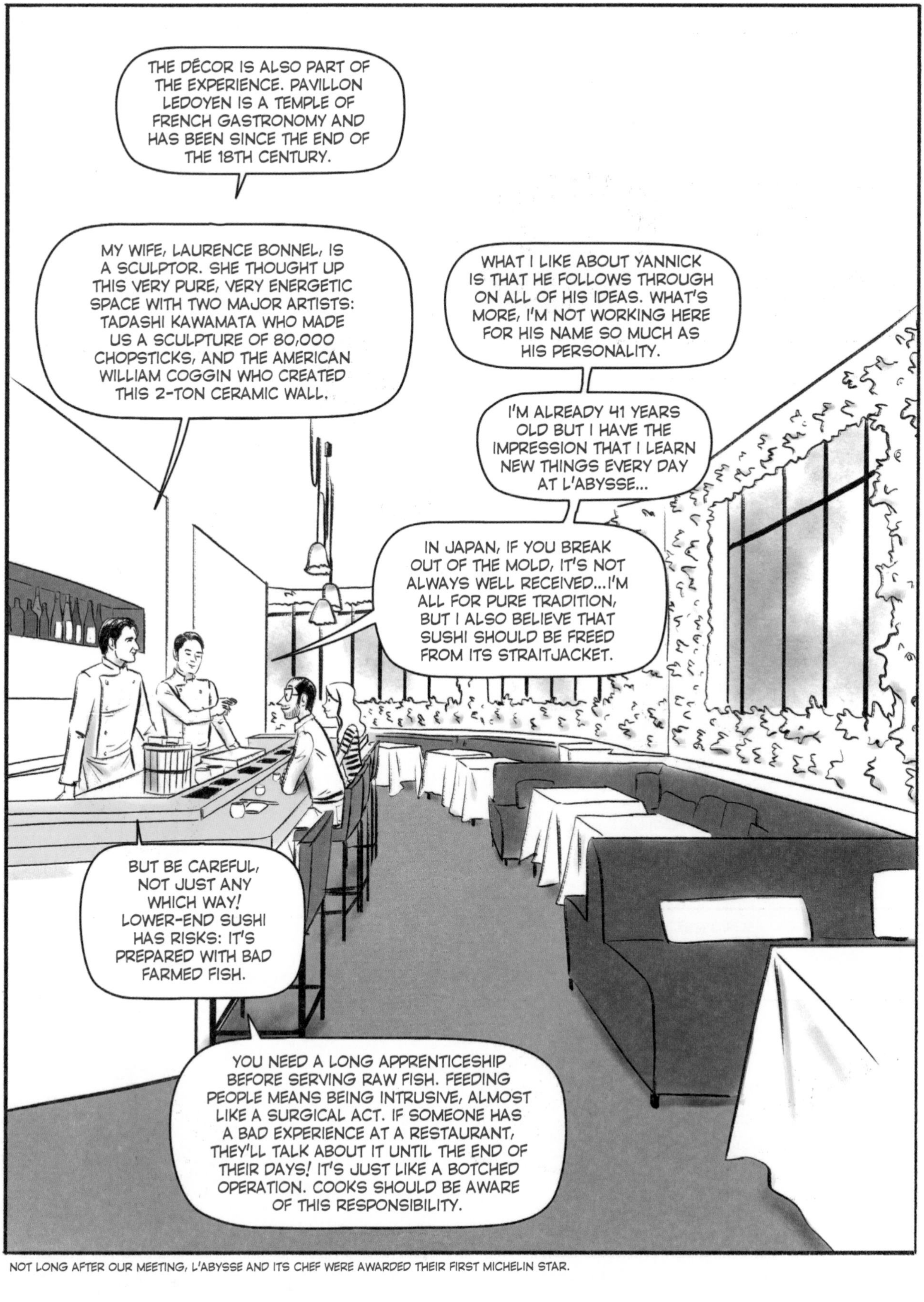
THE DÉCOR IS ALSO PART OF THE EXPERIENCE. PAVILLON LEDOYEN IS A TEMPLE OF FRENCH GASTRONOMY AND HAS BEEN SINCE THE END OF THE 18TH CENTURY.
MY WIFE, LAURENCE BONNEL, IS A SCULPTOR. SHE THOUGHT UP THIS VERY PURE, VERY ENERGETIC SPACE WITH TWO MAJOR ARTISTS: TADASHI KAWAMATA WHO MADE US A SCULPTURE OF 80,000 CHOPSTICKS, AND THE AMERICAN WILLIAM COGGIN WHO CREATED THIS 2-TON CERAMIC WALL.
WHAT I LIKE ABOUT YANNICK IS THAT HE FOLLOWS THROUGH ON ALL OF HIS IDEAS. WHAT'S MORE, I'M NOT WORKING HERE FOR HIS NAME SO MUCH AS HIS PERSONALITY.
I'M ALREADY 41 YEARS OLD BUT I HAVE THE IMPRESSION THAT I LEARN NEW THINGS EVERY DAY AT L'ABYSSE...
IN JAPAN, IF YOU BREAK OUT OF THE MOLD, IT'S NOT ALWAYS WELL RECEIVED...I'M ALL FOR PURE TRADITION, BUT I ALSO BELIEVE THAT SUSHI SHOULD BE FREED FROM ITS STRAITJACKET.
BUT BE CAREFUL, NOT JUST ANY WHICH WAY! LOWER-END SUSHI HAS RISKS: IT'S PREPARED WITH BAD FARMED FISH.
YOU NEED A LONG APPRENTICESHIP BEFORE SERVING RAW FISH. FEEDING PEOPLE MEANS BEING INTRUSIVE, ALMOST LIKE A SURGICAL ACT. IF SOMEONE HAS A BAD EXPERIENCE AT A RESTAURANT, THEY'LL TALK ABOUT IT UNTIL THE END OF THEIR DAYS! IT'S JUST LIKE A BOTCHED OPERATION. COOKS SHOULD BE AWARE OF THIS RESPONSIBILITY.

NOT LONG AFTER OUR MEETING, L'ABYSSE AND ITS CHEF WERE AWARDED THEIR FIRST MICHELIN STAR.

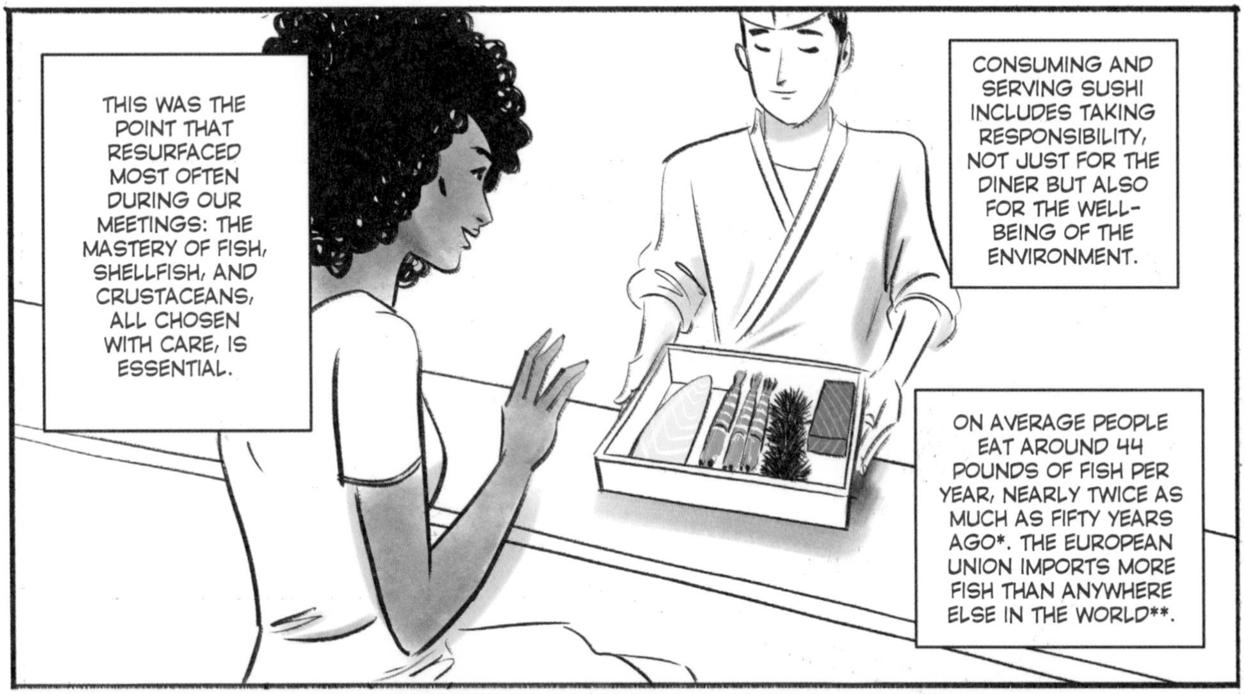
THIS WAS THE POINT THAT RESURFACED MOST OFTEN DURING OUR MEETINGS: THE MASTERY OF FISH, SHELLFISH, AND CRUSTACEANS, ALL CHOSEN WITH CARE, IS ESSENTIAL.
CONSUMING AND SERVING SUSHI INCLUDES TAKING RESPONSIBILITY, NOT JUST FOR THE DINER BUT ALSO FOR THE WELL-BEING OF THE ENVIRONMENT.
ON AVERAGE PEOPLE EAT AROUND 44 POUNDS OF FISH PER YEAR, NEARLY TWICE AS MUCH AS FIFTY YEARS AGO*. THE EUROPEAN UNION IMPORTS MORE FISH THAN ANYWHERE ELSE IN THE WORLD**.

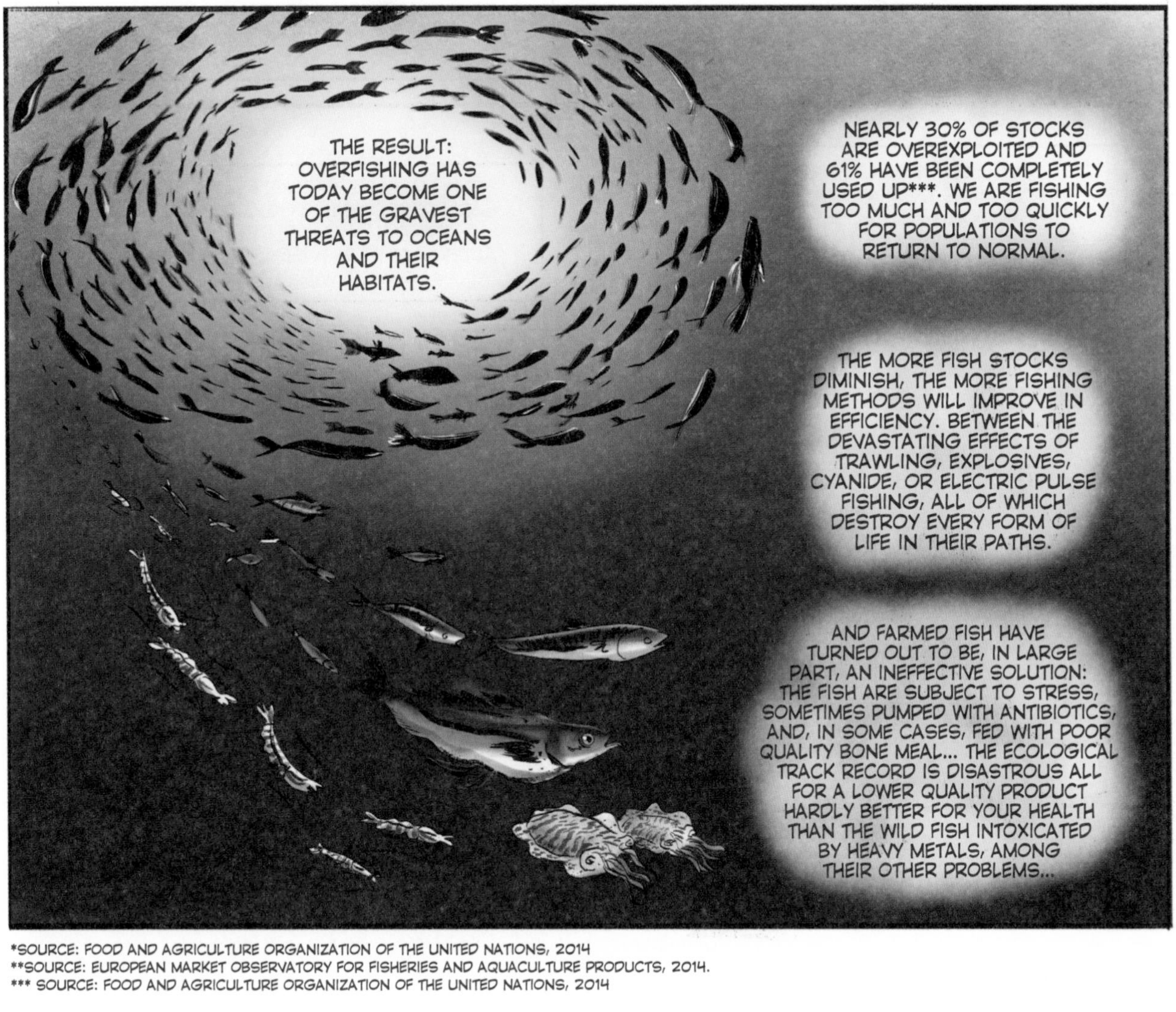
THE RESULT: OVERFISHING HAS TODAY BECOME ONE OF THE GRAVEST THREATS TO OCEANS AND THEIR HABITATS.
NEARLY 30% OF STOCKS ARE OVEREXPLOITED AND 61% HAVE BEEN COMPLETELY USED UP***. WE ARE FISHING TOO MUCH AND TOO QUICKLY FOR POPULATIONS TO RETURN TO NORMAL.
THE MORE FISH STOCKS DIMINISH, THE MORE FISHING METHODS WILL IMPROVE IN EFFICIENCY. BETWEEN THE DEVASTATING EFFECTS OF TRAWLING, EXPLOSIVES, CYANIDE, OR ELECTRIC PULSE FISHING, ALL OF WHICH DESTROY EVERY FORM OF LIFE IN THEIR PATHS.
AND FARMED FISH HAVE TURNED OUT TO BE, IN LARGE PART, AN INEFFECTIVE SOLUTION: THE FISH ARE SUBJECT TO STRESS, SOMETIMES PUMPED WITH ANTIBIOTICS, AND, IN SOME CASES, FED WITH POOR QUALITY BONE MEAL... THE ECOLOGICAL TRACK RECORD IS DISASTROUS ALL FOR A LOWER QUALITY PRODUCT HARDLY BETTER FOR YOUR HEALTH THAN THE WILD FISH INTOXICATED BY HEAVY METALS, AMONG THEIR OTHER PROBLEMS...

*SOURCE: FOOD AND AGRICULTURE ORGANIZATION OF THE UNITED NATIONS, 2014
**SOURCE: EUROPEAN MARKET OBSERVATORY FOR FISHERIES AND AQUACULTURE PRODUCTS, 2014.
*** SOURCE: FOOD AND AGRICULTURE ORGANIZATION OF THE UNITED NATIONS, 2014

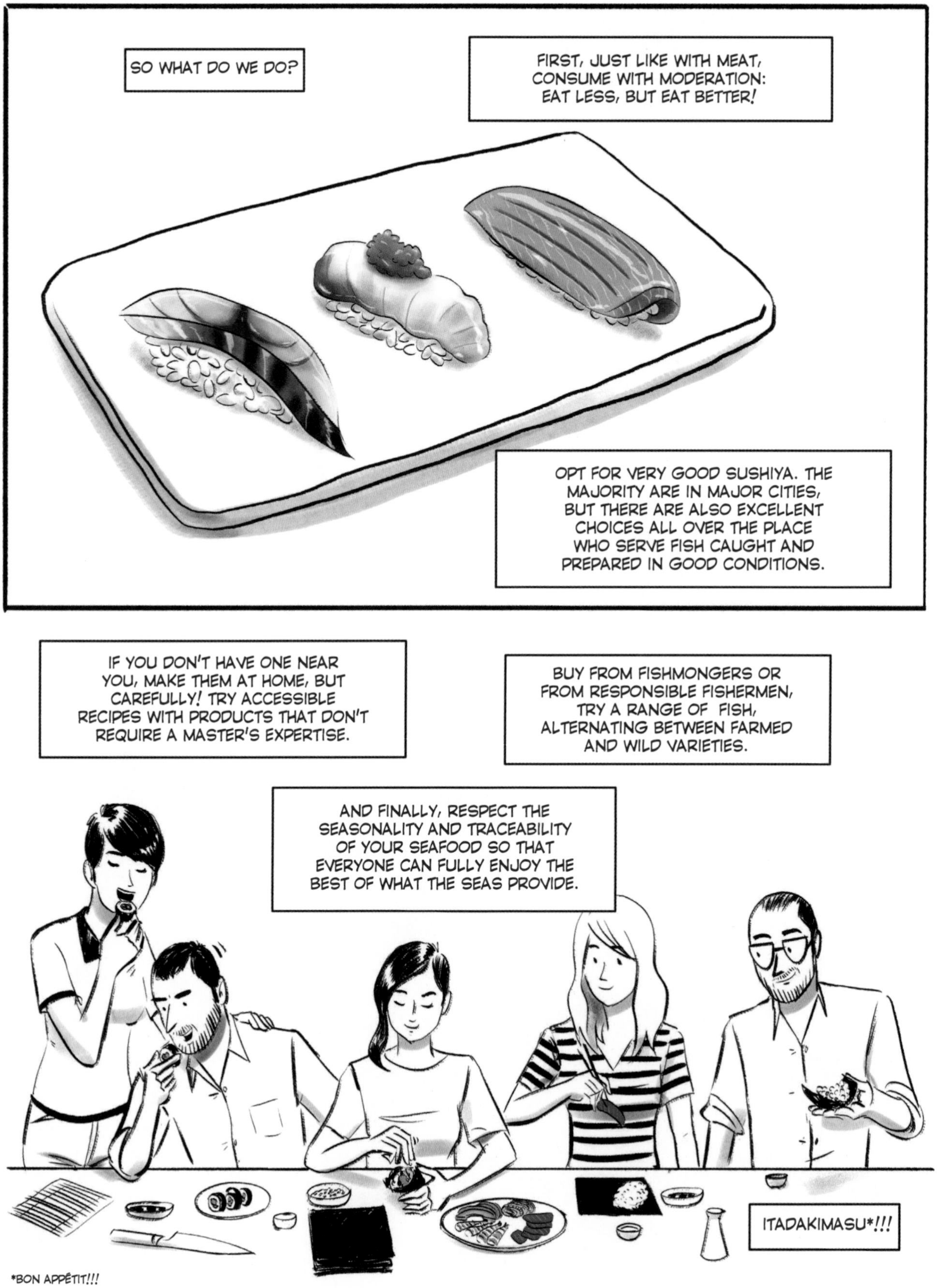
SO WHAT DO WE DO?
FIRST, JUST LIKE WITH MEAT, CONSUME WITH MODERATION: EAT LESS, BUT EAT BETTER!
OPT FOR VERY GOOD SUSHIYA. THE MAJORITY ARE IN MAJOR CITIES, BUT THERE ARE ALSO EXCELLENT CHOICES ALL OVER THE PLACE WHO SERVE FISH CAUGHT AND PREPARED IN GOOD CONDITIONS.
IF YOU DON'T HAVE ONE NEAR YOU, MAKE THEM AT HOME, BUT CAREFULLY! TRY ACCESSIBLE RECIPES WITH PRODUCTS THAT DON'T REQUIRE A MASTER'S EXPERTISE.
BUY FROM FISHMONGERS OR FROM RESPONSIBLE FISHERMEN, TRY A RANGE OF FISH, ALTERNATING BETWEEN FARMED AND WILD VARIETIES.
AND FINALLY, RESPECT THE SEASONALITY AND TRACEABILITY OF YOUR SEAFOOD SO THAT EVERYONE CAN FULLY ENJOY THE BEST OF WHAT THE SEAS PROVIDE.
ITADAKIMASU*!!!

*BON APPÉTIT!!!

Recipes

Here are some distinctly Japanese recipes that
were shared with us by the people we met with
or who helped us to make this book.

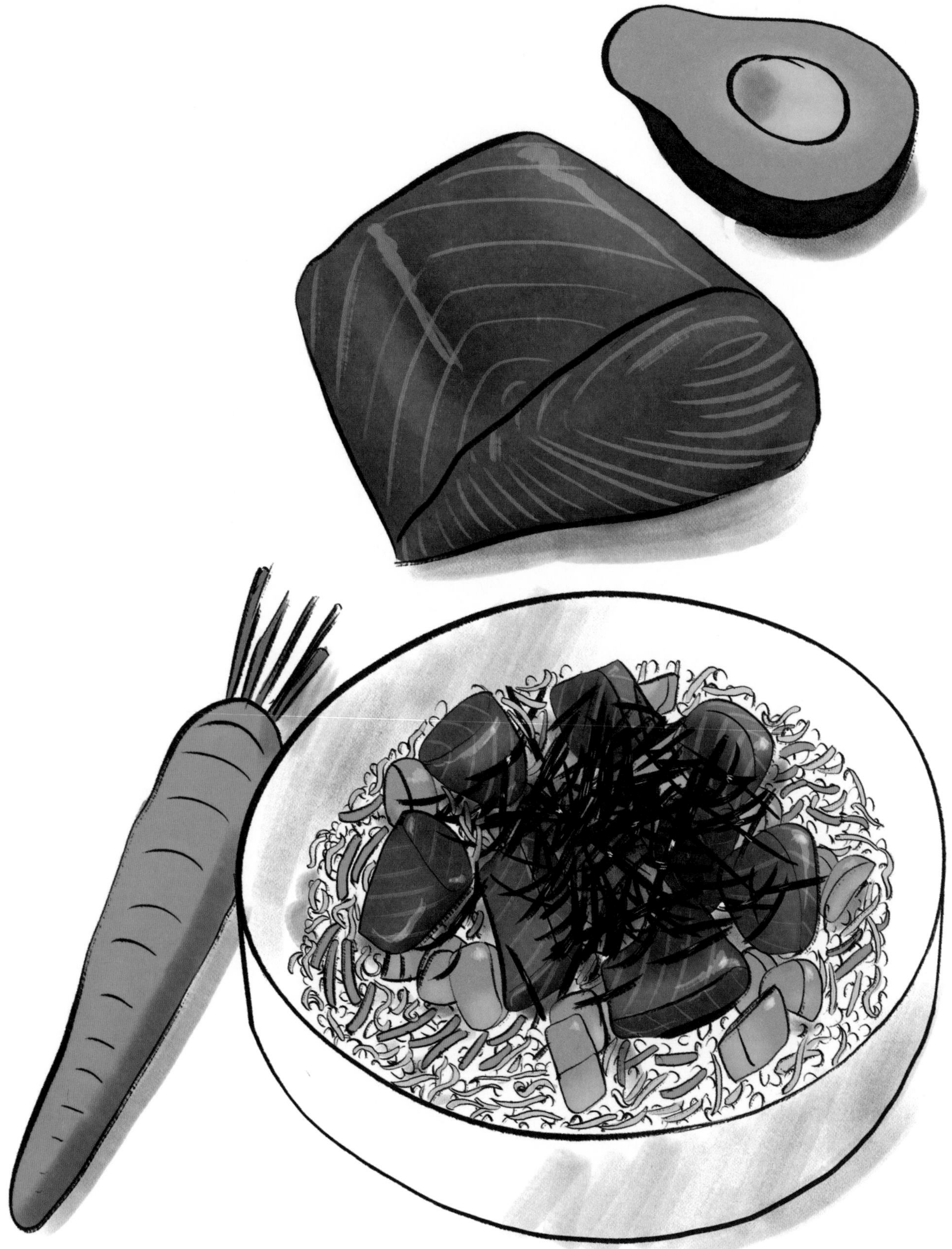

Rica's Chirashi

Chirashi is a deconstructed sushi where the ingredients are placed in a bowl of seasoned rice

INGREDIENTS FOR 6 PEOPLE: :

VINEGARED RICE:

- 450 g rice (about 2 cups)
- 400 g water (a bit more than 1½ cups) + 3 tablespoons of sake (or white wine)
- One square of kombu around 6 in. x 6 in.
- 5 tablespoons vinegar
- 2 tablespoons sugar
- 1 teaspoon salt

- - - - - - - - - - - - - - - - - - -

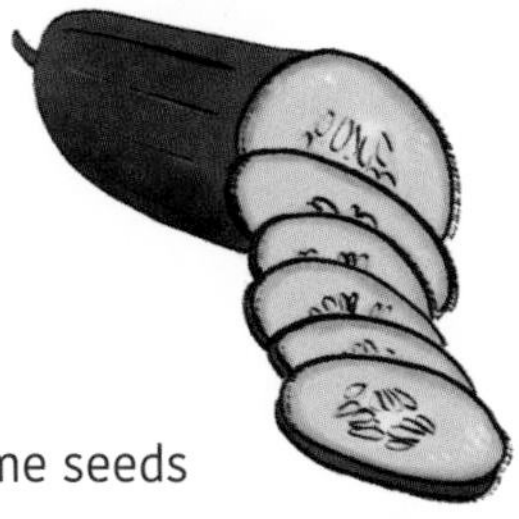

TOPPINGS :

- 1 carrot
- 1 cucumber
- 2 or 3 eggs
- White sesame seeds
- 2½ tablespoons sugar
- 1 tablespoon mirin
- 2½ tablespoons soy sauce
- Salt
- Nori
- Optional: bluefin tuna/ avocado or grilled eel

INSTRUCTIONS :

1 • For the vinegared rice

Wash the rice several times under the tap until the water under the rice runs clear. Drain the rice by putting it in a colander and leaving it to rest for 1 to 3 hours.
Put the rice in a heavy pot with the water, sake, and kombu. When the water boils, remove the kombu and cover the pot. Let it cook on low for around 10 minutes.

2 • For the toppings

Dice or julienne the carrot. Boil first in hot water before cooking them in water, sugar, mirin, and soy sauce. You can replace the carrot with lotus, green beans, shiitakes, etc.
Slice the cucumber very thinly. Lightly salt it and leave it to rest for a couple of minutes. Wash it quickly in water and drain.
Whisk the eggs in a bowl. Lightly oil a pan. Pour a small quantity of the mixture into the pan and cook like a crepe by moving the pan over the flame so the mixture spreads out in one thin layer. Remove and repeat until you have used all the mixture. Stack all the egg crepes then roll them together. Slice the roll very finely.

3 • Assembly

Put the rice in a bowl. Add the mixture of vinegar, sugar, and salt (see the quantities in Ingredients, part 1). Mix them together delicately, venting the rice.
Add the cucumber and carrot, white sesame seeds, and the sliced eggs. Sprinkle on some finely sliced nori.
It's possible to add grilled eel or bluefin tuna to this dish.

4 • Variation with marinated bluefin tuna and avocado

Cut the tuna into pieces and marinate them in a mixture of 2 tables-poons of sake, 2 tablespoons of mirin, and 3 tablespoons or soy sauce. Let it rest for at least an hour in the fridge.
You can also marinate the avocado in the same way, add it as it is, or season it with a mixture of mayonnaise and soy sauce.
Mix these ingredients into the prepared rice.

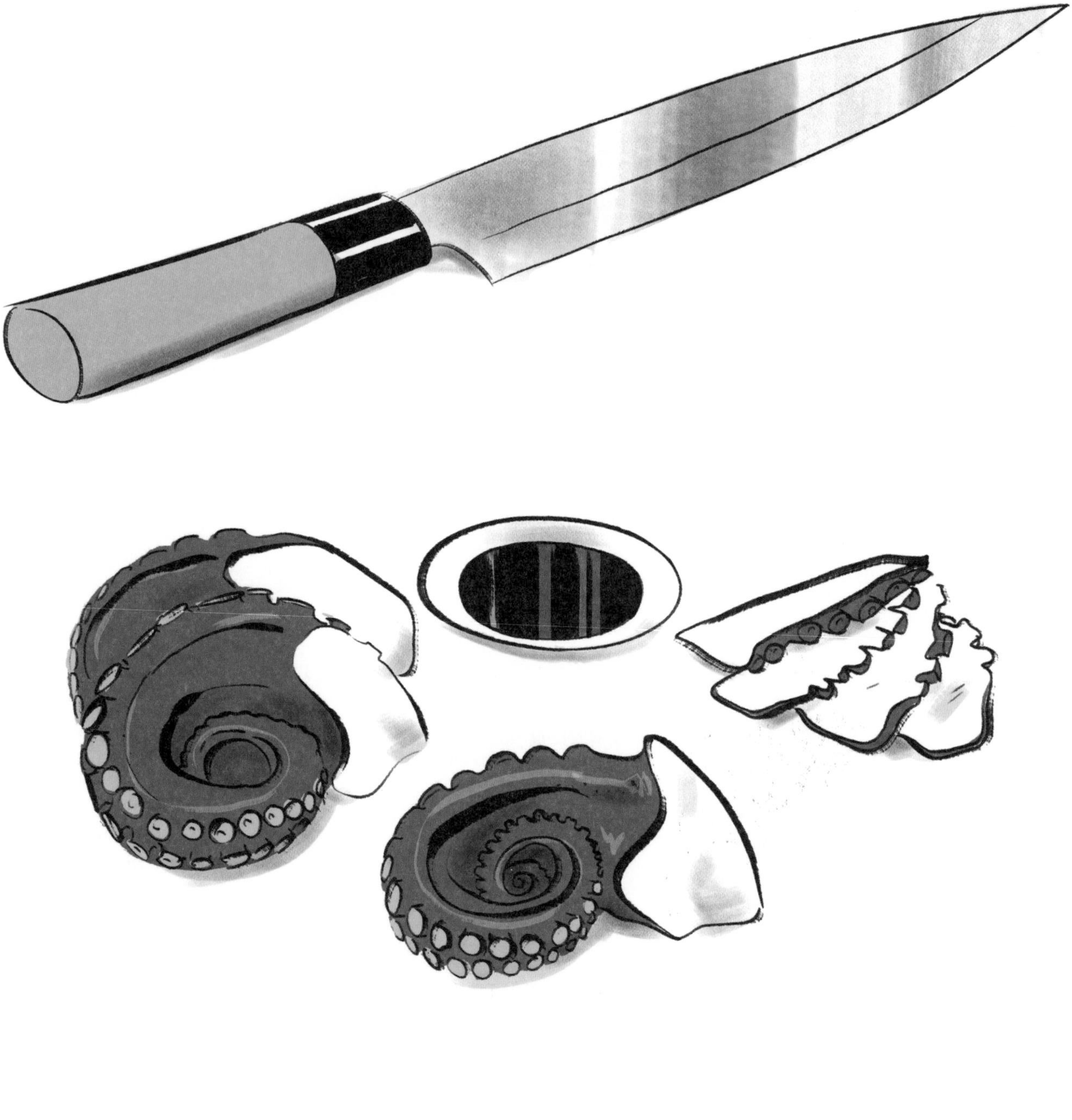

Okada's Green Tea Octopus

Chef Okada's octopus is made with ryokucha green tea which is more mainstream and affordable than matcha.

INGREDIENTS :

- 1 octopus
- Ryokucha green tea powder or leaves
- 1 bag of coarse sea salt

INSTRUCTIONS :

1 • For the whole octopus

The night before cooking the octopus, if not sooner, remove the eyes and the beak with a knife. Make an incision at the base of the head and empty it of its contents. Freeze the octopus to break down its structural fibers and tenderize it.
When you're ready to prepare it, put the thawed octopus in a large bowl and massage it with the salt for a long time (at least 20 minutes). Continue massaging it until its viscosity and any bubbles disappear.
Rinse very well in cold water.

2 • Cooking

Boil water in a large, heavy-bottomed pot and add in enough green tea to get a full-bodied bouillon.
Submerge the octopus in the water, beginning with the ends of its tentacles. (For a more presentable form at the end of the cook time, submerge the octopus little by little so that the tentacles coil up). Cook for around 5 minutes for a smaller octopus. To test for doneness, insert a small skewer into it: if it goes in easily, it's ready! Remove it from the pot and let it cool to room temperature.

3 • Serving

Cut in fine slices and eat the sashimi with soy sauce and wasabi.

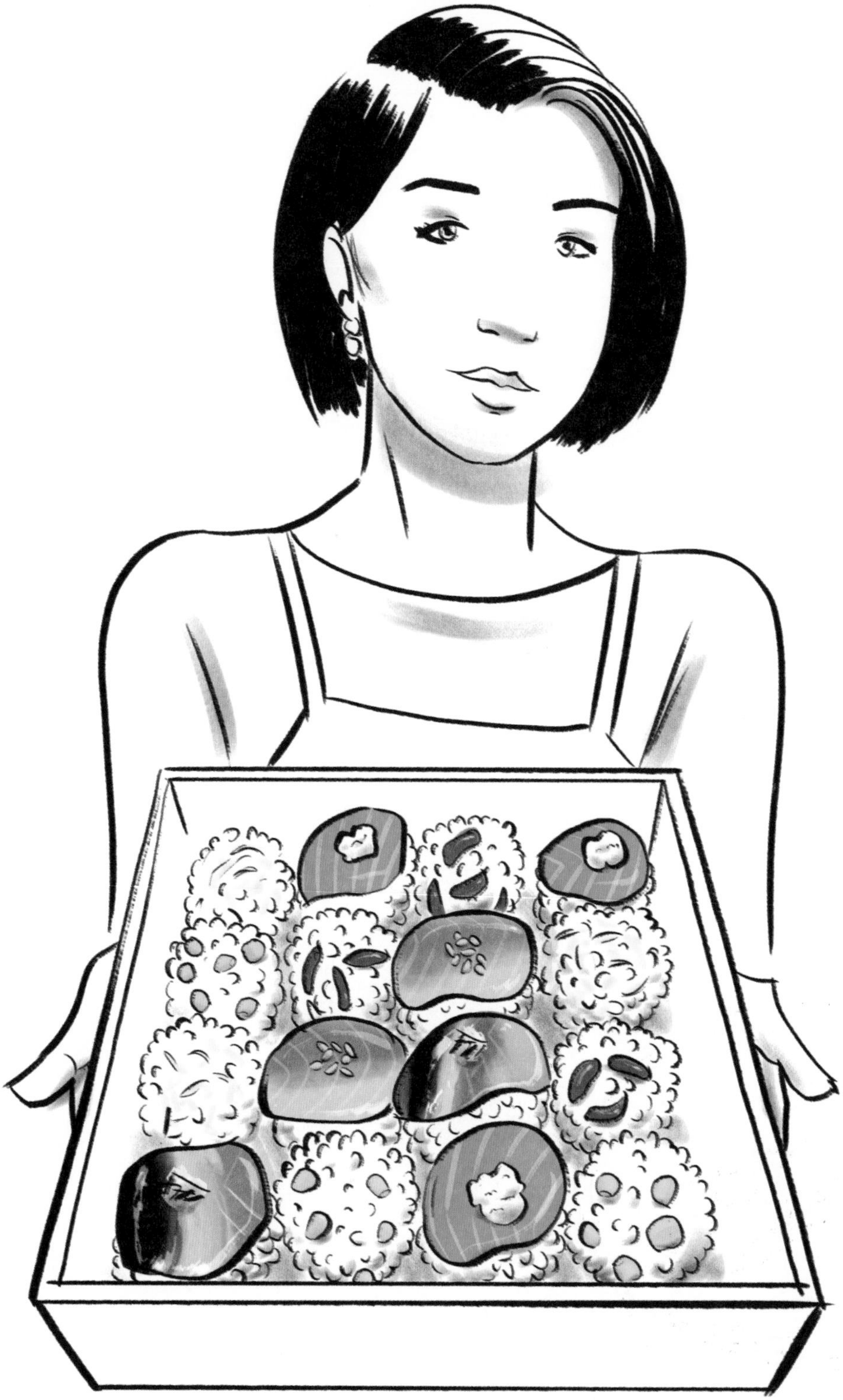

Mrs. Okuda is a professional cook who shares her know-how through Japanese cooking classes, by creating recipes and writing articles. She was our resident expert during our first visit to Tsukiji and here has generously shared her recipe for temari sushi.

Mrs. Okuda's Temari

Taking its name from temari, a traditional decorative ball, this dish is composed of a small ball of rice to which you can add just about any ingredient.

INGREDIENTS:

First prepare the vinegared rice for versions 1, 2, and 3

- 450 g Japanese sushi rice (about 2½ cups)
- 620 g water (2½ cups or about 250 ml)
- 55 ml of rice vinegar (3½ tablespoons or so)
- 1 teaspoon of sugar
- 1 teaspoon of salt
- White sesame seeds

Cook the rice in a covered pot or in a rice cooker.
While the rice is cooking, mix together the rice vinegar, sugar, and salt.
When the rice is cooked, drizzle the mixture of rice vinegar, sugar and salt over the top of it. Stir delicately with a spatula as if you were cutting the rice while ventilating it to remove any excess water. Repeat.
You can then add the toasted sesame

INSTRUCTIONS:

1 • Salmon and feta

Form a ball of cooled vinegared rice and cover it with a slice of smoked salmon.
Add a little bit of feta on top of each sushi.

2 • Sardine or saurel

Filet the sardine or saurel. Lightly salt them and wipe away any excess water with a paper towel. After removing any bones and the skin, cut into slices.
Coat the flesh side of the filet with soy sauce.
Form cold balls of rice and cover each of them with a slice of fish.
Add a little bit of grated ginger on top.

3 • White fish

Filet a sea bream or a turbot, skin it, and remove its bones. Next, place each filet between two pieces of kombu (if the filets are too large, cut them to fit inside the kombu). Wrap them up in plastic wrap and let them rest in the fridge for several hours. Then cut the fish into ¼ inch slices and lightly paint on soy sauce on the flesh side.
Form balls of cold rice and cover them with a slice of fish. Sprinkle on sesame seeds.
Squeeze a few drops of lemon or lime juice over them before serving.

4 • Octopus

Slice 150 g (about 1/3 lb.) of octopus and sauté it in a pot with 30 ml (2 tablespoons) of sake and a pinch of salt. Remove the octopus from the pot and set aside, reserving any cooking juices for the coming steps.
After washing 300 g (around 1½ cups) of rice, put it in a large, heavy-bottomed pot with 430 g (1 1/3 cups) of bouillon (reserved cooking juices + water), 10 ml (2 teaspoons) of sake, a dash of clear soy sauce and a pinch of salt. Cover and heat. When the water boils, add the cooked octopus and let it cook covered on medium heat. When the liquid is almost cooked off, lower the heat. When it begins to crackle, bring the heat up to high again and continue cooking for 10 seconds. Remove from the heat and let it rest, covered, for 10 minutes. When the rice has cooled, form it into balls.

5 • Ginger rice

After washing 300 g (around 1½ cups) of rice, put it in a large, heavy-bottomed pot with 430 g (1 ¼ cups) of water, 10 ml (2 teaspoons) of sake, a dash of clear soy sauce and a pinch of salt.
When the rice is cooked, add 20 g (3/4 oz.) of fresh ground ginger. Mix them together and shape into balls.

6 • Riz au maïs

After washing 300 g (around 1½ cups) of rice, cook it covered in 430 g (1¾ cups) of water, a pinch of salt and a dash of sake. When the water boils, add some corn kernels (fresh or frozen), cover again, and let cook on medium heat. When it crackles, bring the heat up to high and continue cooking for 10 seconds. Turn off the heat and let it sit for 10 minutes, covered. When the rice has cooled, shape into balls.

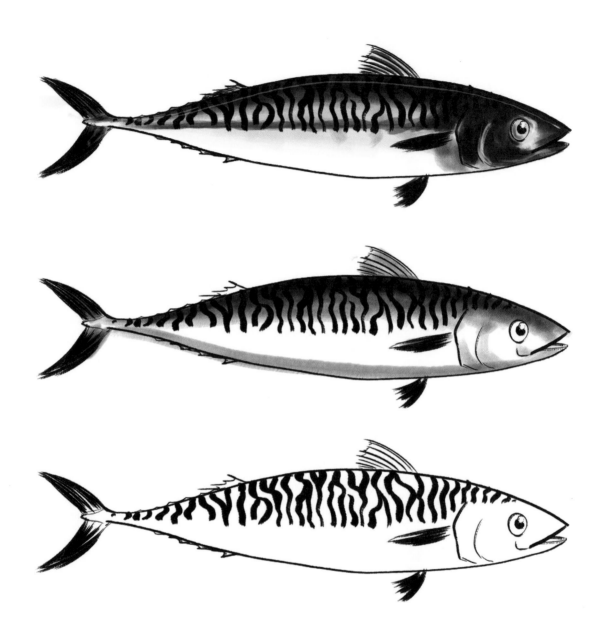

Sasa Sushi

Fisherman's pressed mackerel sushi: sasa sushi

INGREDIENTS:

- 4 or 6 mackerel
- 450 g of rice (around 2½ cups)
- Water
- Rice vinegar
- Apple vinegar
- Salt
- Sugar
- 8 shiso leaves
- Fresh ginger
- Toasted white sesame seeds
- Kombu

This recipe requires a wooden sushi mold. You can buy one in Japanese specialty shops and other Asian grocery stores. This recipe uses 4 molds.

INSTRUCTIONS:

1 • Mackerel

Filet the fish, debone them, and remove as much skin as possible (it's okay if there is a little bit left). Salt the fish and leave them to rest for around 2 hours.
Mix together 6 tablespoons of rice vinegar, 2 tablespoons apple vinegar, and 2 tablespoons of sugar.
Quickly pass the fish under running water before drying them. Marinate them in the vinegar-sugar mixture for a day.

2 • Rice

Clean the rice thoroughly and let drain for around a half-hour in a colander. Cook it in a rice cooker with a piece of kombu, a pinch of salt, and 50 cl water (just over 2 cups).
Finely grind the ginger.
Lightly wipe the fish and cut them so that their size corresponds to that of the mold.
Put the cooked rice in a large bowl and add a mixture of 6 cl (just under ¼ cup) of rice vinegar,
and 2 tablespoons of sugar. Stir the rice to vent it.
Add the ginger and the toasted sesame seeds.

3 • Assembly

Cover the interior of the mold with plastic wrap leaving plenty of excess on the sides.
Add a layer of fish (skin side down).
Add a layer of shiso leaves, the bottom side of the leaf towards you.
Add the rice and lightly shape it by spreading it out over the surface of the previous layers.
Cover with plastic wrap, then replace the cover of the mold being sure to press down firmly with both hands so the sushi will be compact. Leave it to rest for a while. Unmold and cut into 5 or 6 pieces, wiping your knife with a wet towel before each cut.

The Sake Mojito

Mr. Yoshikubo's mojito made with Ippin sake

INGREDIENTS (FOR ONE GLASS):

- 75 ml (2½ oz.) of sake
- 10 ml (1/3 oz.) of cane sugar syrup
- 1/2 lime cut into quarters
- 12 green shiso leaves *
- Carbonated water

INSTRUCTIONS :

In a glass, add the shiso leaves.
Add the cane sugar syrup and the lime, the sake, and ice.
Top the drink off with some carbonated water.

If you don't have shiso you can use mint instead.

Address Book

- RESTAURANTS IN JAPAN

Sumeshiya
2-6-8 Suido, Bunkyō, Tokyo
www.sumeshiya.com/cafe/

Family eel restaurant
7-11 Uminokōen, Kanazawa-ku
Yokohama-shi, Kanagawa-ken 236-0013
http://karinnnoki.blogspot.com

- RESTAURANTS IN FRANCE

L'Abysse
Pavillon Ledoyen
Carré des Champs-Élysées
8, avenue Dutuit 75008 Paris, France
www.yannick-alleno.com/fr/abysse-bar-a-sushis.html

Hinoki
6, rue des 11 Martyrs 29200 Brest, France

Jin
6, rue de la Sourdière 75001 Paris, France

- GROCERY STORES

Katagiri Japanese Grocery
370 Lexington Ave.
New York, New York 10017
http://katagiri.com/

Dainobu
36 W 56th St.
New York, NY 10019
https://dainobunyc.com/

Mitsuwa - Chicago
100 E. Algonquin Road
Arlington Heights, IL 60005
https://mitsuwa.com/ch/

Nijiya Market San Francisco Store
1737 Post St. #333
San Francisco, CA 94115
https://www.nijiya.com/

Seiwa Market
21815 Hawthorne Blvd.
Torrance, CA 90503
https://www.seiwamarket.com/

- ONLINE GROCERY STORES

The Japanese Pantry
https://thejapanesepantry.myshopify.com/

Umami Insider
https://umami-insider.store/

- WHERE TO BUY SAKE?

Sakaya
324 E 9th St.
New York, NY 10003

Minoru's Sake Shop
167 W 23rd St.
New York, NY 10011

- WHERE TO BUY MARUYAMA NORI?

Takaski
www.takaski.com

- WHERE TO BUY COOKING UTENSILS?

Korin
57 Warren St.
New York, NY 10007
https://www.korin.com/

- WEBSITES FOR OUR JAPANESE EXPERTS

Chihiro Masui :
https://chihiromasui.com

Ikejime in the US :
ikejimefederation.com

Fujita, tuna supplier :
@magura.fujita

Hide and Kana:
https://www.ebisudou-tamt.com/

Maruyama nori :
https://www.maruyamanori.com/en/history/index.html

Mrs. Koko Okuda :
https://kokookuda.com/
@kokookuda

Sake Ippin :
www.ippin.co.jp

Shikamaru Takeshita Ceramics :
@shikamaru.t

Tsunahiro Yamamura Cutlery :
www.sword-masamune.com

Yugeta Shoyu :
http://yugeta.com/

- AND ALSO

Japan National Tourism Organization
One Grand Central Place
60 East 42nd Street, Suite 448
New York, NY 10165
https//us.jnto.go.jp

Japan Experience
https://www.japan-experience.com/